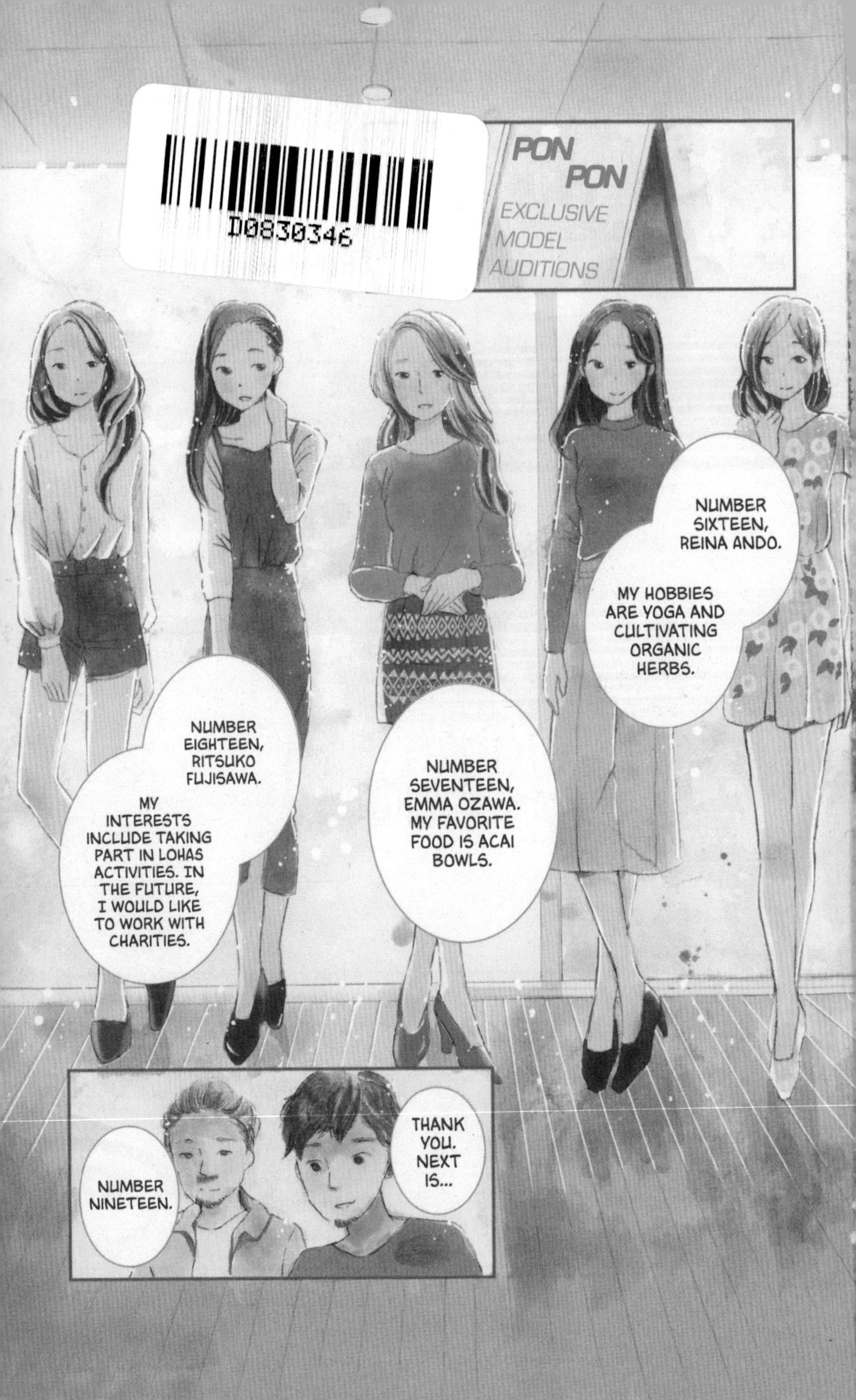
PON PON
EXCLUSIVE MODEL AUDITIONS
NUMBER SIXTEEN, REINA ANDO.
MY HOBBIES ARE YOGA AND CULTIVATING ORGANIC HERBS.
NUMBER SEVENTEEN, EMMA OZAWA. MY FAVORITE FOOD IS ACAI BOWLS.
NUMBER EIGHTEEN, RITSUKO FUJISAWA.
MY INTERESTS INCLUDE TAKING PART IN LOHAS ACTIVITIES. IN THE FUTURE, I WOULD LIKE TO WORK WITH CHARITIES.
THANK YOU. NEXT IS...
NUMBER NINETEEN.

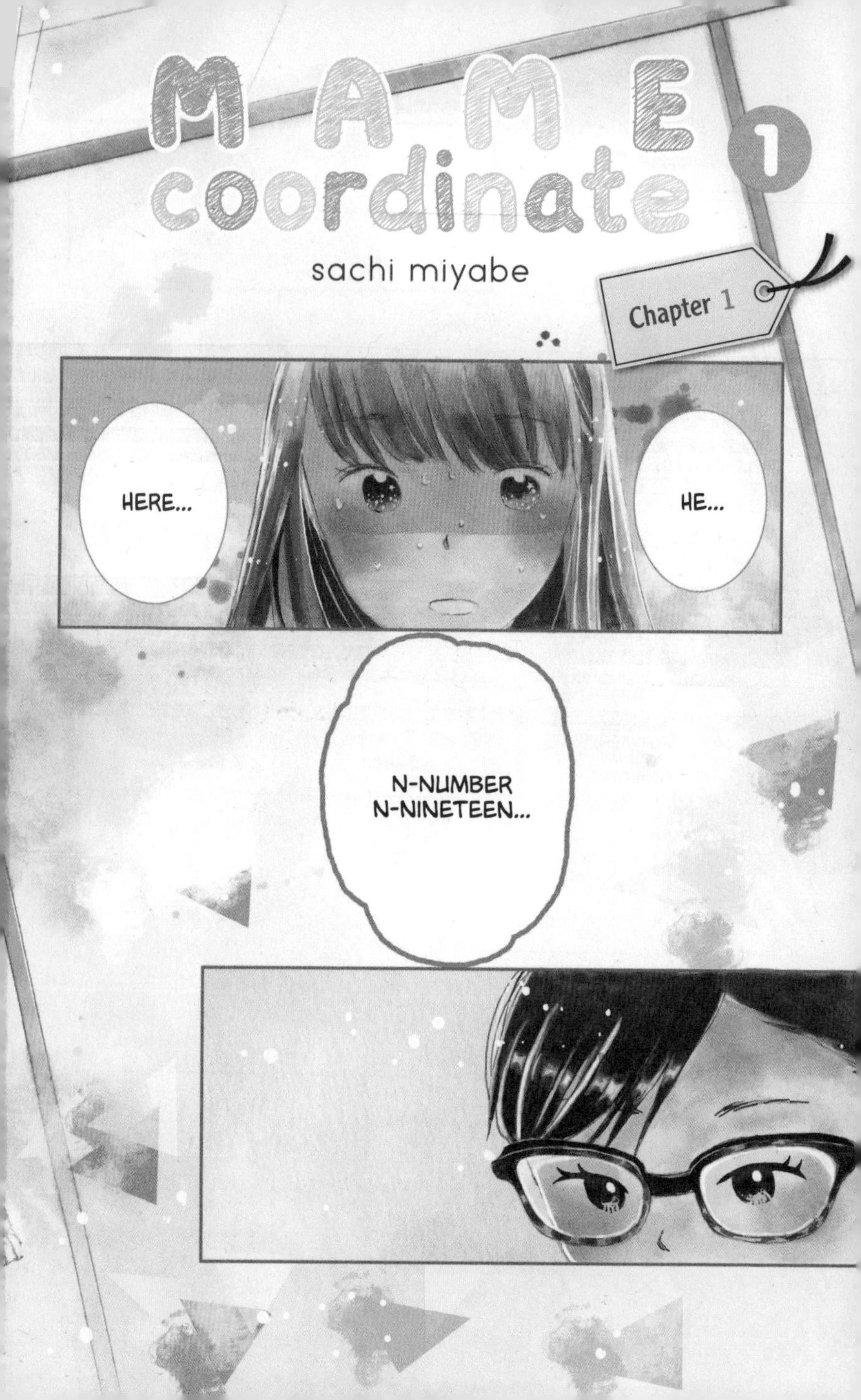
MAME coordinate
1
sachi miyabe
Chapter 1
HE...
HERE...
N-NUMBER N-NINETEEN...

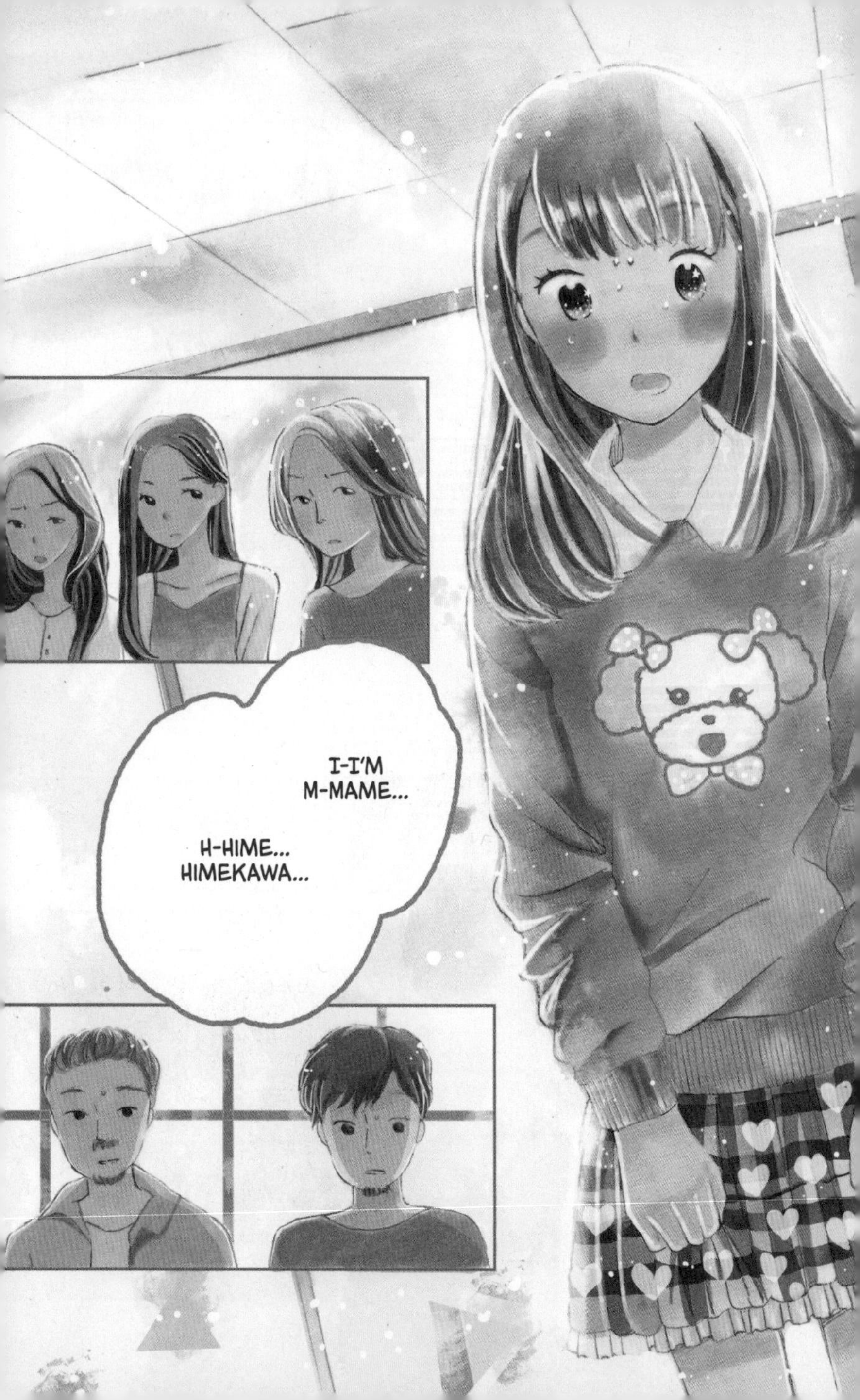
I-I'M M-MAME...
H-HIME... HIMEKAWA...

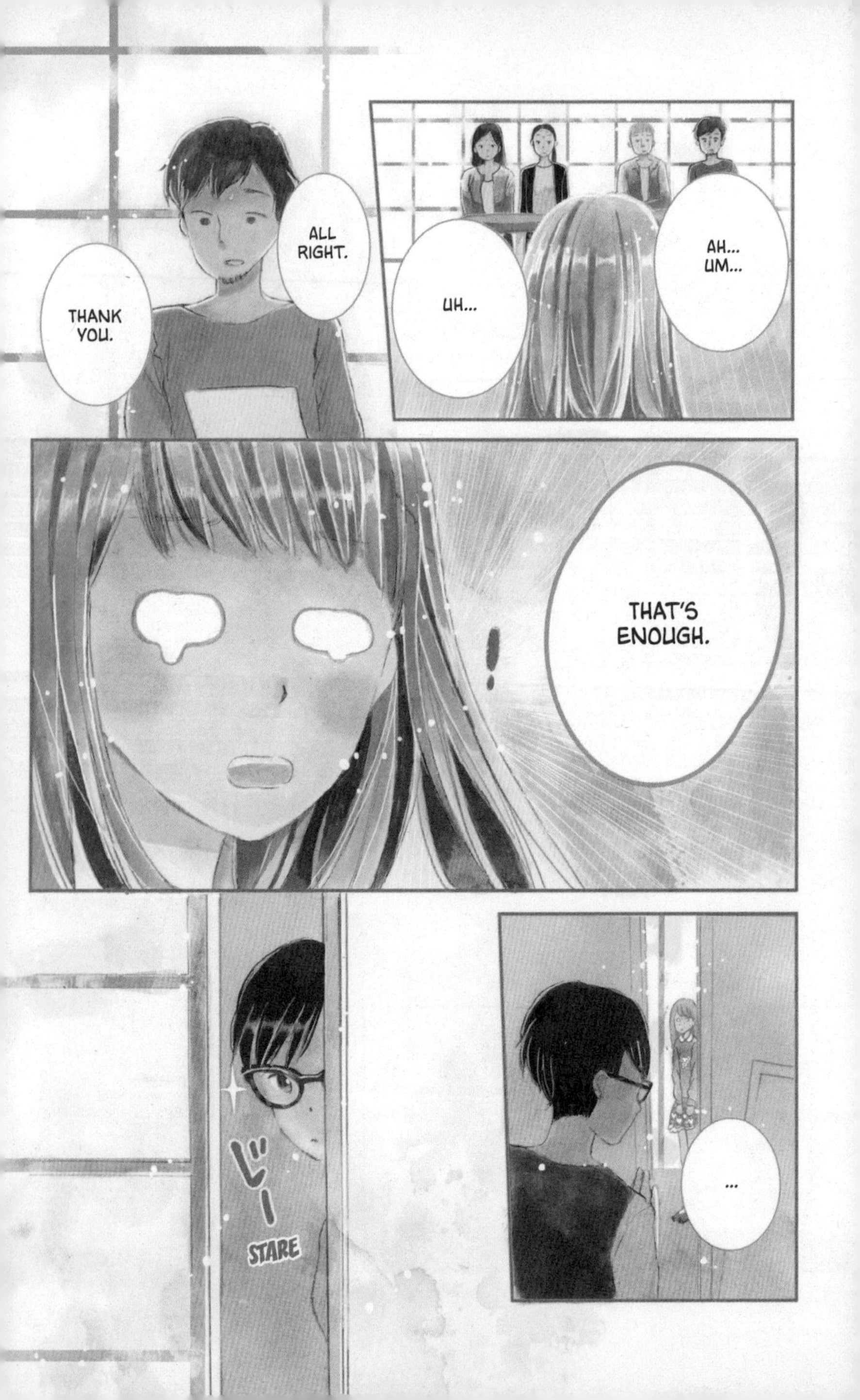
AH... UM...
UH...
ALL RIGHT.
THANK YOU.
THAT'S ENOUGH.
...
STARE

Contents

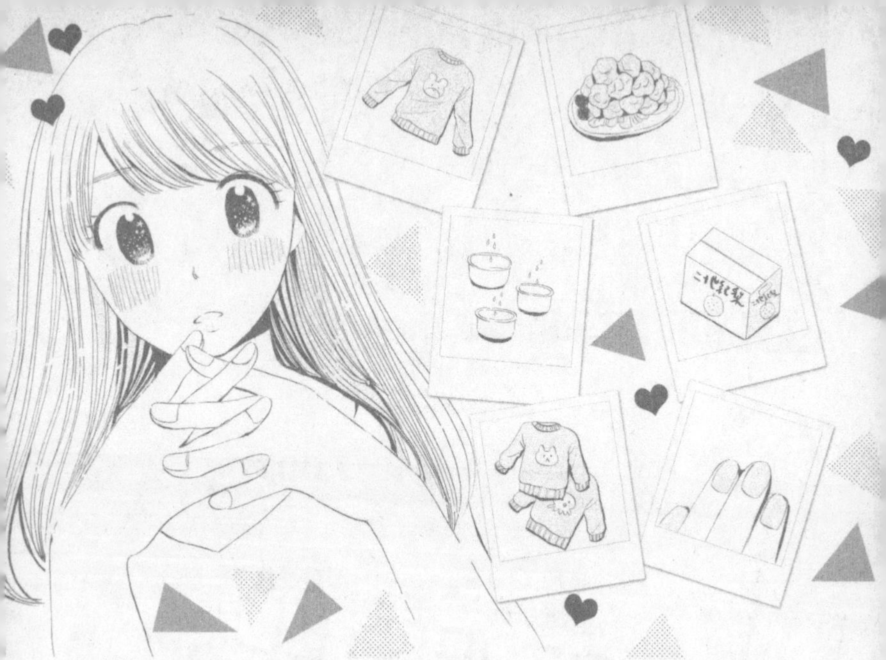

MAME coordinate 1

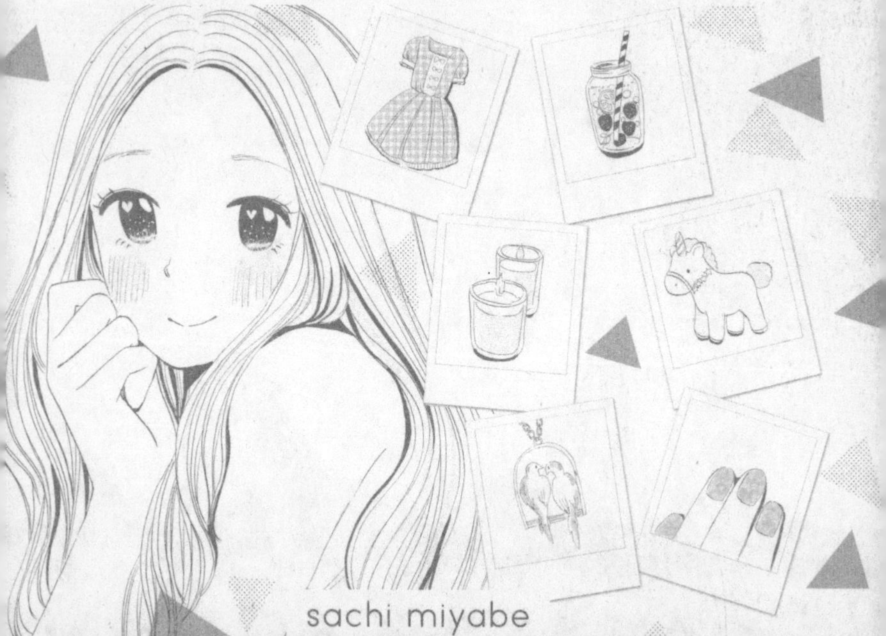

sachi miyabe

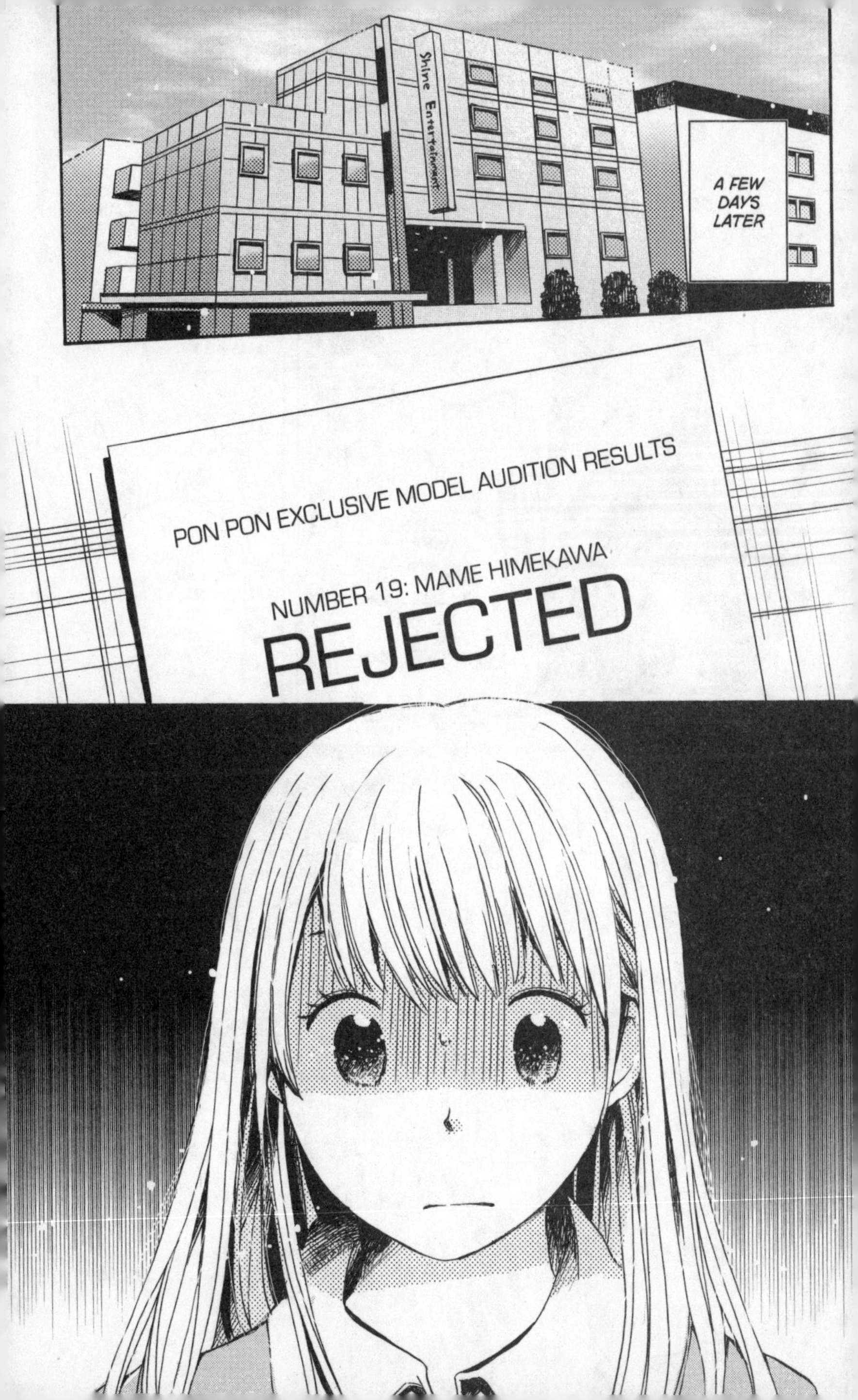
A FEW DAYS LATER
Shine Entertainment
PON PON EXCLUSIVE MODEL AUDITION RESULTS
NUMBER 19: MAME HIMEKAWA
REJECTED

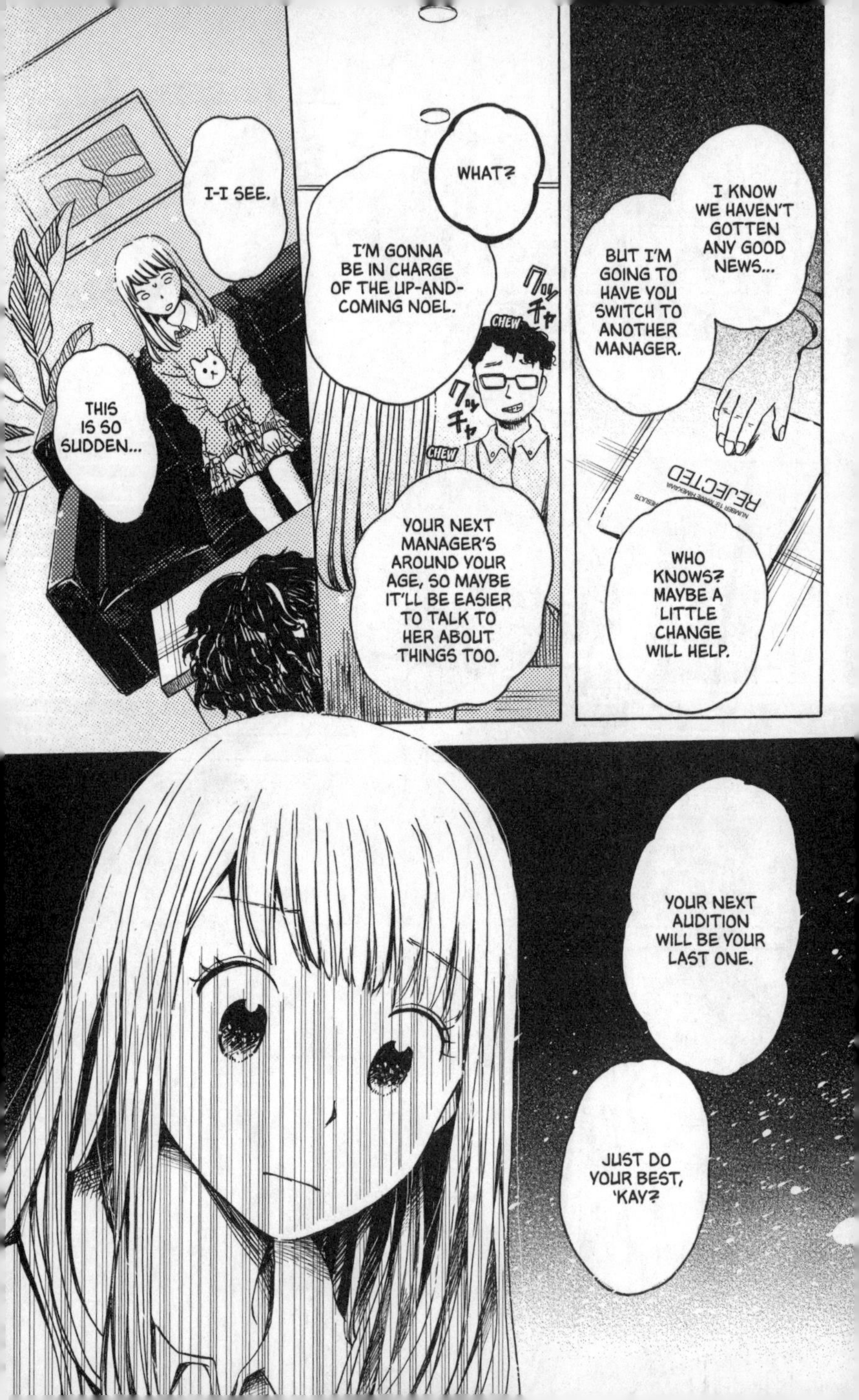
I KNOW WE HAVEN'T GOTTEN ANY GOOD NEWS...
BUT I'M GOING TO HAVE YOU SWITCH TO ANOTHER MANAGER.
REJECTED
WHO KNOWS? MAYBE A LITTLE CHANGE WILL HELP.
WHAT?
I'M GONNA BE IN CHARGE OF THE UP-AND-COMING NOEL.
CHEW
CHEW
YOUR NEXT MANAGER'S AROUND YOUR AGE, SO MAYBE IT'LL BE EASIER TO TALK TO HER ABOUT THINGS TOO.
I-I SEE.
THIS IS SO SUDDEN...
YOUR NEXT AUDITION WILL BE YOUR LAST ONE.
JUST DO YOUR BEST, 'KAY?

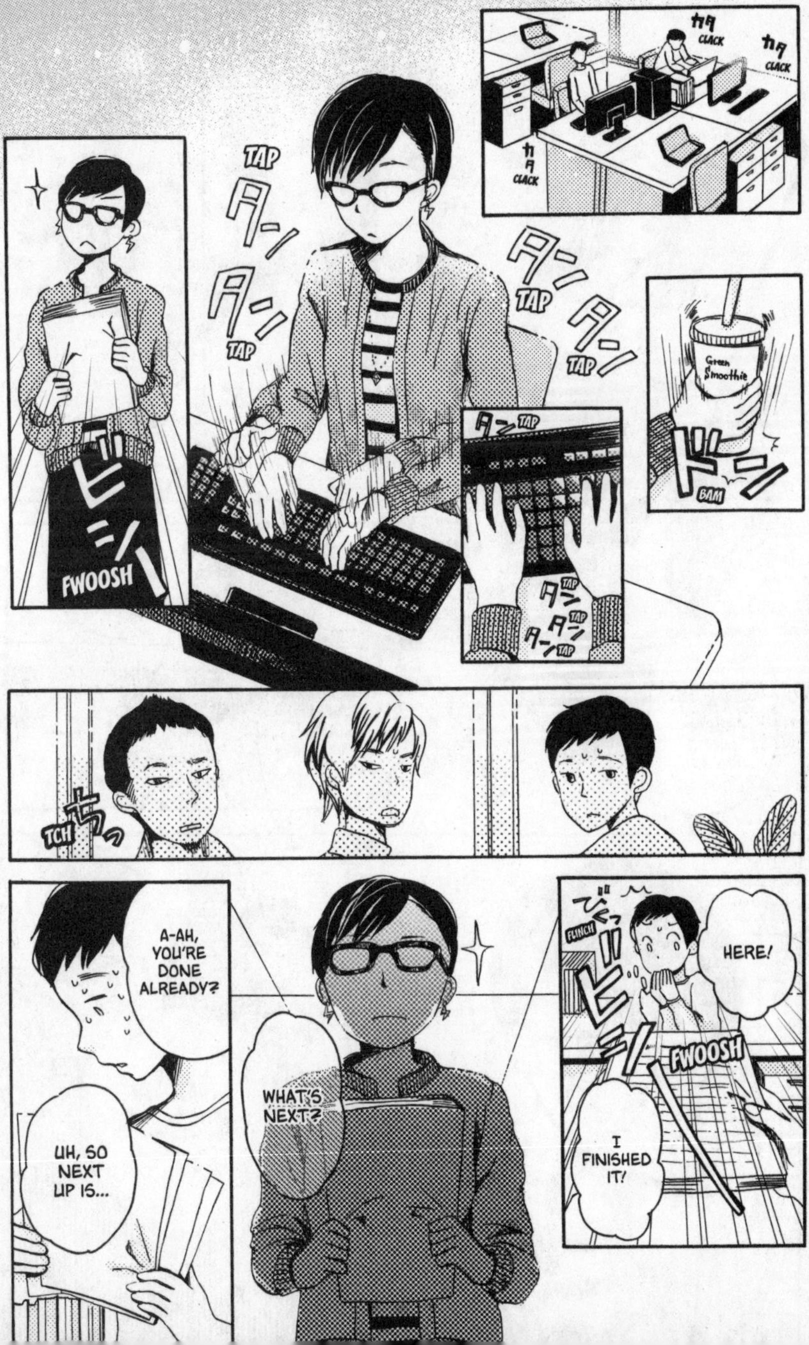
カタ CLACK
カタ CLACK
カタ CLACK
TAP
TAP
TAP
TAP
Green Smoothie
BAM
TAP
TAP
TAP
TAP
FWOOSH
TCH
FLINCH
HERE!
FWOOSH
I FINISHED IT!
WHAT'S NEXT?
A-AH, YOU'RE DONE ALREADY?
UH, SO NEXT UP IS...

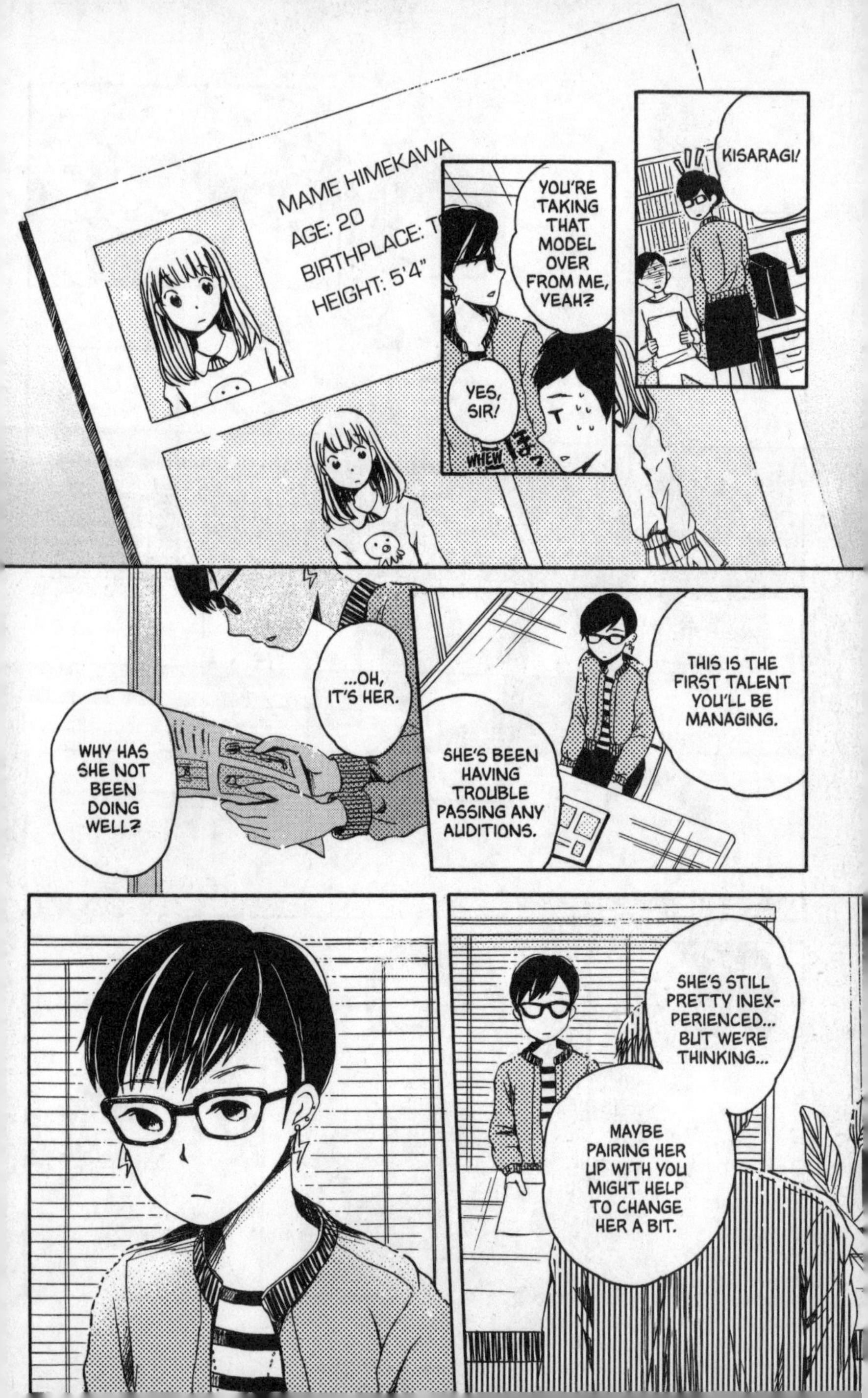
KISARAGI!
YOU'RE TAKING THAT MODEL OVER FROM ME, YEAH?
YES, SIR!
WHEW
MAME HIMEKAWA
AGE: 20
BIRTHPLACE: T
HEIGHT: 5'4"
THIS IS THE FIRST TALENT YOU'LL BE MANAGING.
SHE'S BEEN HAVING TROUBLE PASSING ANY AUDITIONS.
...OH, IT'S HER.
WHY HAS SHE NOT BEEN DOING WELL?
SHE'S STILL PRETTY INEXPERIENCED... BUT WE'RE THINKING...
MAYBE PAIRING HER UP WITH YOU MIGHT HELP TO CHANGE HER A BIT.

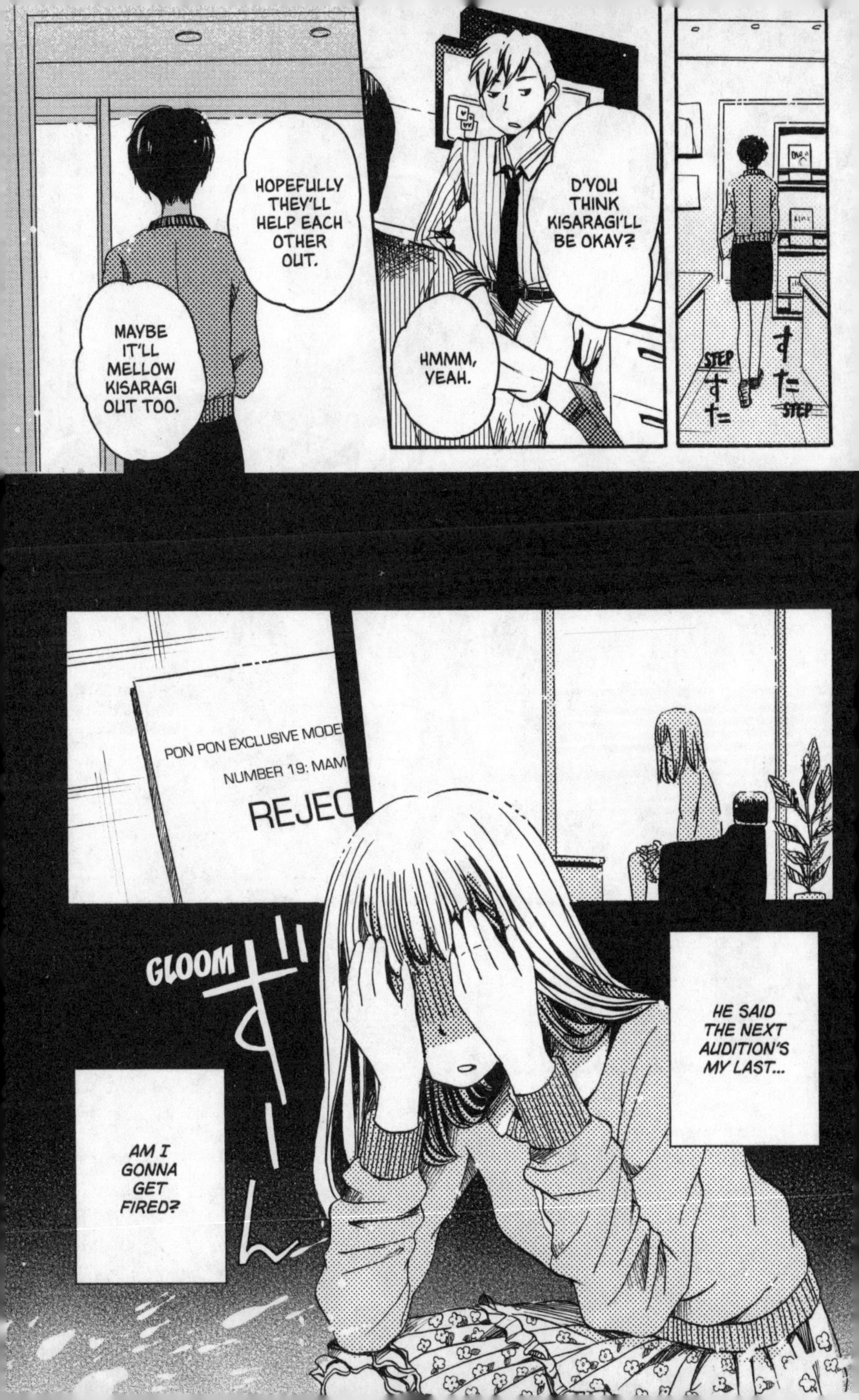

STEP
すた
STEP
すた
D'YOU THINK KISARAGI'LL BE OKAY?
HMMM, YEAH.
HOPEFULLY THEY'LL HELP EACH OTHER OUT.
MAYBE IT'LL MELLOW KISARAGI OUT TOO.
PON PON EXCLUSIVE MODE
NUMBER 19: MAM
REJEC
HE SAID THE NEXT AUDITION'S MY LAST...
GLOOM
ずーん
AM I GONNA GET FIRED?

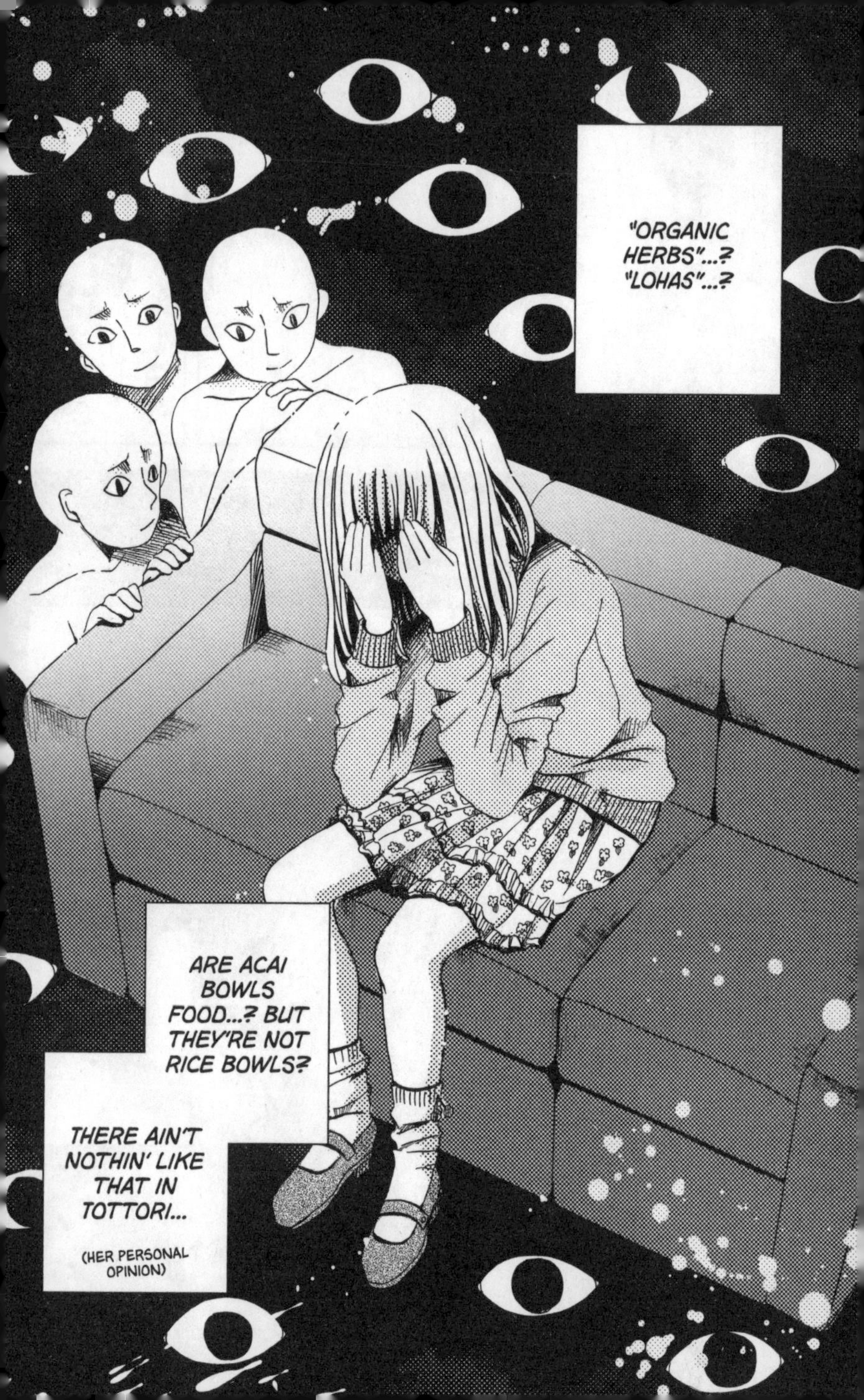
"ORGANIC HERBS"...? "LOHAS"...?
ARE ACAI BOWLS FOOD...? BUT THEY'RE NOT RICE BOWLS?
THERE AIN'T NOTHIN' LIKE THAT IN TOTTORI...
(HER PERSONAL OPINION)

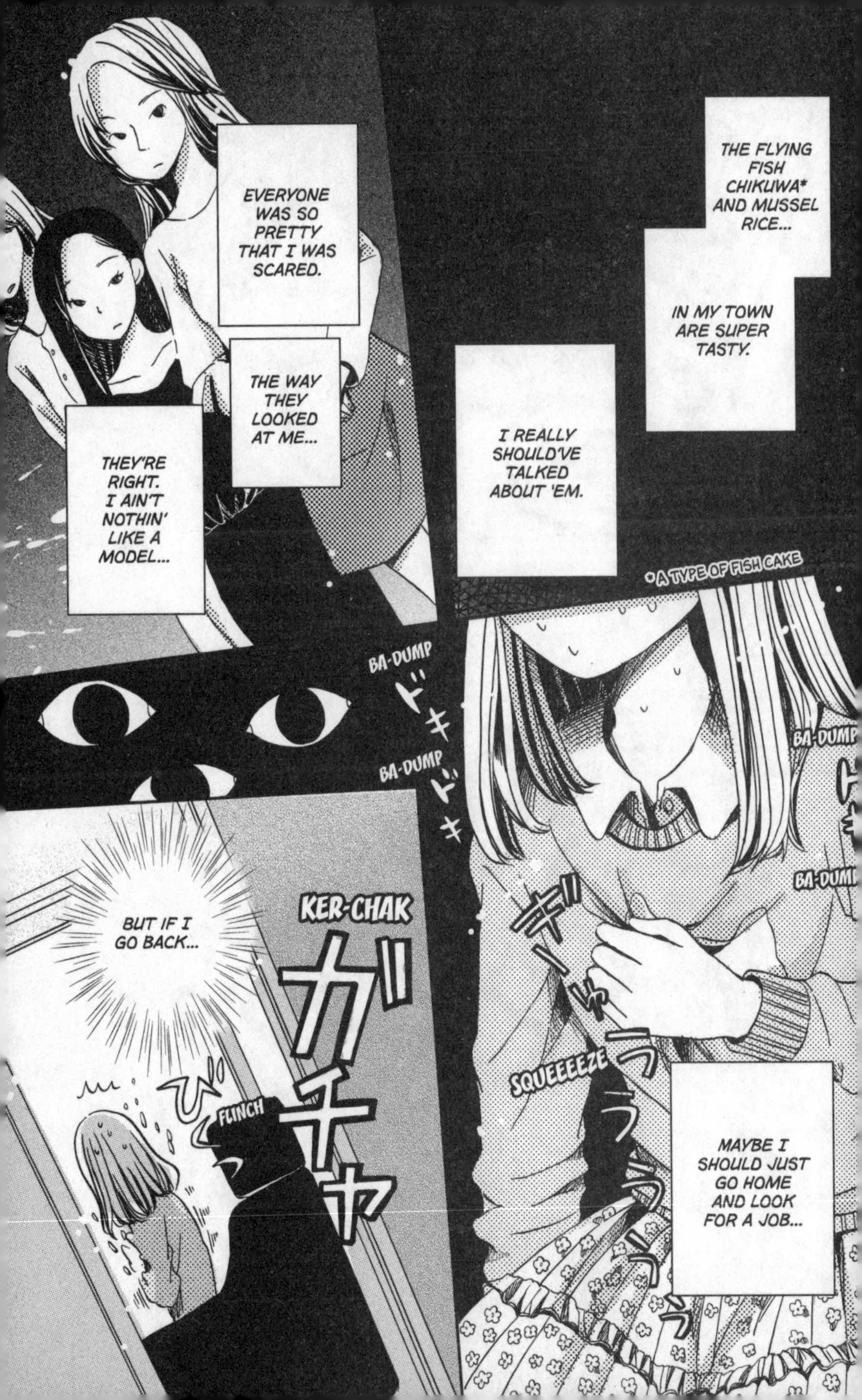
THE FLYING FISH CHIKUWA* AND MUSSEL RICE...
IN MY TOWN ARE SUPER TASTY.
I REALLY SHOULD'VE TALKED ABOUT 'EM.
*A TYPE OF FISH CAKE
EVERYONE WAS SO PRETTY THAT I WAS SCARED.
THE WAY THEY LOOKED AT ME...
THEY'RE RIGHT. I AIN'T NOTHIN' LIKE A MODEL...
BA-DUMP
BA-DUMP
SQUEEEEZE
MAYBE I SHOULD JUST GO HOME AND LOOK FOR A JOB...
BA-DUMP
BA-DUMP
KER-CHAK
BUT IF I GO BACK...
FLINCH

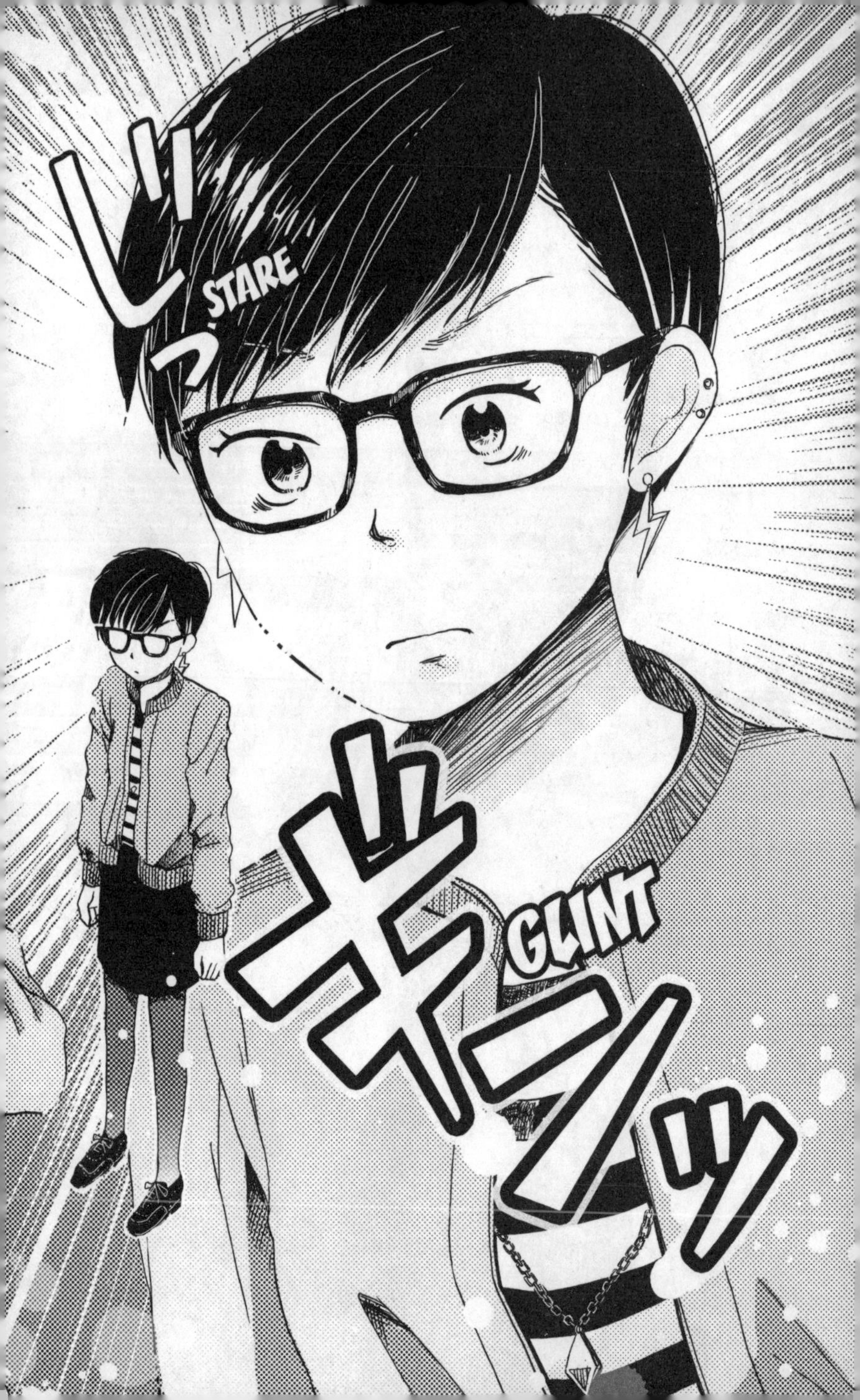
じーっ
STARE
ギーンッ
GLINT

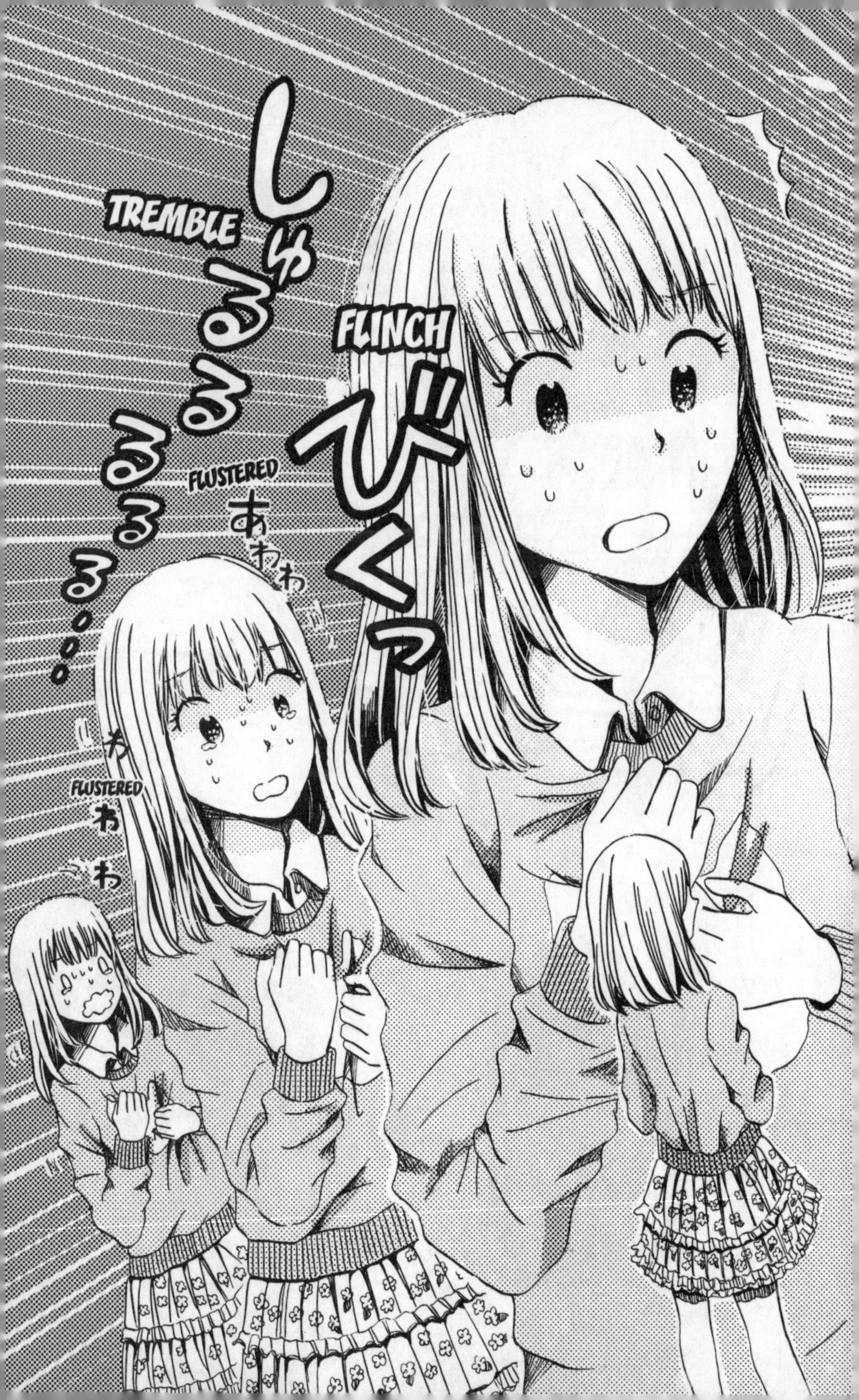FLINCH
びくぅ
TREMBLE
しゅるるるるる…
FLUSTERED
あわわ
FLUSTERED
わわわ

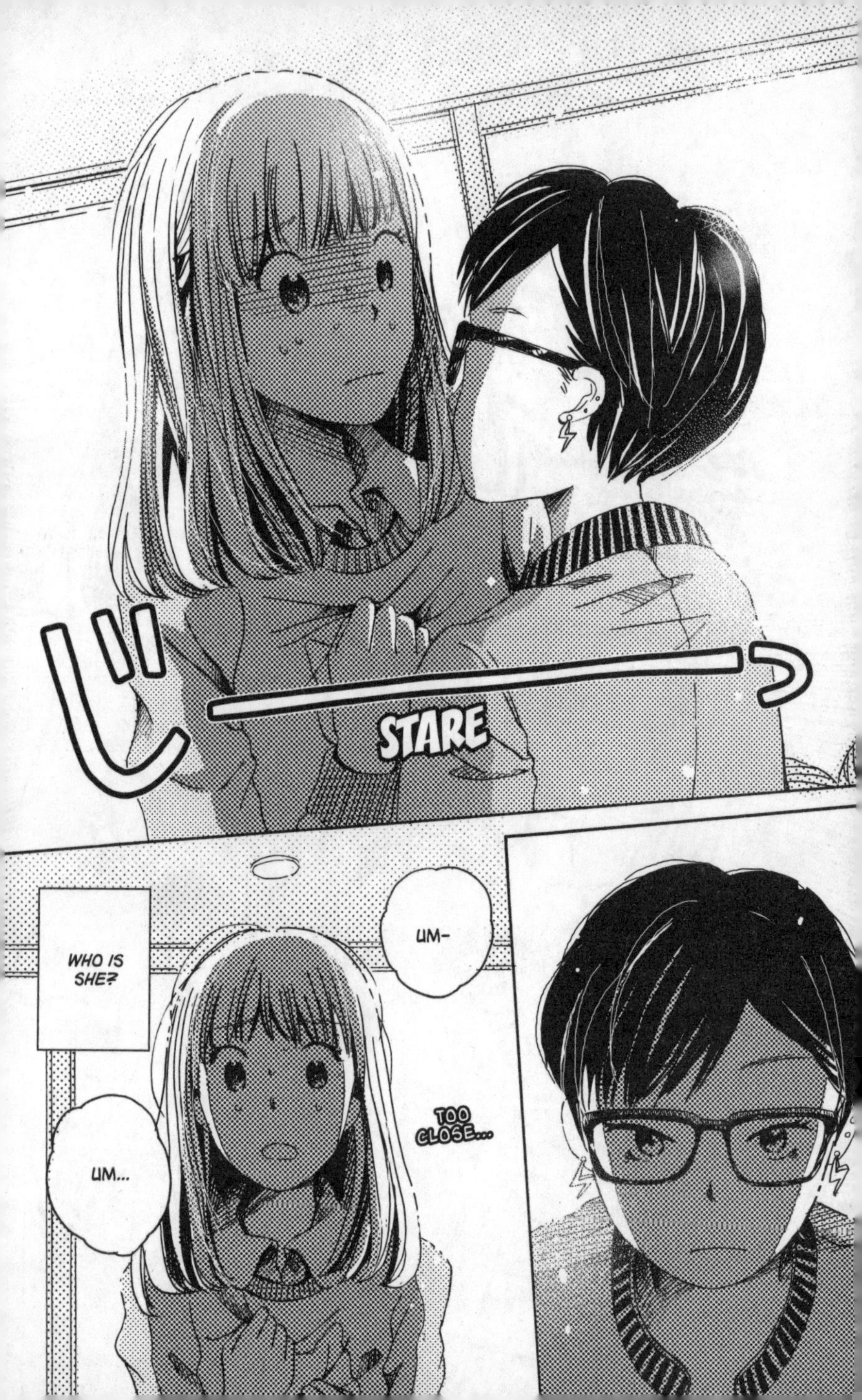
じーっ
STARE
UM-
WHO IS SHE?
TOO CLOSE...
UM...

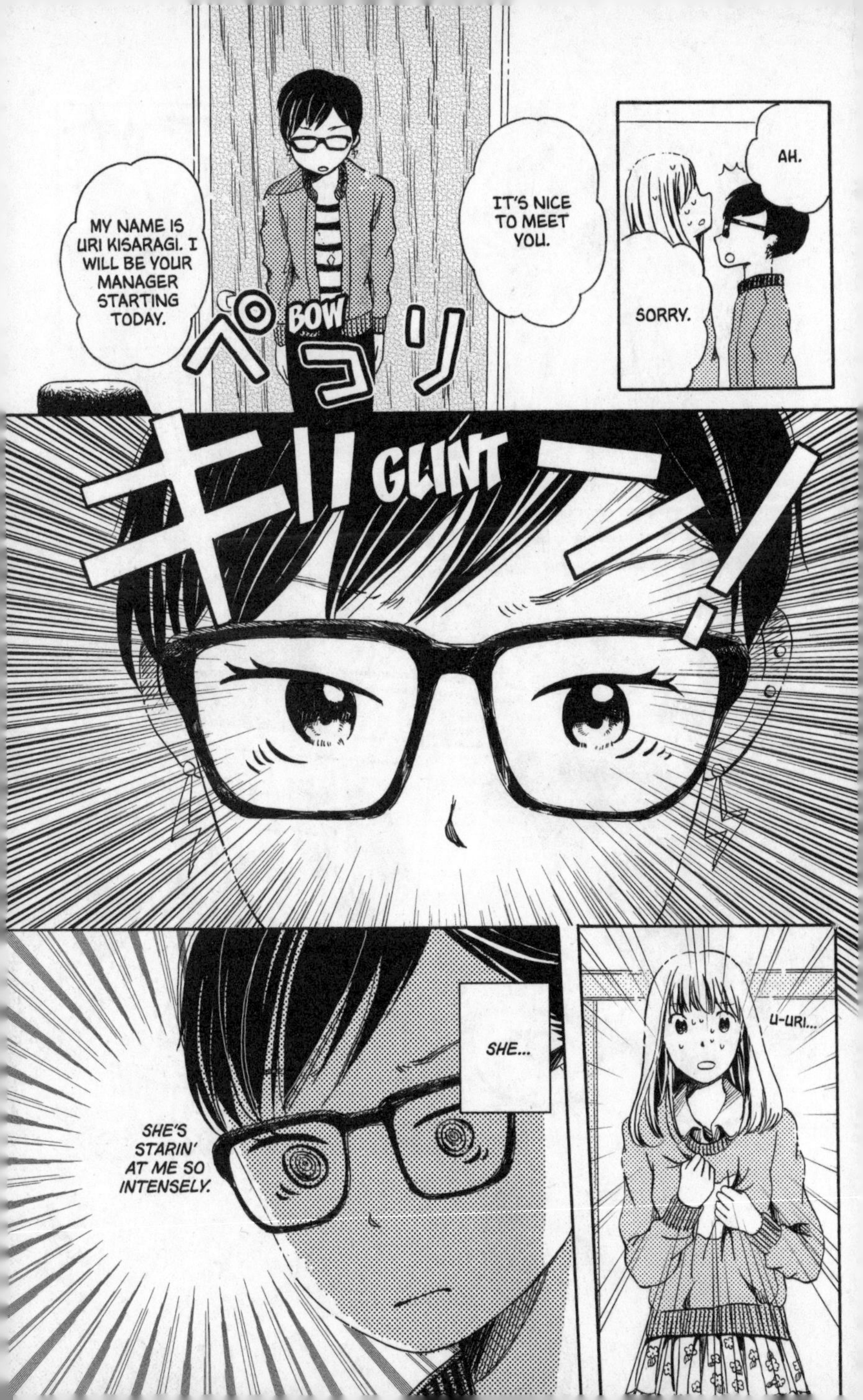
AH.
SORRY.
IT'S NICE TO MEET YOU.
MY NAME IS URI KISARAGI. I WILL BE YOUR MANAGER STARTING TODAY.
ペコリ
BOW
キーン!
GLINT
U-URI...
SHE...
SHE'S STARIN' AT ME SO INTENSELY.

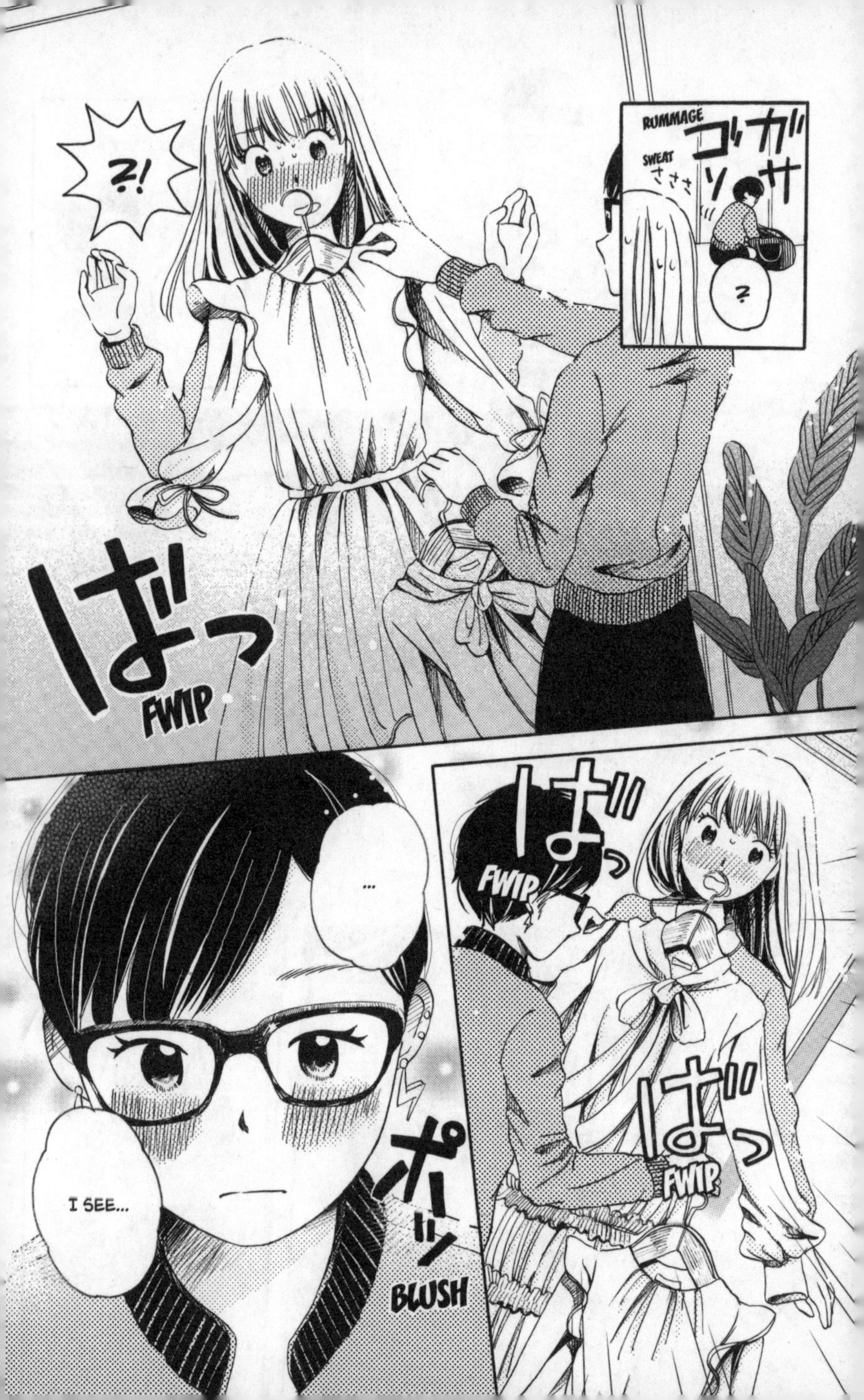

ガサゴソ
RUMMAGE
さささ
SWEAT
?
?!
ぱっ
FWIP
ぱっ
FWIP
ぱっ
FWIP
...
I SEE...
ポーッ
BLUSH

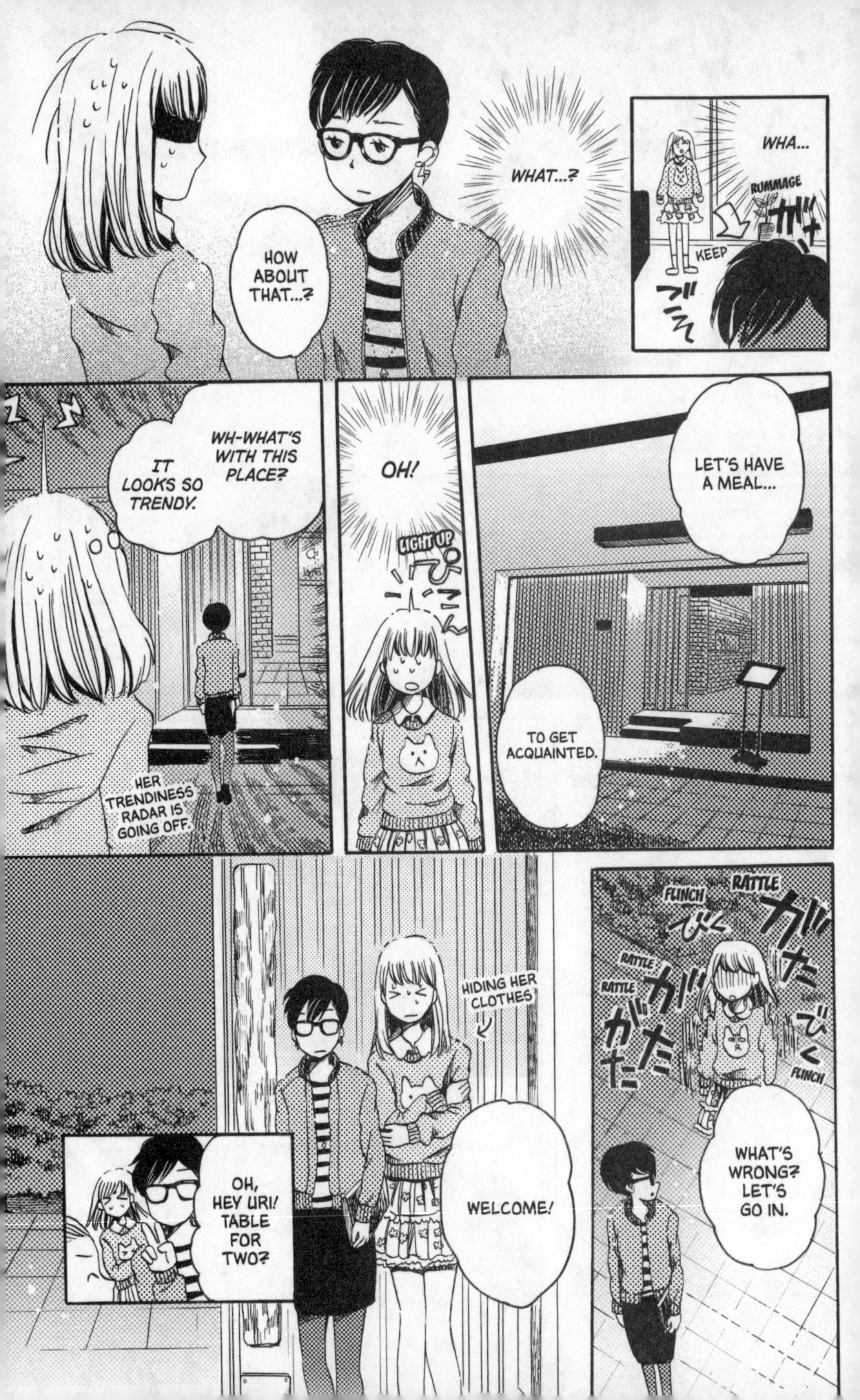
WHA...
RUMMAGE
KEEP
WHAT...?
HOW ABOUT THAT...?
LET'S HAVE A MEAL...
TO GET ACQUAINTED.
OH!
LIGHT UP
WH-WHAT'S WITH THIS PLACE?
IT LOOKS SO TRENDY.
HER TRENDINESS RADAR IS GOING OFF.
RATTLE
FLINCH
RATTLE
RATTLE
FLINCH
WHAT'S WRONG? LET'S GO IN.
WELCOME!
HIDING HER CLOTHES
OH, HEY URI! TABLE FOR TWO?

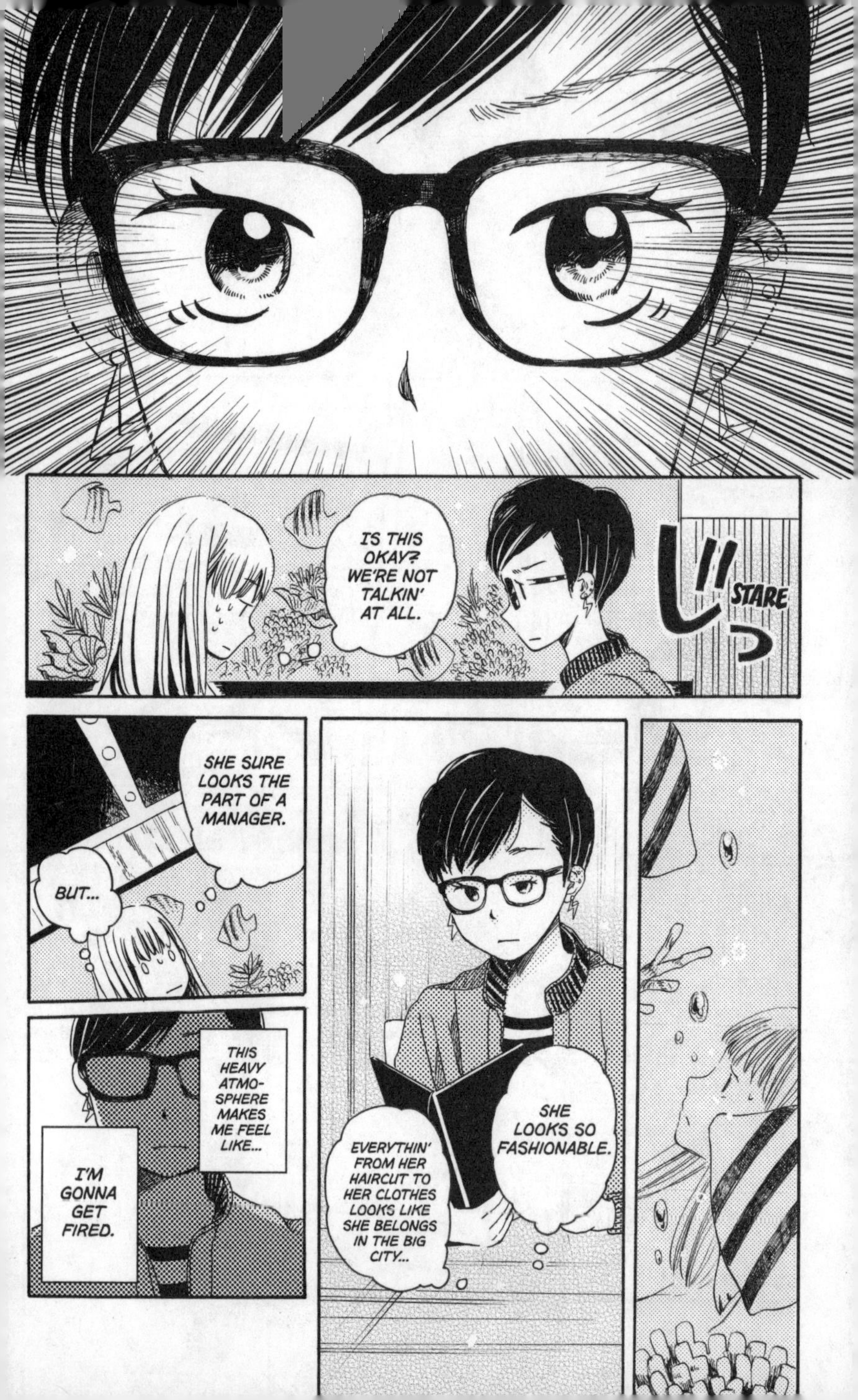

じーっ
STARE
IS THIS OKAY? WE'RE NOT TALKIN' AT ALL.
SHE LOOKS SO FASHIONABLE.
EVERYTHIN' FROM HER HAIRCUT TO HER CLOTHES LOOKS LIKE SHE BELONGS IN THE BIG CITY...
SHE SURE LOOKS THE PART OF A MANAGER.
BUT...
THIS HEAVY ATMOSPHERE MAKES ME FEEL LIKE...
I'M GONNA GET FIRED.

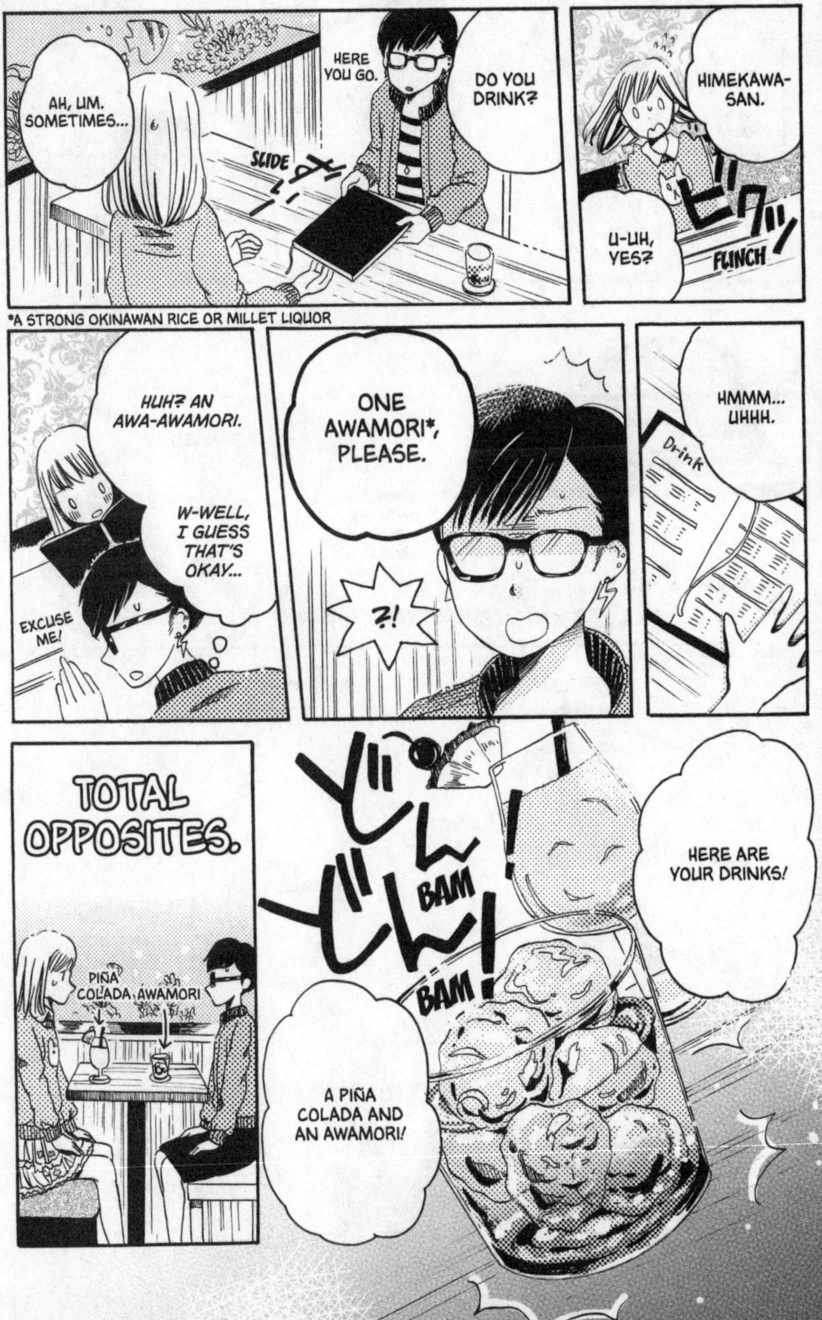
HIMEKAWA-SAN.
U-UH, YES?
FLINCH
HERE YOU GO.
DO YOU DRINK?
SLIDE
AH, UM. SOMETIMES...
HMMM... UHHH.
Drink
ONE AWAMORI*, PLEASE.
?!
HUH? AN AWA-AWAMORI.
W-WELL, I GUESS THAT'S OKAY...
EXCUSE ME!
HERE ARE YOUR DRINKS!
BAM
BAM
A PIÑA COLADA AND AN AWAMORI!
TOTAL OPPOSITES.
PIÑA COLADA
AWAMORI

*A STRONG OKINAWAN RICE OR MILLET LIQUOR

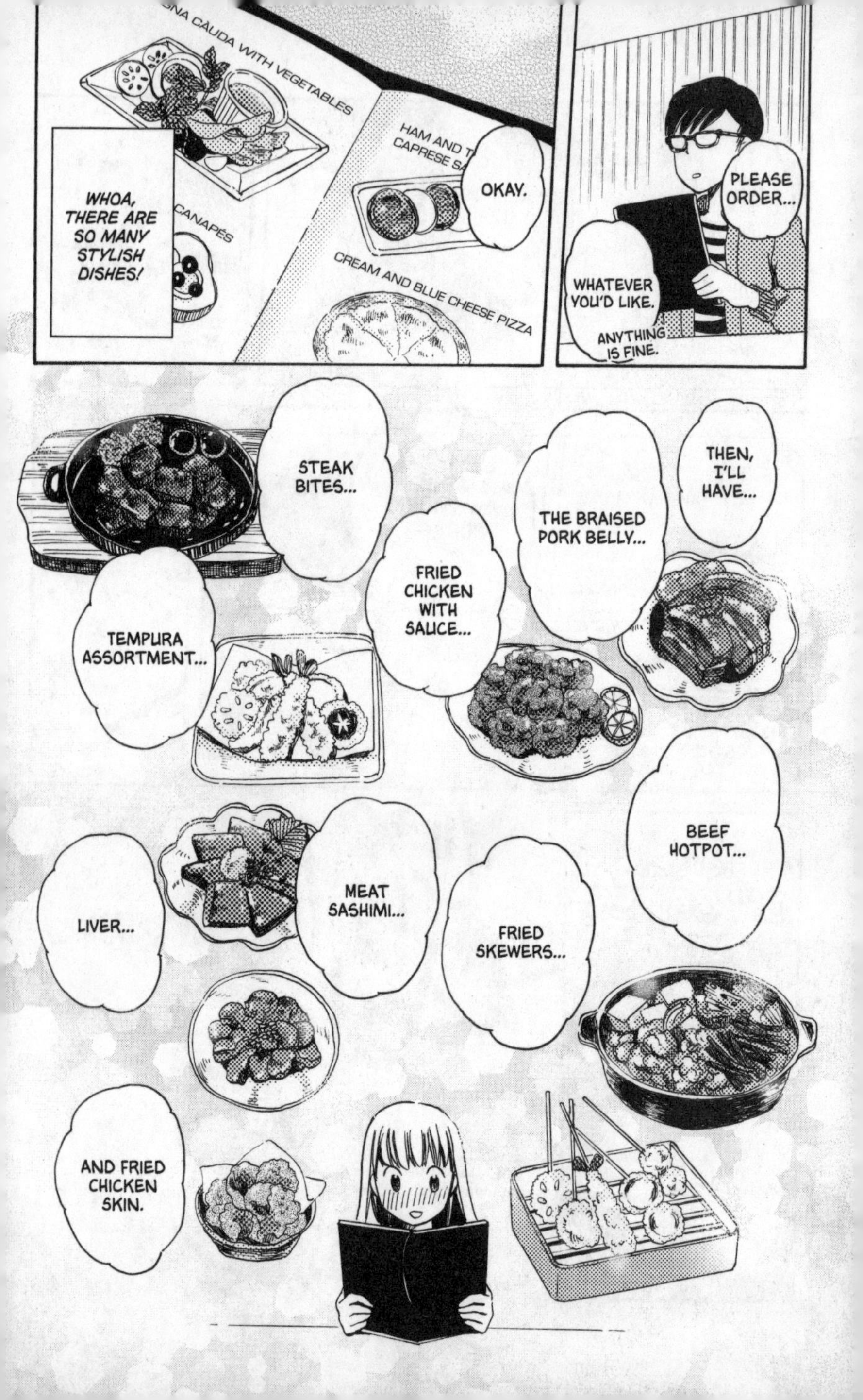
PLEASE ORDER...
WHATEVER YOU'D LIKE.
ANYTHING IS FINE.
OKAY.
CAPRESE SA
CREAM AND BLUE CHEESE PIZZA
CANAPÉS
WHOA, THERE ARE SO MANY STYLISH DISHES!
THEN, I'LL HAVE...
THE BRAISED PORK BELLY...
STEAK BITES...
FRIED CHICKEN WITH SAUCE...
TEMPURA ASSORTMENT...
BEEF HOTPOT...
FRIED SKEWERS...
MEAT SASHIMI...
LIVER...
AND FRIED CHICKEN SKIN.

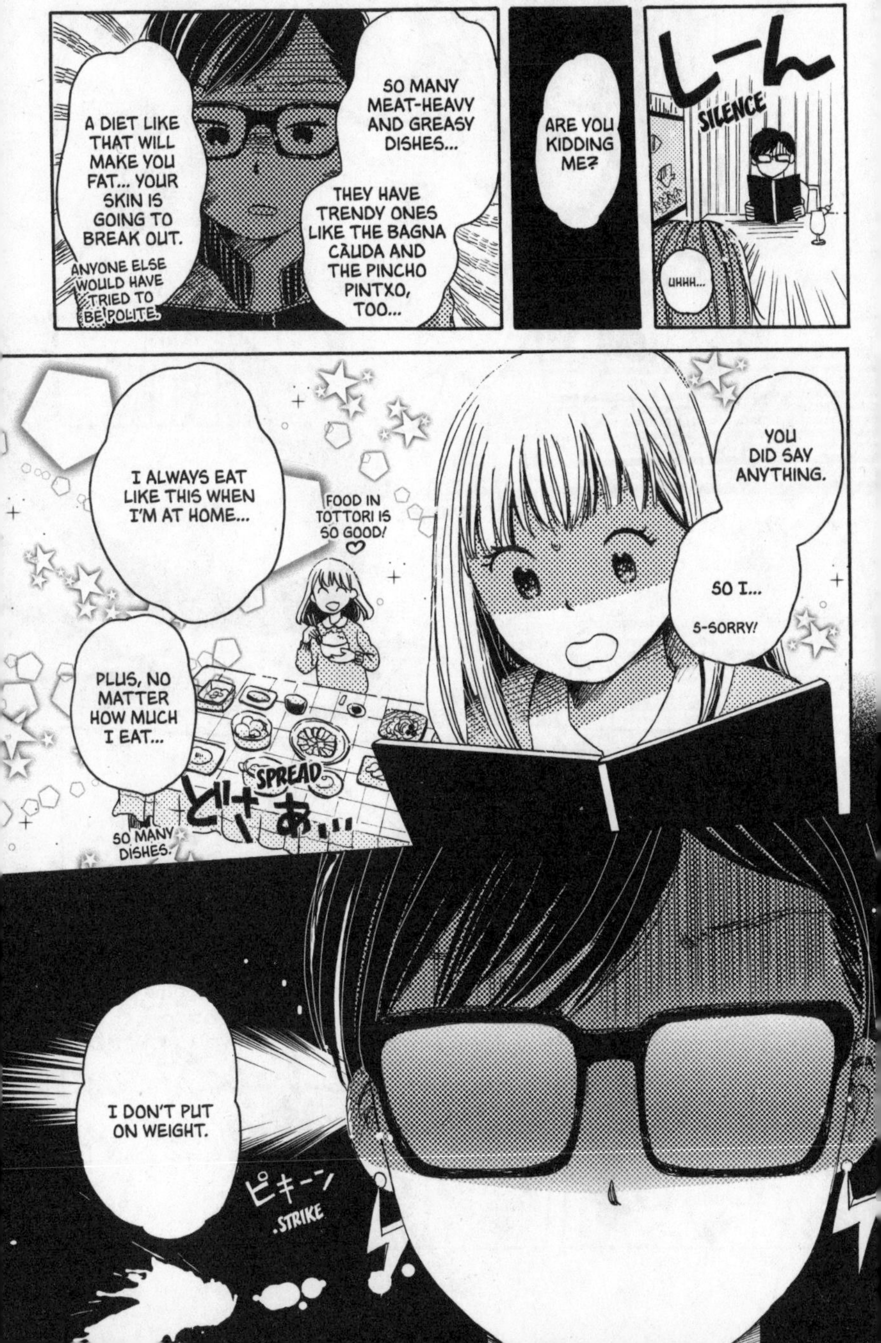
しーん
SILENCE
UHHH...
ARE YOU KIDDING ME?
SO MANY MEAT-HEAVY AND GREASY DISHES...
THEY HAVE TRENDY ONES LIKE THE BAGNA CAUDA AND THE PINCHO PINTXO, TOO...
A DIET LIKE THAT WILL MAKE YOU FAT... YOUR SKIN IS GOING TO BREAK OUT.
ANYONE ELSE WOULD HAVE TRIED TO BE POLITE.
YOU DID SAY ANYTHING.
SO I...
S-SORRY!
I ALWAYS EAT LIKE THIS WHEN I'M AT HOME...
FOOD IN TOTTORI IS SO GOOD!
PLUS, NO MATTER HOW MUCH I EAT...
どさぁっ
SPREAD
SO MANY DISHES.
I DON'T PUT ON WEIGHT.
ピキーン
STRIKE

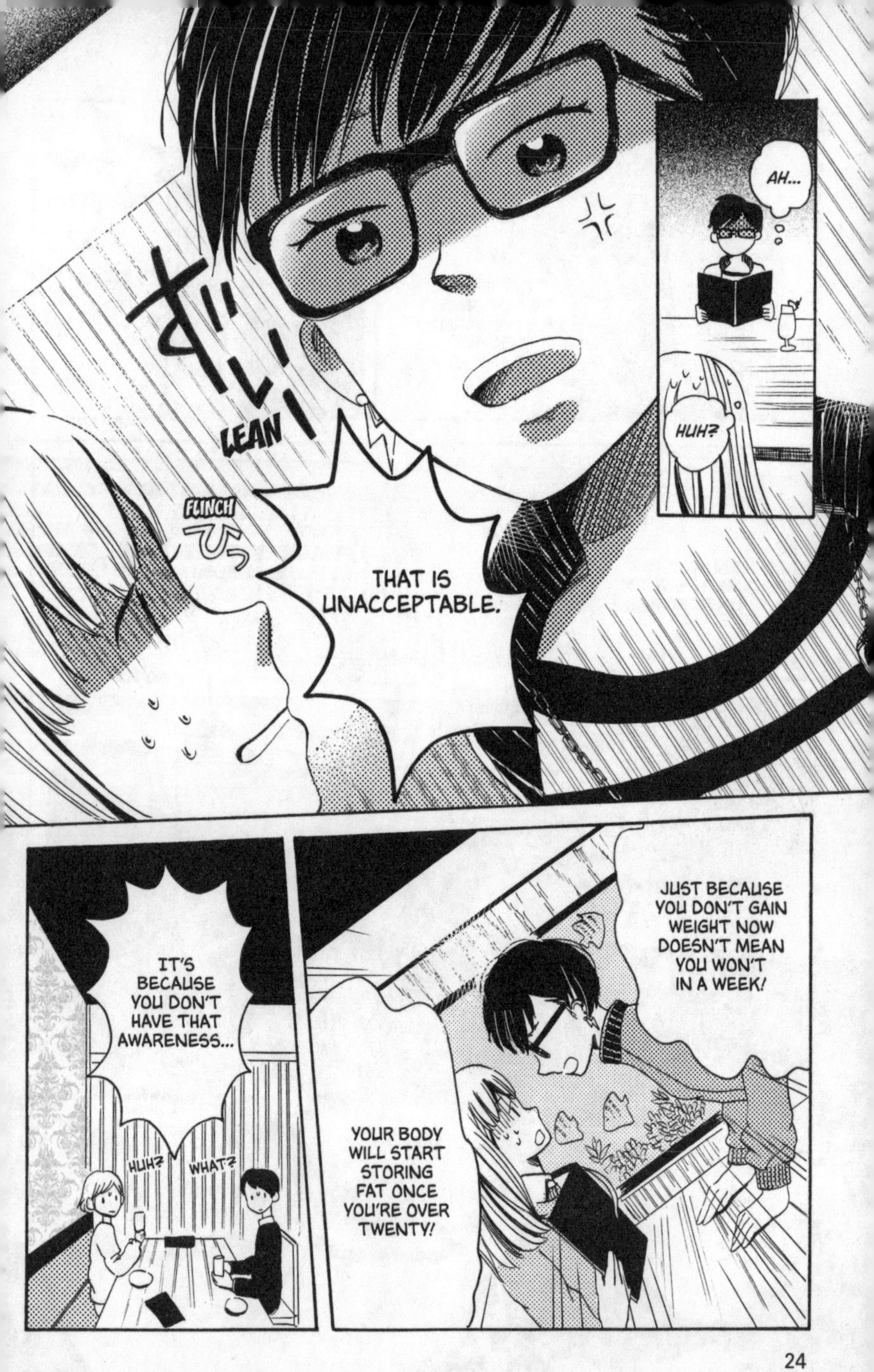
AH...
HUH?
LEAN
FLINCH
THAT IS UNACCEPTABLE.
JUST BECAUSE YOU DON'T GAIN WEIGHT NOW DOESN'T MEAN YOU WON'T IN A WEEK!
YOUR BODY WILL START STORING FAT ONCE YOU'RE OVER TWENTY!
IT'S BECAUSE YOU DON'T HAVE THAT AWARENESS...
WHAT?
HUH?

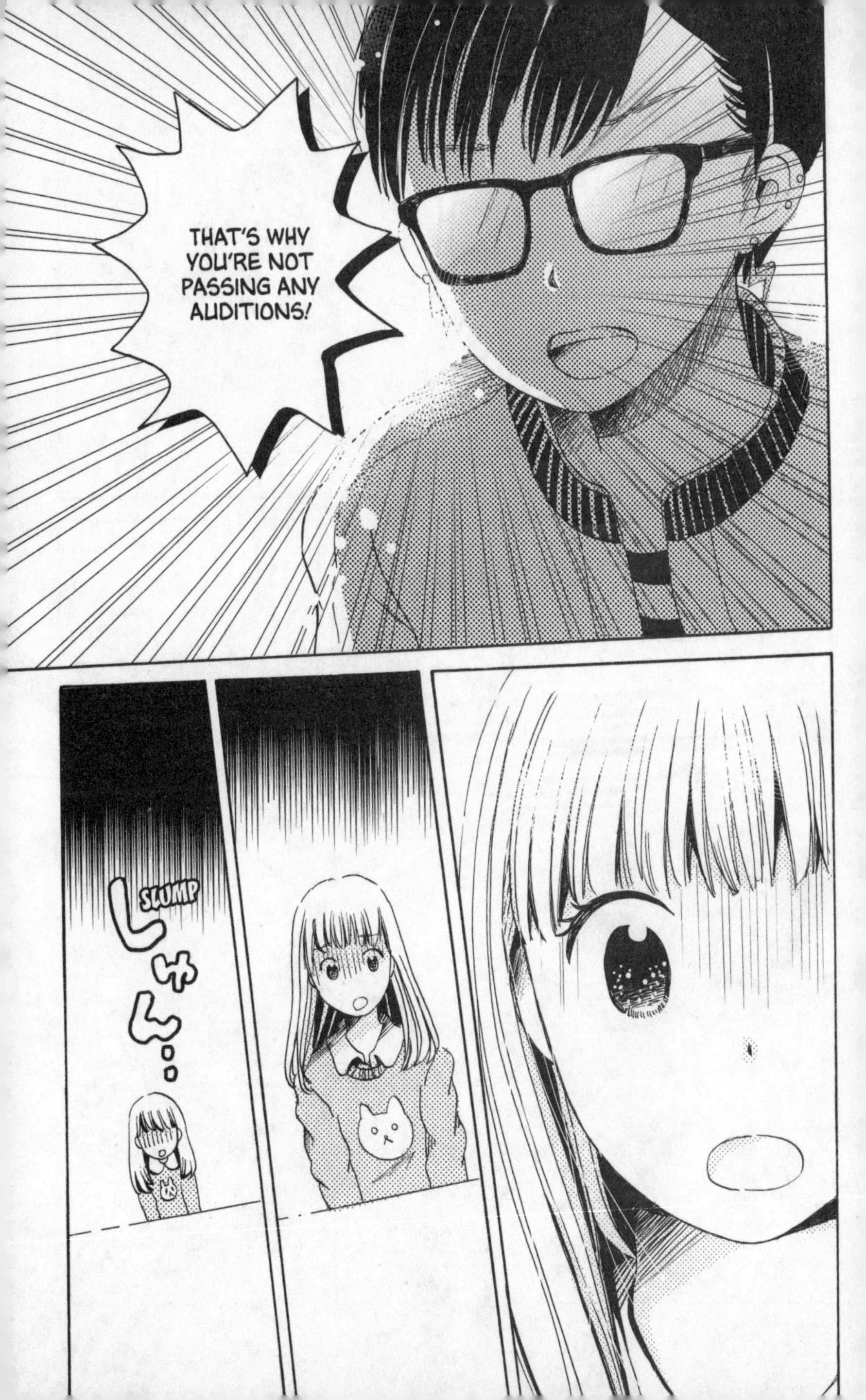
THAT'S WHY YOU'RE NOT PASSING ANY AUDITIONS!
SLUMP
しゅん。。

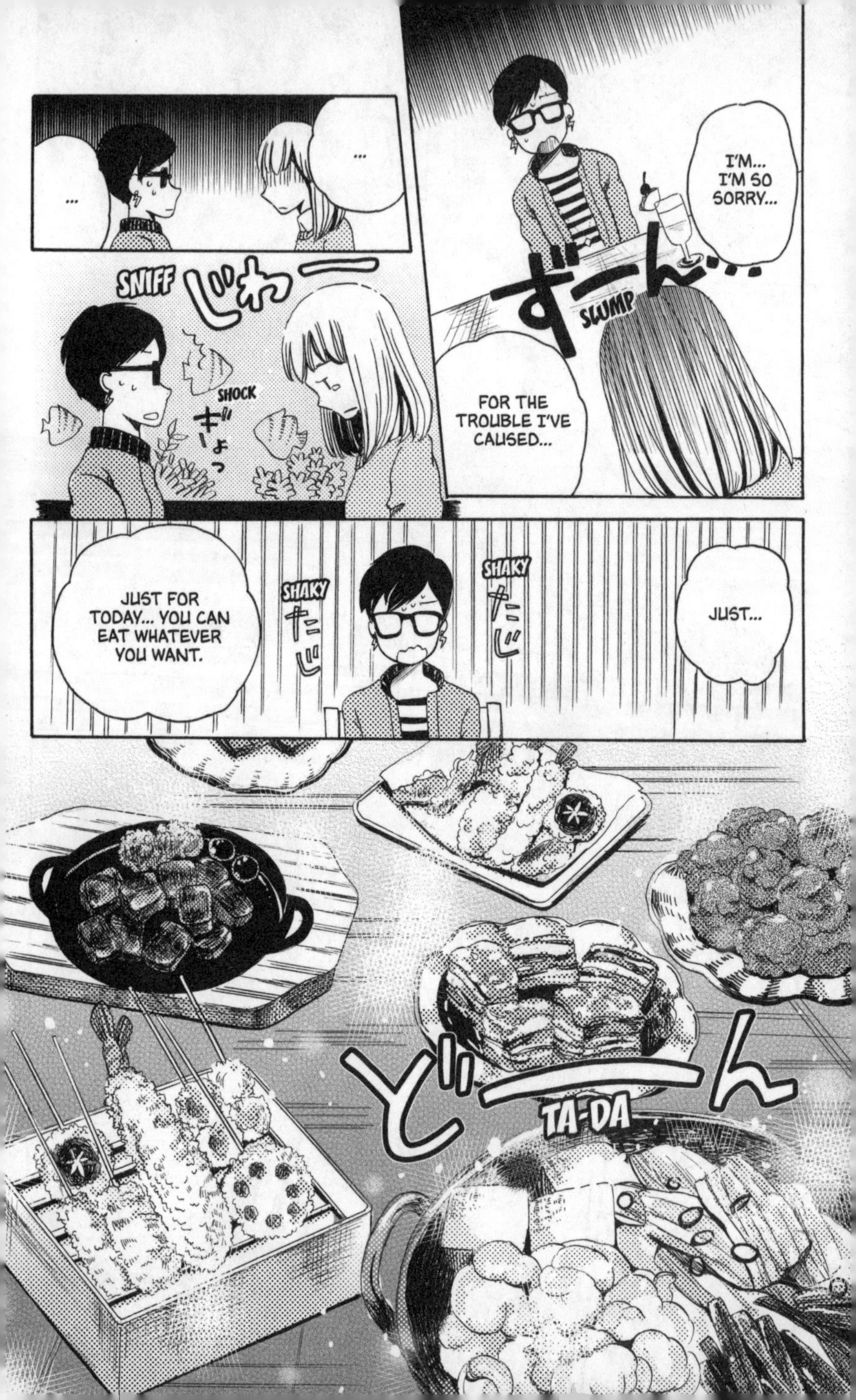
I'M... I'M SO SORRY...
ずーん…
SLUMP
FOR THE TROUBLE I'VE CAUSED...
...
...
じわー
SNIFF
SHOCK
ぎょっ
JUST...
SHAKY
たじ
SHAKY
たじ
JUST FOR TODAY... YOU CAN EAT WHATEVER YOU WANT.
どーん
TA-DA

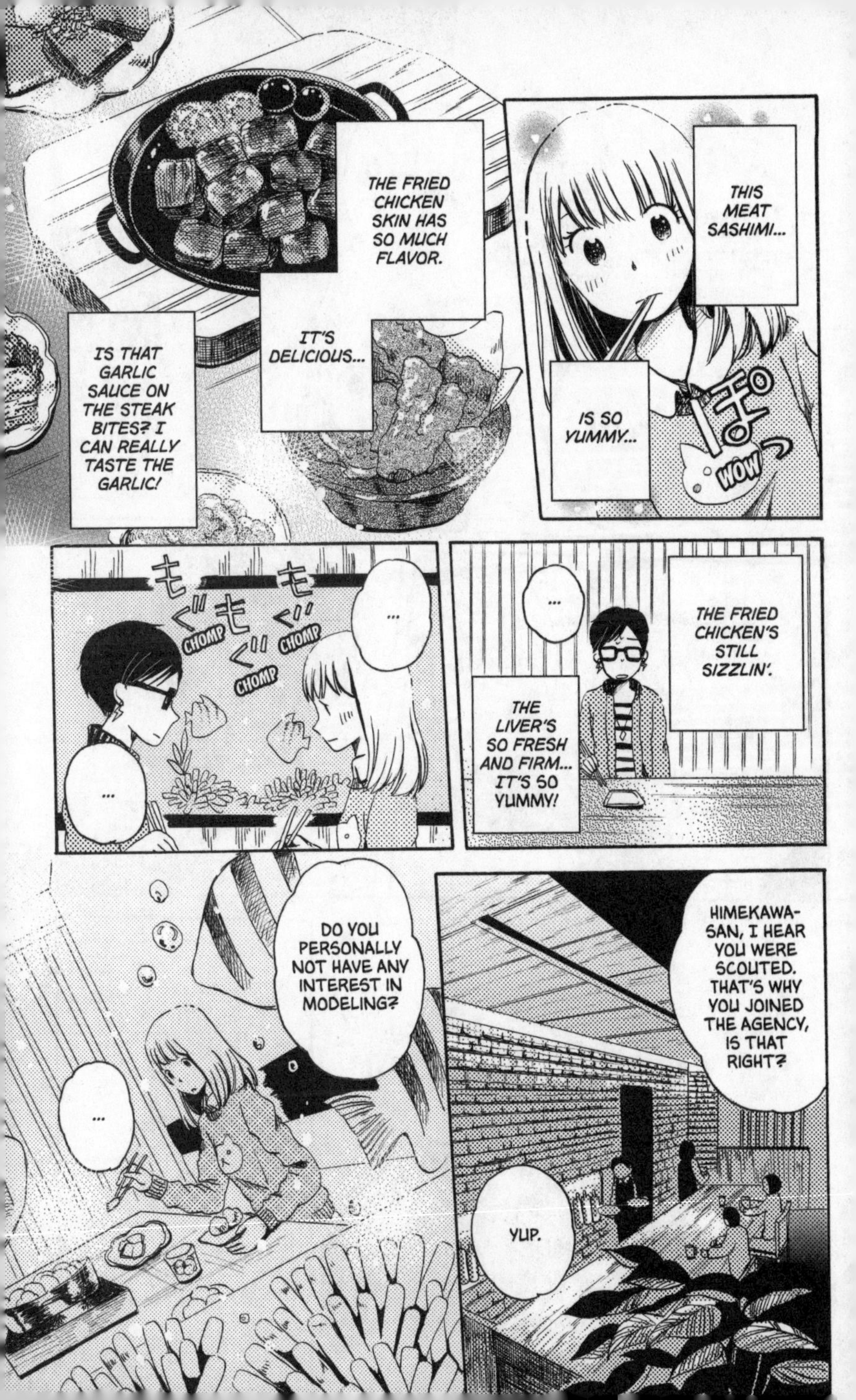
THIS MEAT SASHIMI...
IS SO YUMMY...
ぽっ
WOW
THE FRIED CHICKEN SKIN HAS SO MUCH FLAVOR.
IT'S DELICIOUS...
IS THAT GARLIC SAUCE ON THE STEAK BITES? I CAN REALLY TASTE THE GARLIC!
THE FRIED CHICKEN'S STILL SIZZLIN'.
...
THE LIVER'S SO FRESH AND FIRM... IT'S SO YUMMY!
...
もぐ CHOMP
もぐ CHOMP
もぐ CHOMP
...
HIMEKAWA-SAN, I HEAR YOU WERE SCOUTED. THAT'S WHY YOU JOINED THE AGENCY, IS THAT RIGHT?
YUP.
DO YOU PERSONALLY NOT HAVE ANY INTEREST IN MODELING?
...

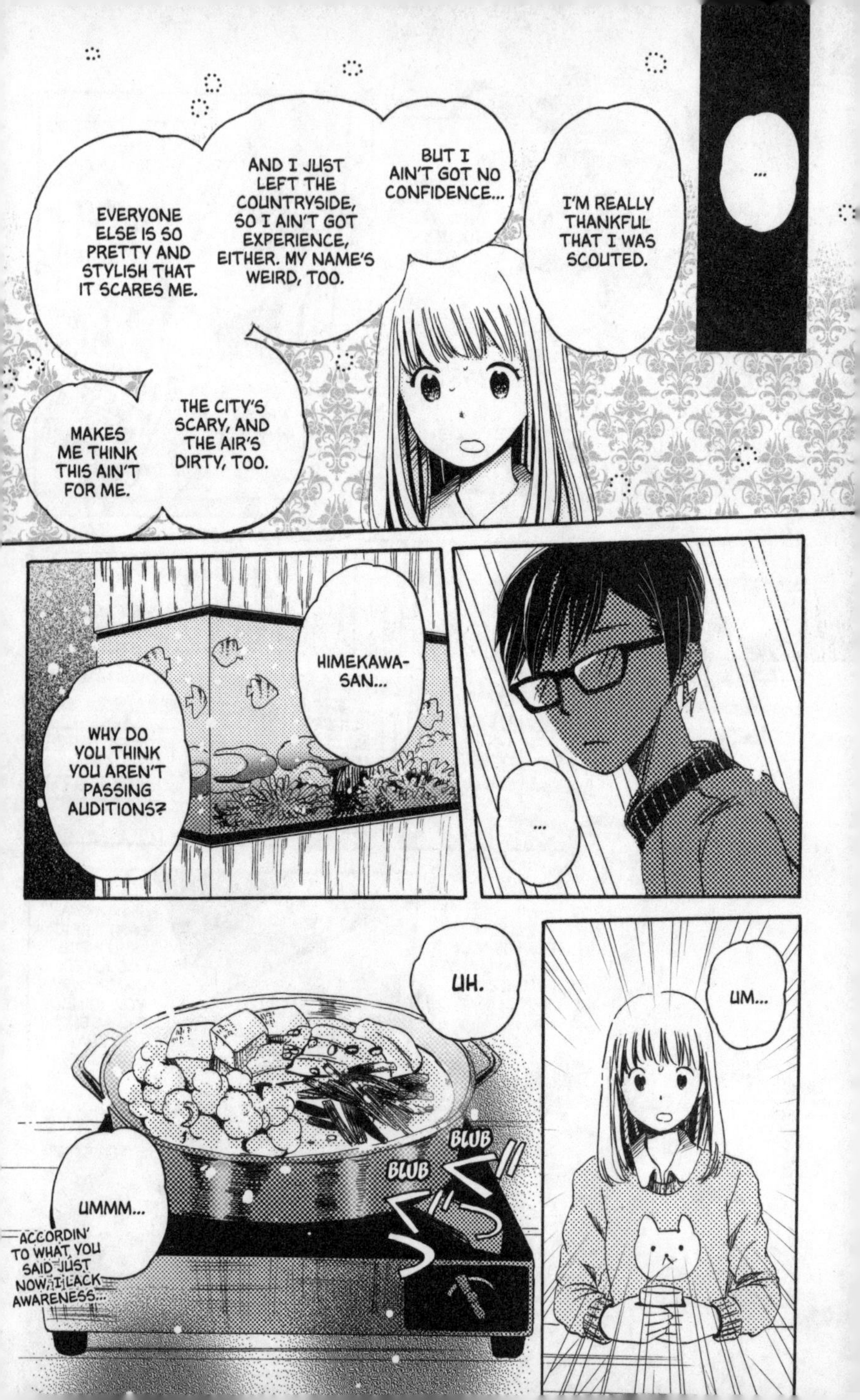
...
I'M REALLY THANKFUL THAT I WAS SCOUTED.
BUT I AIN'T GOT NO CONFIDENCE...
AND I JUST LEFT THE COUNTRYSIDE, SO I AIN'T GOT EXPERIENCE, EITHER. MY NAME'S WEIRD, TOO.
EVERYONE ELSE IS SO PRETTY AND STYLISH THAT IT SCARES ME.
THE CITY'S SCARY, AND THE AIR'S DIRTY, TOO.
MAKES ME THINK THIS AIN'T FOR ME.
...
HIMEKAWA-SAN...
WHY DO YOU THINK YOU AREN'T PASSING AUDITIONS?
UM...
UH.
BLUB
BLUB
UMMM...
ACCORDIN' TO WHAT YOU SAID JUST NOW, I LACK AWARENESS...

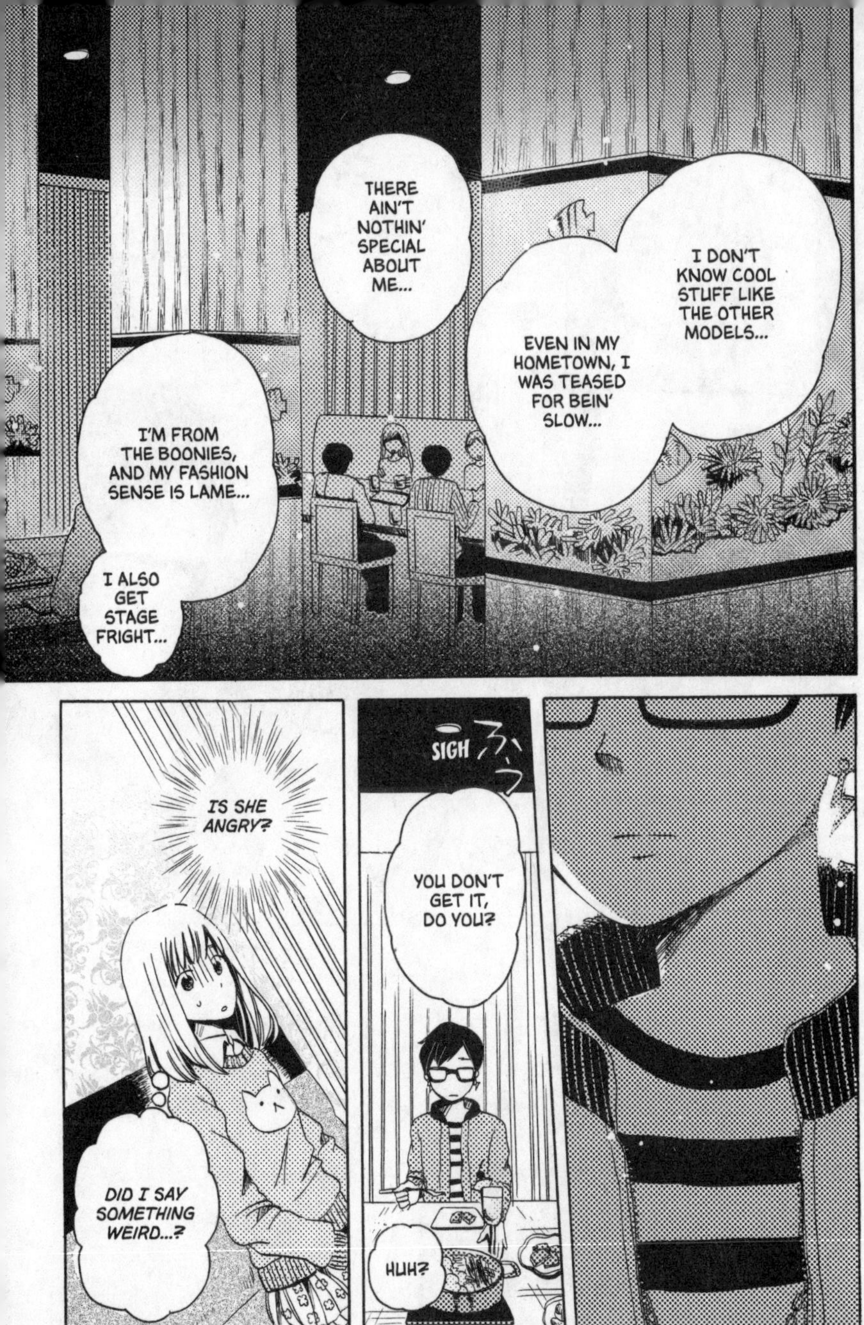
I DON'T KNOW COOL STUFF LIKE THE OTHER MODELS...
EVEN IN MY HOMETOWN, I WAS TEASED FOR BEIN' SLOW...
THERE AIN'T NOTHIN' SPECIAL ABOUT ME...
I'M FROM THE BOONIES, AND MY FASHION SENSE IS LAME...
I ALSO GET STAGE FRIGHT...
SIGH
YOU DON'T GET IT, DO YOU?
HUH?
IS SHE ANGRY?
DID I SAY SOMETHING WEIRD...?

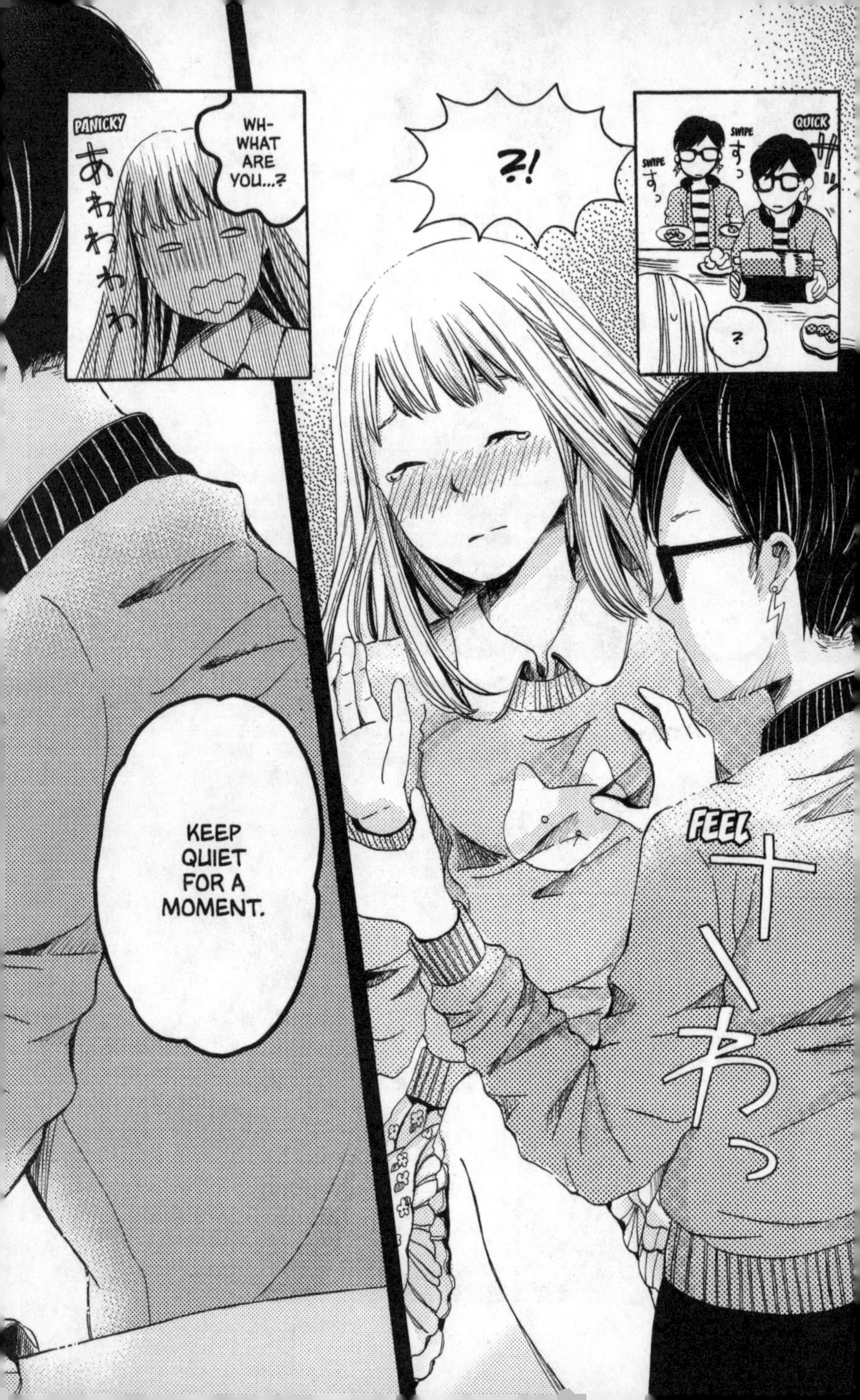
QUICK
SWIPE
すっ
SWIPE
すっ
?
?!
FEEL
さわっ
PANICKY
あわわわわ
WH-WHAT ARE YOU...?
KEEP QUIET FOR A MOMENT.

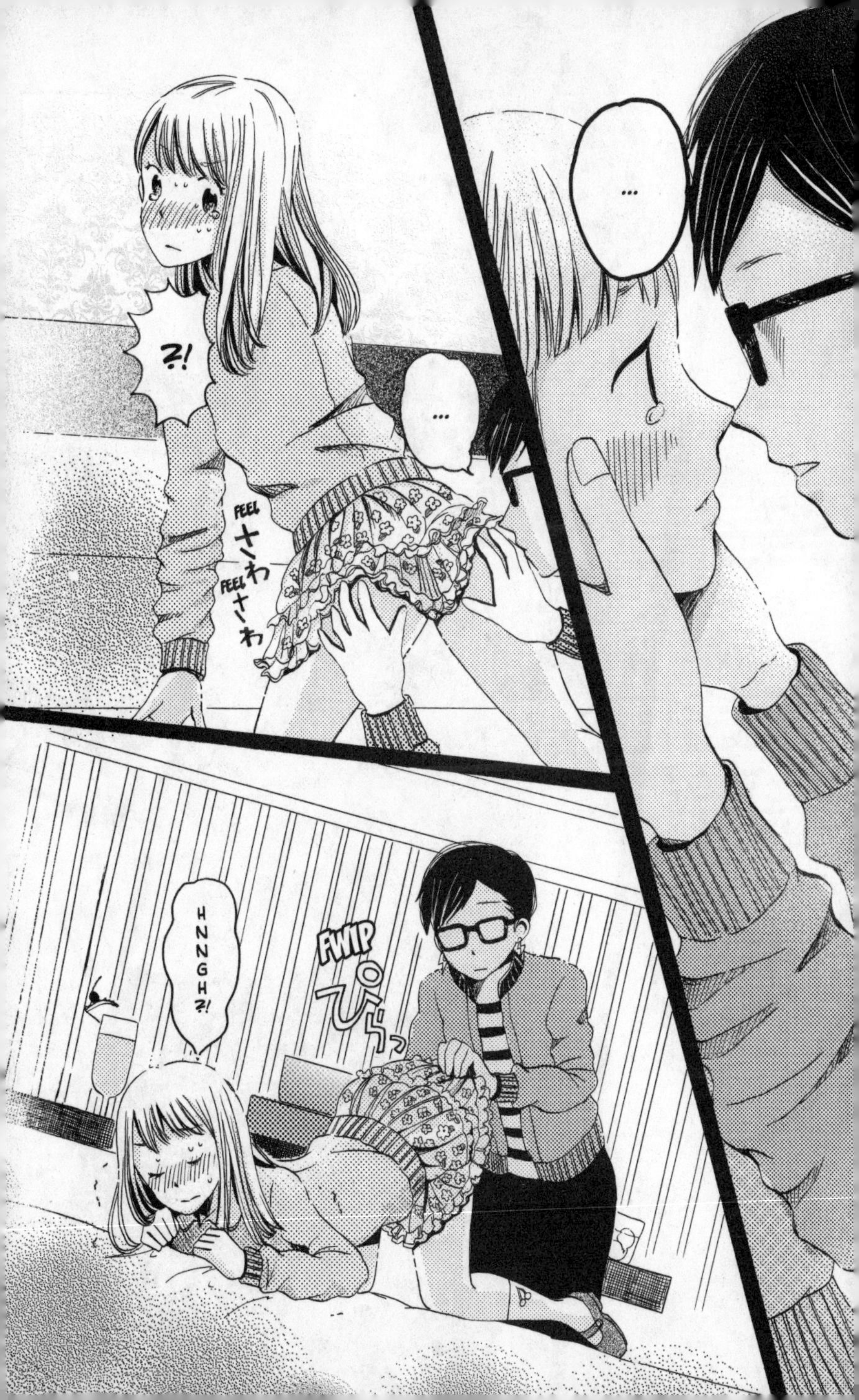
...
?!
...
FEEL さわ
FEEL さわ
FWIP ぴらっ
HNNGH?!

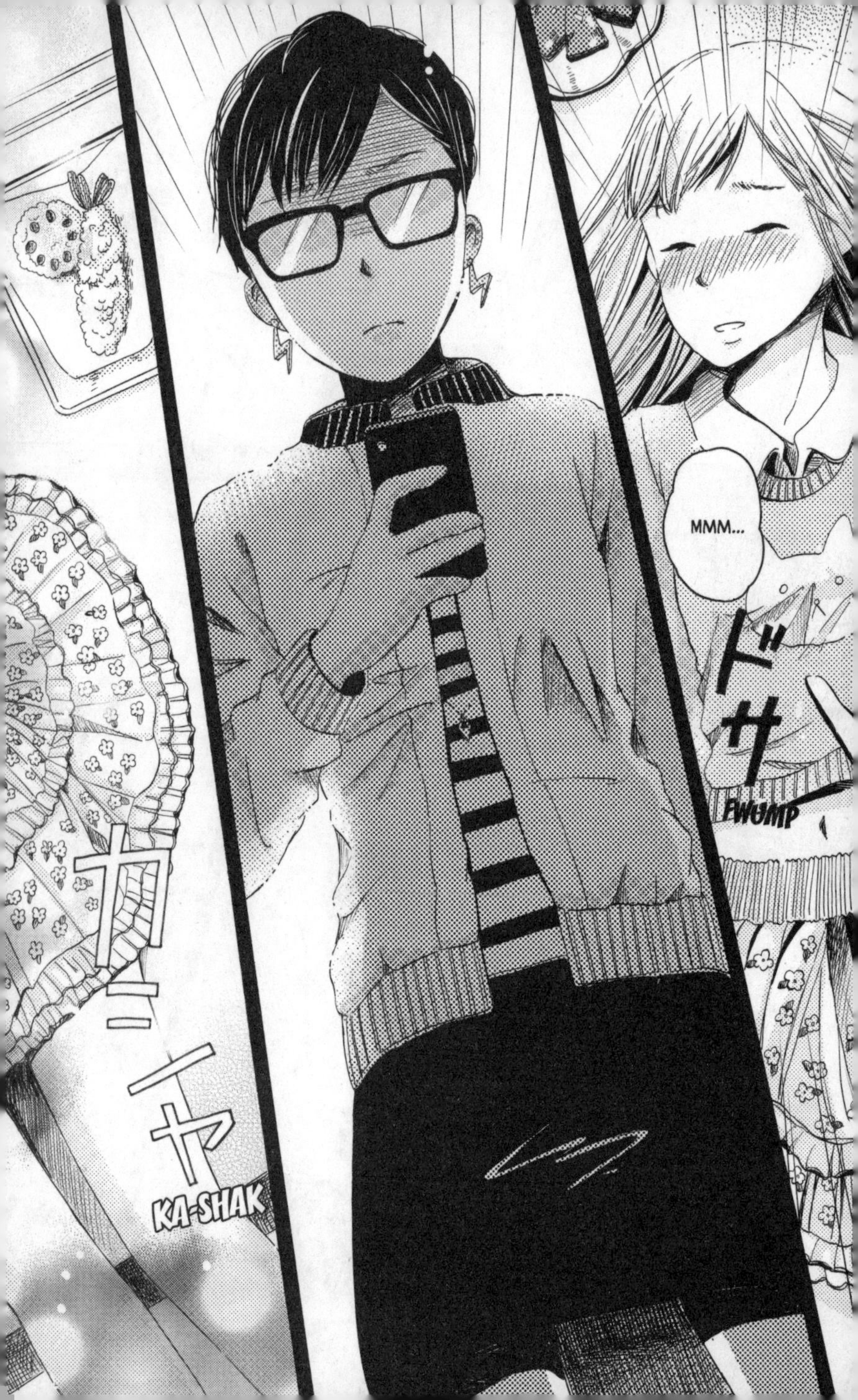
MMM...
ドサ
FWUMP
カシャ
KA-SHAK

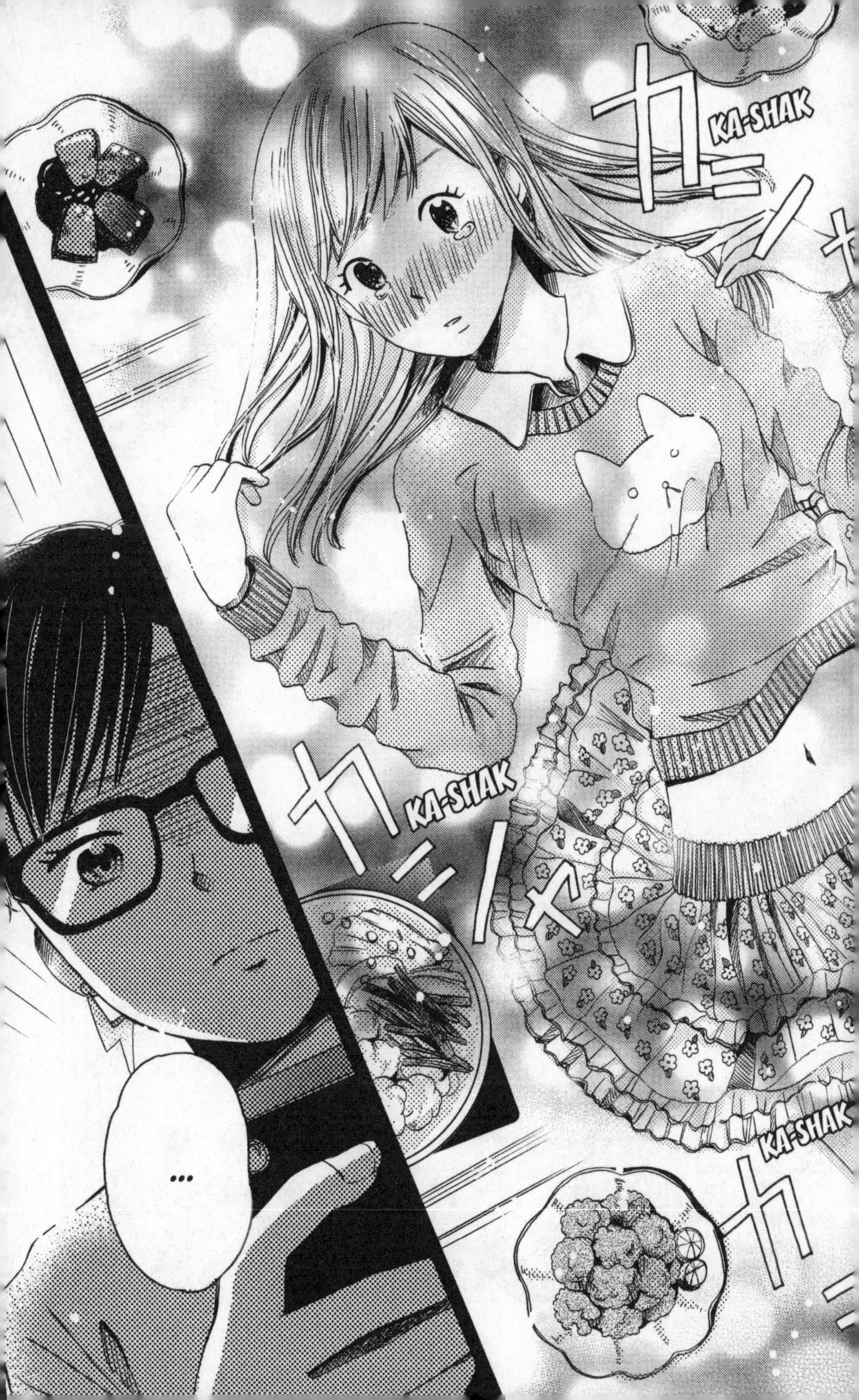
KA-SHAK
KA-SHAK
KA-SHAK
...

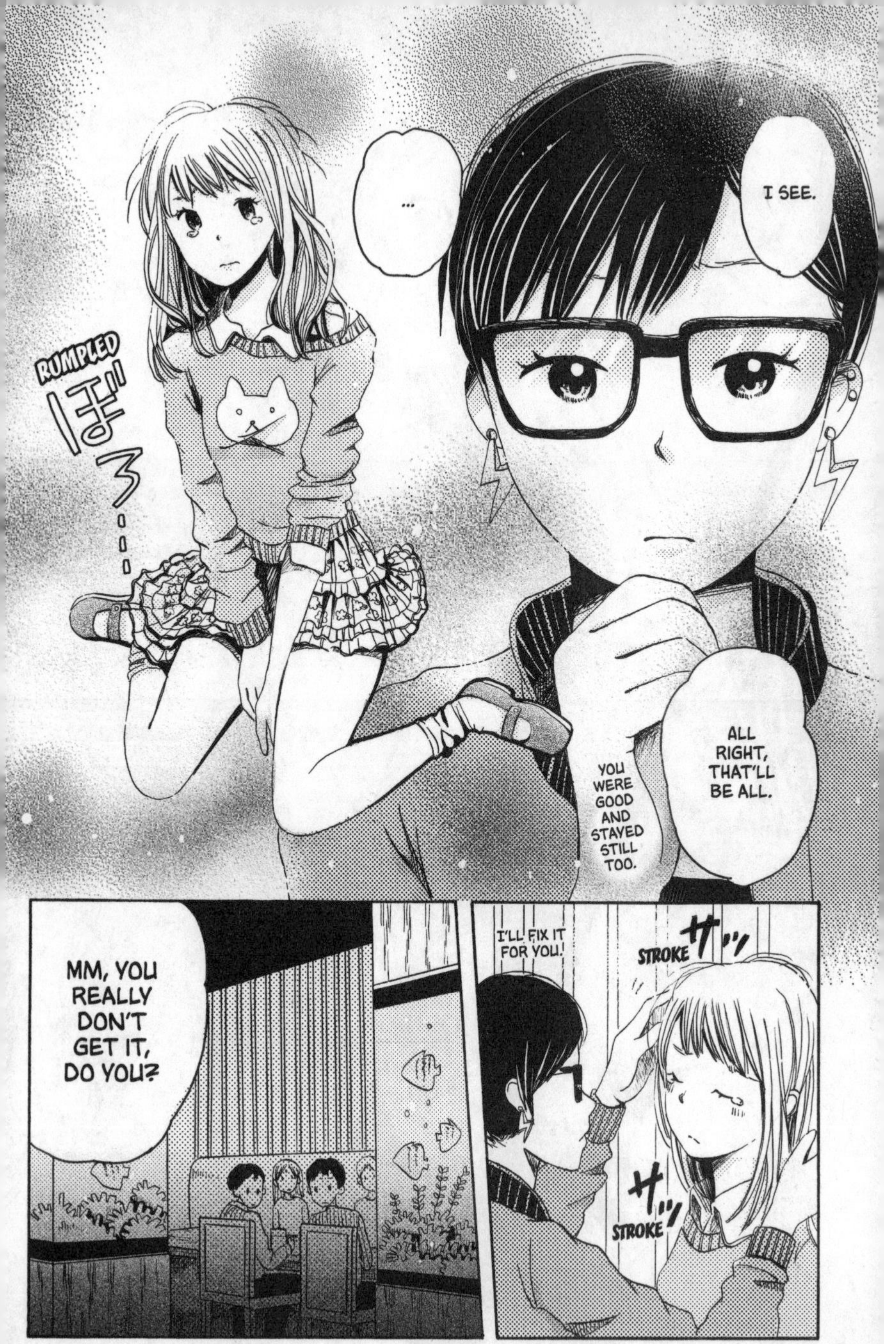
I SEE.
...
RUMPLED
ぼろ…
ALL RIGHT, THAT'LL BE ALL.
YOU WERE GOOD AND STAYED STILL TOO.
I'LL FIX IT FOR YOU!
STROKE
ザッ
ザッ
STROKE
MM, YOU REALLY DON'T GET IT, DO YOU?

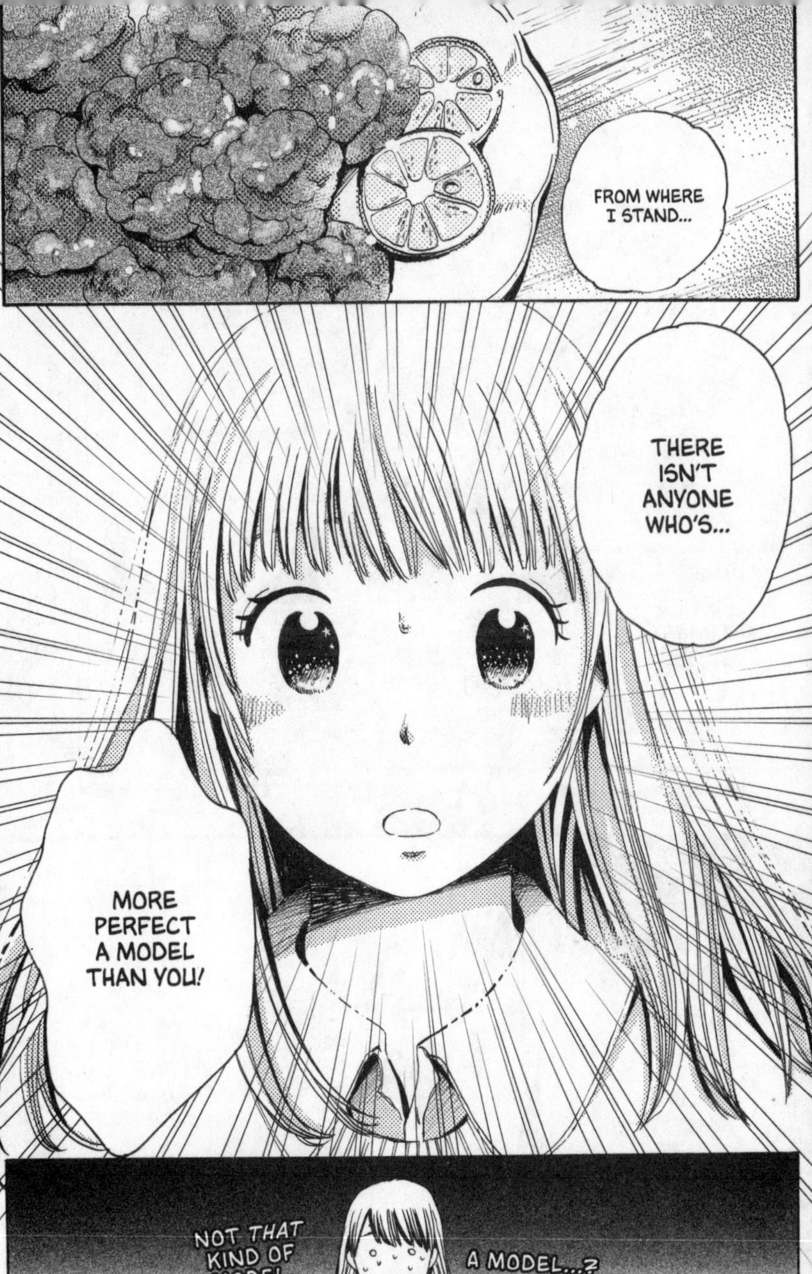
FROM WHERE I STAND...
THERE ISN'T ANYONE WHO'S...
MORE PERFECT A MODEL THAN YOU!
A MODEL...?
NOT *THAT* KIND OF MODEL, RIGHT...?

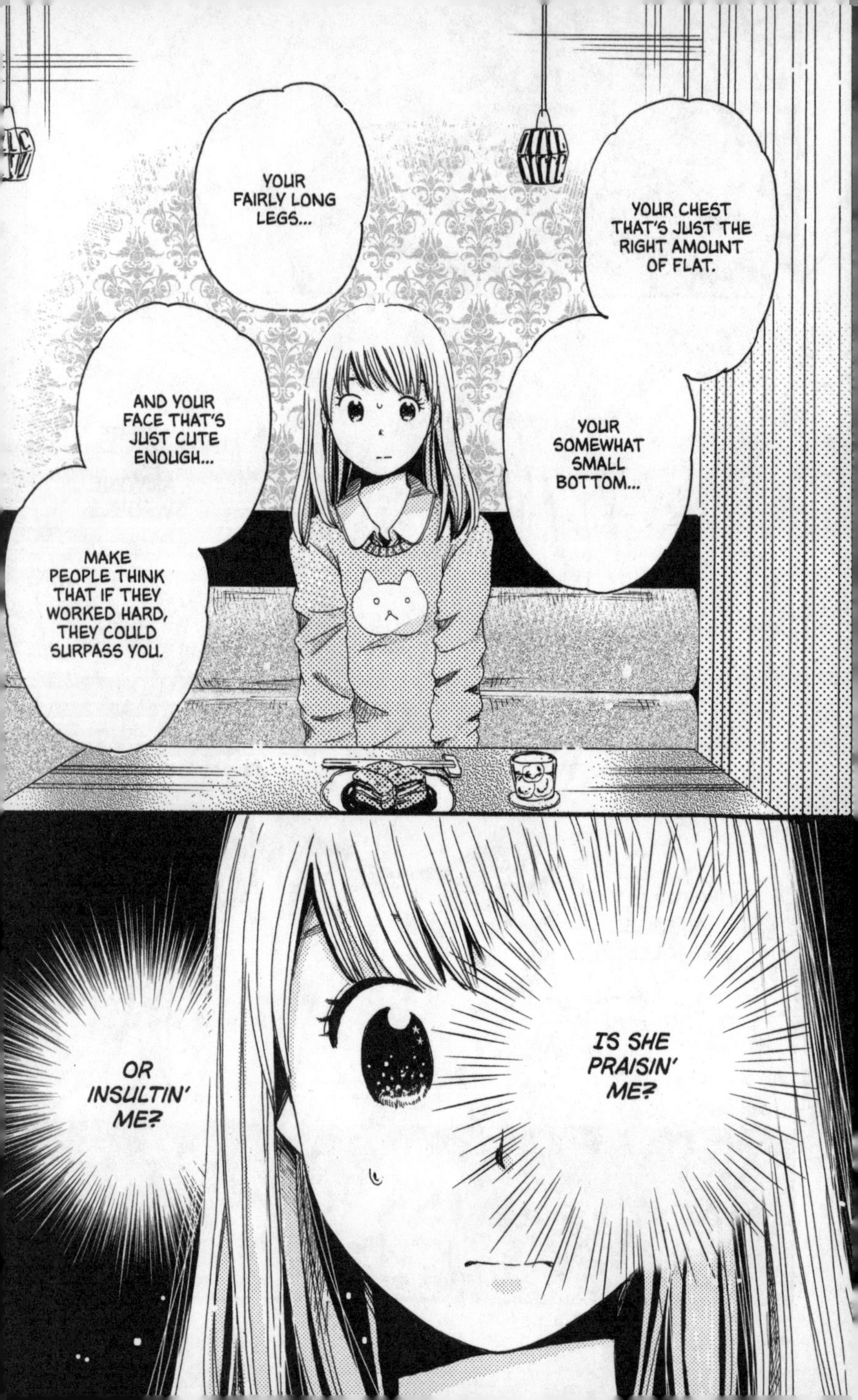
YOUR CHEST THAT'S JUST THE RIGHT AMOUNT OF FLAT.
YOUR FAIRLY LONG LEGS...
YOUR SOMEWHAT SMALL BOTTOM...
AND YOUR FACE THAT'S JUST CUTE ENOUGH...
MAKE PEOPLE THINK THAT IF THEY WORKED HARD, THEY COULD SURPASS YOU.
IS SHE PRAISIN' ME?
OR INSULTIN' ME?

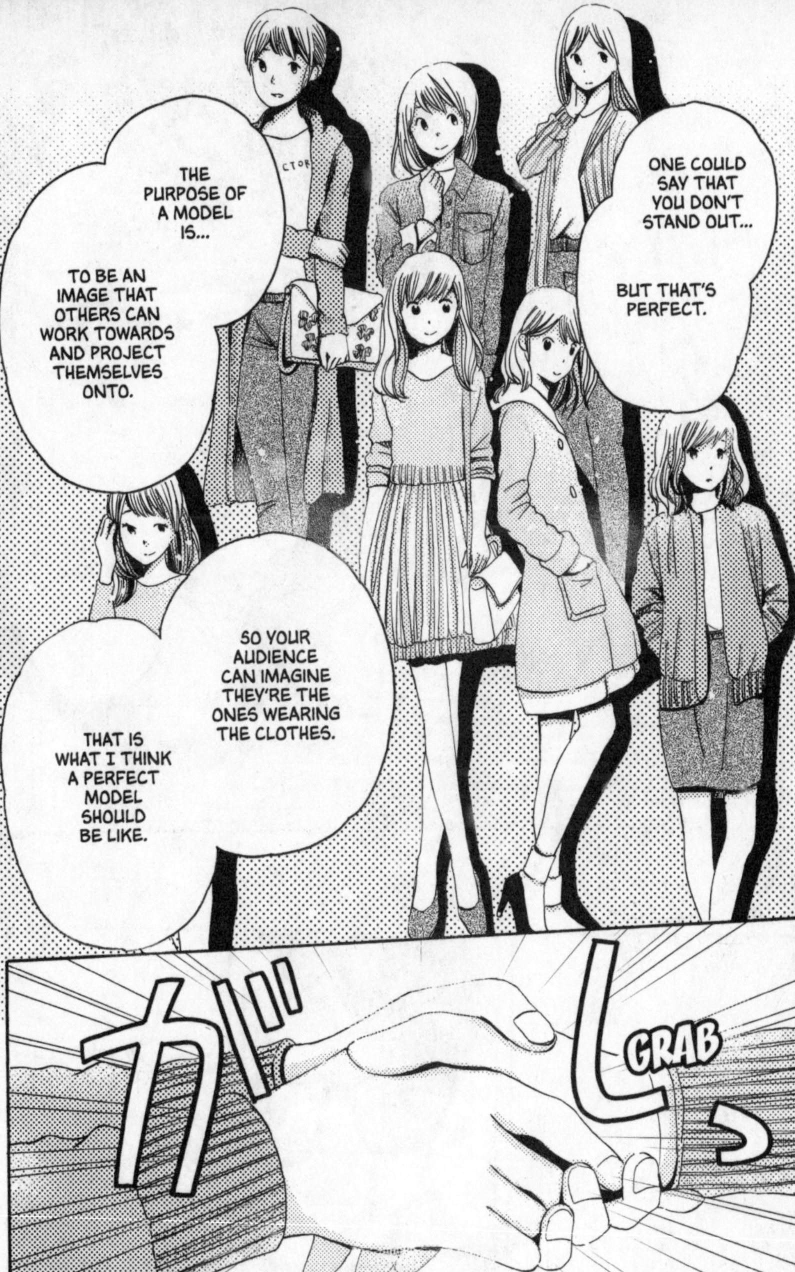
ONE COULD SAY THAT YOU DON'T STAND OUT... BUT THAT'S PERFECT.
THE PURPOSE OF A MODEL IS... TO BE AN IMAGE THAT OTHERS CAN WORK TOWARDS AND PROJECT THEMSELVES ONTO.
SO YOUR AUDIENCE CAN IMAGINE THEY'RE THE ONES WEARING THE CLOTHES.
THAT IS WHAT I THINK A PERFECT MODEL SHOULD BE LIKE.
GRAB

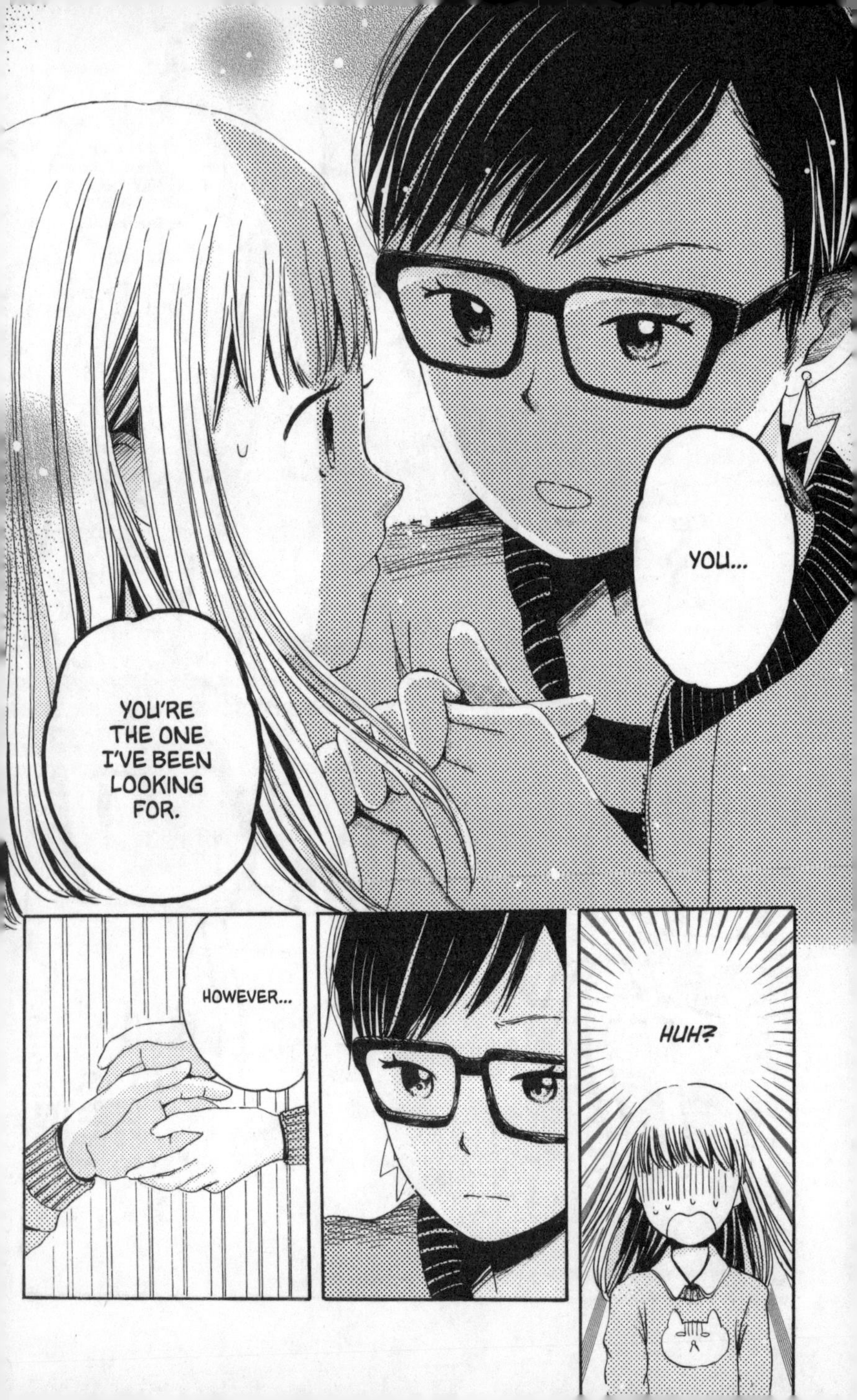
YOU...
YOU'RE THE ONE I'VE BEEN LOOKING FOR.
HUH?
HOWEVER...

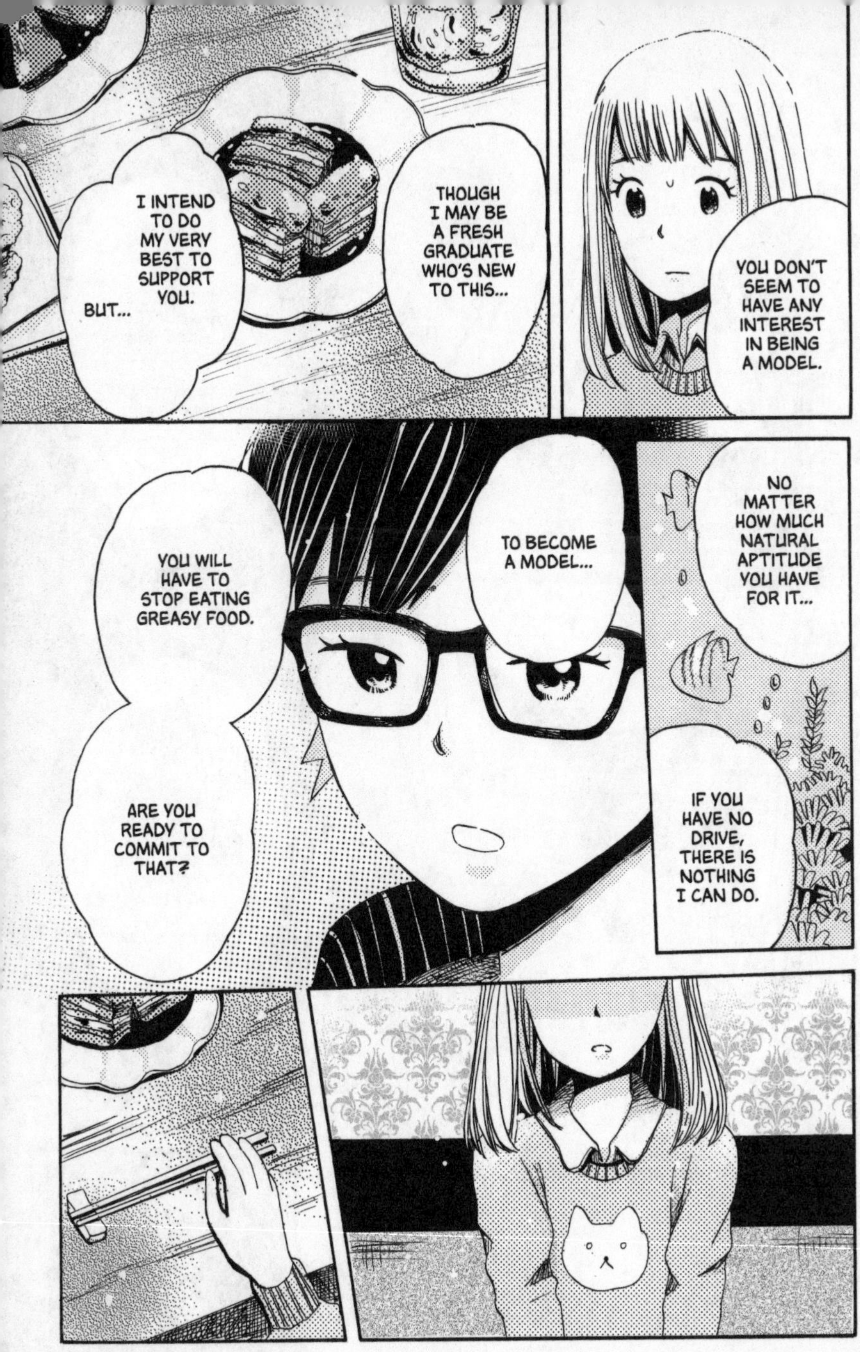
YOU DON'T SEEM TO HAVE ANY INTEREST IN BEING A MODEL.
THOUGH I MAY BE A FRESH GRADUATE WHO'S NEW TO THIS...
I INTEND TO DO MY VERY BEST TO SUPPORT YOU.
BUT...
NO MATTER HOW MUCH NATURAL APTITUDE YOU HAVE FOR IT...
IF YOU HAVE NO DRIVE, THERE IS NOTHING I CAN DO.
TO BECOME A MODEL...
YOU WILL HAVE TO STOP EATING GREASY FOOD.
ARE YOU READY TO COMMIT TO THAT?

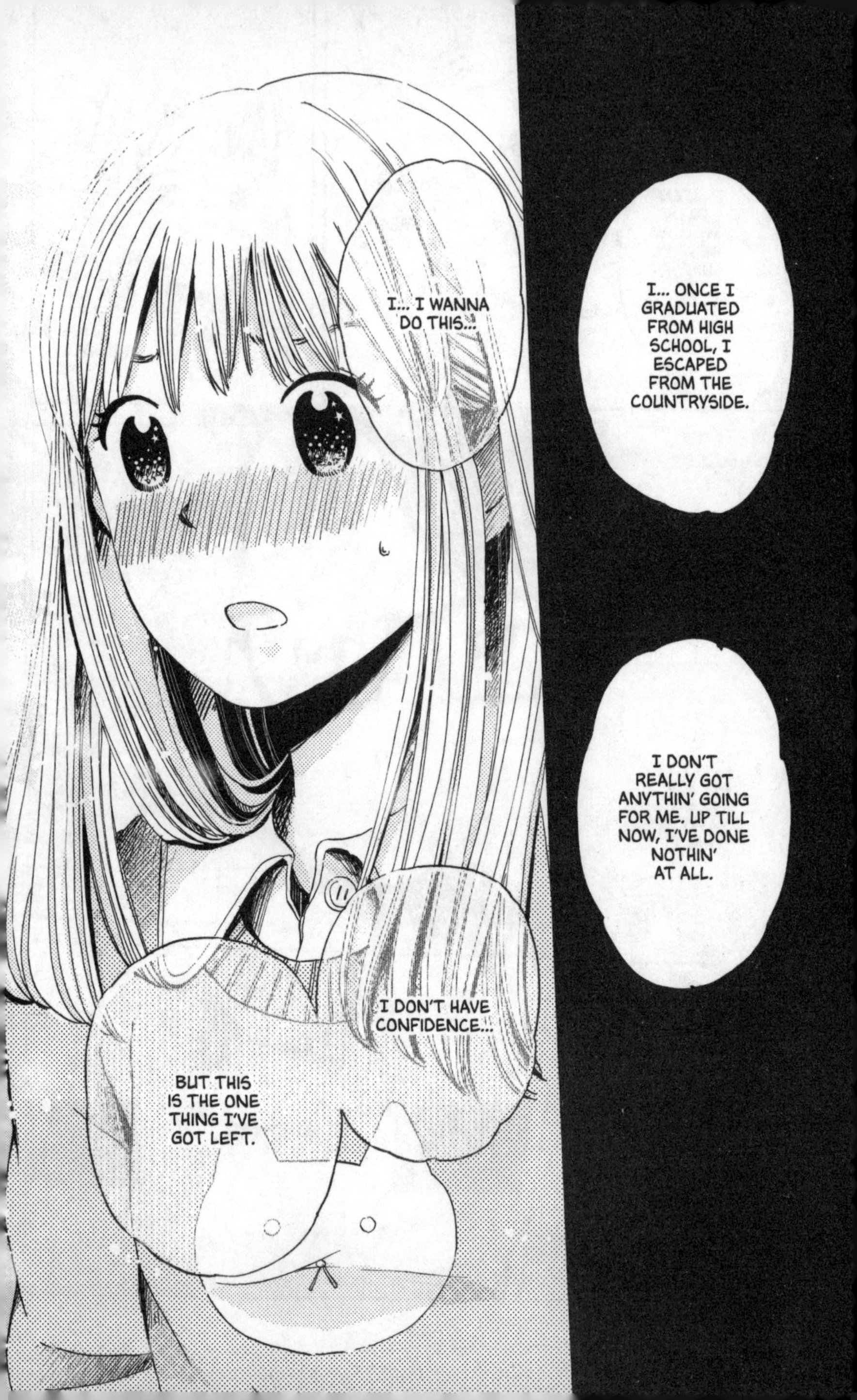
I... ONCE I GRADUATED FROM HIGH SCHOOL, I ESCAPED FROM THE COUNTRYSIDE.
I DON'T REALLY GOT ANYTHIN' GOING FOR ME. UP TILL NOW, I'VE DONE NOTHIN' AT ALL.
I... I WANNA DO THIS...
I DON'T HAVE CONFIDENCE...
BUT THIS IS THE ONE THING I'VE GOT LEFT.

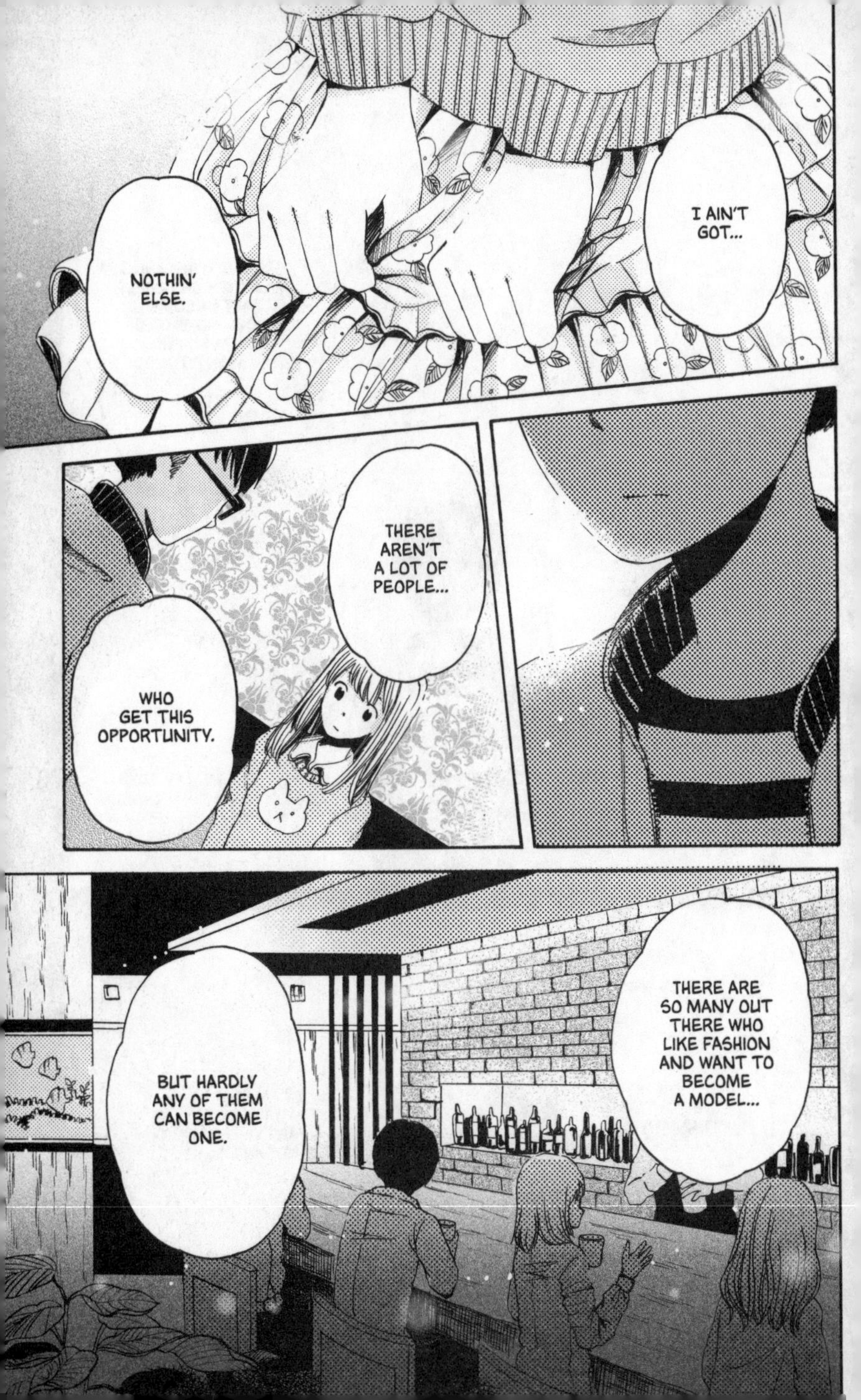
I AIN'T GOT...
NOTHIN' ELSE.
THERE AREN'T A LOT OF PEOPLE...
WHO GET THIS OPPORTUNITY.
THERE ARE SO MANY OUT THERE WHO LIKE FASHION AND WANT TO BECOME A MODEL...
BUT HARDLY ANY OF THEM CAN BECOME ONE.

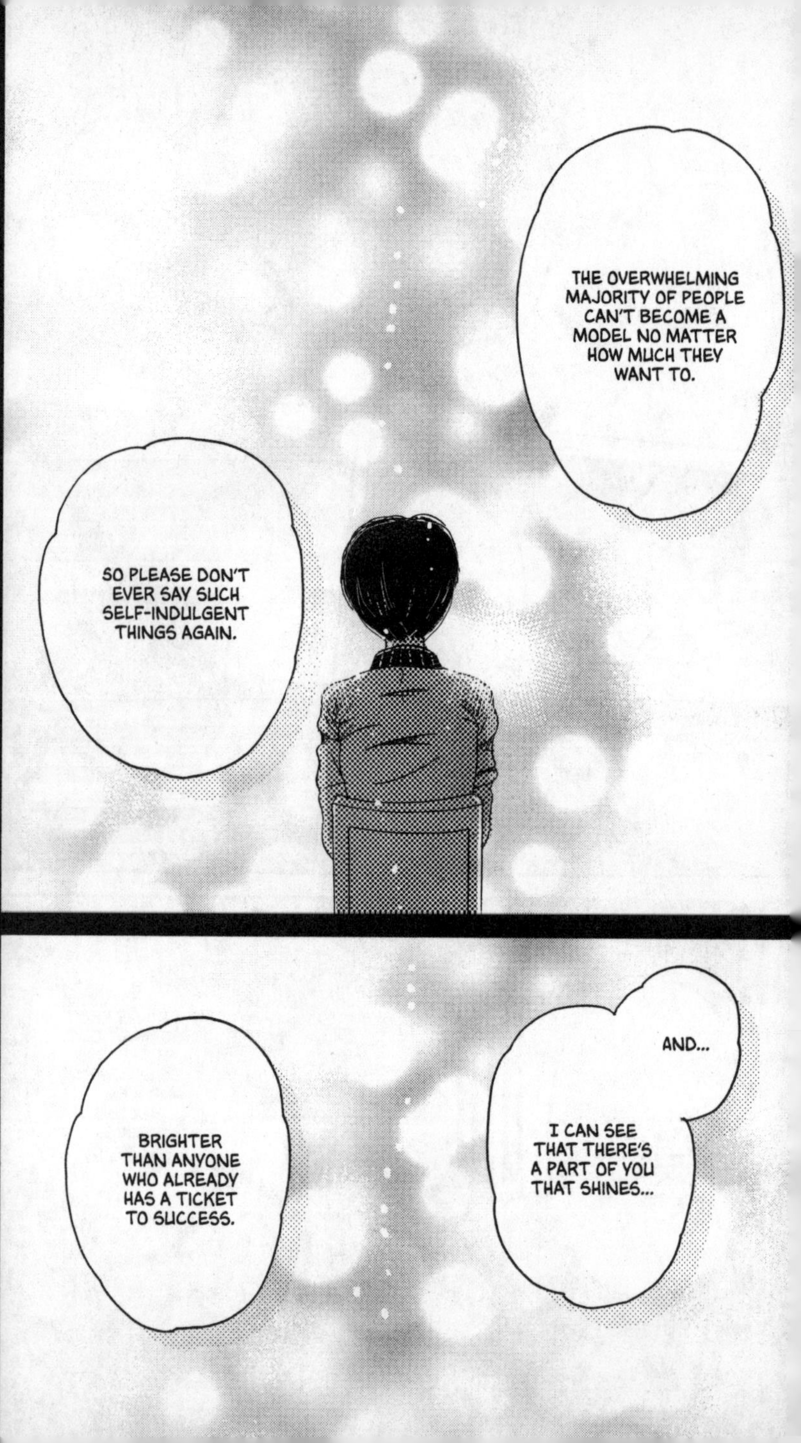
THE OVERWHELMING MAJORITY OF PEOPLE CAN'T BECOME A MODEL NO MATTER HOW MUCH THEY WANT TO.
SO PLEASE DON'T EVER SAY SUCH SELF-INDULGENT THINGS AGAIN.
AND...
I CAN SEE THAT THERE'S A PART OF YOU THAT SHINES...
BRIGHTER THAN ANYONE WHO ALREADY HAS A TICKET TO SUCCESS.

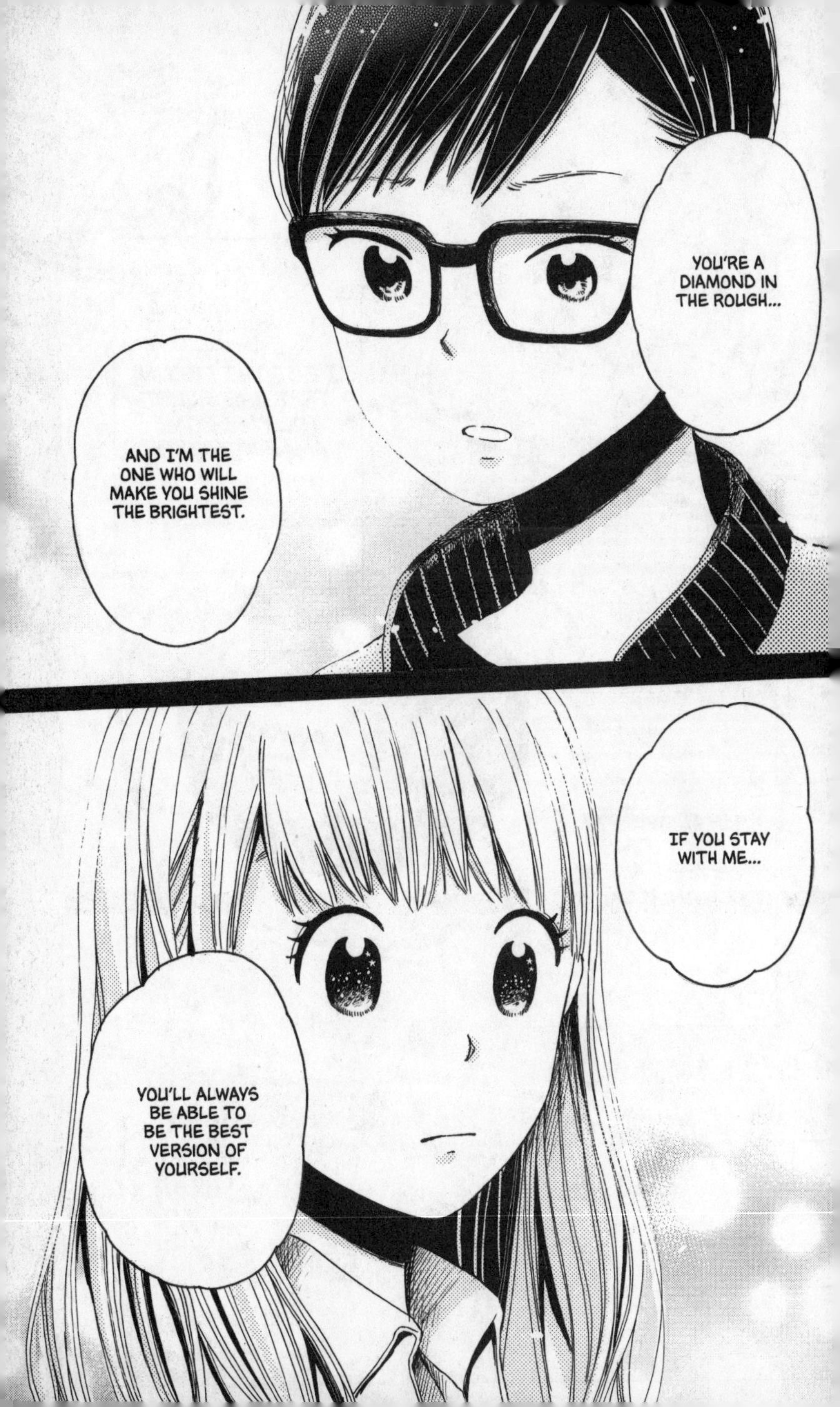
YOU'RE A DIAMOND IN THE ROUGH...
AND I'M THE ONE WHO WILL MAKE YOU SHINE THE BRIGHTEST.
IF YOU STAY WITH ME...
YOU'LL ALWAYS BE ABLE TO BE THE BEST VERSION OF YOURSELF.

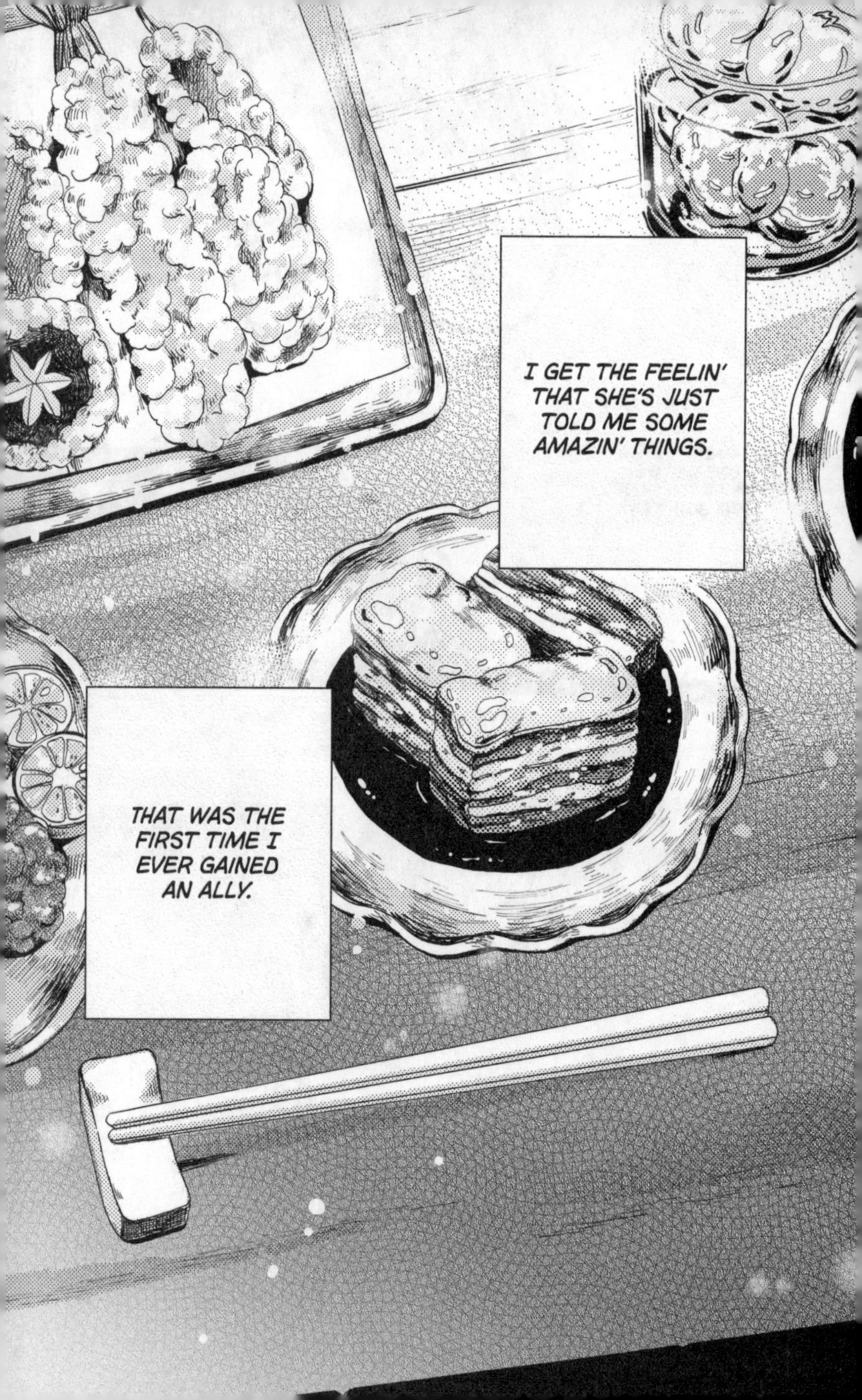
I GET THE FEELIN' THAT SHE'S JUST TOLD ME SOME AMAZIN' THINGS.
THAT WAS THE FIRST TIME I EVER GAINED AN ALLY.

MAME
coordinate

OOTD*
CORNER
CONCEPT: A TOMBOYISH LOOK
STRIPED JERSEY KNIT CREWNECK
KHAKI BOMBER JACKET
BLACK PENCIL SKIRT
BLACK CLUTCH BAG
30 DENIER TIGHTS
BLACK LACE-UP SHOES
CONCEPT: 5TH GRADER
BLOUSE FROM HER HIGH SCHOOL UNIFORM
CAT SWEATSHIRT (THE CAT IS SENTIENT.)
FLOWER-PRINTED FRILLY SKIRT WITH TWO LAYERS
SOCKS THAT HAVE TINY CHERRY-SHAPED POM-POMS
SHOES WITH STRAPS
*OUTFIT OF THE DAY

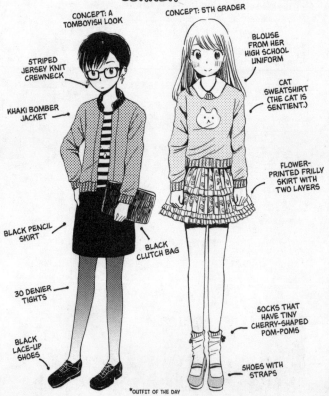

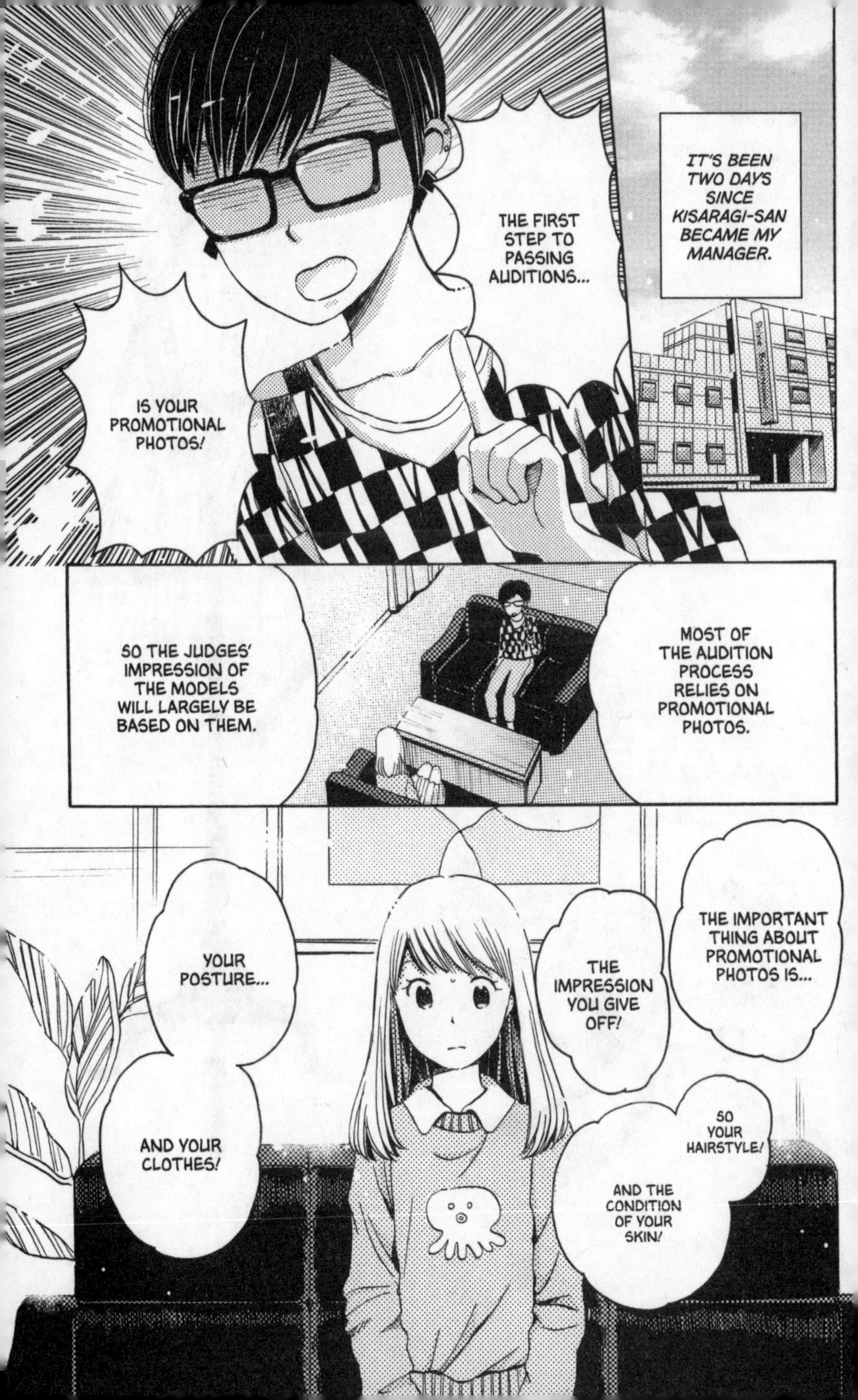
IT'S BEEN TWO DAYS SINCE KISARAGI-SAN BECAME MY MANAGER.
THE FIRST STEP TO PASSING AUDITIONS...
IS YOUR PROMOTIONAL PHOTOS!
MOST OF THE AUDITION PROCESS RELIES ON PROMOTIONAL PHOTOS.
SO THE JUDGES' IMPRESSION OF THE MODELS WILL LARGELY BE BASED ON THEM.
THE IMPORTANT THING ABOUT PROMOTIONAL PHOTOS IS...
THE IMPRESSION YOU GIVE OFF!
YOUR POSTURE...
SO YOUR HAIRSTYLE!
AND THE CONDITION OF YOUR SKIN!
AND YOUR CLOTHES!

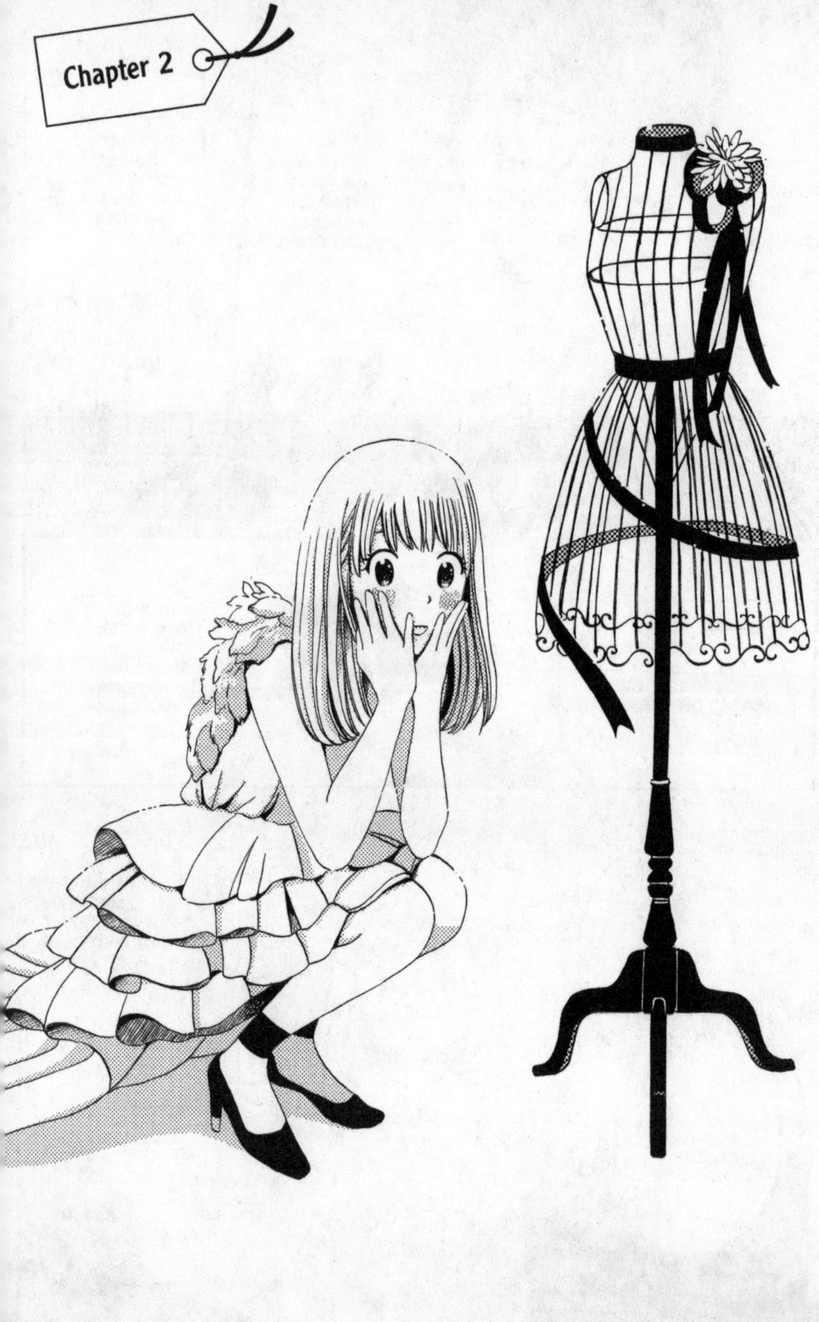
Chapter 2

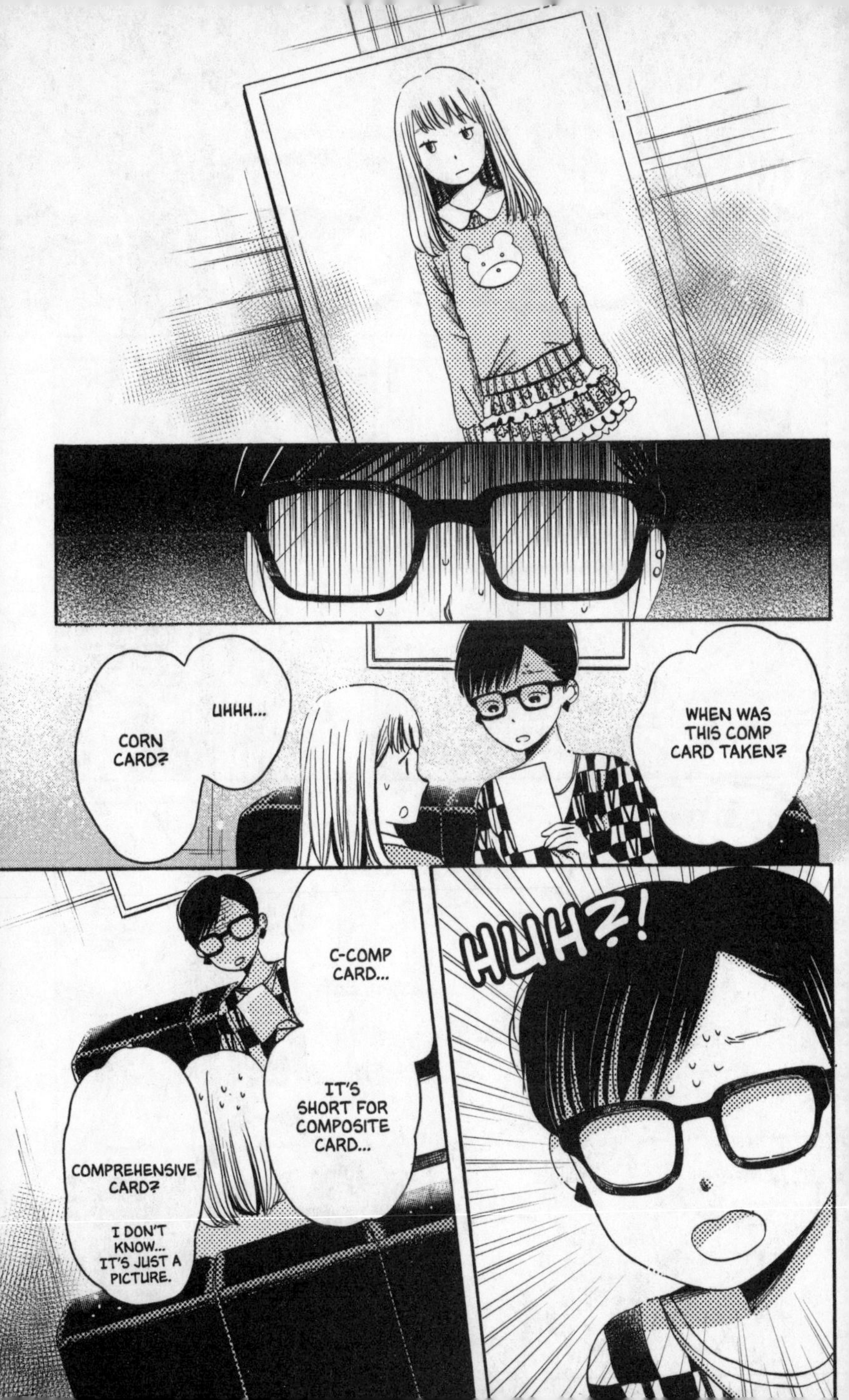
WHEN WAS THIS COMP CARD TAKEN?
UHHH... CORN CARD?
HUH?!
C-COMP CARD...
IT'S SHORT FOR COMPOSITE CARD...
COMPREHENSIVE CARD?
I DON'T KNOW... IT'S JUST A PICTURE.

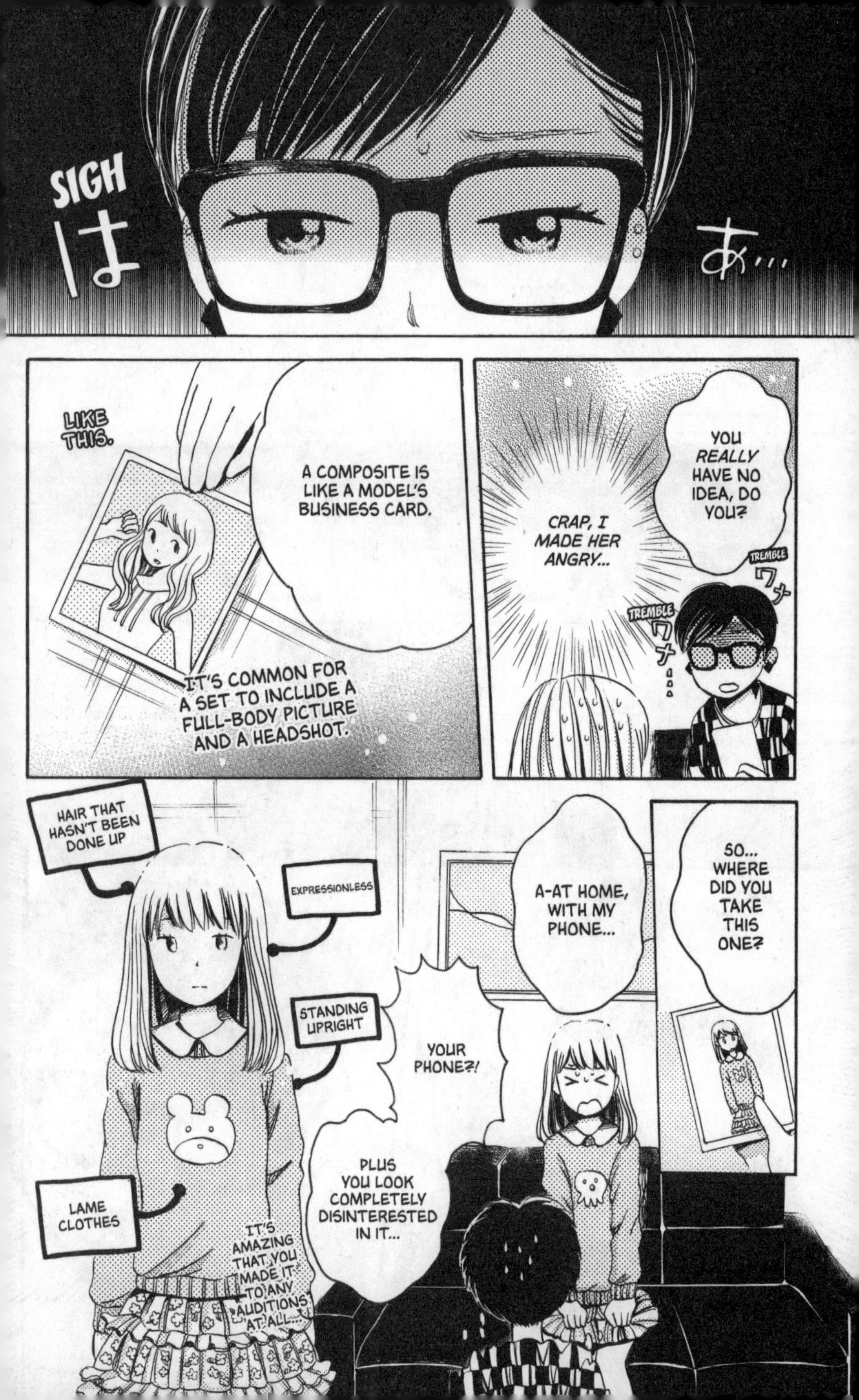

SIGH
は
あ...
YOU *REALLY* HAVE NO IDEA, DO YOU?
CRAP, I MADE HER ANGRY...
TREMBLE
ワナ
TREMBLE
ワナ...
A COMPOSITE IS LIKE A MODEL'S BUSINESS CARD.
LIKE THIS.
IT'S COMMON FOR A SET TO INCLUDE A FULL-BODY PICTURE AND A HEADSHOT.
SO... WHERE DID YOU TAKE THIS ONE?
A-AT HOME, WITH MY PHONE...
YOUR PHONE?!
PLUS YOU LOOK COMPLETELY DISINTERESTED IN IT...
HAIR THAT HASN'T BEEN DONE UP
EXPRESSIONLESS
STANDING UPRIGHT
LAME CLOTHES
IT'S AMAZING THAT YOU MADE IT TO ANY AUDITIONS AT ALL...

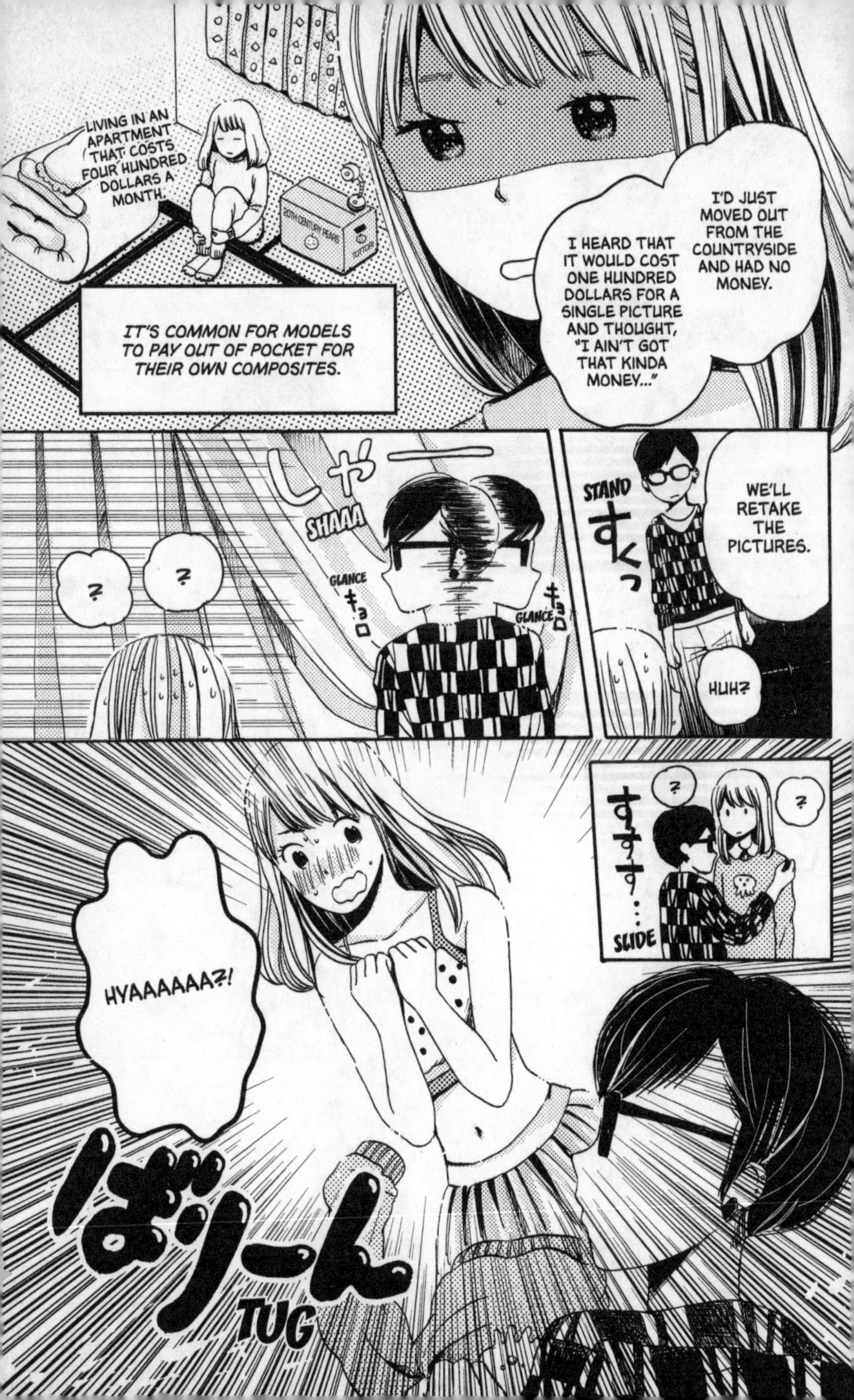
I'D JUST MOVED OUT FROM THE COUNTRYSIDE AND HAD NO MONEY.
I HEARD THAT IT WOULD COST ONE HUNDRED DOLLARS FOR A SINGLE PICTURE AND THOUGHT, "I AIN'T GOT THAT KINDA MONEY..."
LIVING IN AN APARTMENT THAT COSTS FOUR HUNDRED DOLLARS A MONTH.
20TH CENTURY PEARS
TOTTORI
IT'S COMMON FOR MODELS TO PAY OUT OF POCKET FOR THEIR OWN COMPOSITES.
WE'LL RETAKE THE PICTURES.
すくっ
STAND
HUH?
しゃー
SHAAA
キョロ
GLANCE
キョロ
GLANCE
?
?
?
?
すすす…
SLIDE
HYAAAAAA?!
TUG

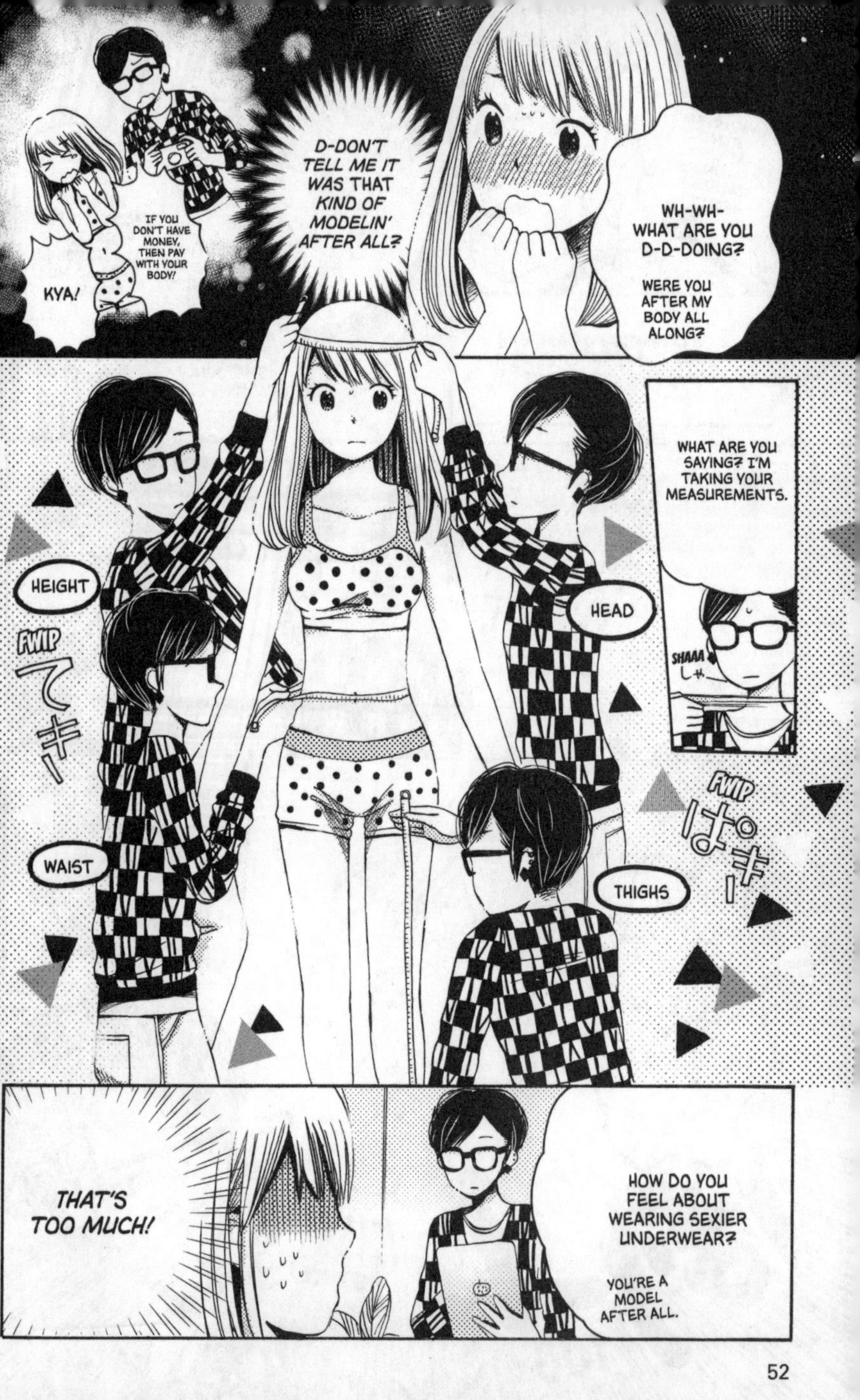
WH-WH-WHAT ARE YOU D-D-DOING?
WERE YOU AFTER MY BODY ALL ALONG?
D-DON'T TELL ME IT WAS THAT KIND OF MODELIN' AFTER ALL?
IF YOU DON'T HAVE MONEY, THEN PAY WITH YOUR BODY!
KYA!
WHAT ARE YOU SAYING? I'M TAKING YOUR MEASUREMENTS.
SHAAA
しゃ
HEAD
HEIGHT
FWIP
てきー
WAIST
THIGHS
FWIP
ぱきー
HOW DO YOU FEEL ABOUT WEARING SEXIER UNDERWEAR?
YOU'RE A MODEL AFTER ALL.
THAT'S TOO MUCH!

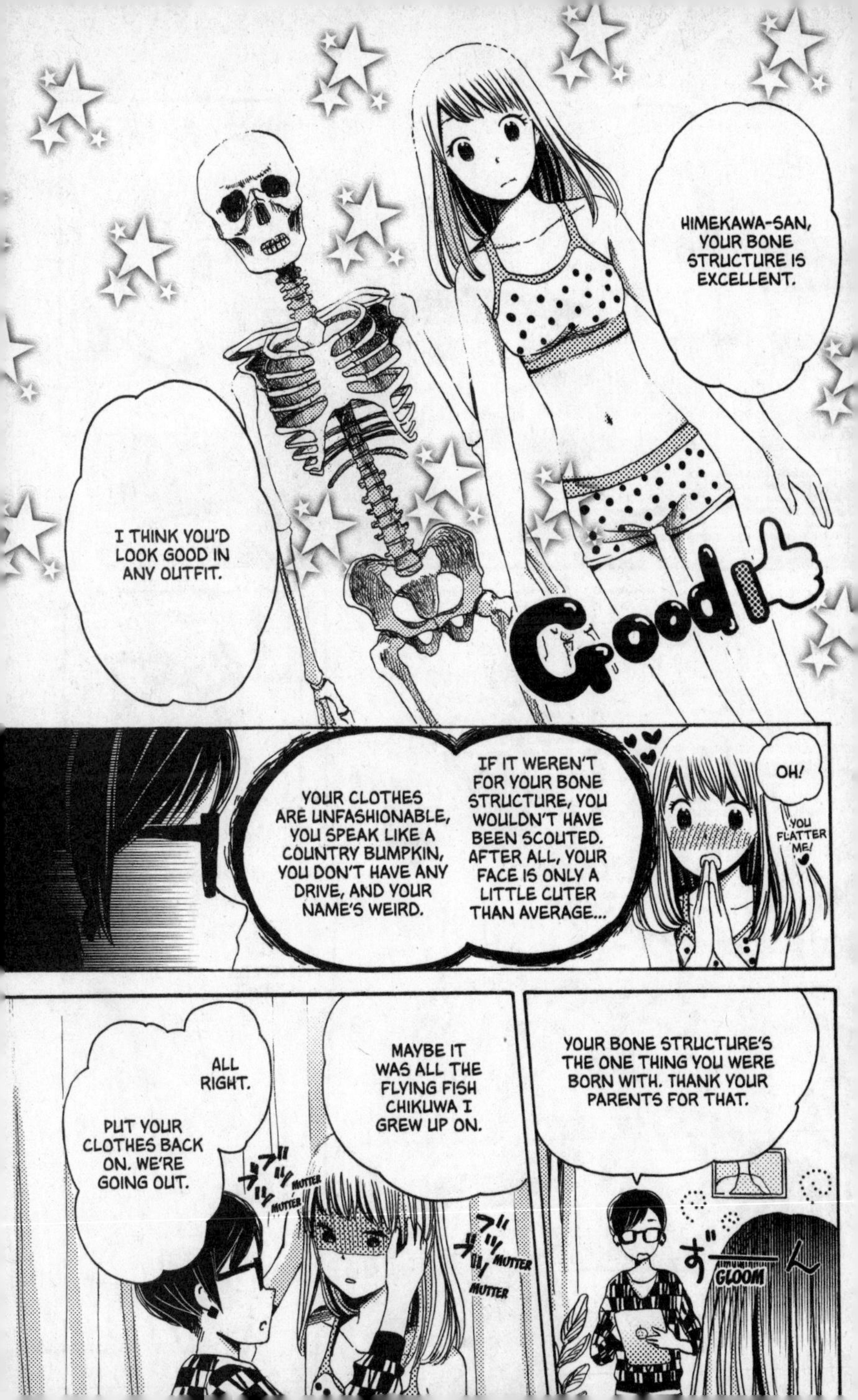
HIMEKAWA-SAN, YOUR BONE STRUCTURE IS EXCELLENT.
I THINK YOU'D LOOK GOOD IN ANY OUTFIT.
GOOD!
OH!
YOU FLATTER ME!
IF IT WEREN'T FOR YOUR BONE STRUCTURE, YOU WOULDN'T HAVE BEEN SCOUTED. AFTER ALL, YOUR FACE IS ONLY A LITTLE CUTER THAN AVERAGE...
YOUR CLOTHES ARE UNFASHIONABLE, YOU SPEAK LIKE A COUNTRY BUMPKIN, YOU DON'T HAVE ANY DRIVE, AND YOUR NAME'S WEIRD.
YOUR BONE STRUCTURE'S THE ONE THING YOU WERE BORN WITH. THANK YOUR PARENTS FOR THAT.
GLOOM
MAYBE IT WAS ALL THE FLYING FISH CHIKUWA I GREW UP ON.
MUTTER
MUTTER
MUTTER
MUTTER
ALL RIGHT.
PUT YOUR CLOTHES BACK ON. WE'RE GOING OUT.

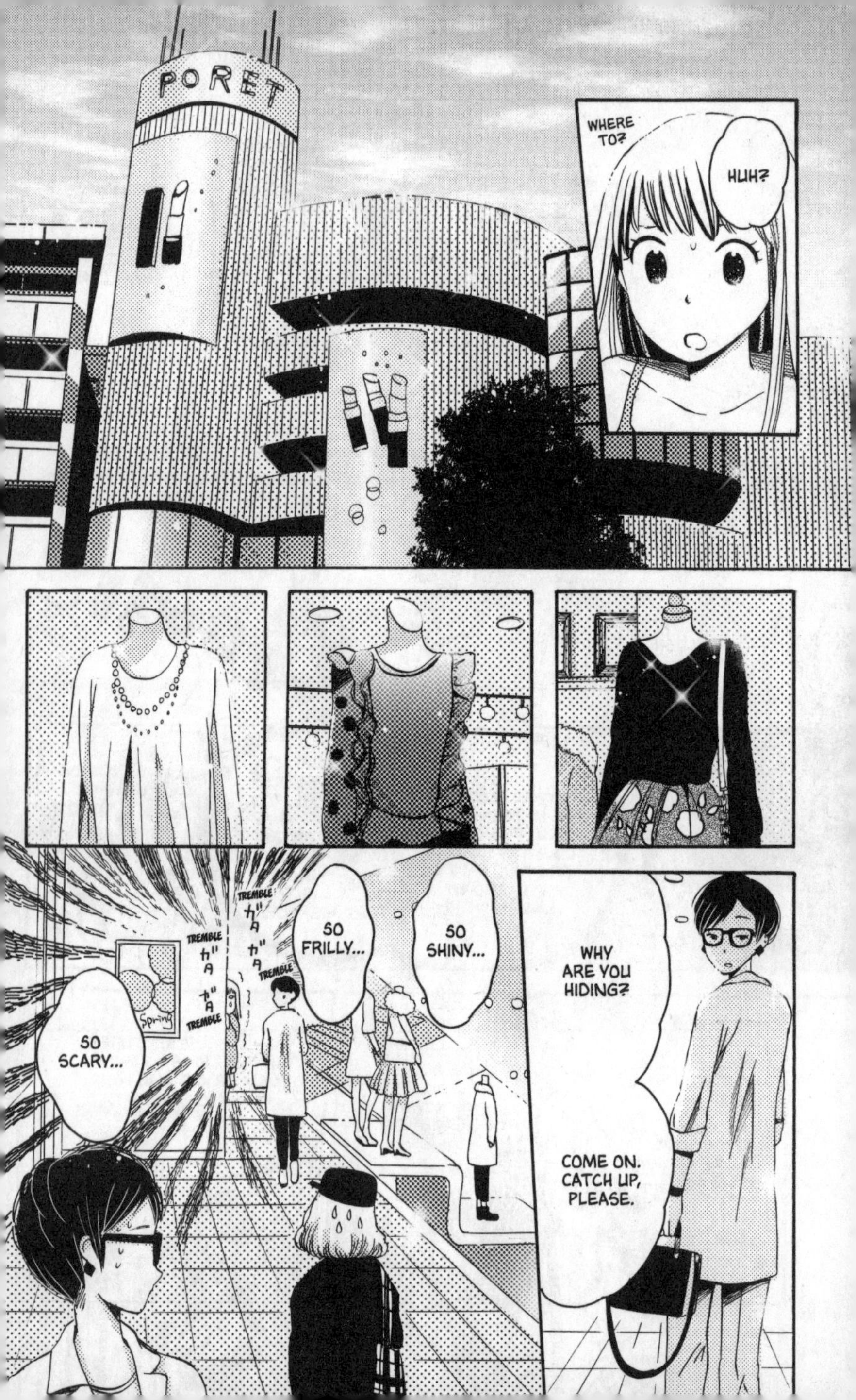
HUH?
WHERE TO?
PORET
WHY ARE YOU HIDING?
COME ON. CATCH UP, PLEASE.
SO SHINY...
SO FRILLY...
TREMBLE ガタ
TREMBLE ガタ
TREMBLE ガタ
TREMBLE ガタ
Spring
SO SCARY...

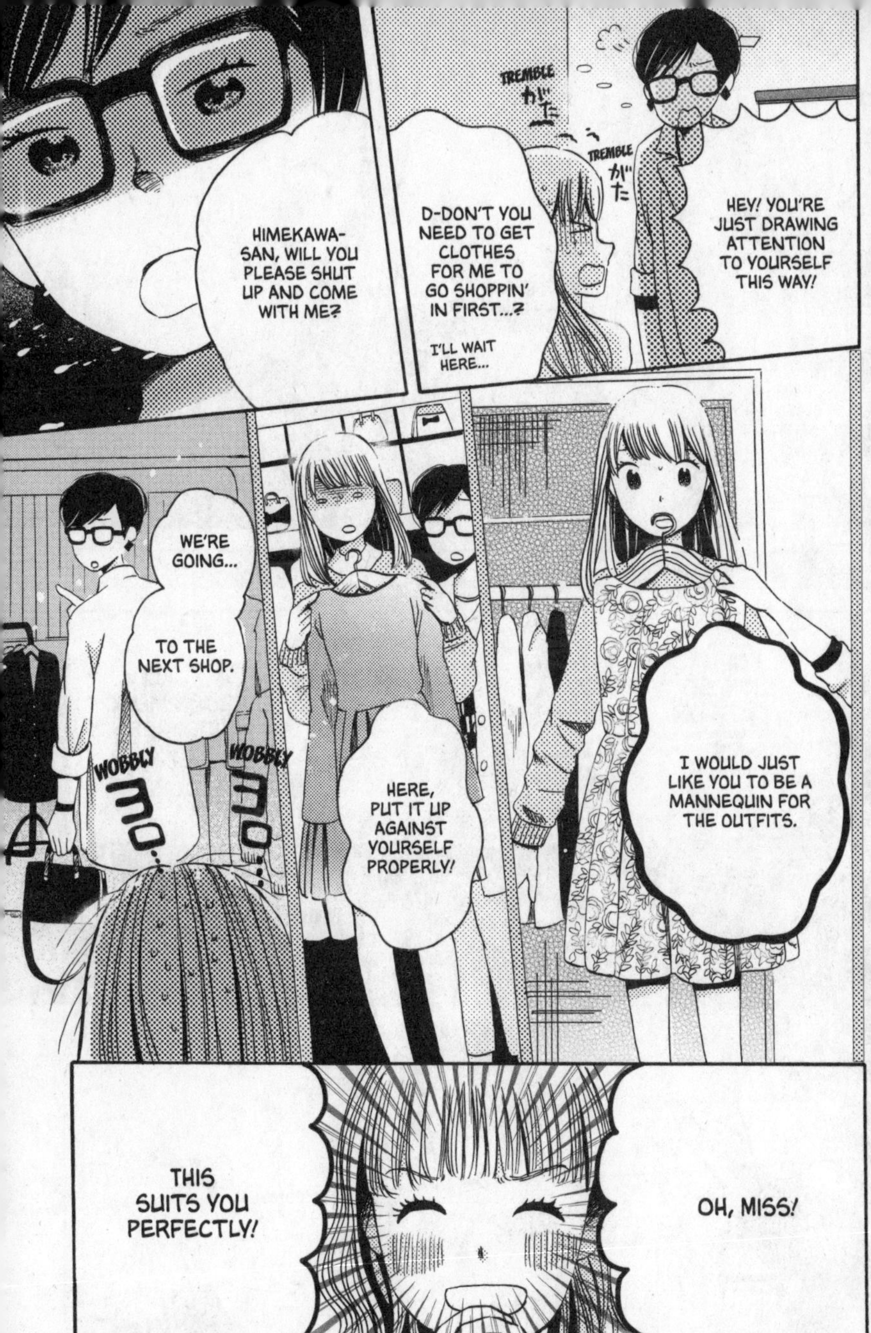
TREMBLE がた
TREMBLE がた
HEY! YOU'RE JUST DRAWING ATTENTION TO YOURSELF THIS WAY!
D-DON'T YOU NEED TO GET CLOTHES FOR ME TO GO SHOPPIN' IN FIRST...?
I'LL WAIT HERE...
HIMEKAWA-SAN, WILL YOU PLEASE SHUT UP AND COME WITH ME?
I WOULD JUST LIKE YOU TO BE A MANNEQUIN FOR THE OUTFITS.
HERE, PUT IT UP AGAINST YOURSELF PROPERLY!
WE'RE GOING...
TO THE NEXT SHOP.
WOBBLY ヨロ...
WOBBLY ヨロ...
OH, MISS!
THIS SUITS YOU PERFECTLY!

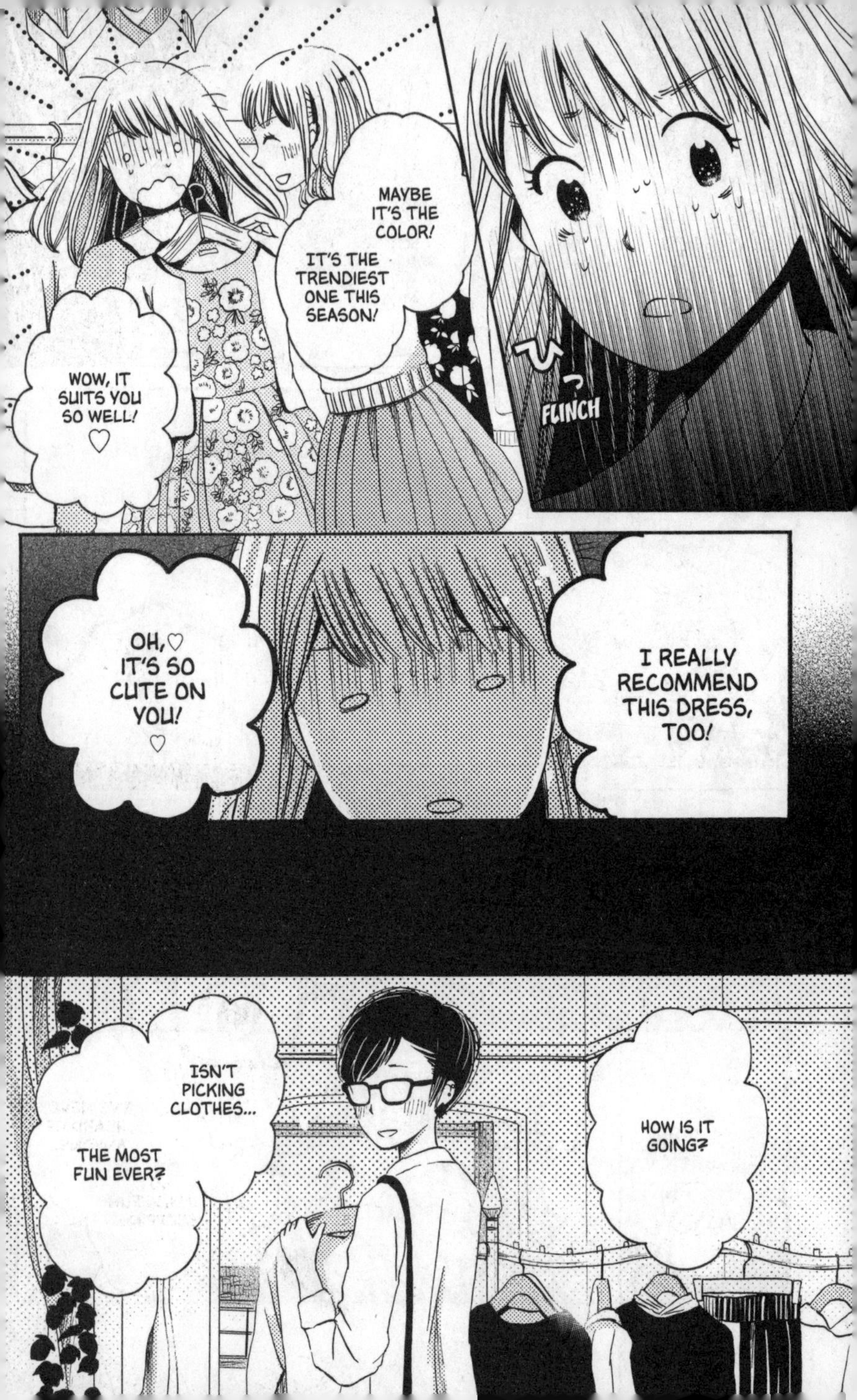
FLINCH
MAYBE IT'S THE COLOR! IT'S THE TRENDIEST ONE THIS SEASON!
WOW, IT SUITS YOU SO WELL! ♡
I REALLY RECOMMEND THIS DRESS, TOO!
OH, ♡ IT'S SO CUTE ON YOU! ♡
HOW IS IT GOING?
ISN'T PICKING CLOTHES... THE MOST FUN EVER?

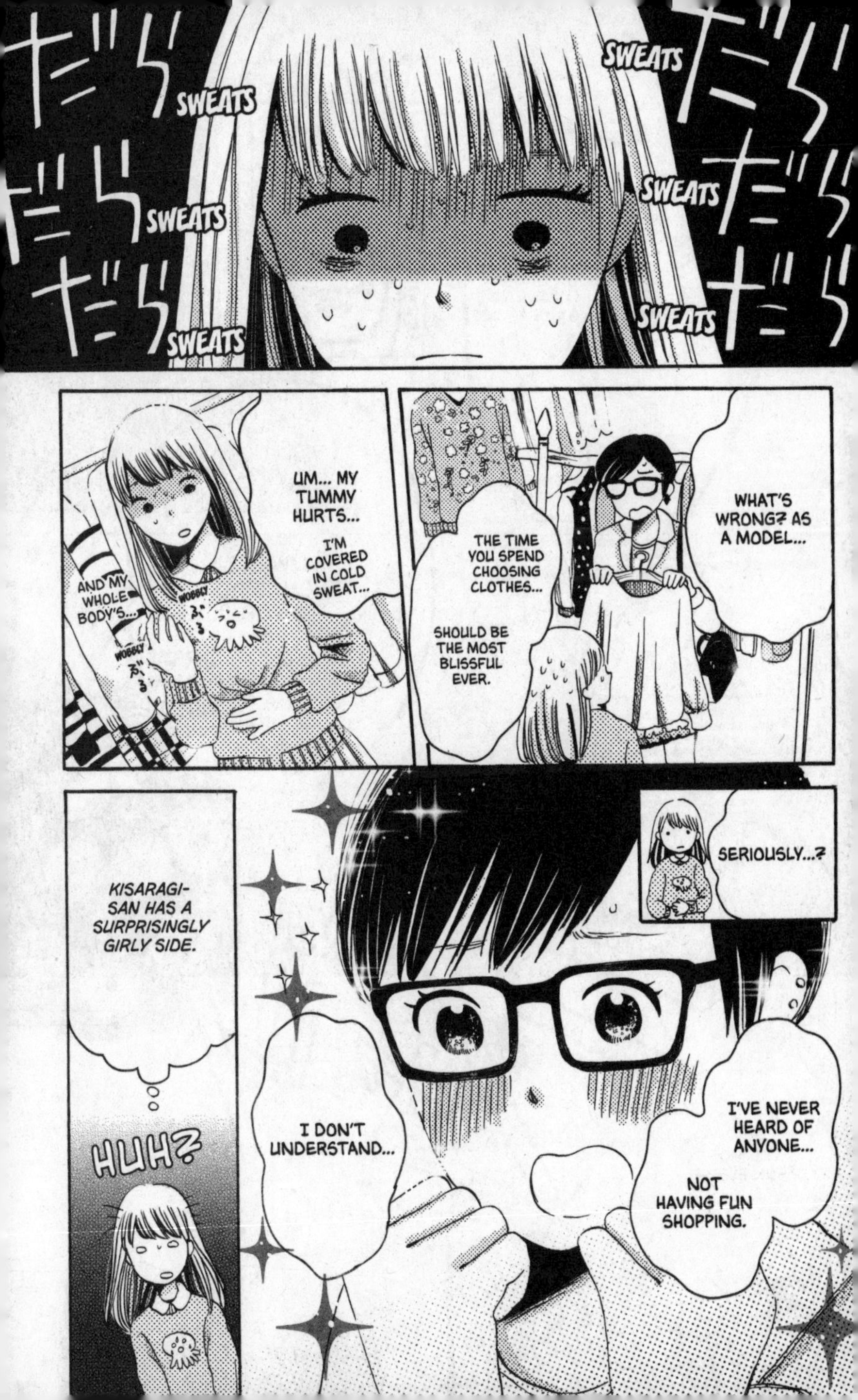
だらだらだら
SWEATS
SWEATS
SWEATS
だらだらだら
SWEATS
SWEATS
SWEATS
WHAT'S WRONG? AS A MODEL...
THE TIME YOU SPEND CHOOSING CLOTHES...
SHOULD BE THE MOST BLISSFUL EVER.
UM... MY TUMMY HURTS...
I'M COVERED IN COLD SWEAT...
AND MY WHOLE BODY'S...
WOBBLY ぶる
WOBBLY ぶるる
SERIOUSLY...?
I'VE NEVER HEARD OF ANYONE...
NOT HAVING FUN SHOPPING.
I DON'T UNDERSTAND...
KISARAGI-SAN HAS A SURPRISINGLY GIRLY SIDE.
HUH?

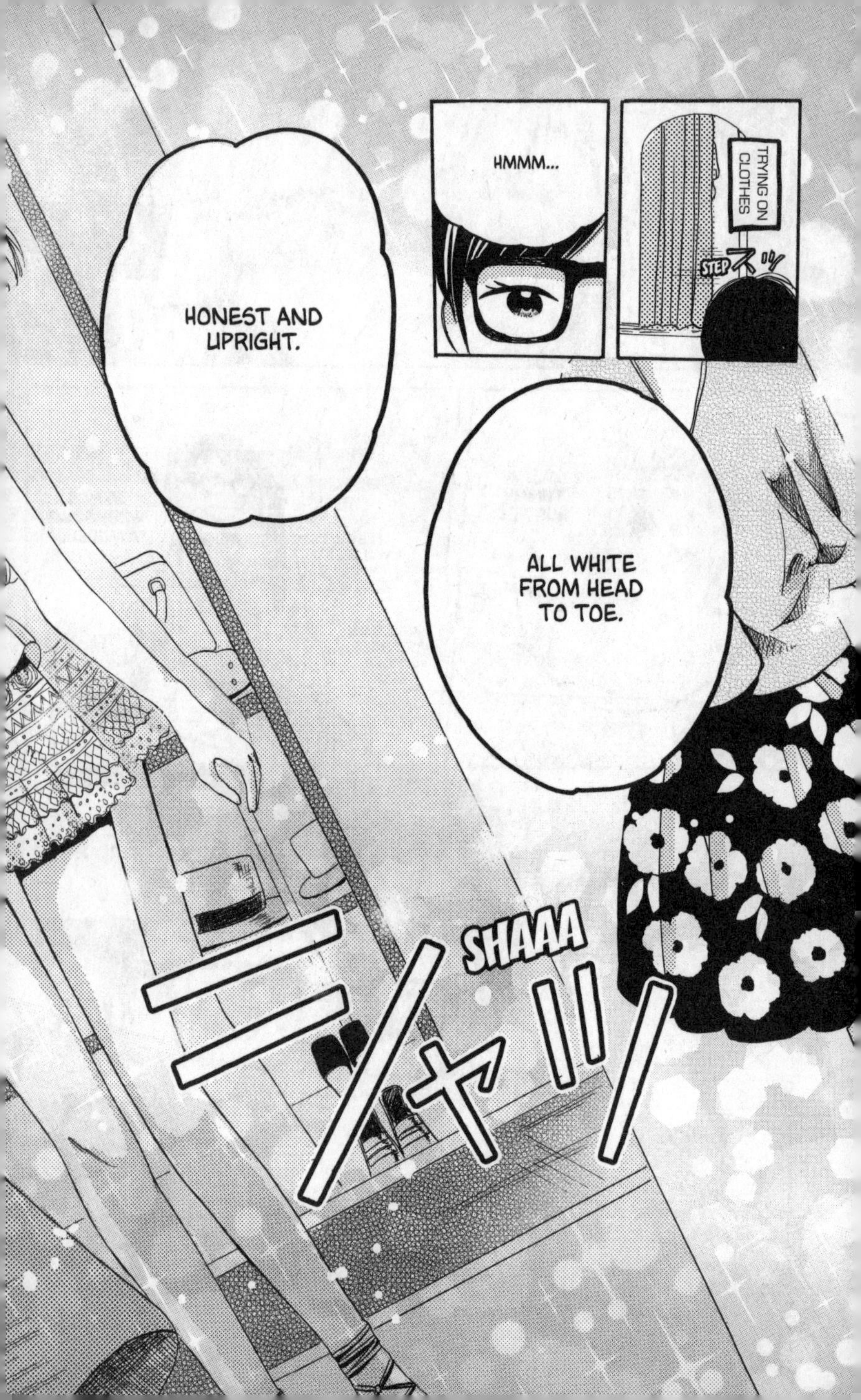
TRYING ON CLOTHES
STEP
HMMM...
ALL WHITE FROM HEAD TO TOE.
HONEST AND UPRIGHT.
SHAAA

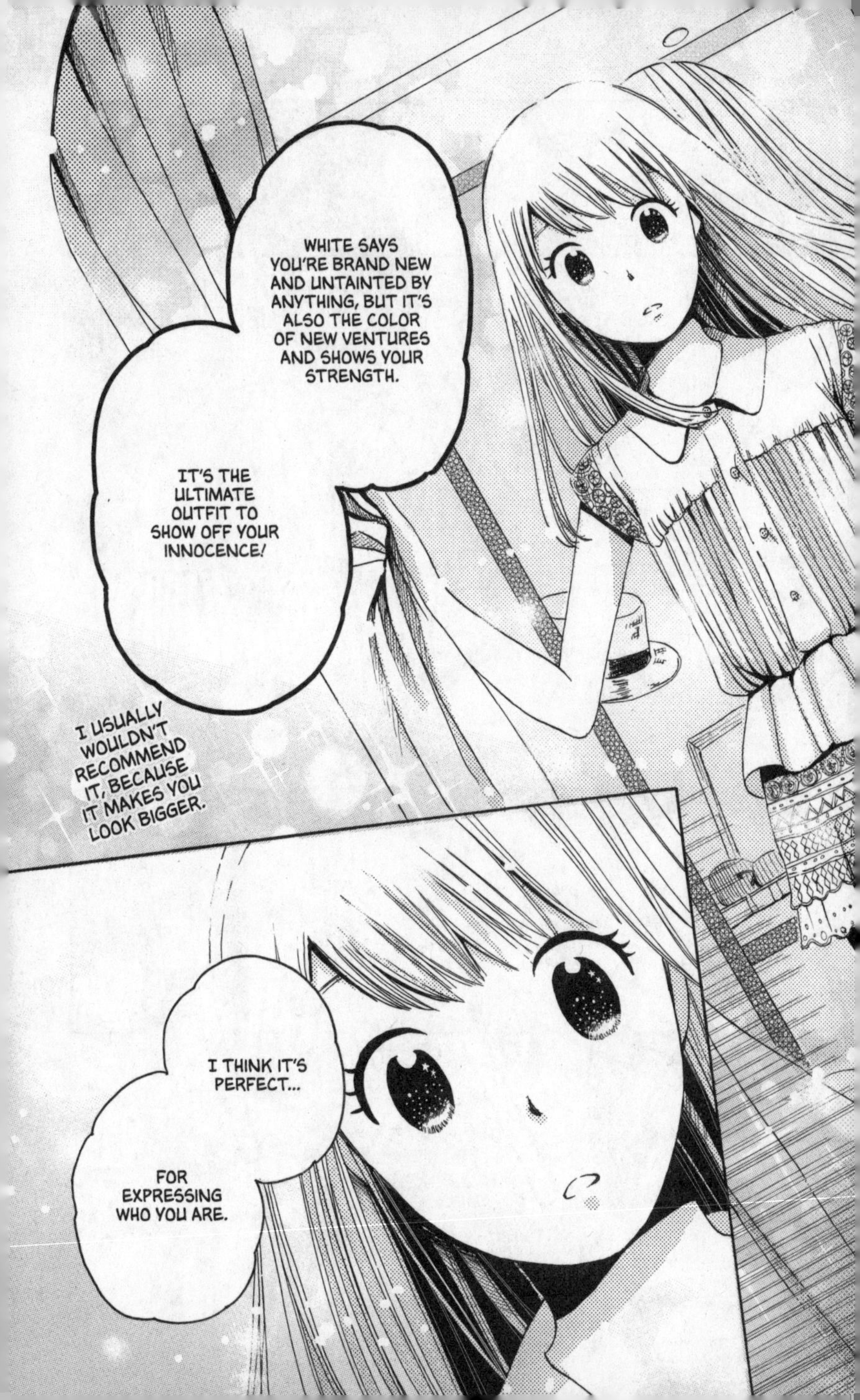
WHITE SAYS YOU'RE BRAND NEW AND UNTAINTED BY ANYTHING, BUT IT'S ALSO THE COLOR OF NEW VENTURES AND SHOWS YOUR STRENGTH.
IT'S THE ULTIMATE OUTFIT TO SHOW OFF YOUR INNOCENCE!
I USUALLY WOULDN'T RECOMMEND IT, BECAUSE IT MAKES YOU LOOK BIGGER.
I THINK IT'S PERFECT...
FOR EXPRESSING WHO YOU ARE.

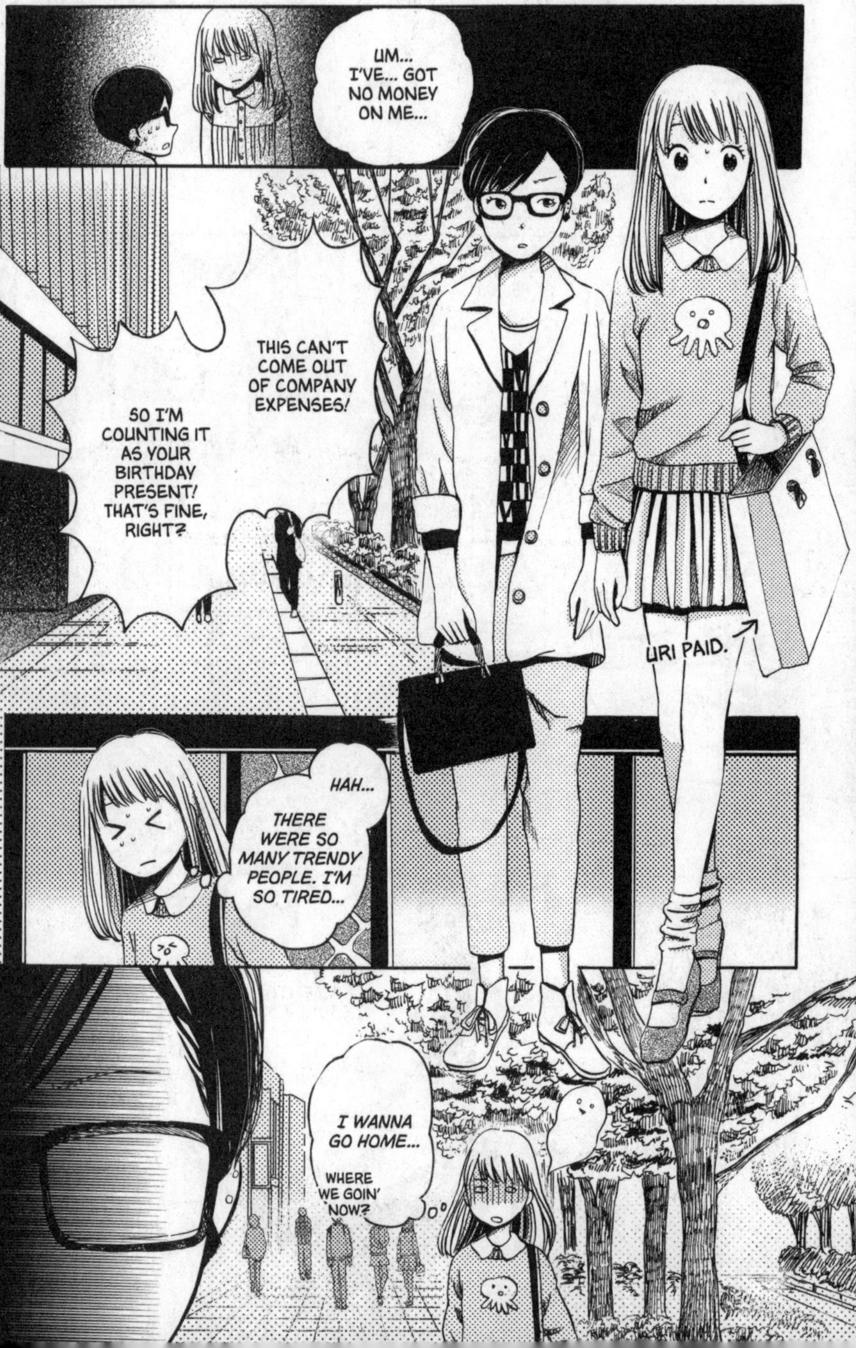
UM... I'VE... GOT NO MONEY ON ME...
THIS CAN'T COME OUT OF COMPANY EXPENSES!
SO I'M COUNTING IT AS YOUR BIRTHDAY PRESENT! THAT'S FINE, RIGHT?
URI PAID.
HAH...
THERE WERE SO MANY TRENDY PEOPLE. I'M SO TIRED...
I WANNA GO HOME...
WHERE WE GOIN' NOW?

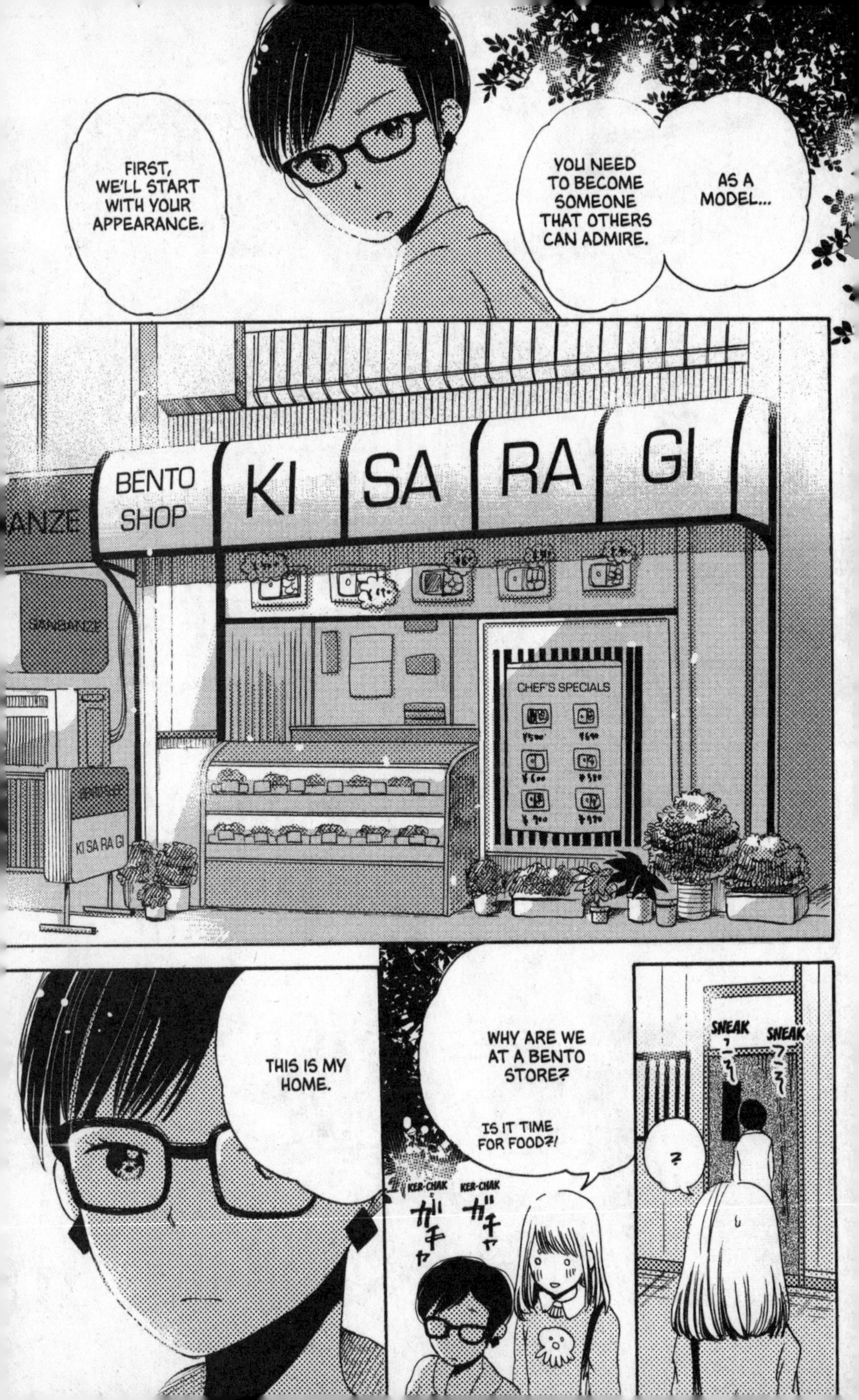
AS A MODEL...
YOU NEED TO BECOME SOMEONE THAT OTHERS CAN ADMIRE.
FIRST, WE'LL START WITH YOUR APPEARANCE.
BENTO SHOP KI SA RA GI
CHEF'S SPECIALS
KI SA RA GI
SNEAK
SNEAK
?
WHY ARE WE AT A BENTO STORE?
IS IT TIME FOR FOOD?!
KER-CHAK
KER-CHAK
ガチャ
ガチャ
THIS IS MY HOME.

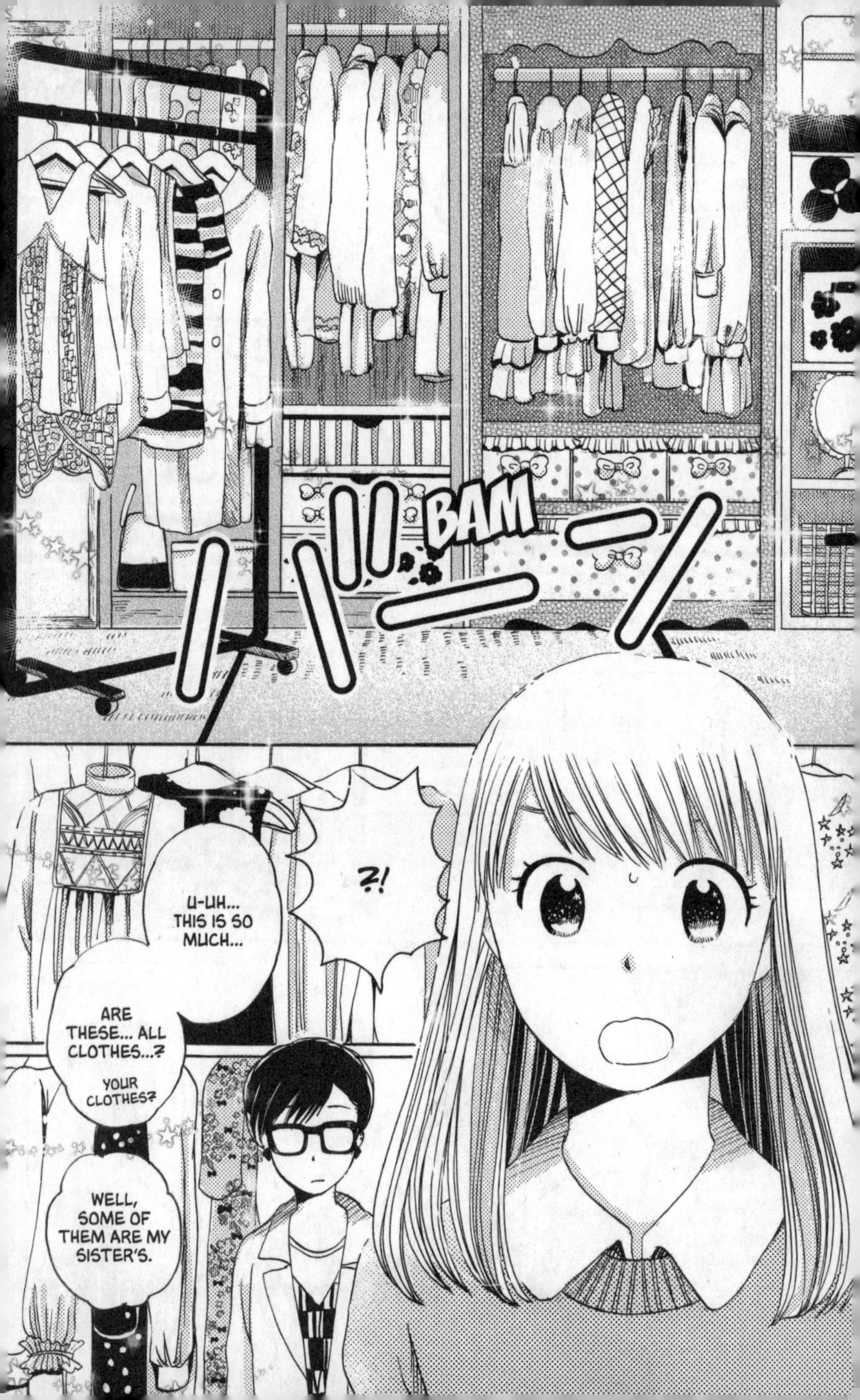
BAM
?!
U-UH... THIS IS SO MUCH...
ARE THESE... ALL CLOTHES...?
YOUR CLOTHES?
WELL, SOME OF THEM ARE MY SISTER'S.

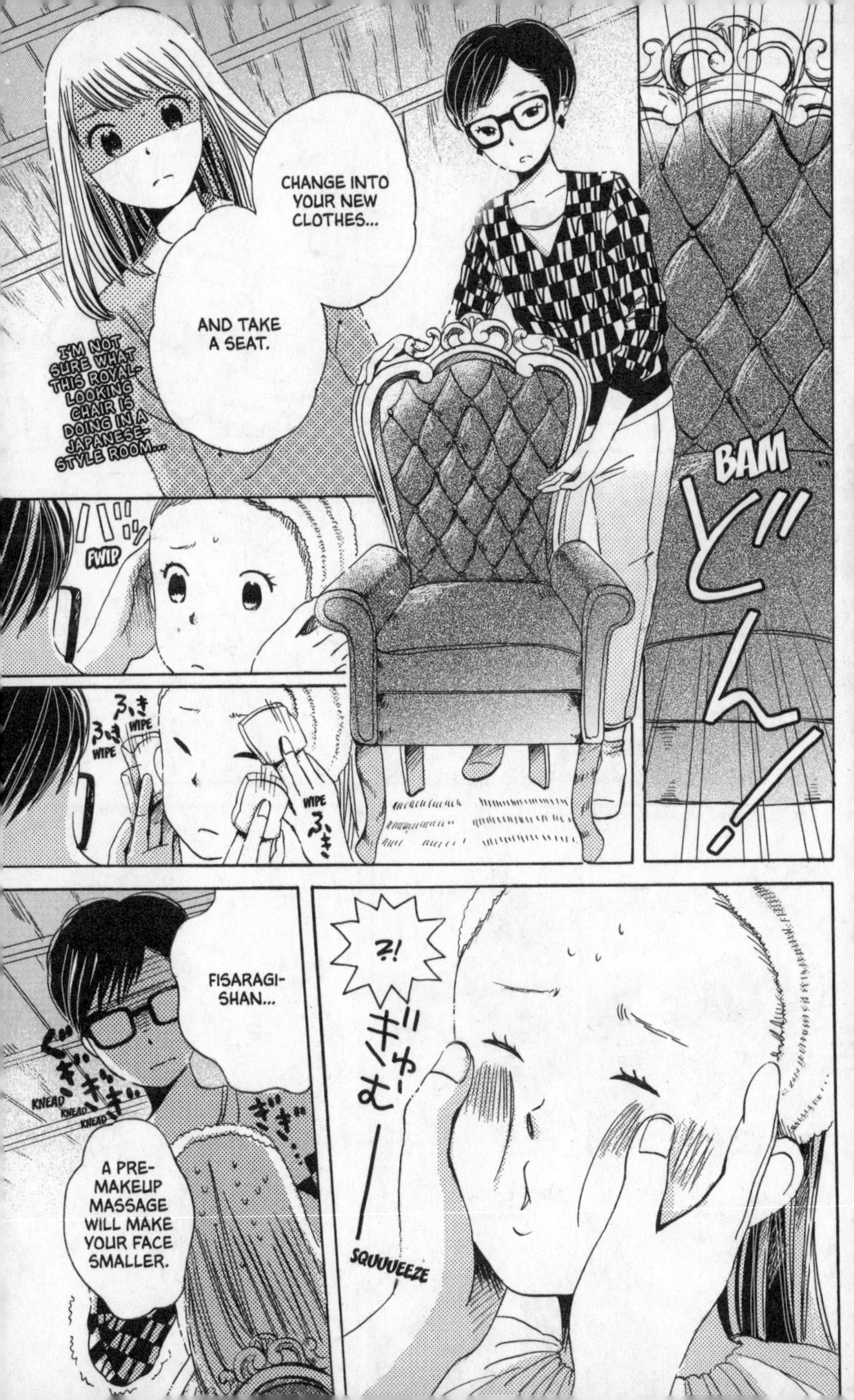
CHANGE INTO YOUR NEW CLOTHES...
AND TAKE A SEAT.
I'M NOT SURE WHAT THIS ROYAL-LOOKING CHAIR IS DOING IN A JAPANESE-STYLE ROOM...
BAM
どどん!
バッ
FWIP
ふき
WIPE
ふき
WIPE
WIPE
ふき
?!
ぎゅむー
SQUUUEEZE
FISARAGI-SHAN...
A PRE-MAKEUP MASSAGE WILL MAKE YOUR FACE SMALLER.
ぐぎぎぎぎ
KNEAD
KNEAD
KNEAD
ぎぎ...

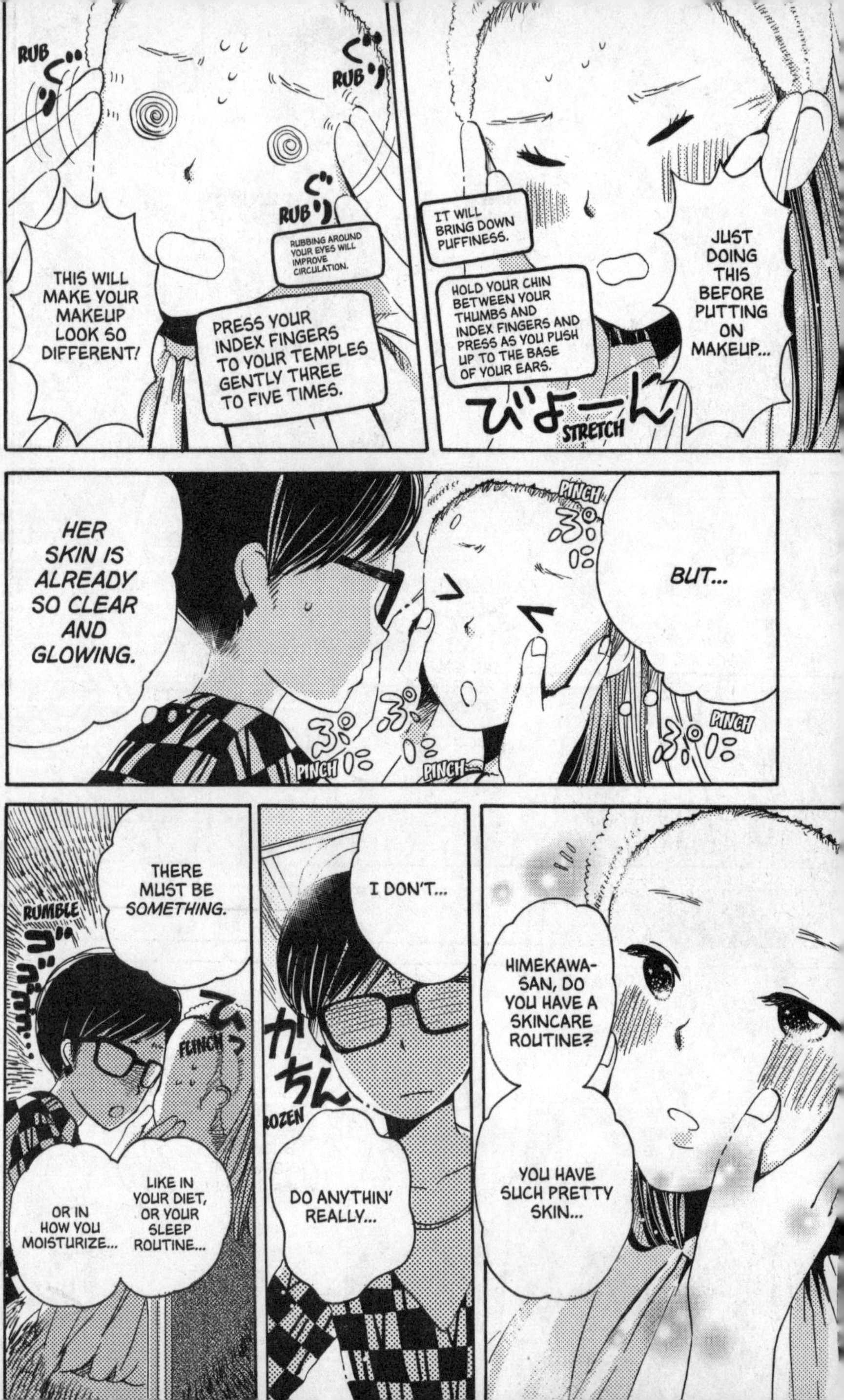
JUST DOING THIS BEFORE PUTTING ON MAKEUP...
IT WILL BRING DOWN PUFFINESS.
HOLD YOUR CHIN BETWEEN YOUR THUMBS AND INDEX FINGERS AND PRESS AS YOU PUSH UP TO THE BASE OF YOUR EARS.
びよーん STRETCH
ぐり RUB
RUB ぐり
RUBBING AROUND YOUR EYES WILL IMPROVE CIRCULATION.
PRESS YOUR INDEX FINGERS TO YOUR TEMPLES GENTLY THREE TO FIVE TIMES.
RUB ぐり
THIS WILL MAKE YOUR MAKEUP LOOK SO DIFFERENT!
BUT...
PINCH ぷに
PINCH ぷに
HER SKIN IS ALREADY SO CLEAR AND GLOWING.
ぷに PINCH
ぷに PINCH
HIMEKAWA-SAN, DO YOU HAVE A SKINCARE ROUTINE?
YOU HAVE SUCH PRETTY SKIN...
I DON'T...
かちん
ROZEN
DO ANYTHIN' REALLY...
THERE MUST BE SOMETHING.
ひっ FLINCH
RUMBLE ゴゴ
LIKE IN YOUR DIET, OR YOUR SLEEP ROUTINE...
OR IN HOW YOU MOISTURIZE...

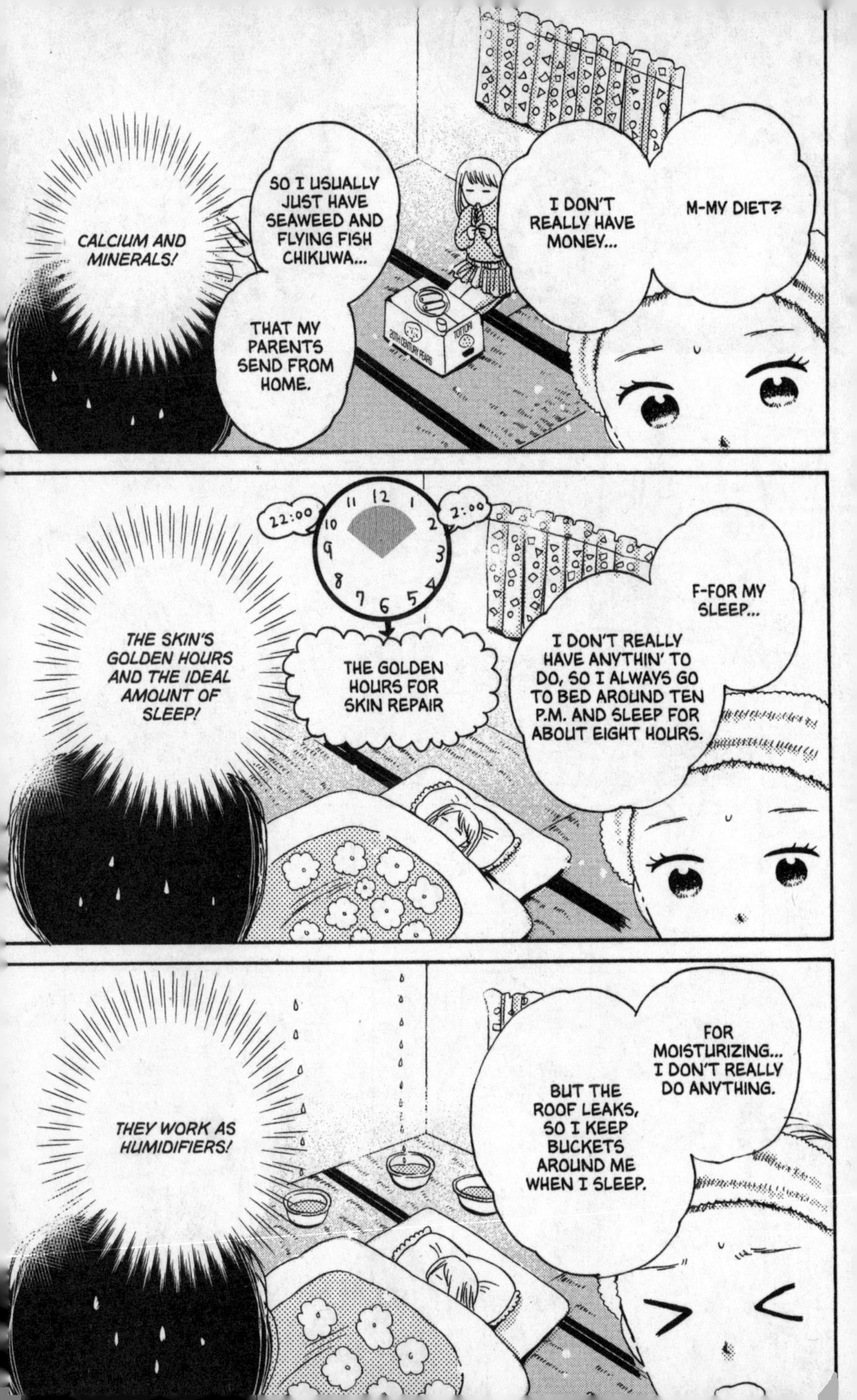
M-MY DIET?
I DON'T REALLY HAVE MONEY...
SO I USUALLY JUST HAVE SEAWEED AND FLYING FISH CHIKUWA...
THAT MY PARENTS SEND FROM HOME.
TOTTORI
20TH CENTURY PEARS
CALCIUM AND MINERALS!
F-FOR MY SLEEP...
I DON'T REALLY HAVE ANYTHIN' TO DO, SO I ALWAYS GO TO BED AROUND TEN P.M. AND SLEEP FOR ABOUT EIGHT HOURS.
2:00
22:00
THE GOLDEN HOURS FOR SKIN REPAIR
THE SKIN'S GOLDEN HOURS AND THE IDEAL AMOUNT OF SLEEP!
FOR MOISTURIZING... I DON'T REALLY DO ANYTHING.
BUT THE ROOF LEAKS, SO I KEEP BUCKETS AROUND ME WHEN I SLEEP.
THEY WORK AS HUMIDIFIERS!

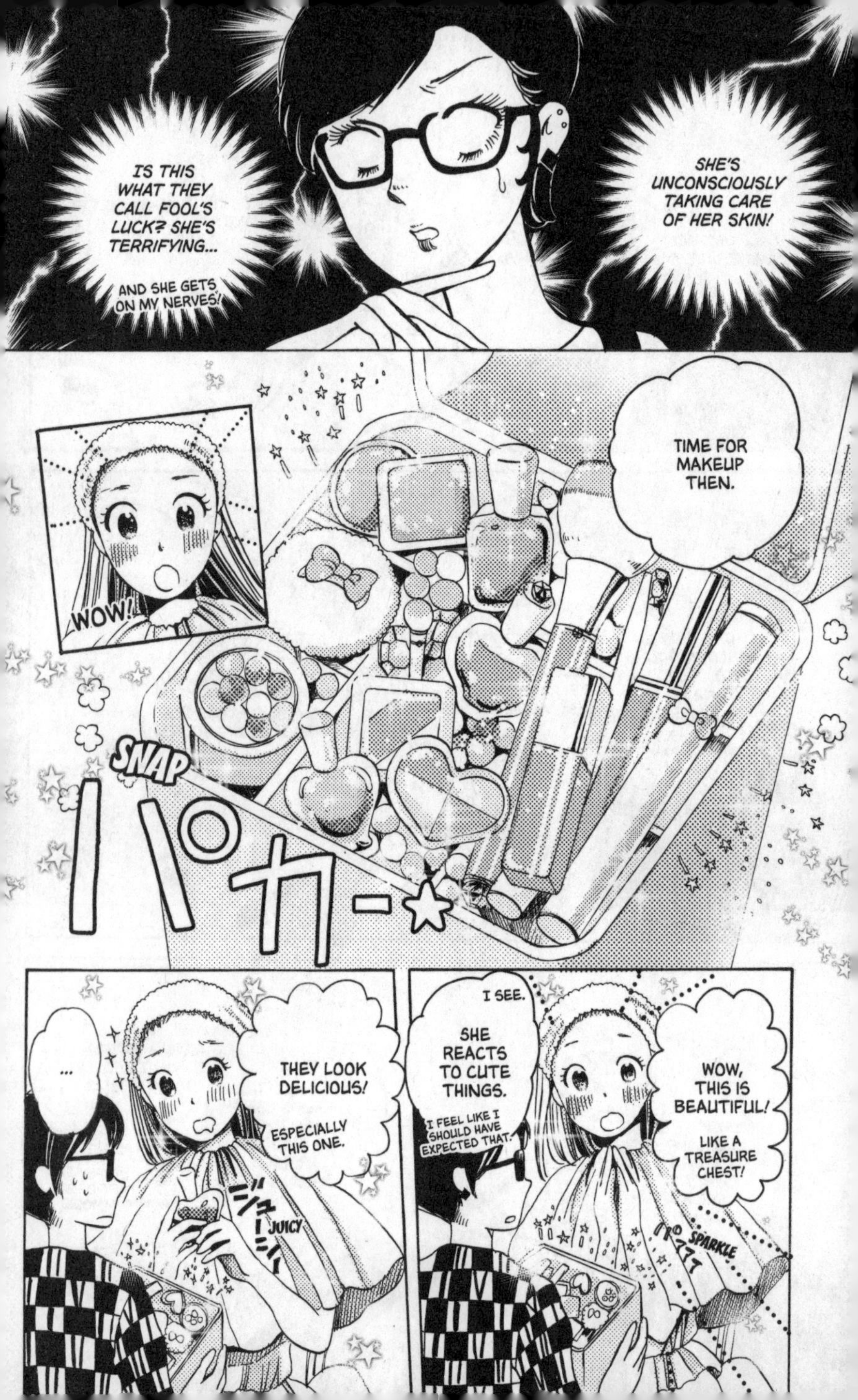
SHE'S UNCONSCIOUSLY TAKING CARE OF HER SKIN!
IS THIS WHAT THEY CALL FOOL'S LUCK? SHE'S TERRIFYING...
AND SHE GETS ON MY NERVES!
TIME FOR MAKEUP THEN.
SNAP
パカー☆
WOW!
WOW, THIS IS BEAUTIFUL!
LIKE A TREASURE CHEST!
SPARKLE
I SEE.
SHE REACTS TO CUTE THINGS.
I FEEL LIKE I SHOULD HAVE EXPECTED THAT.
THEY LOOK DELICIOUS!
ESPECIALLY THIS ONE.
JUICY
...

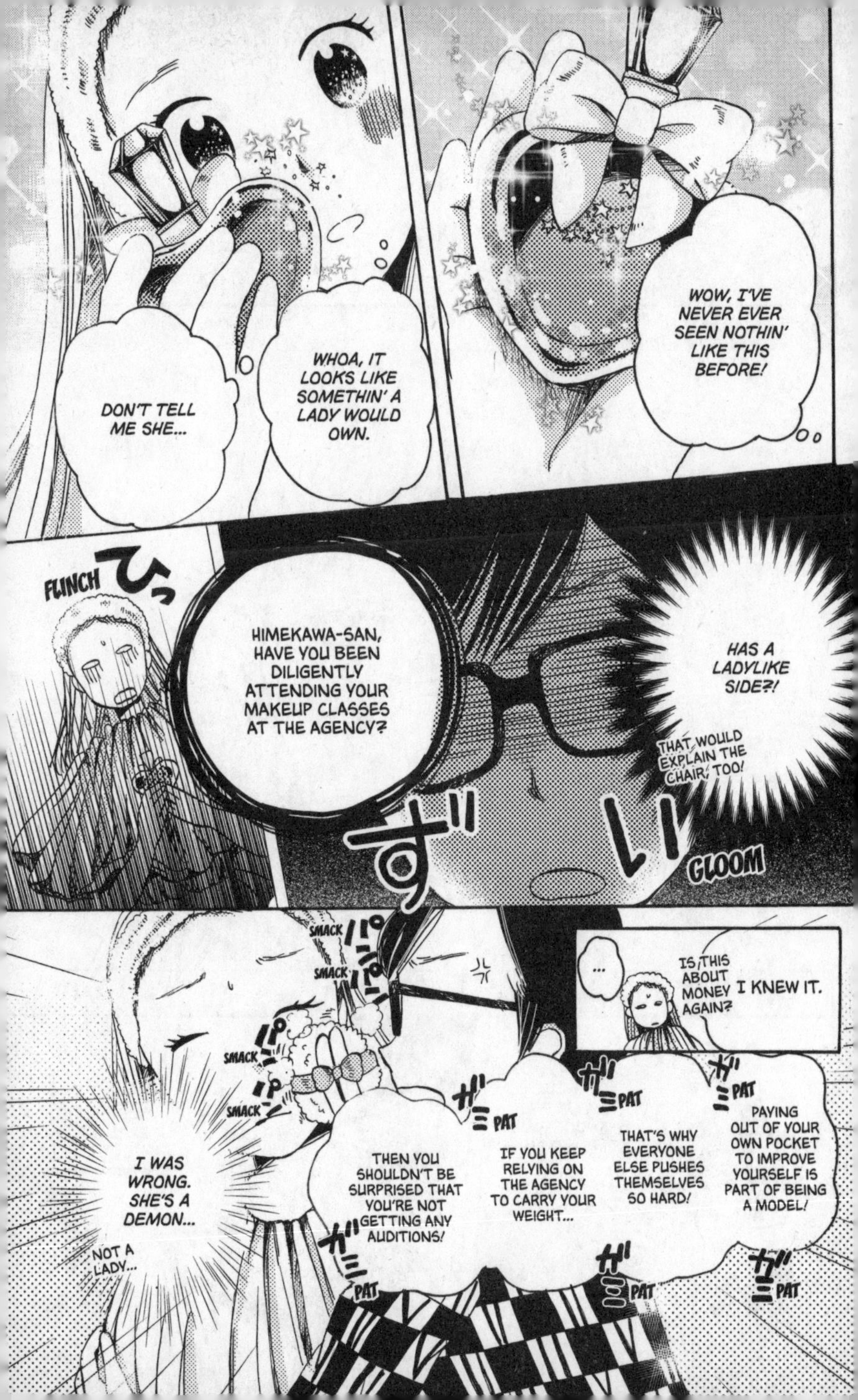
WOW, I'VE NEVER EVER SEEN NOTHIN' LIKE THIS BEFORE!
WHOA, IT LOOKS LIKE SOMETHIN' A LADY WOULD OWN.
DON'T TELL ME SHE...
HAS A LADYLIKE SIDE?!
THAT WOULD EXPLAIN THE CHAIR, TOO!
GLOOM
HIMEKAWA-SAN, HAVE YOU BEEN DILIGENTLY ATTENDING YOUR MAKEUP CLASSES AT THE AGENCY?
FLINCH
I KNEW IT.
IS THIS ABOUT MONEY AGAIN?
...
PAT
PAYING OUT OF YOUR OWN POCKET TO IMPROVE YOURSELF IS PART OF BEING A MODEL!
PAT
THAT'S WHY EVERYONE ELSE PUSHES THEMSELVES SO HARD!
PAT
IF YOU KEEP RELYING ON THE AGENCY TO CARRY YOUR WEIGHT...
THEN YOU SHOULDN'T BE SURPRISED THAT YOU'RE NOT GETTING ANY AUDITIONS!
PAT
PAT
PAT
SMACK
SMACK
SMACK
SMACK
I WAS WRONG. SHE'S A DEMON...
NOT A LADY...

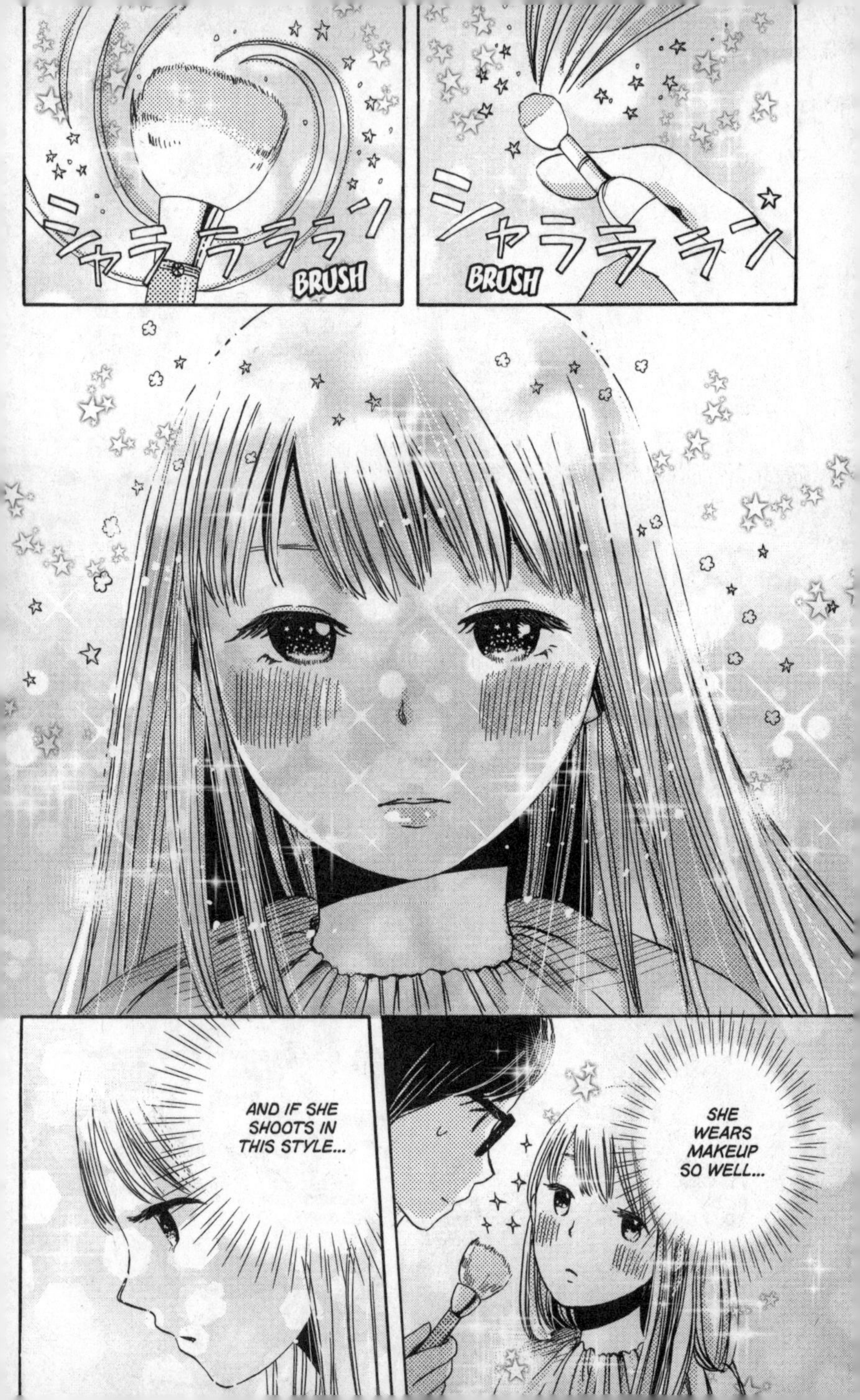
BRUSH
BRUSH
SHE WEARS MAKEUP SO WELL...
AND IF SHE SHOOTS IN THIS STYLE...

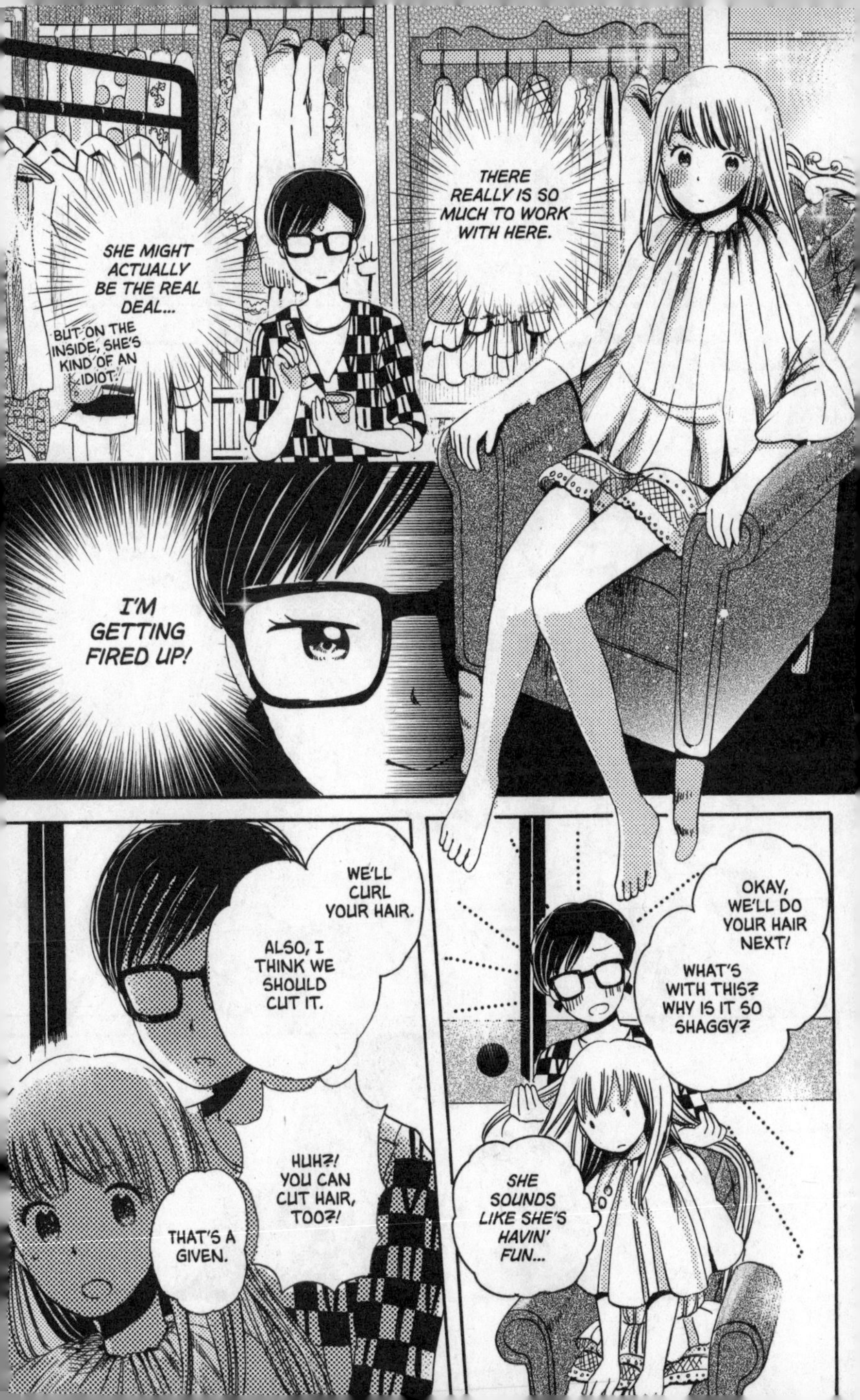
THERE REALLY IS SO MUCH TO WORK WITH HERE.
SHE MIGHT ACTUALLY BE THE REAL DEAL...
BUT ON THE INSIDE, SHE'S KIND OF AN IDIOT.
I'M GETTING FIRED UP!
OKAY, WE'LL DO YOUR HAIR NEXT!
WHAT'S WITH THIS? WHY IS IT SO SHAGGY?
SHE SOUNDS LIKE SHE'S HAVIN' FUN...
WE'LL CURL YOUR HAIR.
ALSO, I THINK WE SHOULD CUT IT.
HUH?! YOU CAN CUT HAIR, TOO?!
THAT'S A GIVEN.

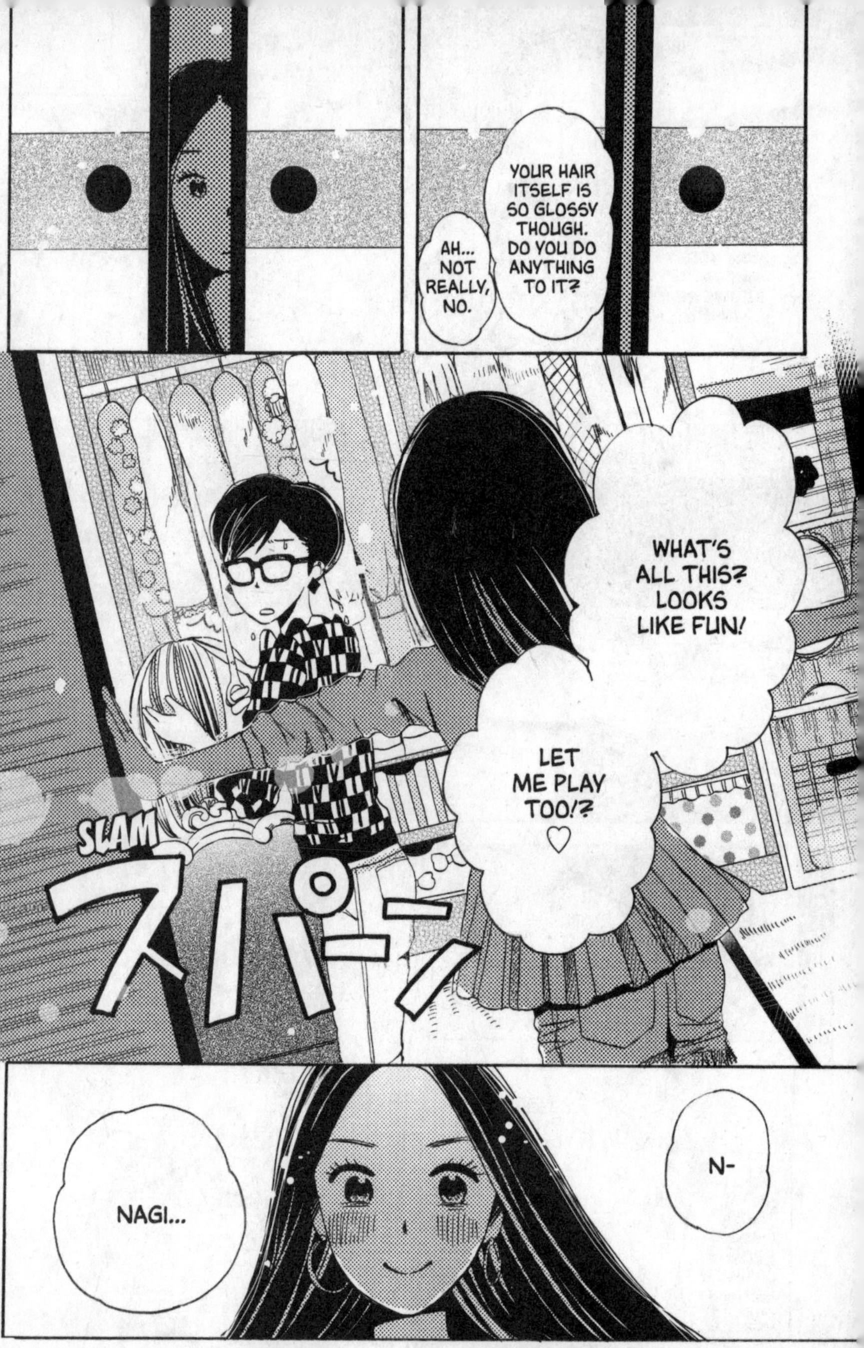
YOUR HAIR ITSELF IS SO GLOSSY THOUGH. DO YOU DO ANYTHING TO IT?
AH... NOT REALLY, NO.
WHAT'S ALL THIS? LOOKS LIKE FUN!
LET ME PLAY TOO!? ♡
SLAM
スパーン
N-
NAGI...

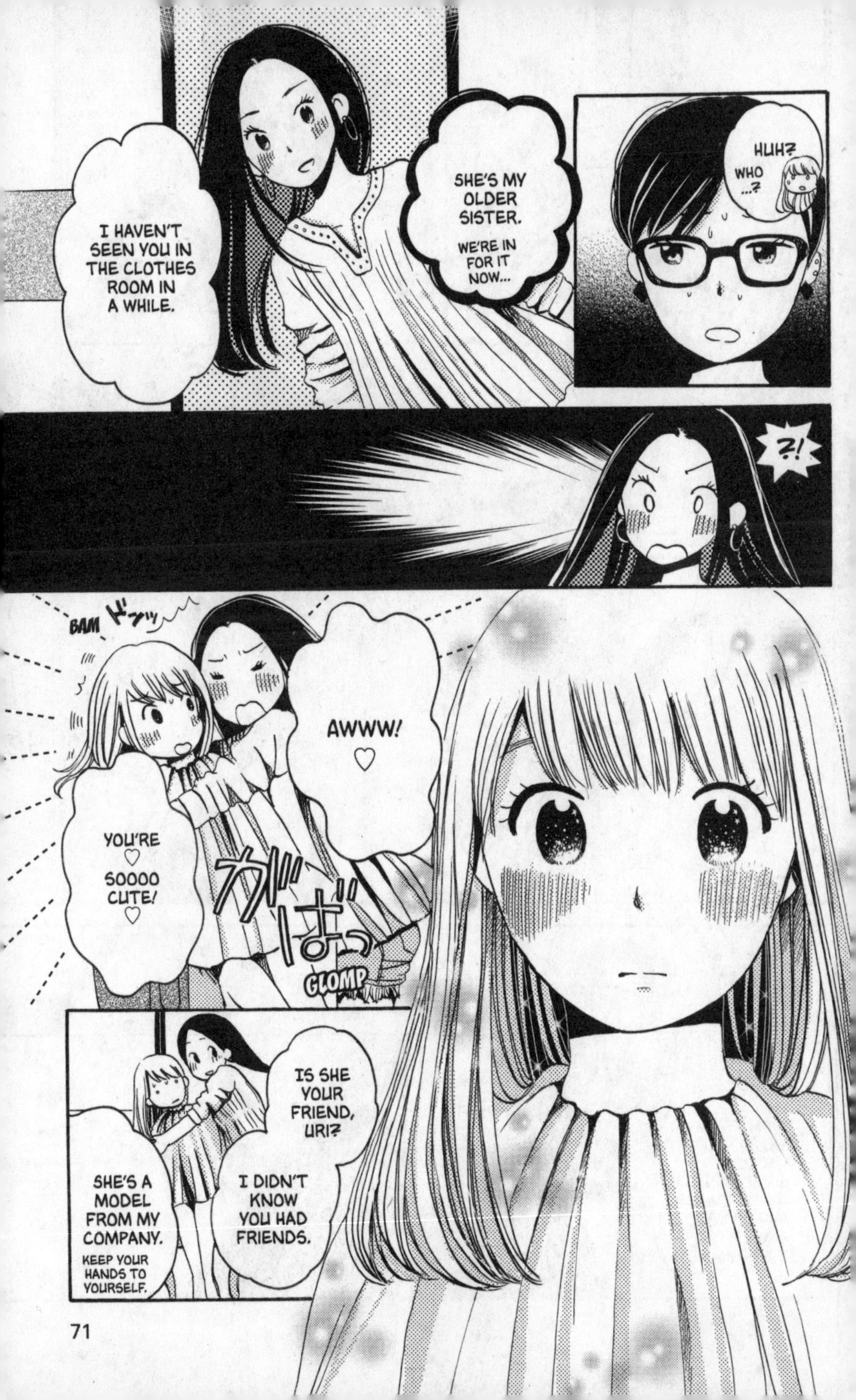
HUH? WHO ...?
SHE'S MY OLDER SISTER. WE'RE IN FOR IT NOW...
I HAVEN'T SEEN YOU IN THE CLOTHES ROOM IN A WHILE.
?!
BAM ドッ
AWWW! ♡
YOU'RE ♡ SOOOO CUTE! ♡
がばっ GLOMP
IS SHE YOUR FRIEND, URI?
I DIDN'T KNOW YOU HAD FRIENDS.
SHE'S A MODEL FROM MY COMPANY. KEEP YOUR HANDS TO YOURSELF.

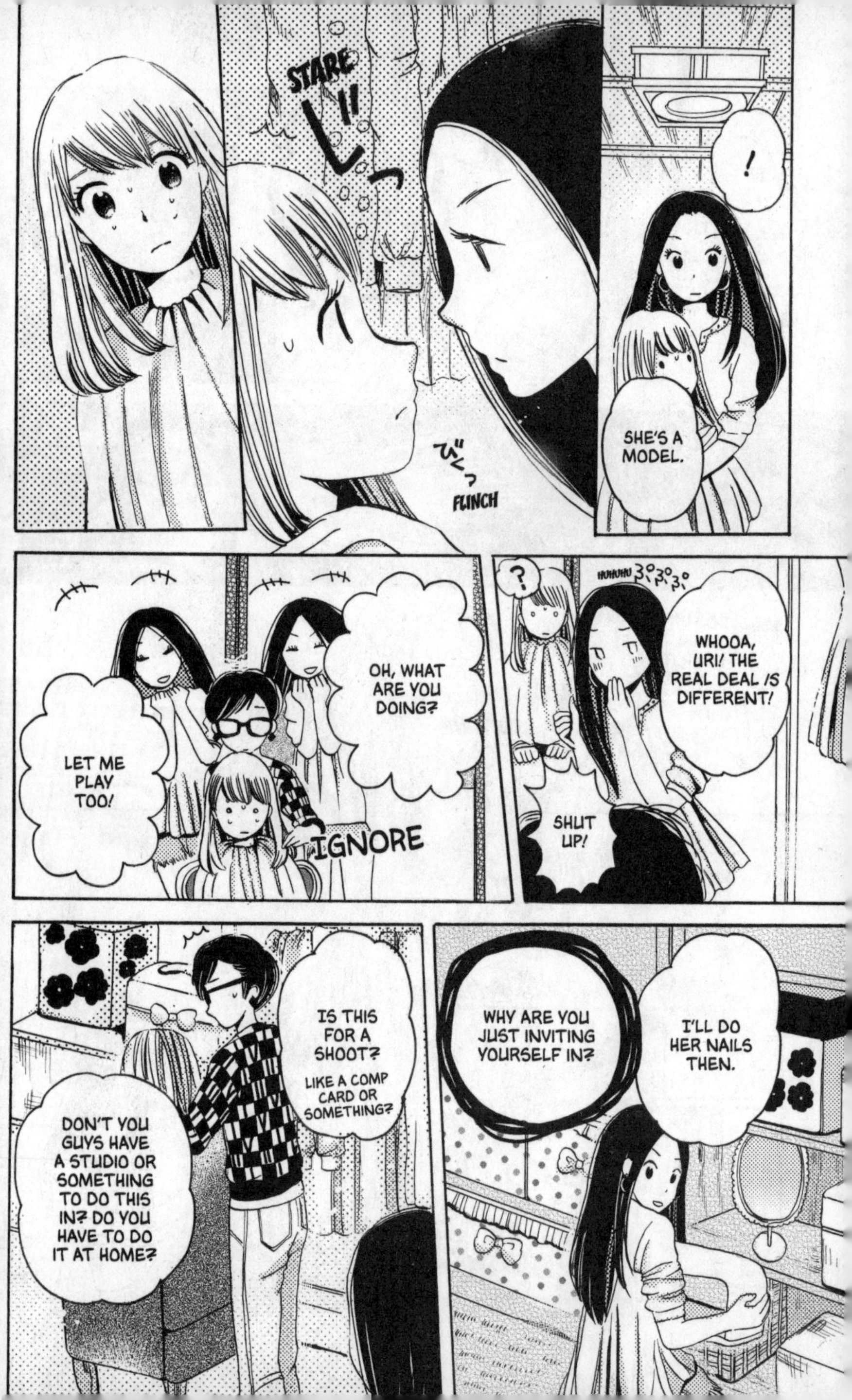
!
SHE'S A MODEL.
STARE
FLINCH
WHOOA, URI! THE REAL DEAL IS DIFFERENT!
HUHUHU
?
SHUT UP!
OH, WHAT ARE YOU DOING?
LET ME PLAY TOO!
IGNORE
I'LL DO HER NAILS THEN.
WHY ARE YOU JUST INVITING YOURSELF IN?
IS THIS FOR A SHOOT?
LIKE A COMP CARD OR SOMETHING?
DON'T YOU GUYS HAVE A STUDIO OR SOMETHING TO DO THIS IN? DO YOU HAVE TO DO IT AT HOME?

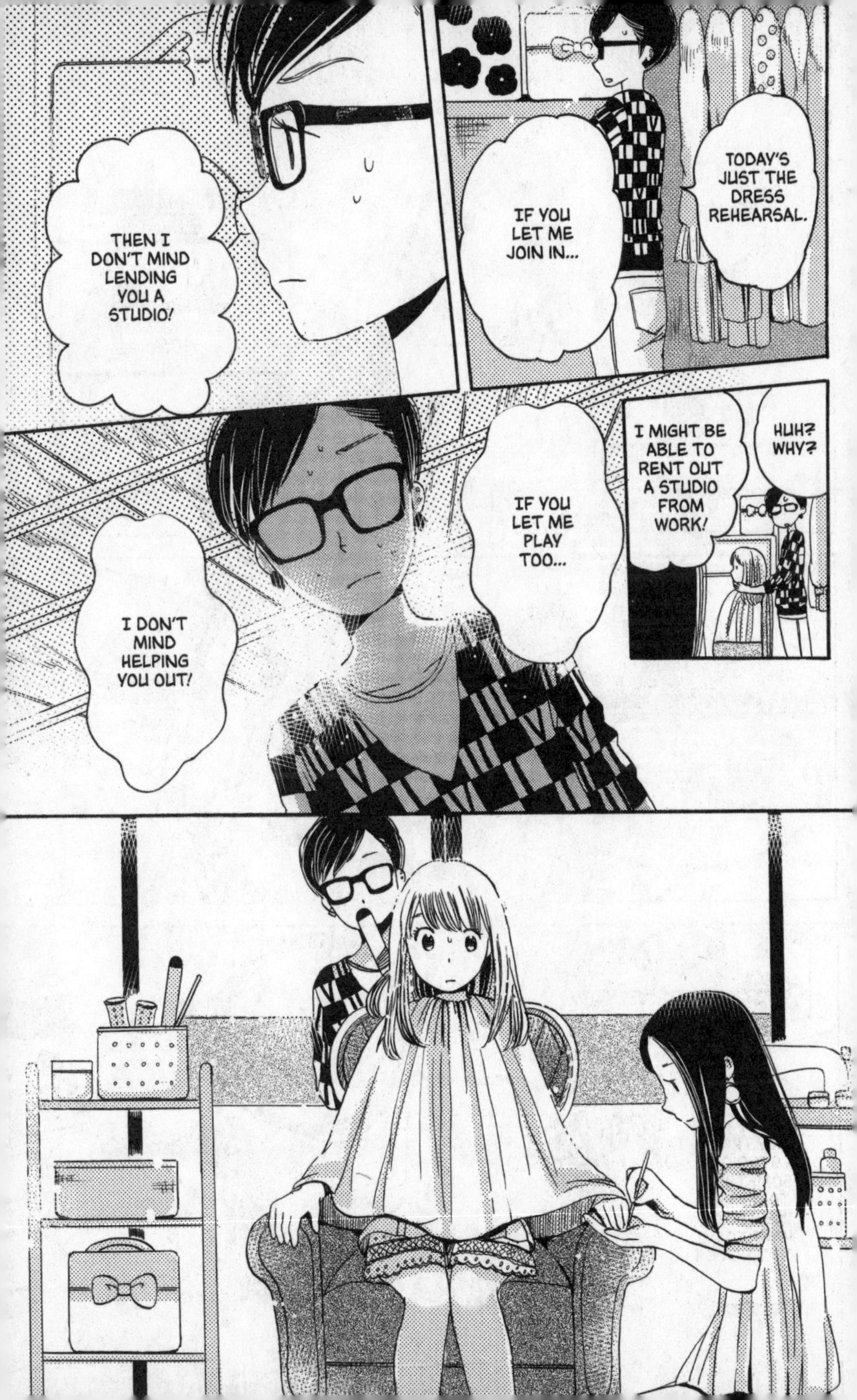
TODAY'S JUST THE DRESS REHEARSAL.
IF YOU LET ME JOIN IN...
THEN I DON'T MIND LENDING YOU A STUDIO!
HUH? WHY?
I MIGHT BE ABLE TO RENT OUT A STUDIO FROM WORK!
IF YOU LET ME PLAY TOO...
I DON'T MIND HELPING YOU OUT!

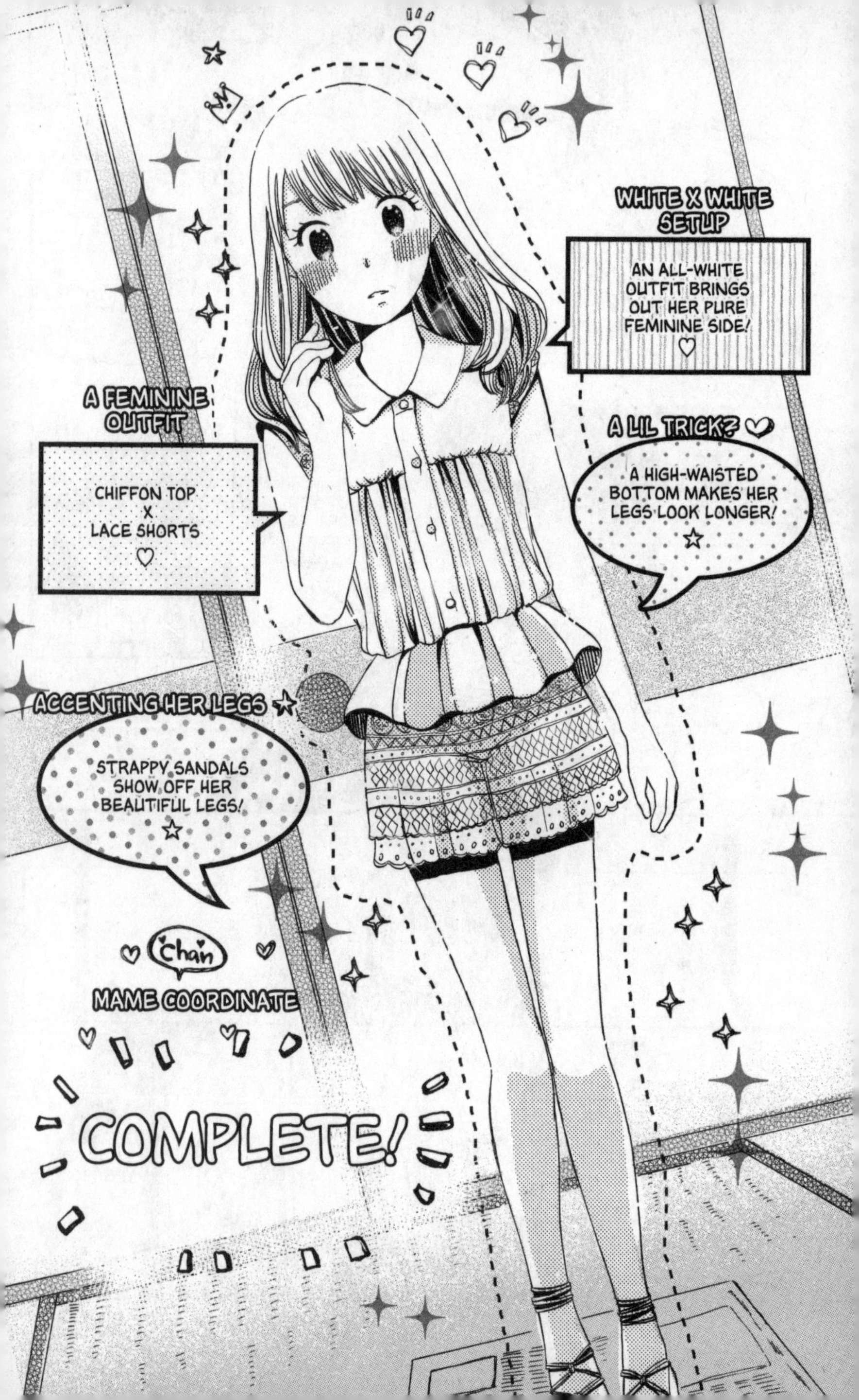
WHITE X WHITE SETUP
AN ALL-WHITE OUTFIT BRINGS OUT HER PURE FEMININE SIDE! ♡
A FEMININE OUTFIT
CHIFFON TOP X LACE SHORTS ♡
A LIL TRICK? ♡
A HIGH-WAISTED BOTTOM MAKES HER LEGS LOOK LONGER! ☆
ACCENTING HER LEGS ☆
STRAPPY SANDALS SHOW OFF HER BEAUTIFUL LEGS! ☆
♡ Chan ♡
MAME COORDINATE
COMPLETE!

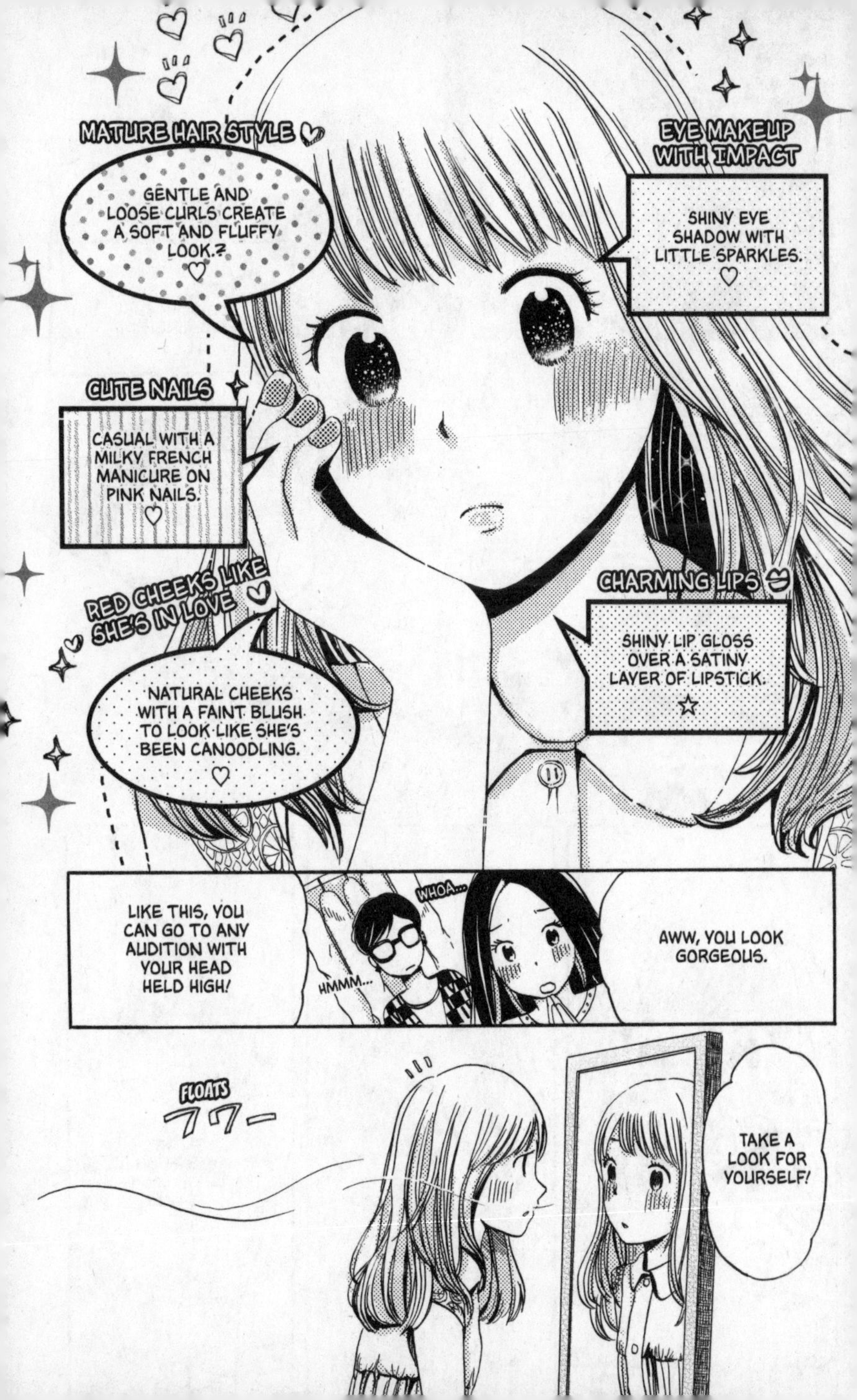
EYE MAKEUP WITH IMPACT
SHINY EYE SHADOW WITH LITTLE SPARKLES. ♡
MATURE HAIR STYLE ♡
GENTLE AND LOOSE CURLS CREATE A SOFT AND FLUFFY LOOK.♪ ♡
CUTE NAILS
CASUAL WITH A MILKY FRENCH MANICURE ON PINK NAILS. ♡
CHARMING LIPS
SHINY LIP GLOSS OVER A SATINY LAYER OF LIPSTICK. ☆
RED CHEEKS LIKE SHE'S IN LOVE ♡
NATURAL CHEEKS WITH A FAINT BLUSH TO LOOK LIKE SHE'S BEEN CANOODLING. ♡
AWW, YOU LOOK GORGEOUS.
WHOA...
HMMM...
LIKE THIS, YOU CAN GO TO ANY AUDITION WITH YOUR HEAD HELD HIGH!
TAKE A LOOK FOR YOURSELF!
FLOATS

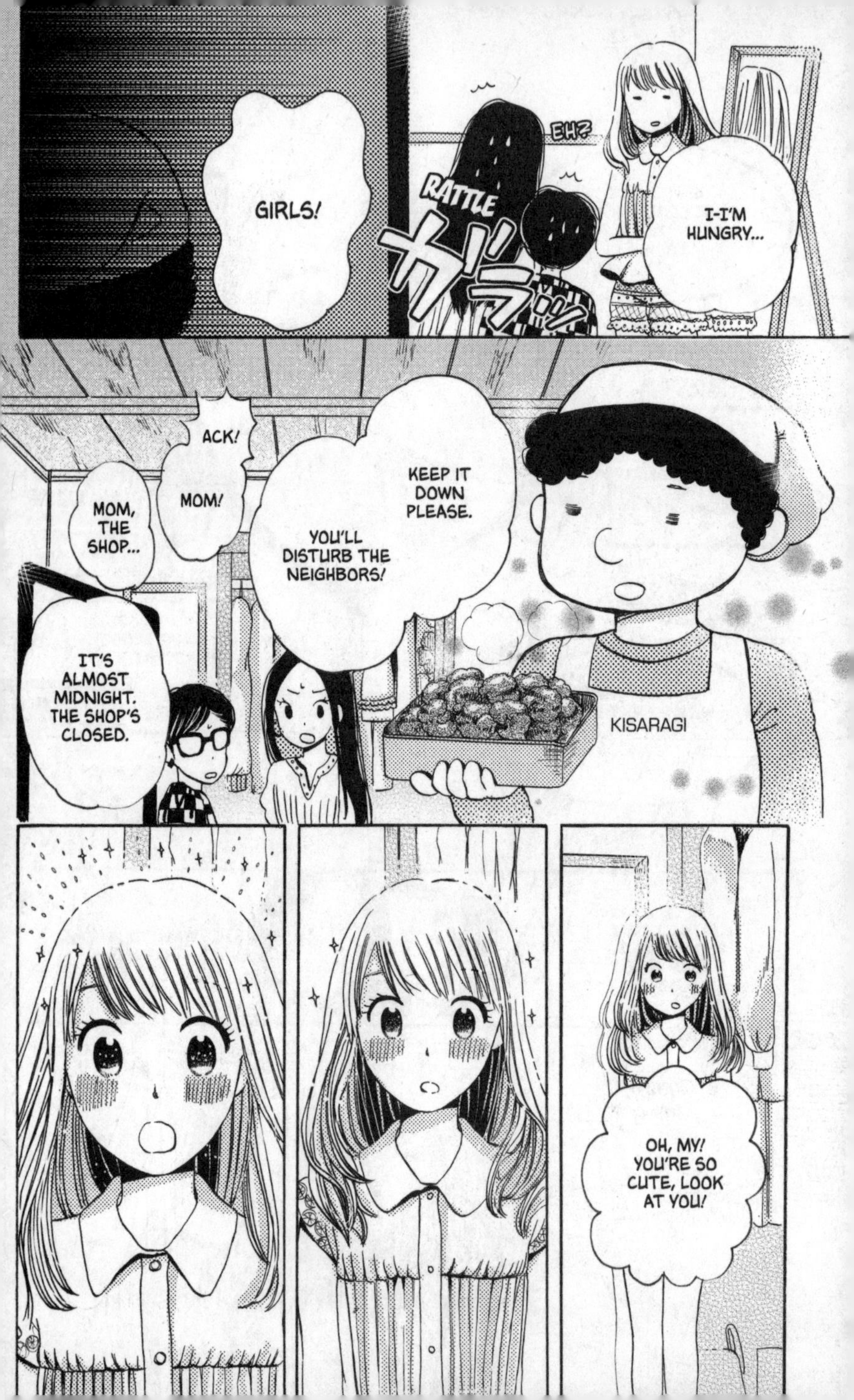
I-I'M HUNGRY...
EH?
RATTLE
GIRLS!
KEEP IT DOWN PLEASE.
YOU'LL DISTURB THE NEIGHBORS!
ACK!
MOM!
MOM, THE SHOP...
KISARAGI
IT'S ALMOST MIDNIGHT. THE SHOP'S CLOSED.
OH, MY! YOU'RE SO CUTE, LOOK AT YOU!

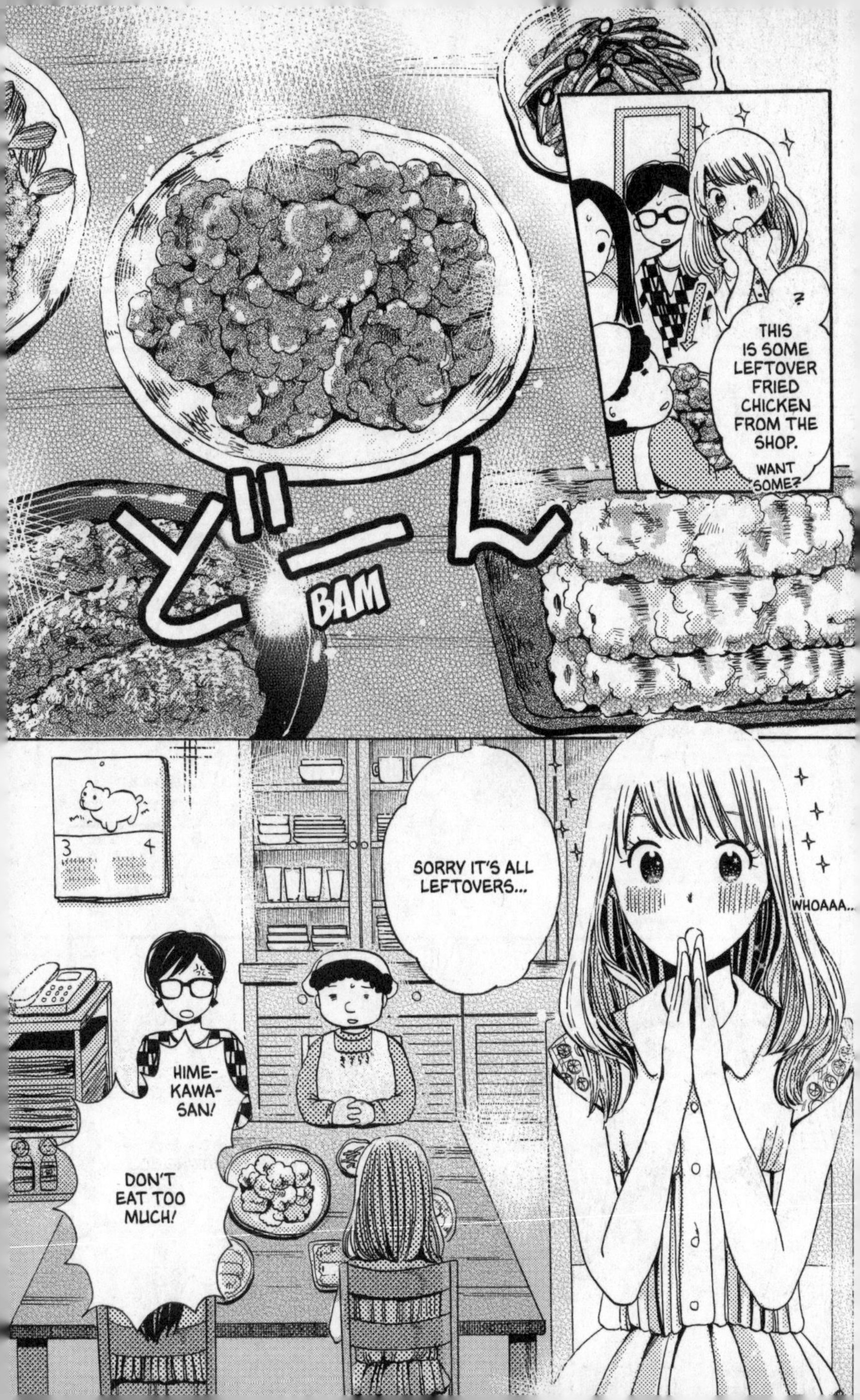
THIS IS SOME LEFTOVER FRIED CHICKEN FROM THE SHOP.
WANT SOME?
ドーン
BAM
WHOAAA...
SORRY IT'S ALL LEFTOVERS...
HIME-KAWA-SAN!
DON'T EAT TOO MUCH!

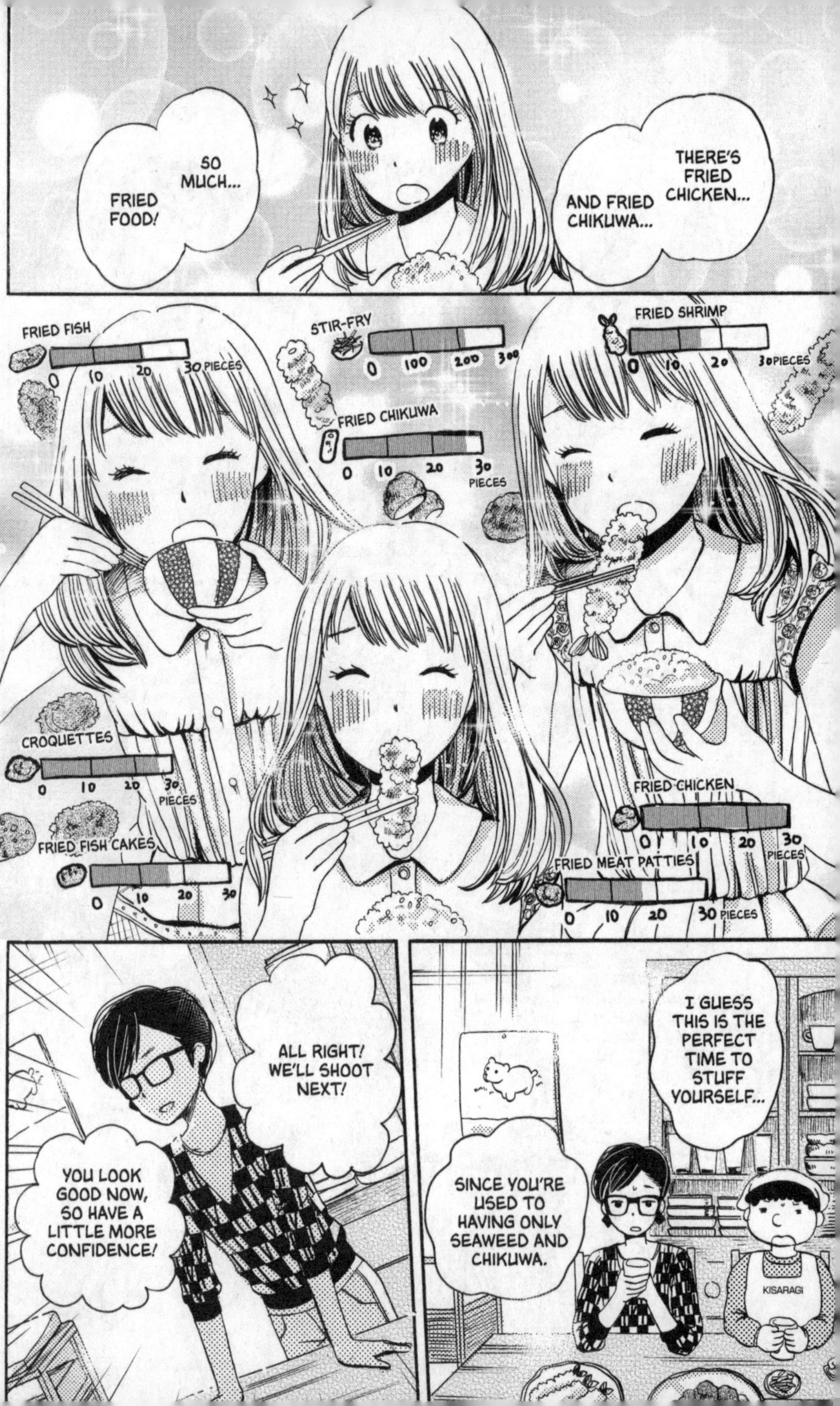
THERE'S FRIED CHICKEN...
AND FRIED CHIKUWA...
SO MUCH...
FRIED FOOD!
FRIED SHRIMP 0 10 20 30 PIECES
STIR-FRY 0 100 200 300
FRIED FISH 0 10 20 30 PIECES
FRIED CHIKUWA 0 10 20 30 PIECES
FRIED CHICKEN 0 10 20 30 PIECES
FRIED MEAT PATTIES 0 10 20 30 PIECES
CROQUETTES 0 10 20 30 PIECES
FRIED FISH CAKES 0 10 20 30
I GUESS THIS IS THE PERFECT TIME TO STUFF YOURSELF...
SINCE YOU'RE USED TO HAVING ONLY SEAWEED AND CHIKUWA.
KISARAGI
ALL RIGHT! WE'LL SHOOT NEXT!
YOU LOOK GOOD NOW, SO HAVE A LITTLE MORE CONFIDENCE!

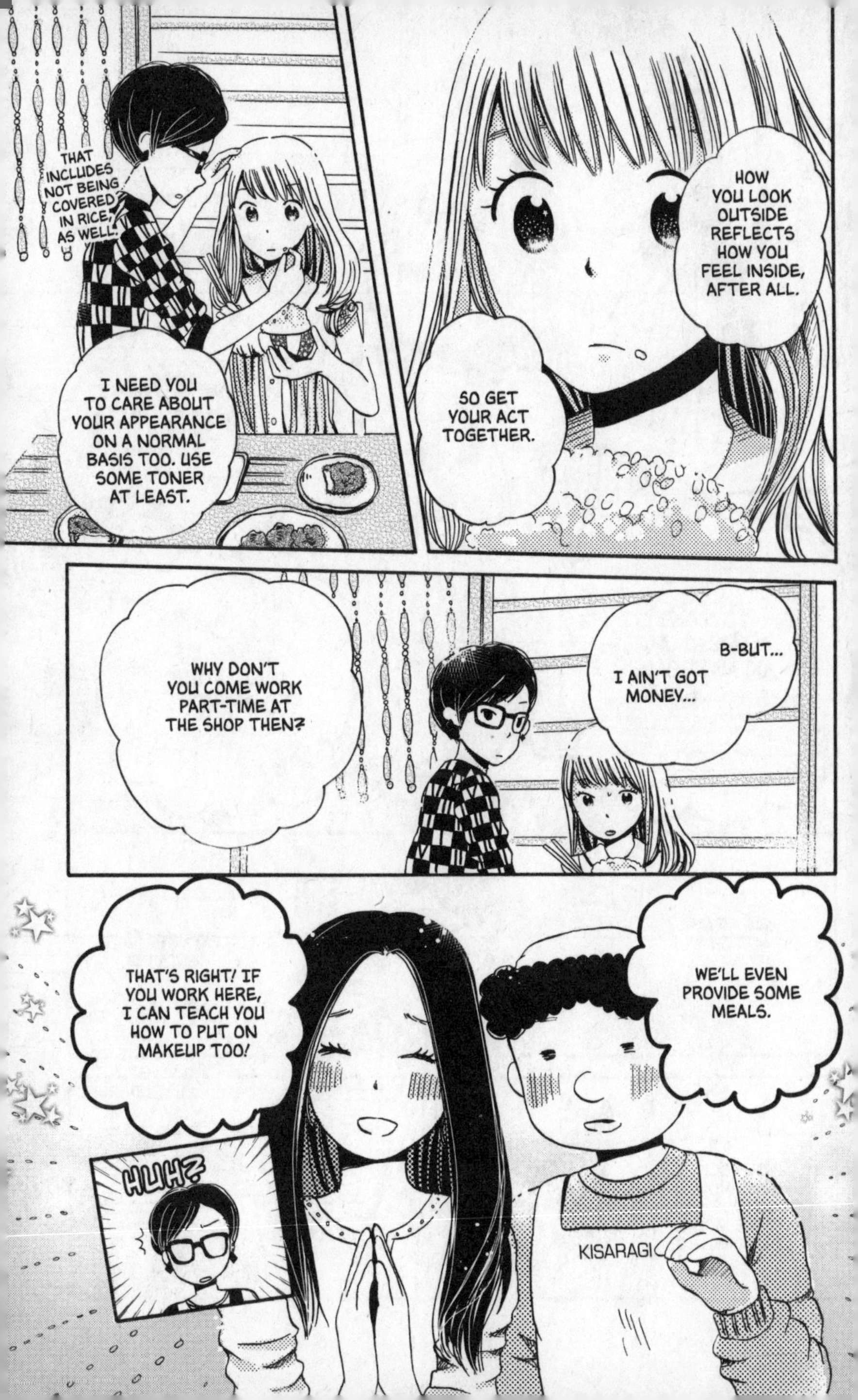
HOW YOU LOOK OUTSIDE REFLECTS HOW YOU FEEL INSIDE, AFTER ALL.
SO GET YOUR ACT TOGETHER.
THAT INCLUDES NOT BEING COVERED IN RICE, AS WELL.
I NEED YOU TO CARE ABOUT YOUR APPEARANCE ON A NORMAL BASIS TOO. USE SOME TONER AT LEAST.
B-BUT...
I AIN'T GOT MONEY...
WHY DON'T YOU COME WORK PART-TIME AT THE SHOP THEN?
WE'LL EVEN PROVIDE SOME MEALS.
THAT'S RIGHT! IF YOU WORK HERE, I CAN TEACH YOU HOW TO PUT ON MAKEUP TOO!
HUH?
KISARAGI

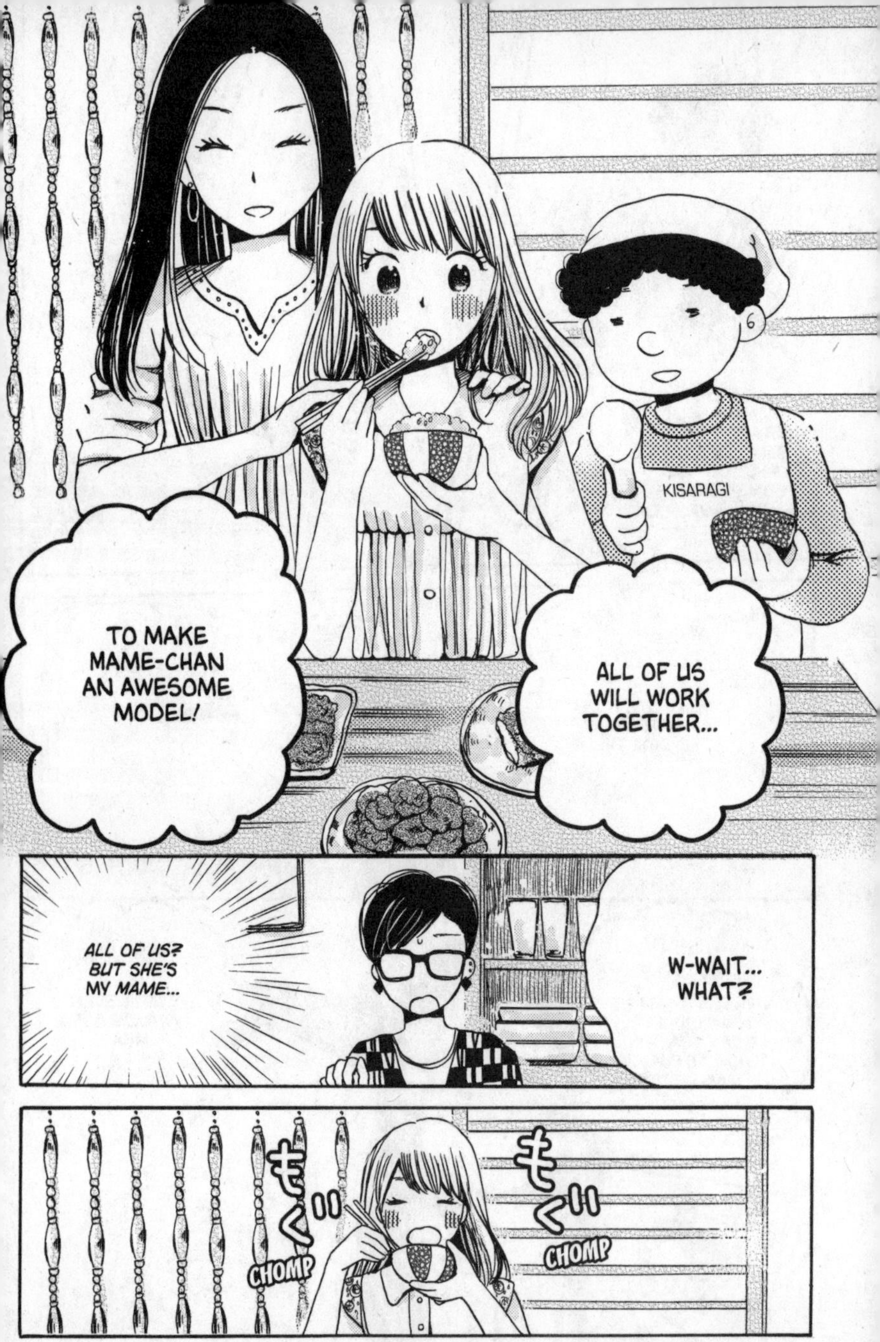
KISARAGI
ALL OF US WILL WORK TOGETHER...
TO MAKE MAME-CHAN AN AWESOME MODEL!
W-WAIT... WHAT?
ALL OF US? BUT SHE'S MY MAME...
もぐ
CHOMP
もぐ
CHOMP

MAME
coordinate

OOTD CORNER
CONCEPT: CASUAL MATURE STYLE (WITH PRINTS)
TOP WITH A MONOCHROME GEOMETRIC PRINT
DROPPED SHOULDER SPRING COAT
CHINOS FOR THE MATURE LOOK
REAL LEATHER BAG
WALLABEE SHOES
CONCEPT: 5TH GRADER
BLOUSE FROM HER HIGH SCHOOL UNIFORM
OCTOPUS SWEATSHIRT (THE OCTOPUS IS SENTIENT.)
SIMPLE PLEATED SKIRT
WRINKLED SOCKS
SHOES WITH STRAPS

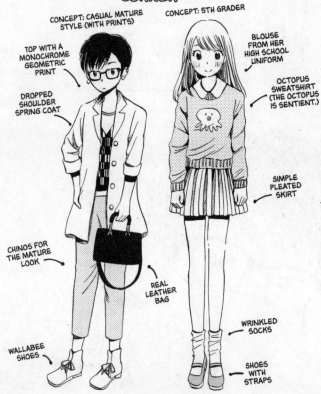

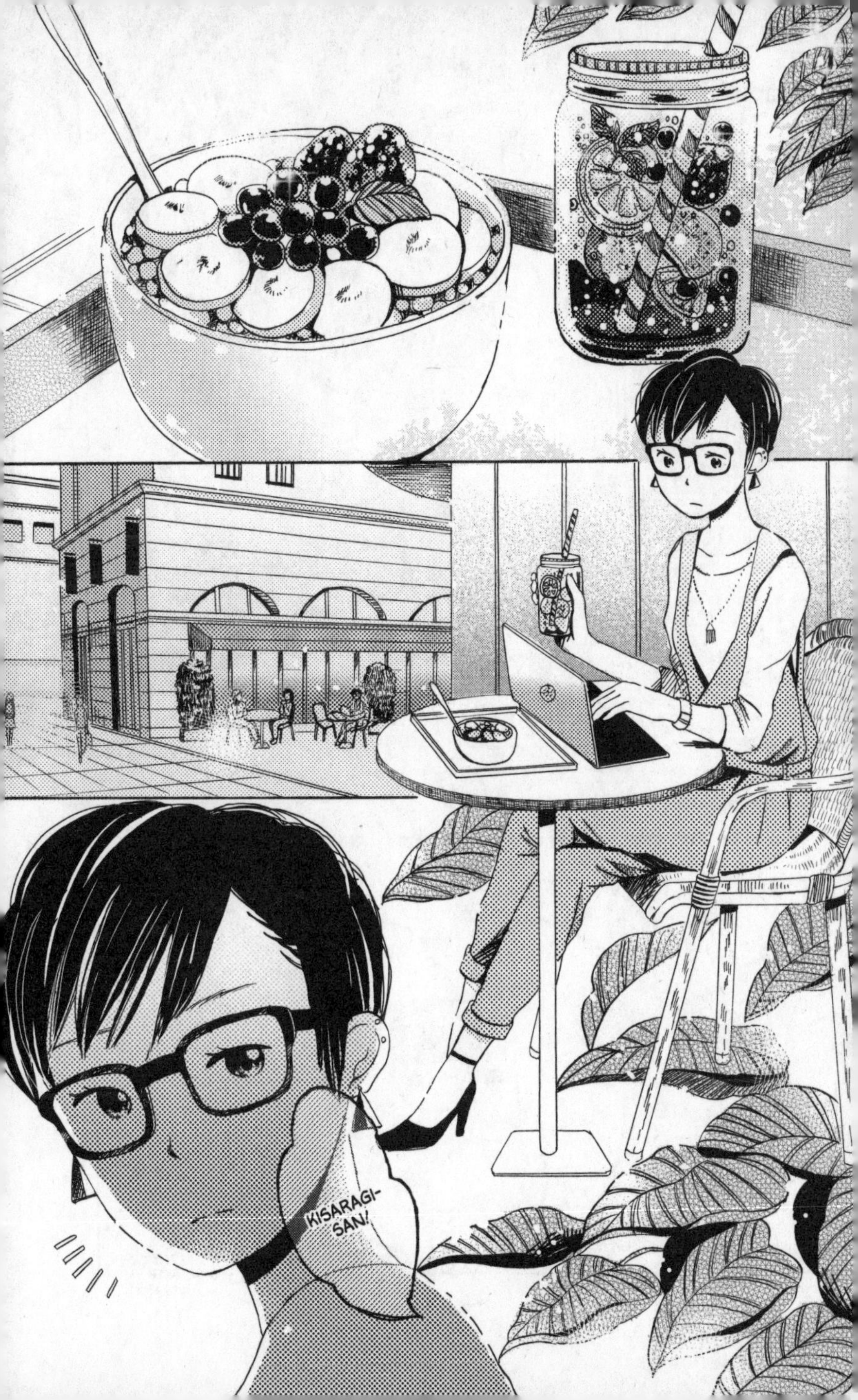
KISARAGI-SAN!

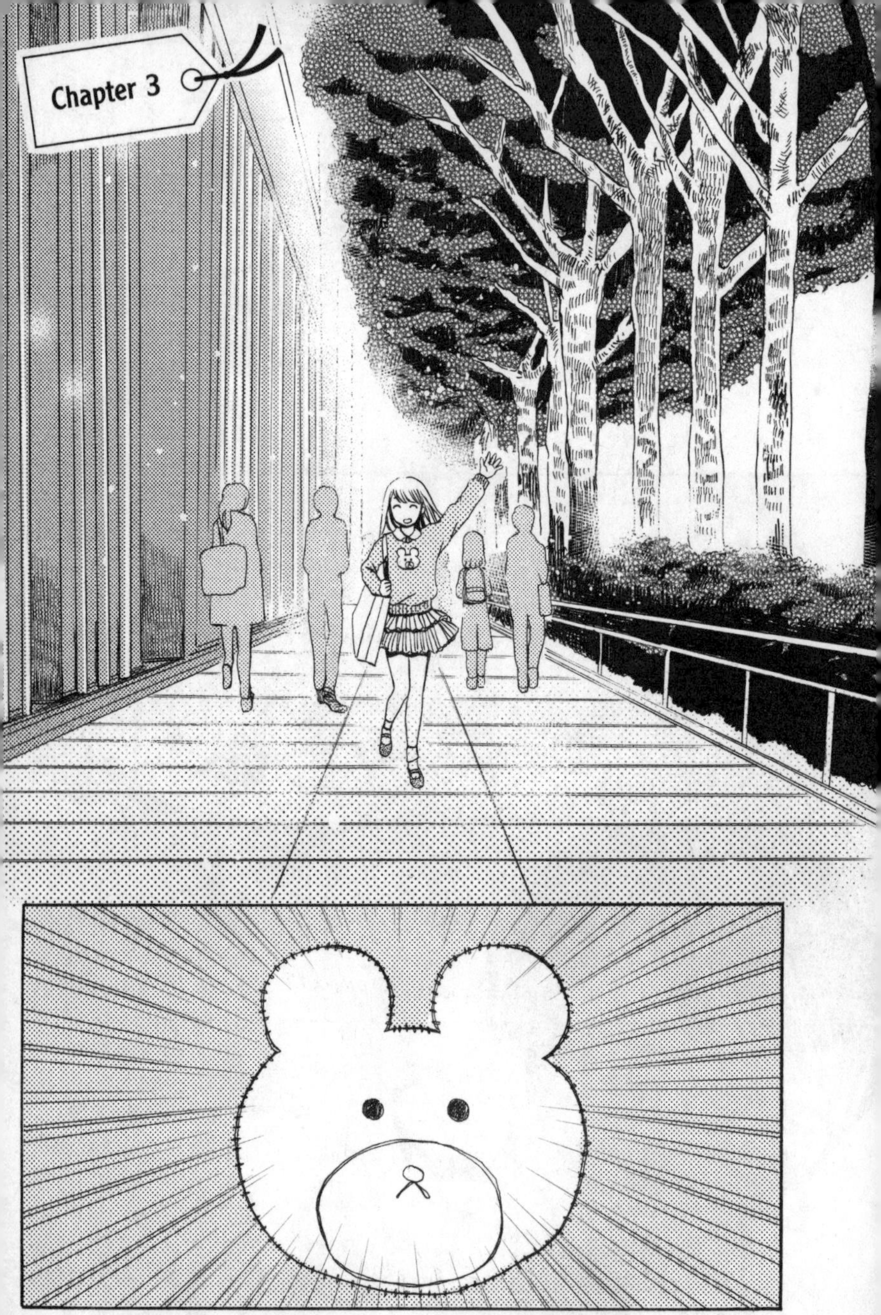
Chapter 3

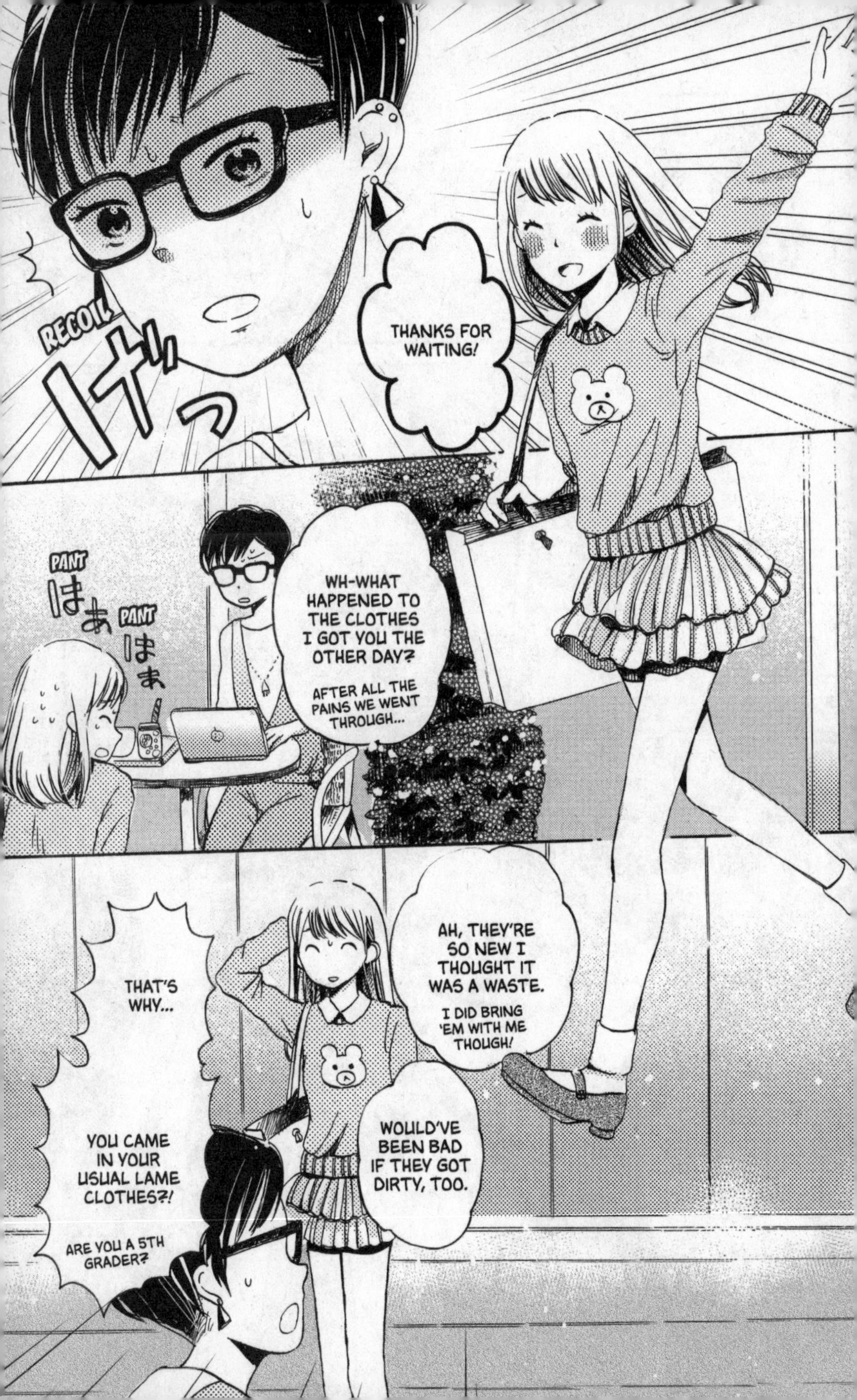
THANKS FOR WAITING!
RECOIL
ゲっ
WH-WHAT HAPPENED TO THE CLOTHES I GOT YOU THE OTHER DAY?
AFTER ALL THE PAINS WE WENT THROUGH...
PANT
はあ
PANT
はぁ
AH, THEY'RE SO NEW I THOUGHT IT WAS A WASTE.
I DID BRING 'EM WITH ME THOUGH!
WOULD'VE BEEN BAD IF THEY GOT DIRTY, TOO.
THAT'S WHY...
YOU CAME IN YOUR USUAL LAME CLOTHES?!
ARE YOU A 5TH GRADER?

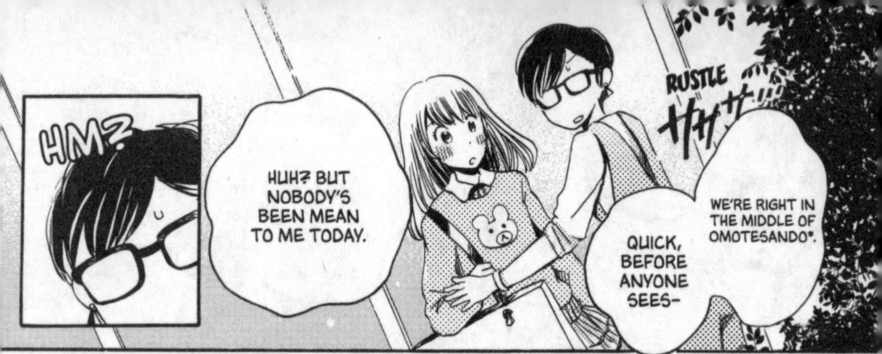
RUSTLE
WE'RE RIGHT IN THE MIDDLE OF OMOTESANDO*.
QUICK, BEFORE ANYONE SEES-
HUH? BUT NOBODY'S BEEN MEAN TO ME TODAY.
HM?

* A HIGH-END SHOPPING DISTRICT IN TOKYO

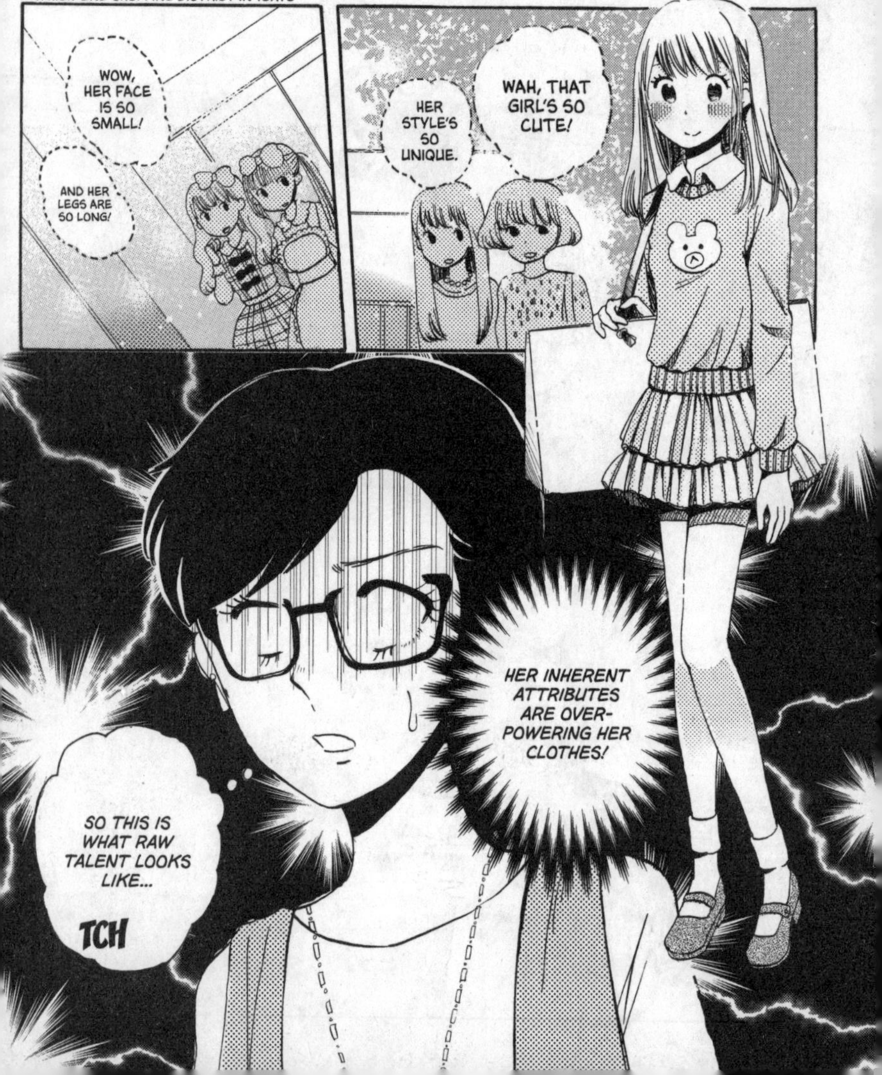
WAH, THAT GIRL'S SO CUTE!
HER STYLE'S SO UNIQUE.
WOW, HER FACE IS SO SMALL!
AND HER LEGS ARE SO LONG!
HER INHERENT ATTRIBUTES ARE OVER-POWERING HER CLOTHES!
SO THIS IS WHAT RAW TALENT LOOKS LIKE...
TCH

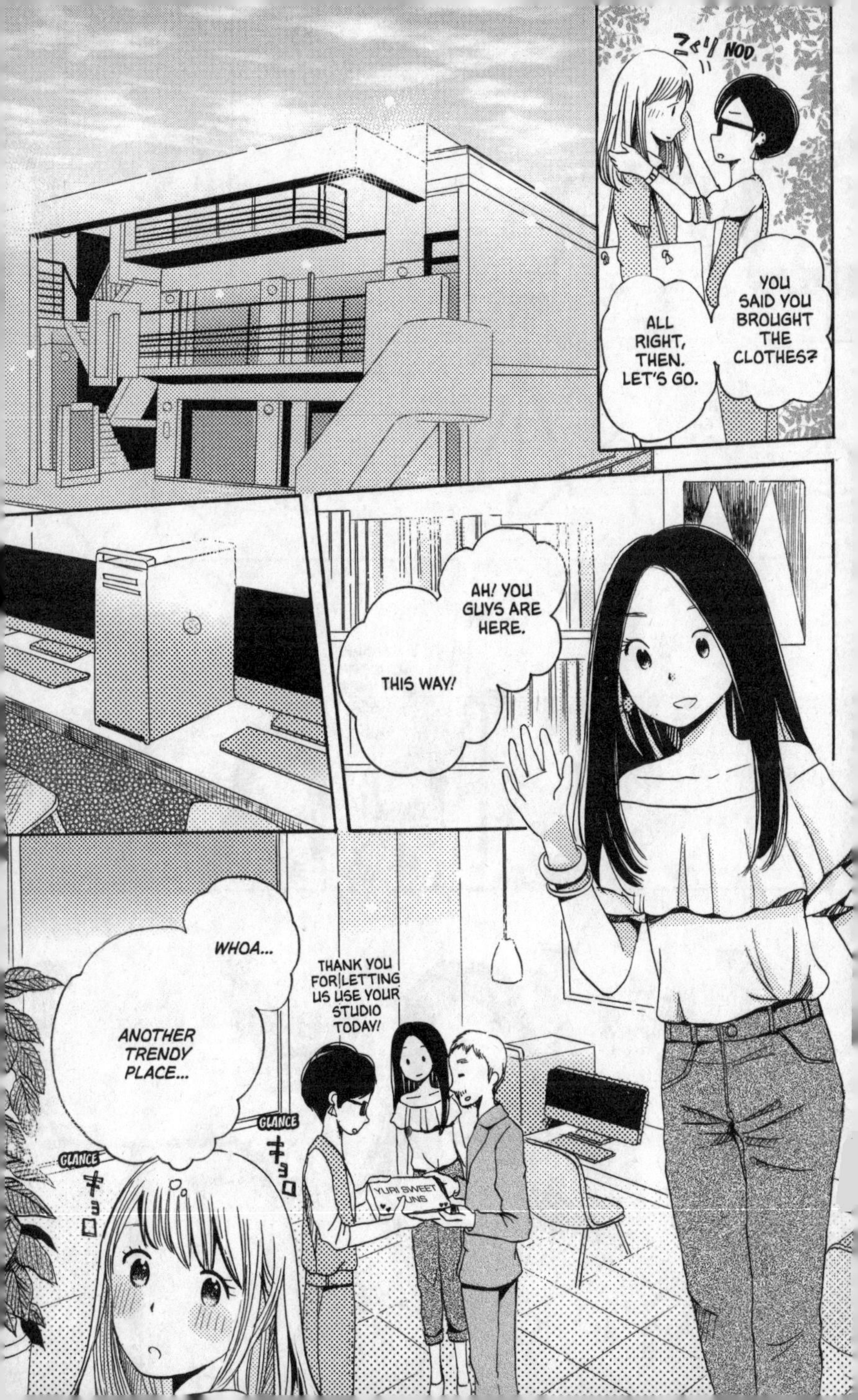
NOD
YOU SAID YOU BROUGHT THE CLOTHES?
ALL RIGHT, THEN. LET'S GO.
AH! YOU GUYS ARE HERE.
THIS WAY!
THANK YOU FOR LETTING US USE YOUR STUDIO TODAY!
YURI SWEET BUNS
WHOA...
ANOTHER TRENDY PLACE...
GLANCE
GLANCE

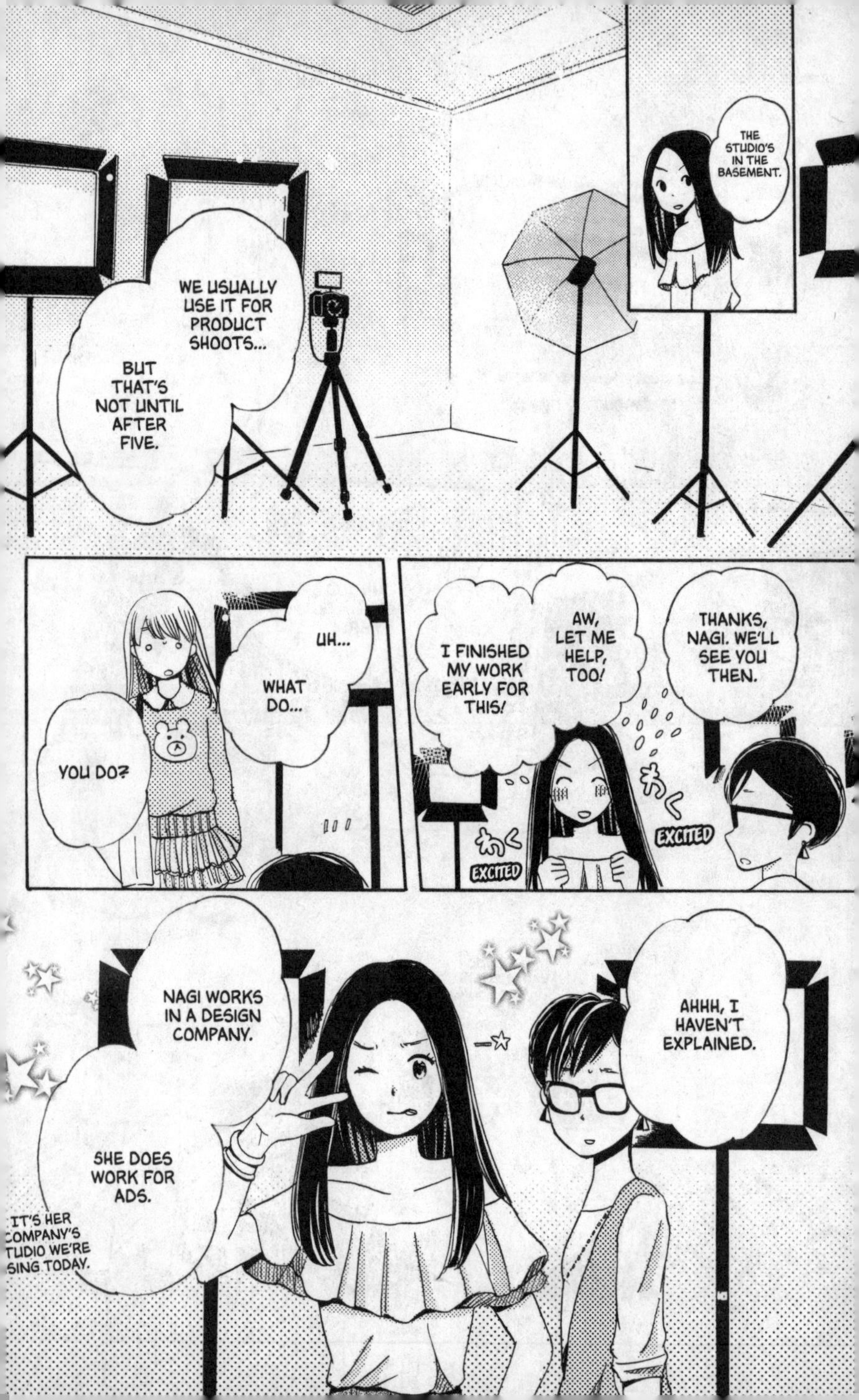
THE STUDIO'S IN THE BASEMENT.
WE USUALLY USE IT FOR PRODUCT SHOOTS...
BUT THAT'S NOT UNTIL AFTER FIVE.
THANKS, NAGI. WE'LL SEE YOU THEN.
AW, LET ME HELP, TOO!
I FINISHED MY WORK EARLY FOR THIS!
わく
EXCITED
わく
EXCITED
UH...
WHAT DO...
YOU DO?
AHHH, I HAVEN'T EXPLAINED.
NAGI WORKS IN A DESIGN COMPANY.
SHE DOES WORK FOR ADS.
IT'S HER COMPANY'S TUDIO WE'RE SING TODAY.

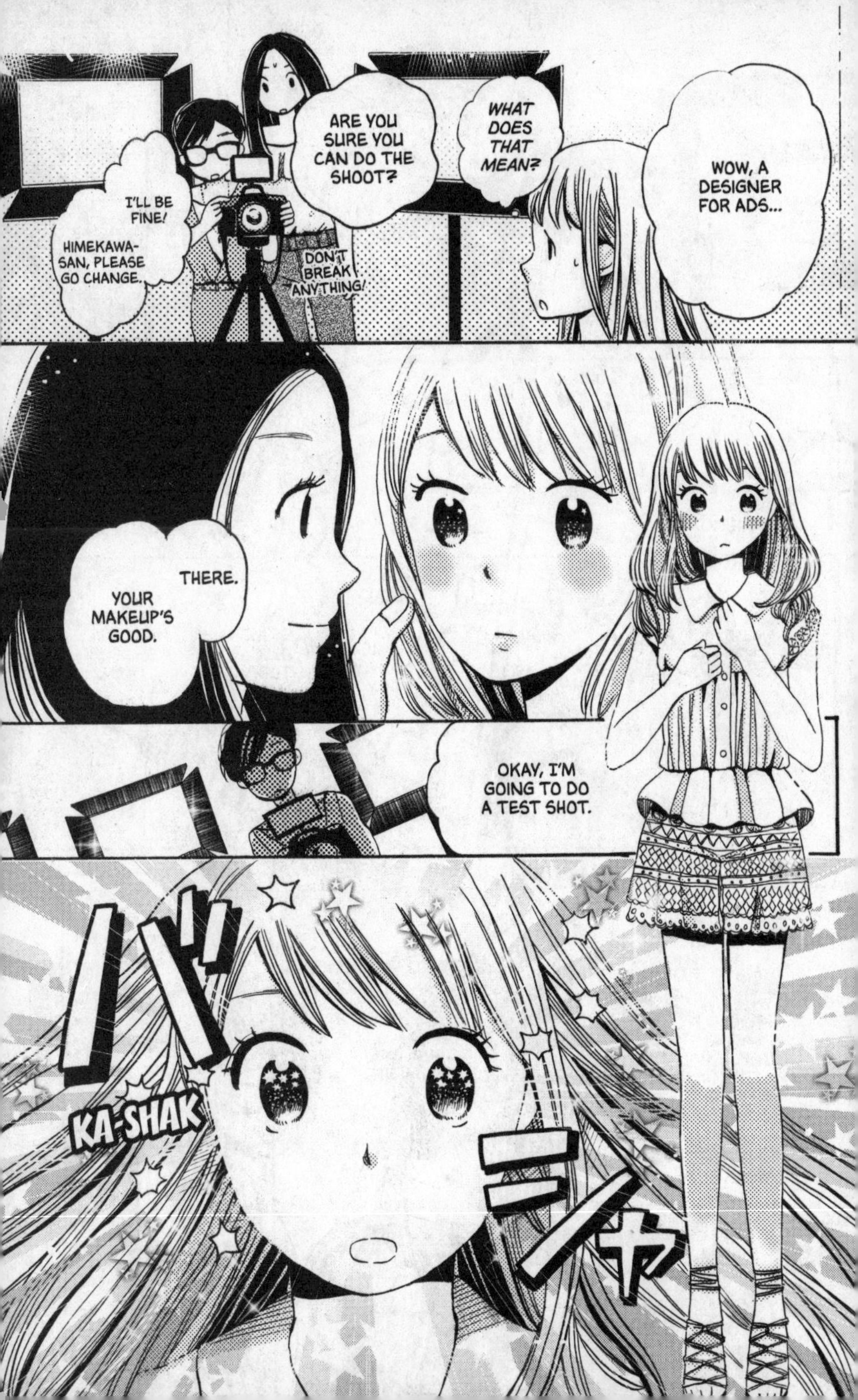
WOW, A DESIGNER FOR ADS...
WHAT DOES THAT MEAN?
ARE YOU SURE YOU CAN DO THE SHOOT?
DON'T BREAK ANYTHING!
I'LL BE FINE!
HIMEKAWA-SAN, PLEASE GO CHANGE.
THERE.
YOUR MAKEUP'S GOOD.
OKAY, I'M GOING TO DO A TEST SHOT.
KA-SHAK

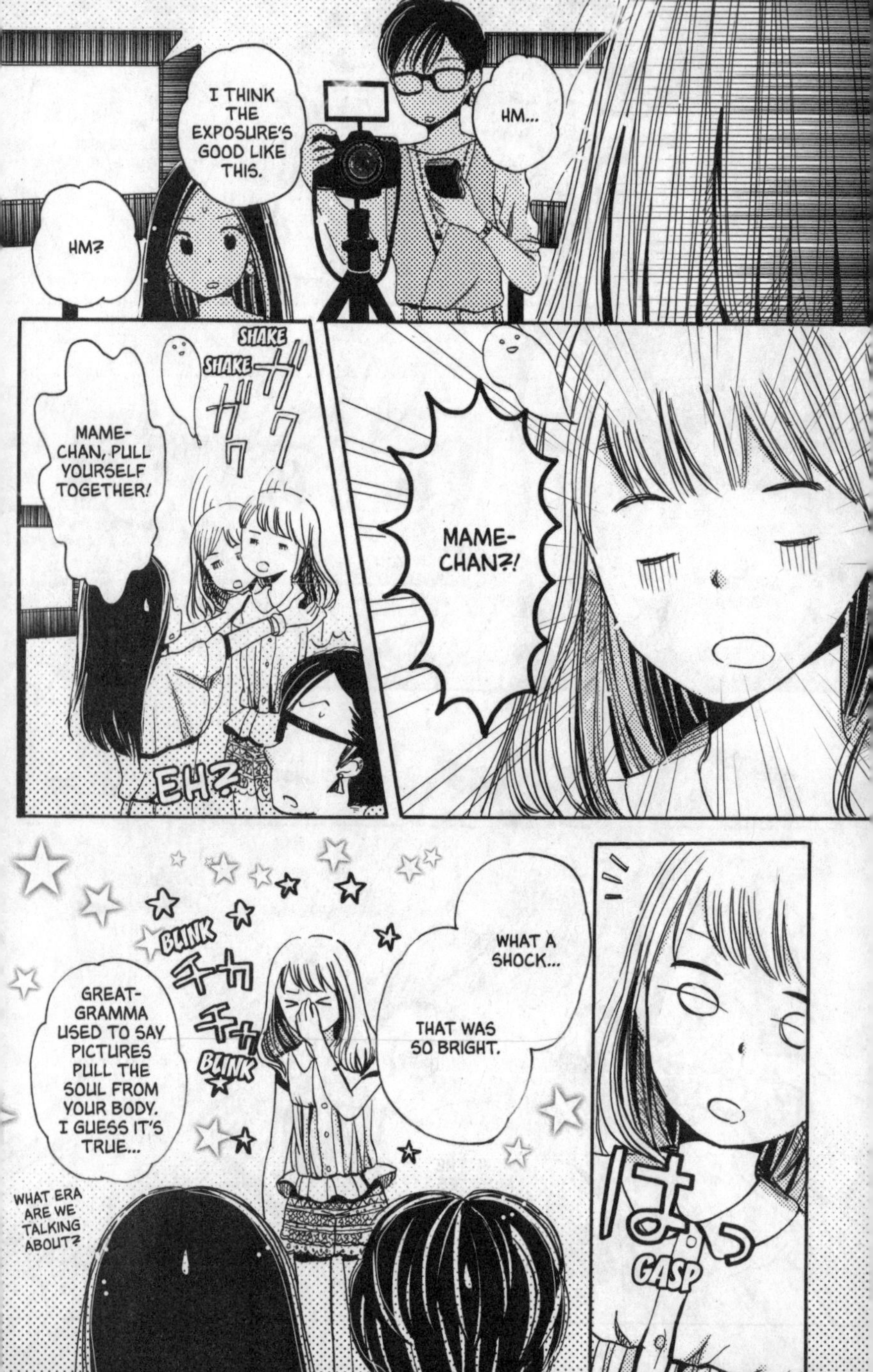
HM...
I THINK THE EXPOSURE'S GOOD LIKE THIS.
HM?
MAME-CHAN?!
SHAKE
SHAKE
MAME-CHAN, PULL YOURSELF TOGETHER!
EH?
GASP
WHAT A SHOCK...
THAT WAS SO BRIGHT.
BLINK
BLINK
GREAT-GRAMMA USED TO SAY PICTURES PULL THE SOUL FROM YOUR BODY. I GUESS IT'S TRUE...
WHAT ERA ARE WE TALKING ABOUT?

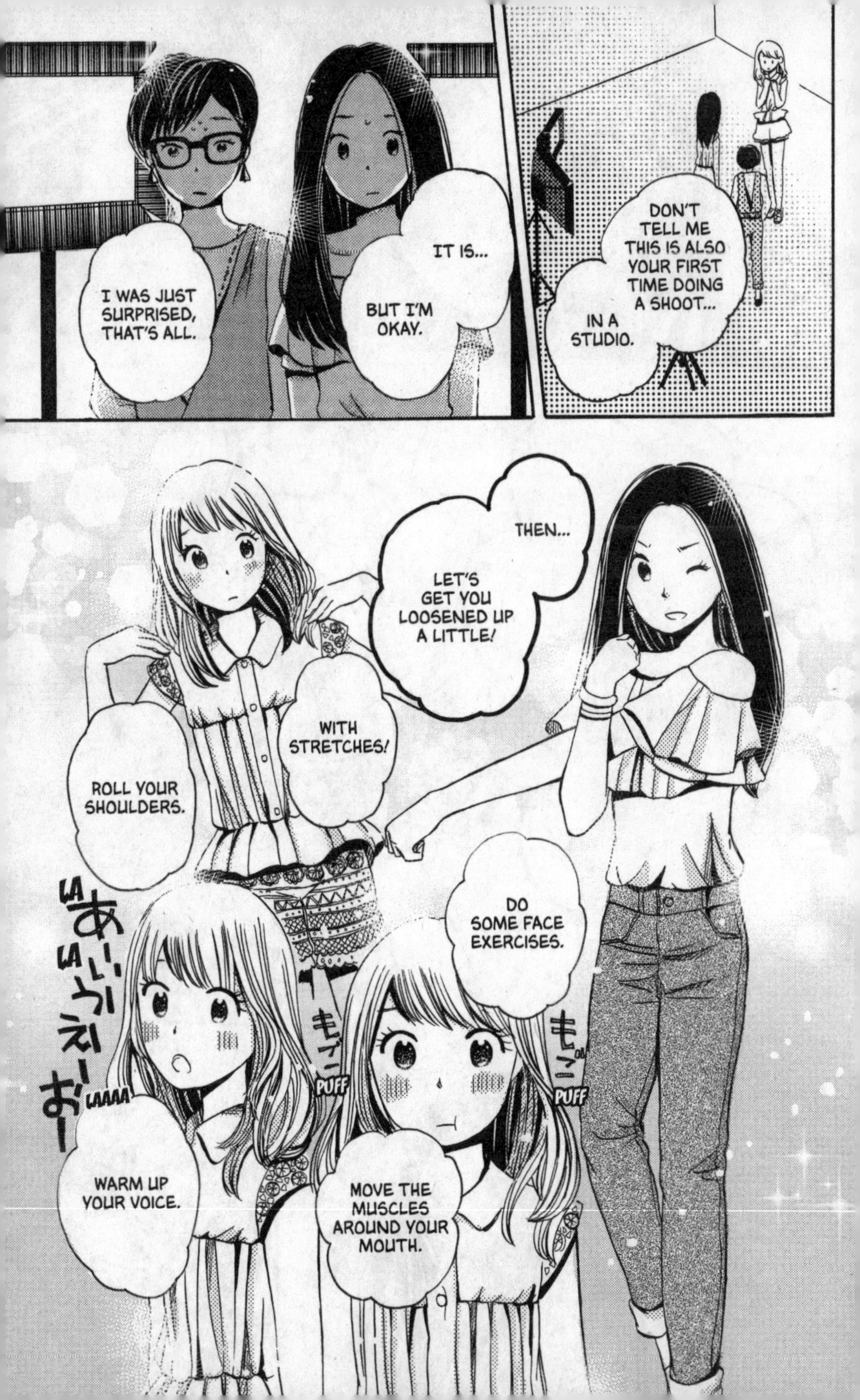
DON'T TELL ME THIS IS ALSO YOUR FIRST TIME DOING A SHOOT...
IN A STUDIO.
IT IS...
BUT I'M OKAY.
I WAS JUST SURPRISED, THAT'S ALL.
THEN...
LET'S GET YOU LOOSENED UP A LITTLE!
WITH STRETCHES!
ROLL YOUR SHOULDERS.
DO SOME FACE EXERCISES.
もごー
PUFF
MOVE THE MUSCLES AROUND YOUR MOUTH.
もごー
PUFF
あーいーうーえーおー
LA LA LAAAA
WARM UP YOUR VOICE.

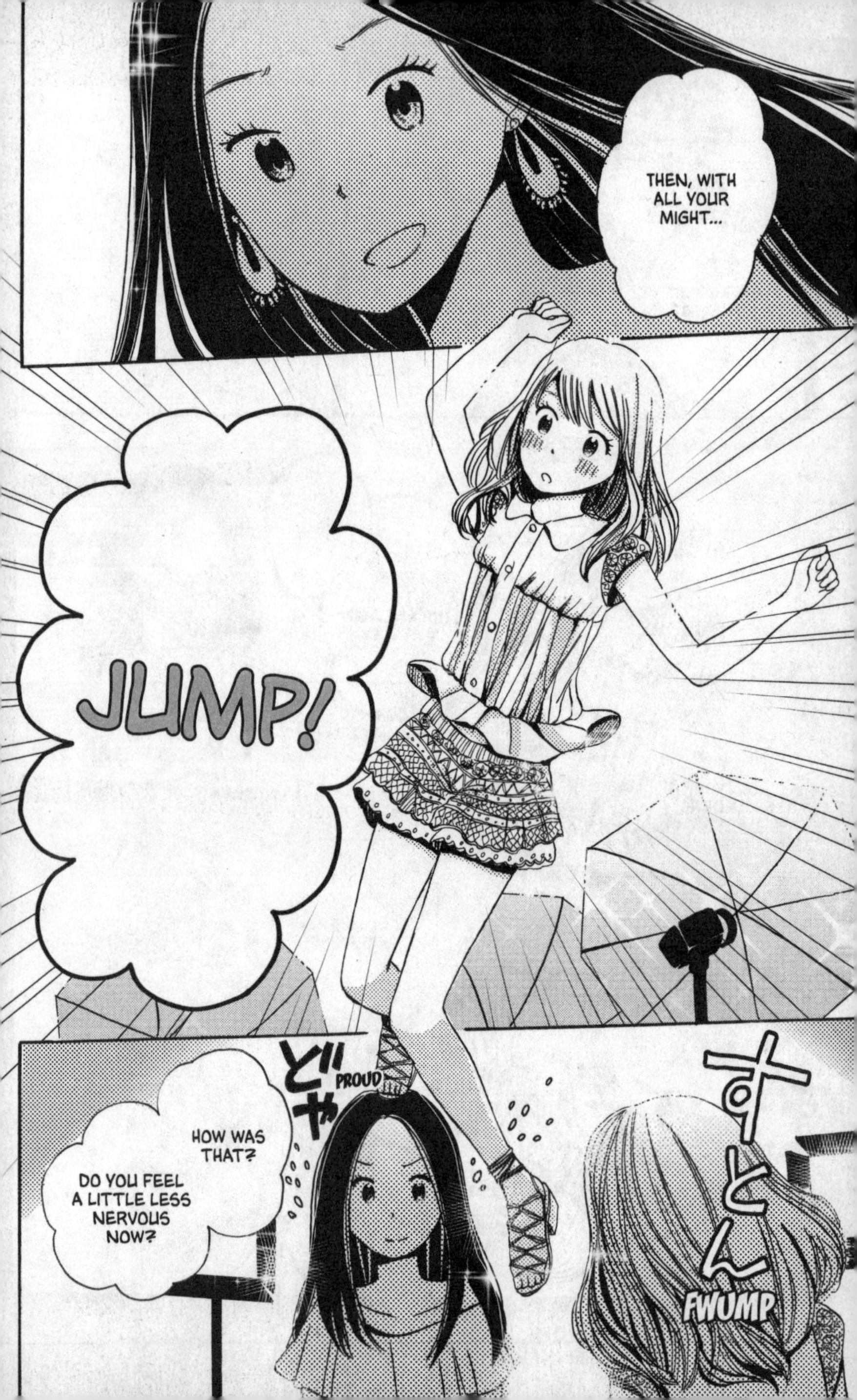
THEN, WITH ALL YOUR MIGHT...
JUMP!
すとん
FWUMP
どや
PROUD
HOW WAS THAT?
DO YOU FEEL A LITTLE LESS NERVOUS NOW?

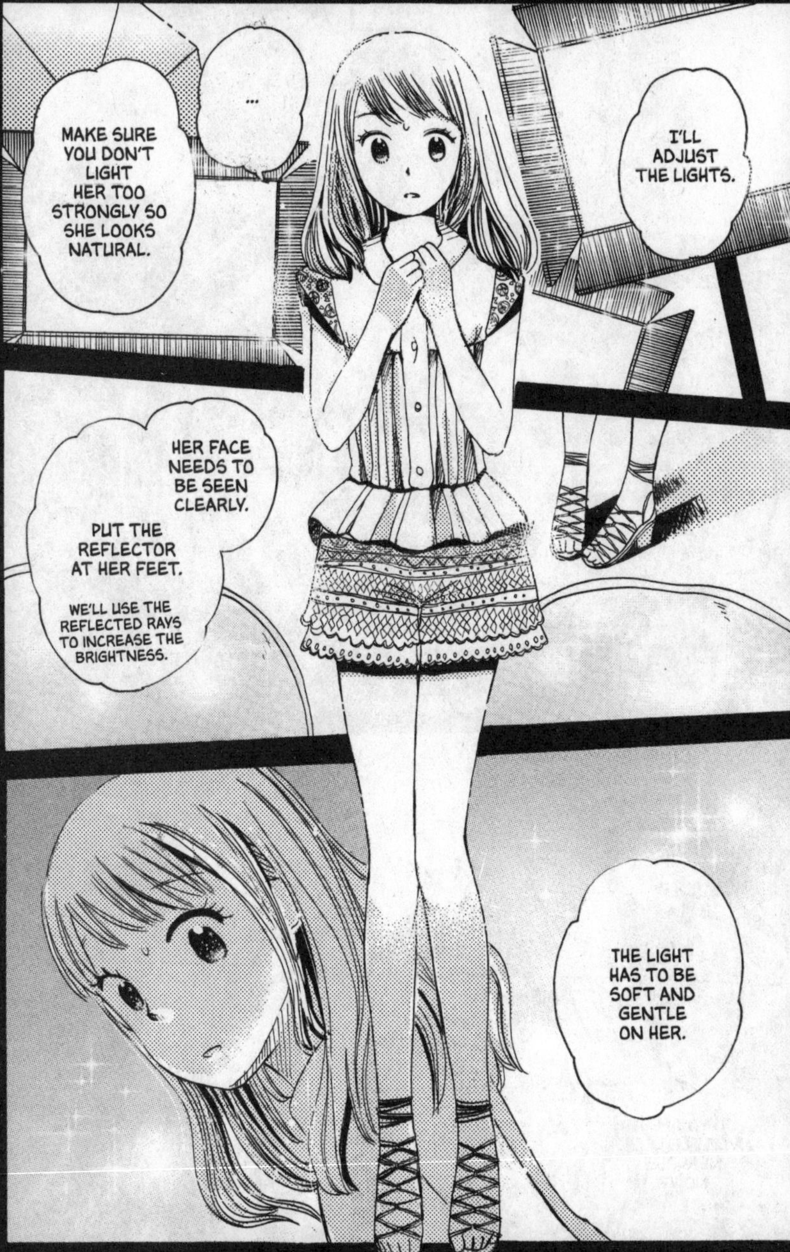
I'LL ADJUST THE LIGHTS.
...
MAKE SURE YOU DON'T LIGHT HER TOO STRONGLY SO SHE LOOKS NATURAL.
HER FACE NEEDS TO BE SEEN CLEARLY.
PUT THE REFLECTOR AT HER FEET.
WE'LL USE THE REFLECTED RAYS TO INCREASE THE BRIGHTNESS.
THE LIGHT HAS TO BE SOFT AND GENTLE ON HER.

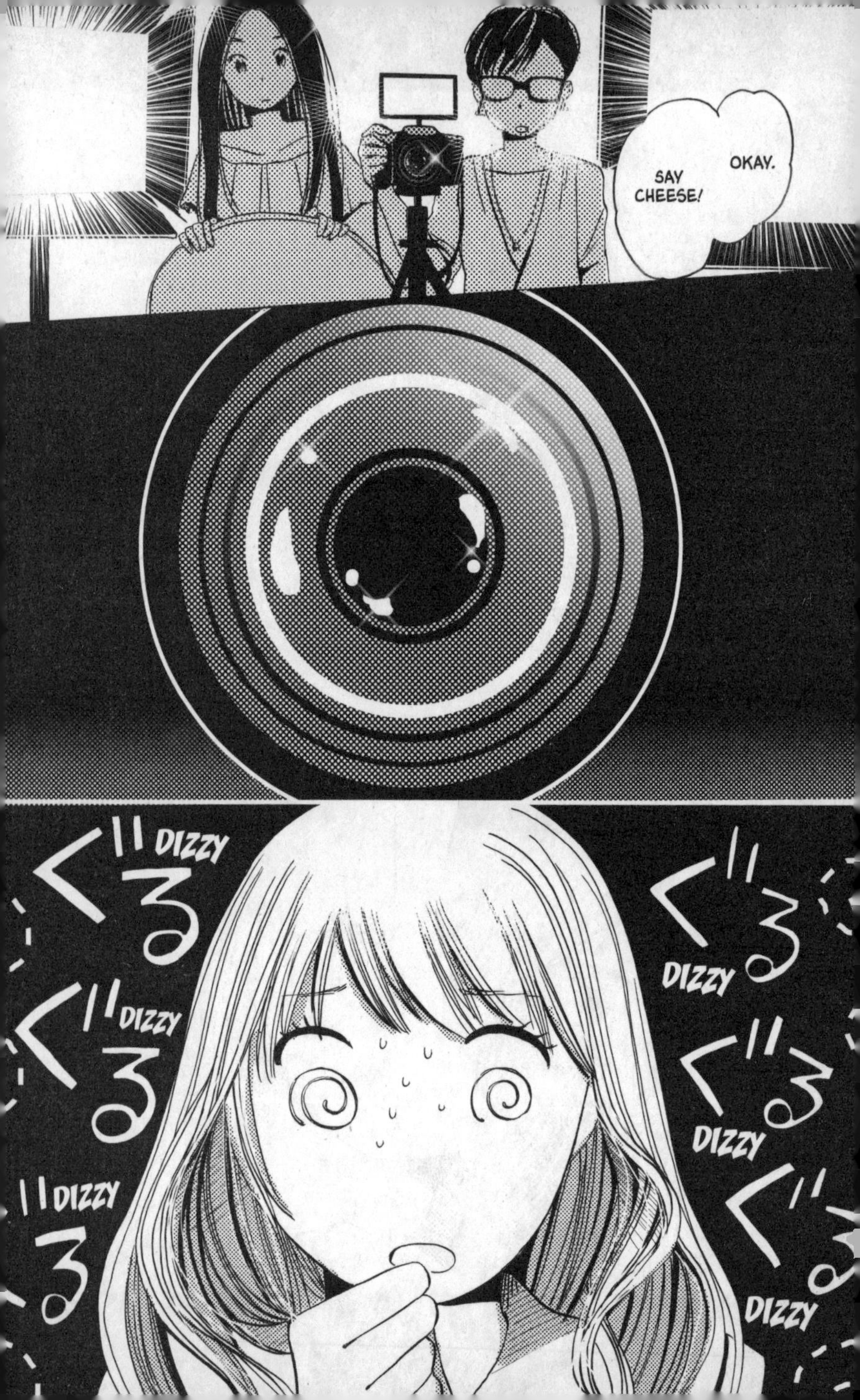
OKAY.
SAY CHEESE!
ぐる DIZZY
ぐる DIZZY
ぐる DIZZY
ぐる DIZZY
ぐる DIZZY
ぐる DIZZY

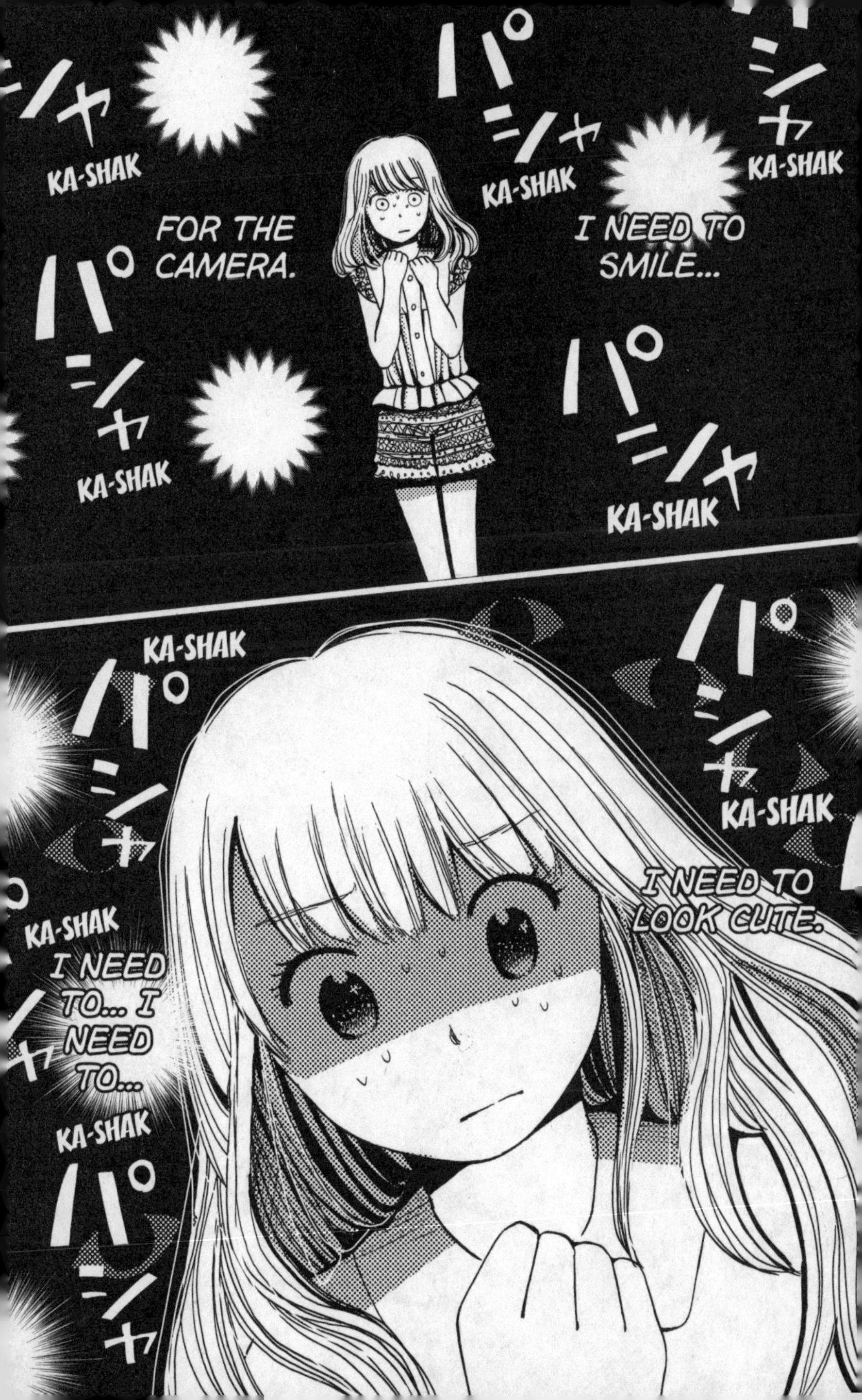
シャ
KA-SHAK
パシャ
KA-SHAK
I NEED TO SMILE...
FOR THE CAMERA.
シャ
KA-SHAK
パシャ
KA-SHAK
パシャ
KA-SHAK
パシャ
KA-SHAK
I NEED TO LOOK CUTE.
KA-SHAK
パシャ
KA-SHAK
I NEED TO... I NEED TO...
KA-SHAK
パシャ

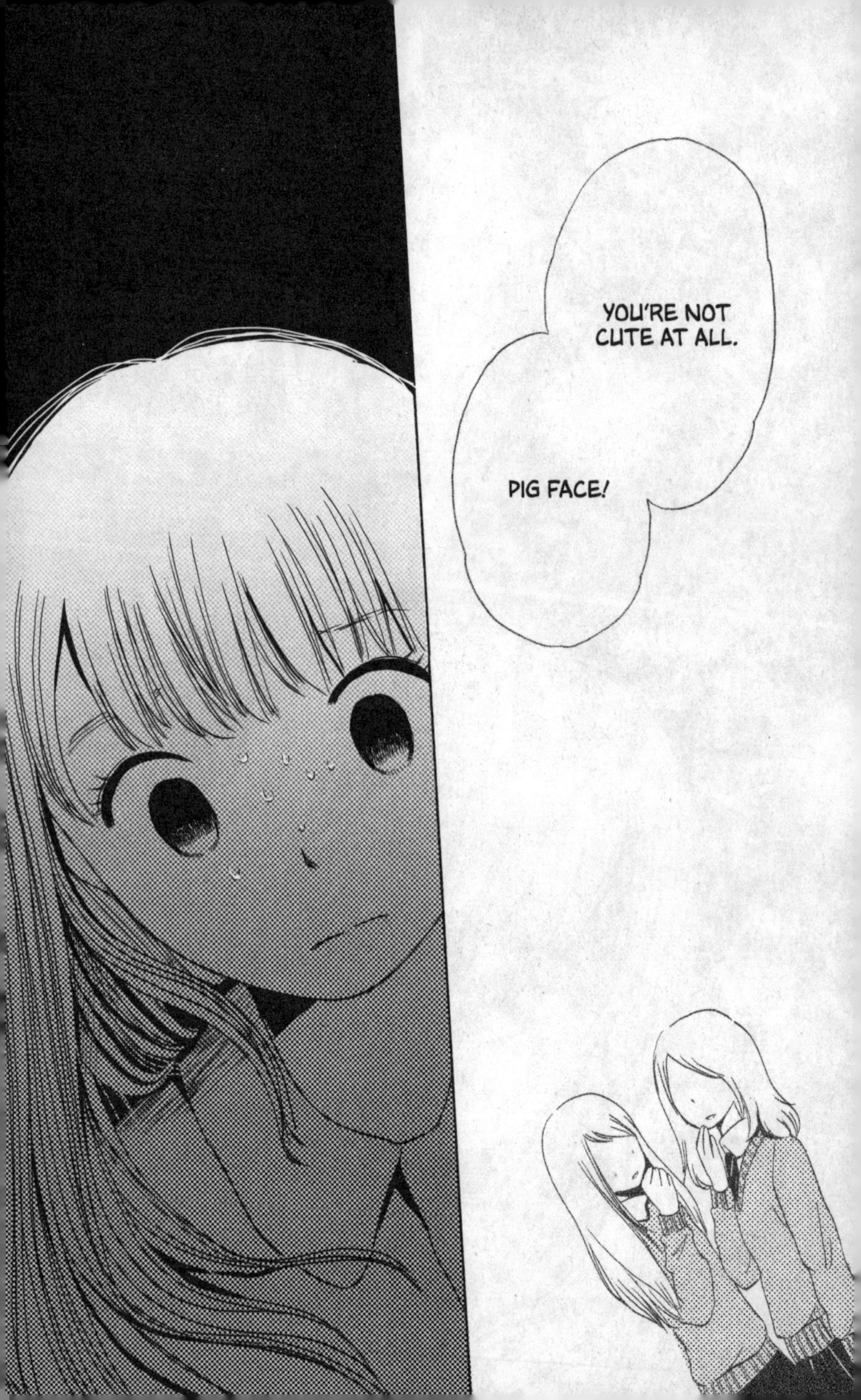
YOU'RE NOT CUTE AT ALL.
PIG FACE!

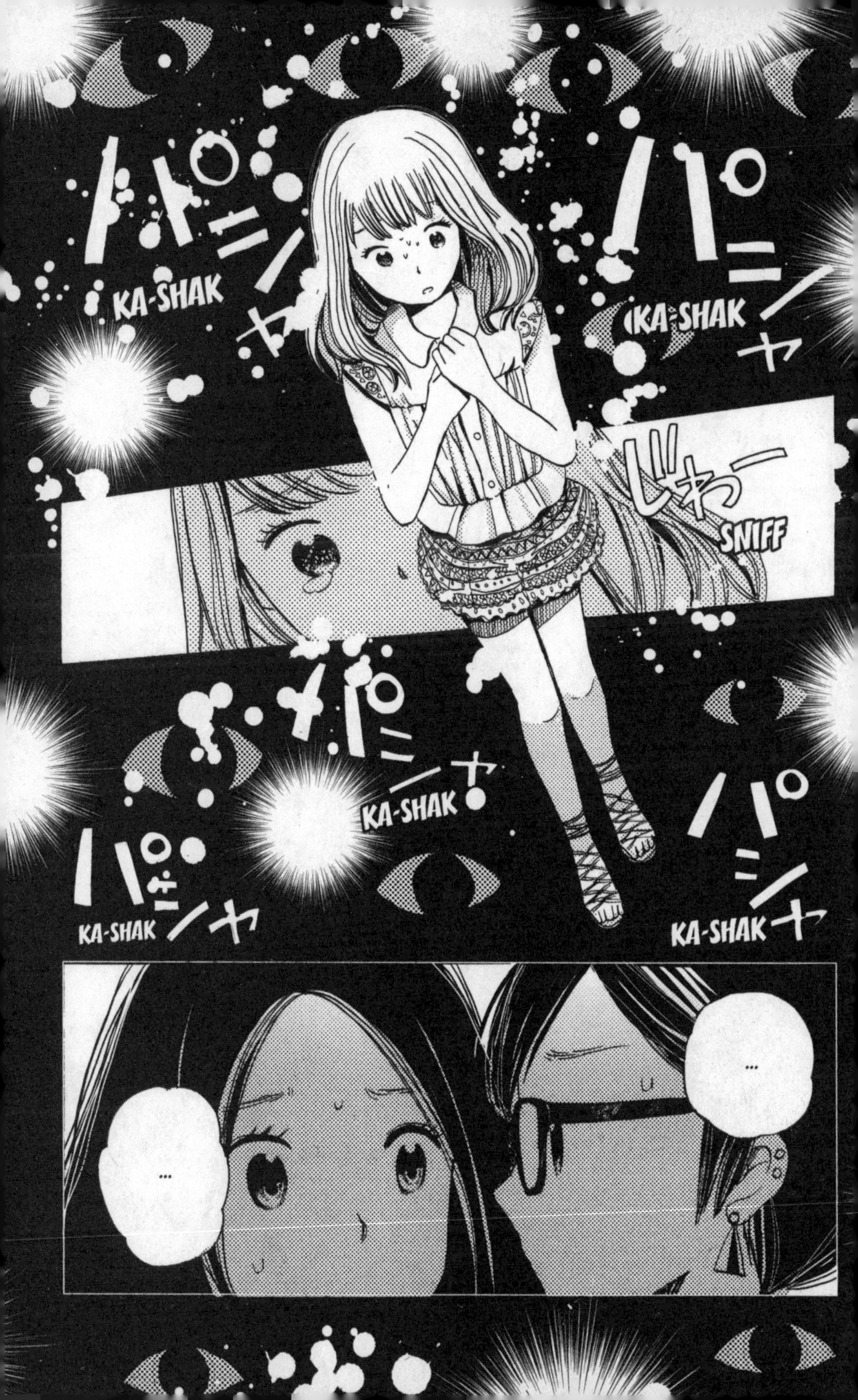
パシャ
KA-SHAK
パシャ
KA-SHAK
じわー
SNIFF
パシャ
KA-SHAK
パシャ
KA-SHAK
パシャ
KA-SHAK
...
...

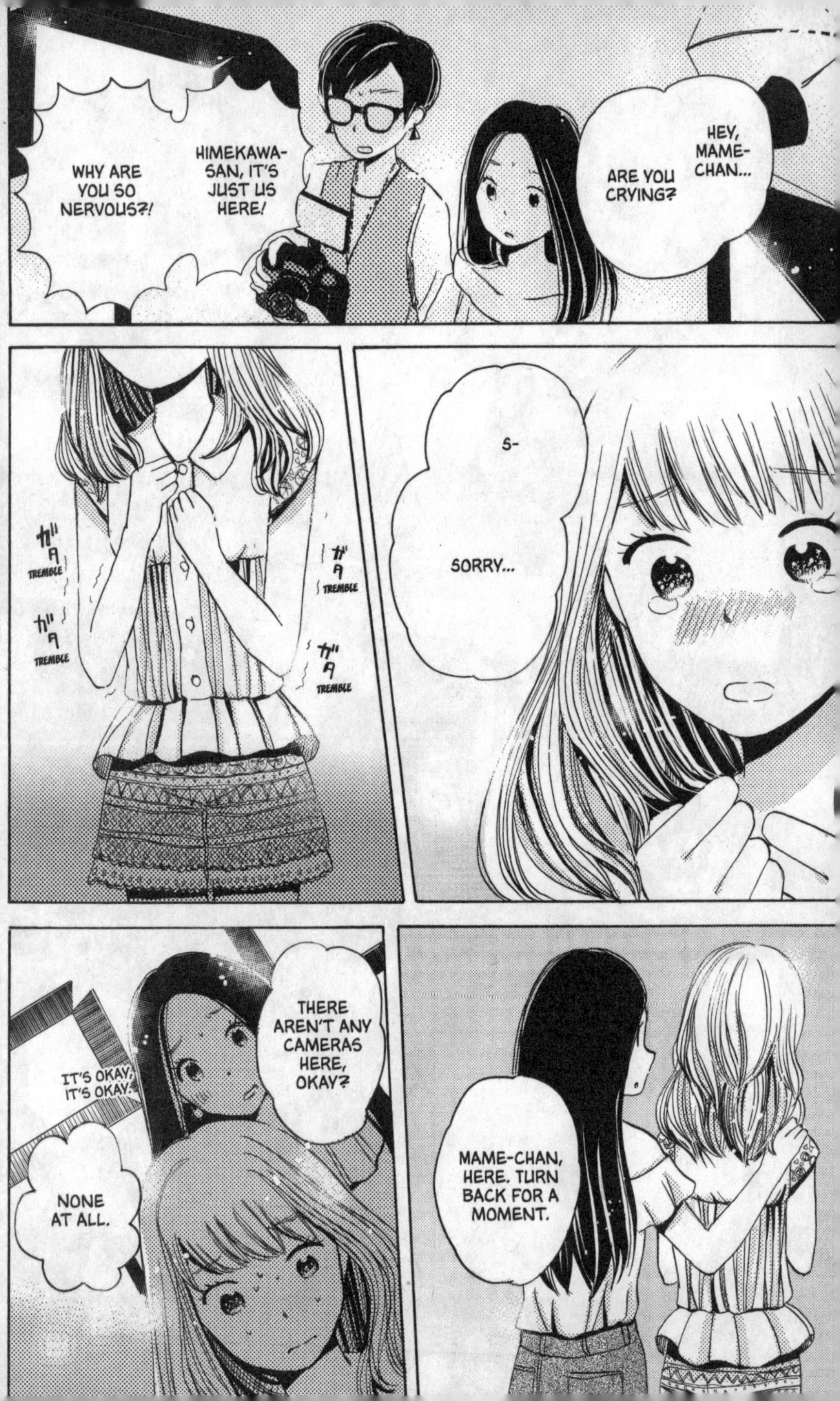
HEY, MAME-CHAN... ARE YOU CRYING?
HIMEKAWA-SAN, IT'S JUST US HERE!
WHY ARE YOU SO NERVOUS?!
S-
SORRY...
ガタ TREMBLE
ガタ TREMBLE
ガタ TREMBLE
ガタ TREMBLE
MAME-CHAN, HERE. TURN BACK FOR A MOMENT.
THERE AREN'T ANY CAMERAS HERE, OKAY?
IT'S OKAY, IT'S OKAY.
NONE AT ALL.

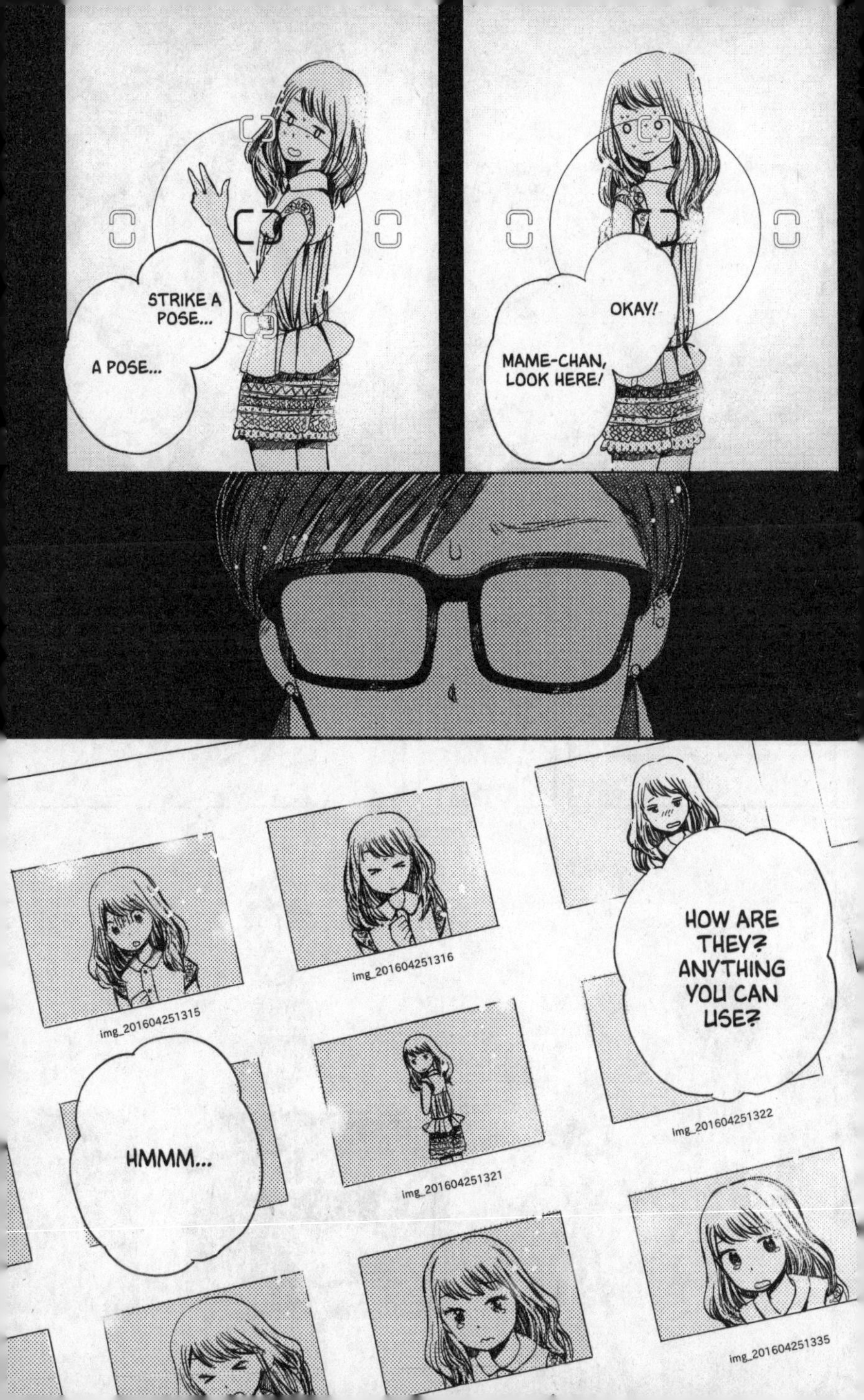
OKAY!
MAME-CHAN, LOOK HERE!
STRIKE A POSE...
A POSE...
HOW ARE THEY? ANYTHING YOU CAN USE?
img_201604251316
img_201604251315
img_201604251322
HMMM...
img_201604251321
img_201604251335

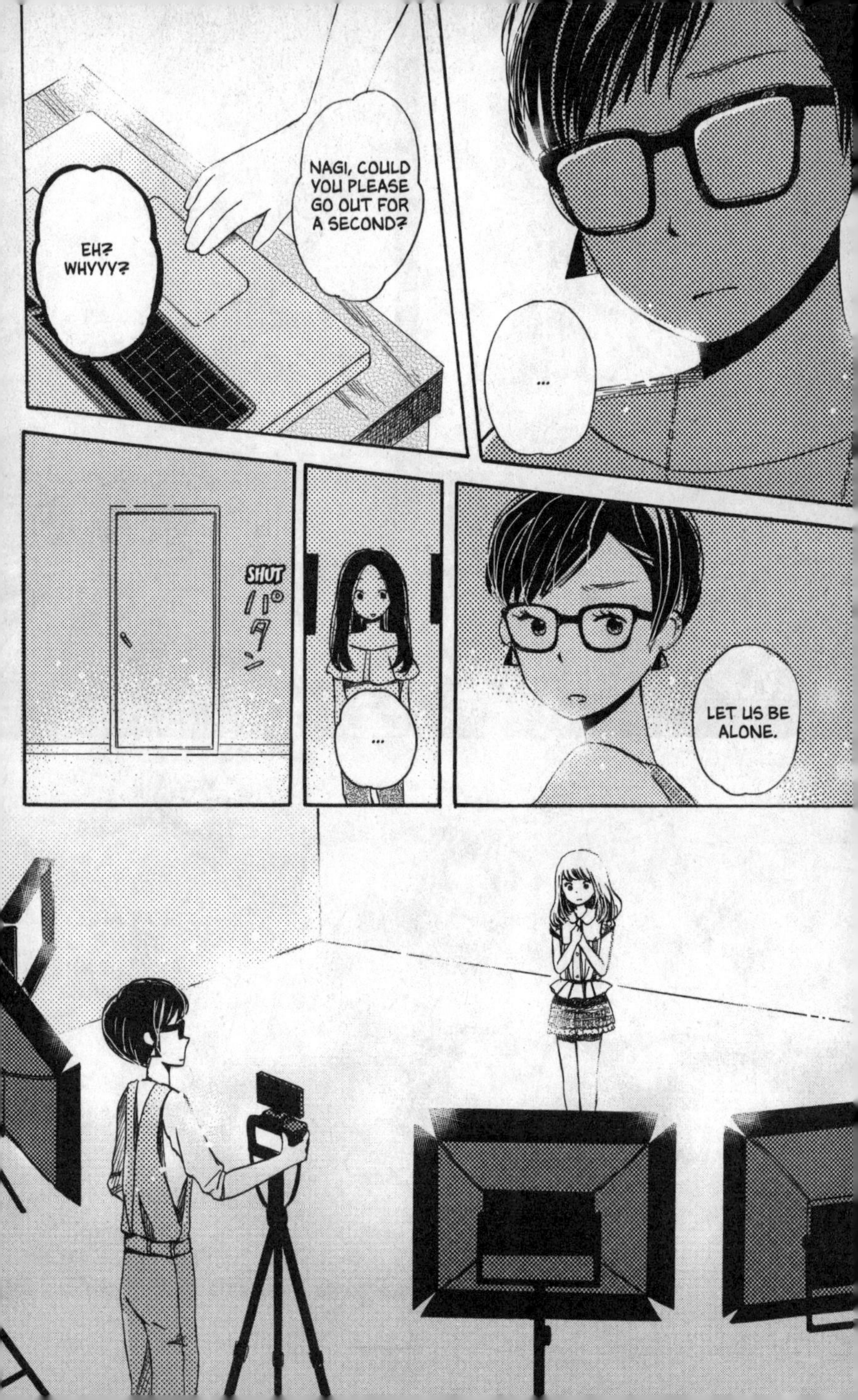
...
NAGI, COULD YOU PLEASE GO OUT FOR A SECOND?
EH? WHYYY?
LET US BE ALONE.
...
SHUT
パタン

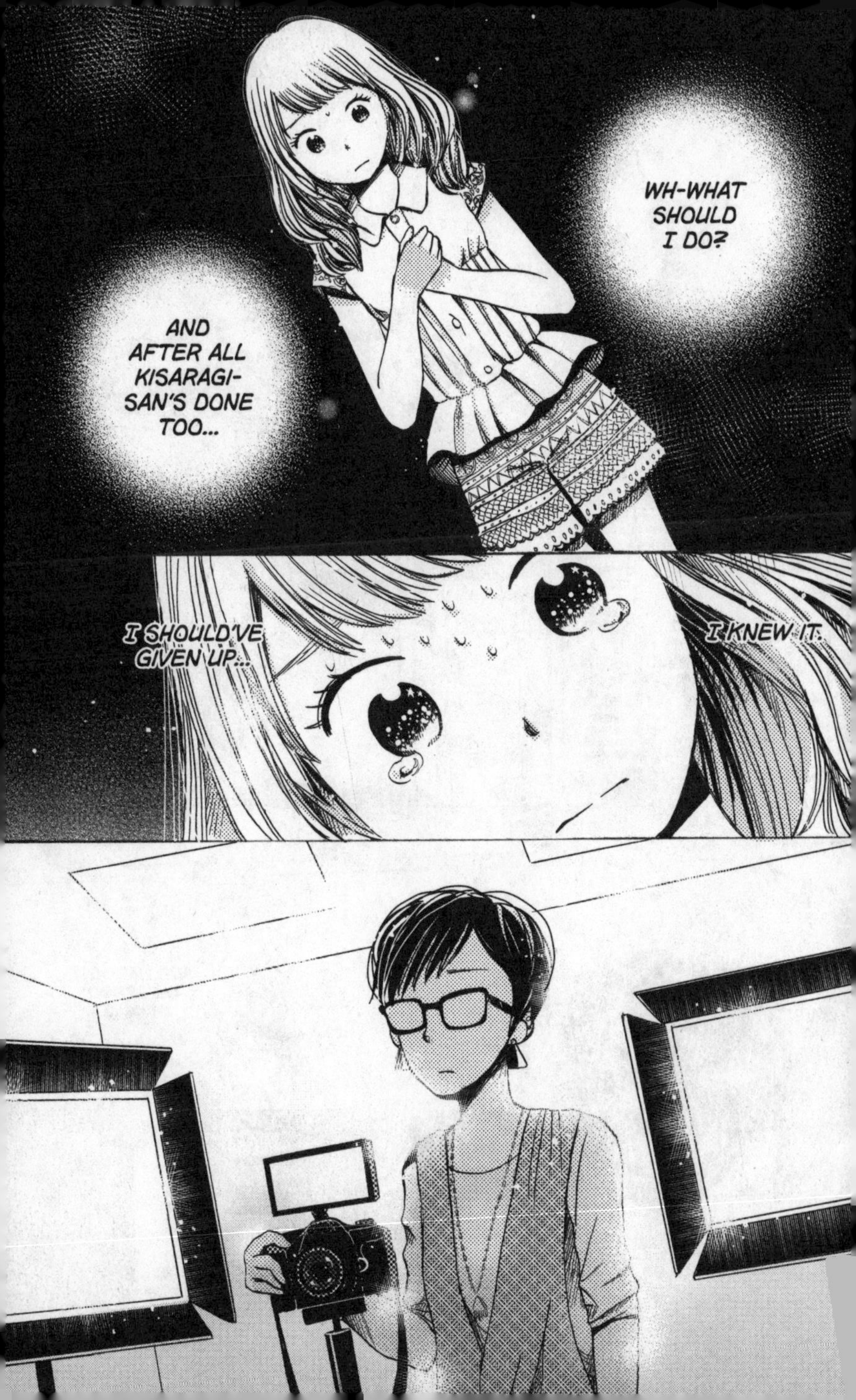
WH-WHAT SHOULD I DO?
AND AFTER ALL KISARAGI-SAN'S DONE TOO...
I KNEW IT.
I SHOULD'VE GIVEN UP...

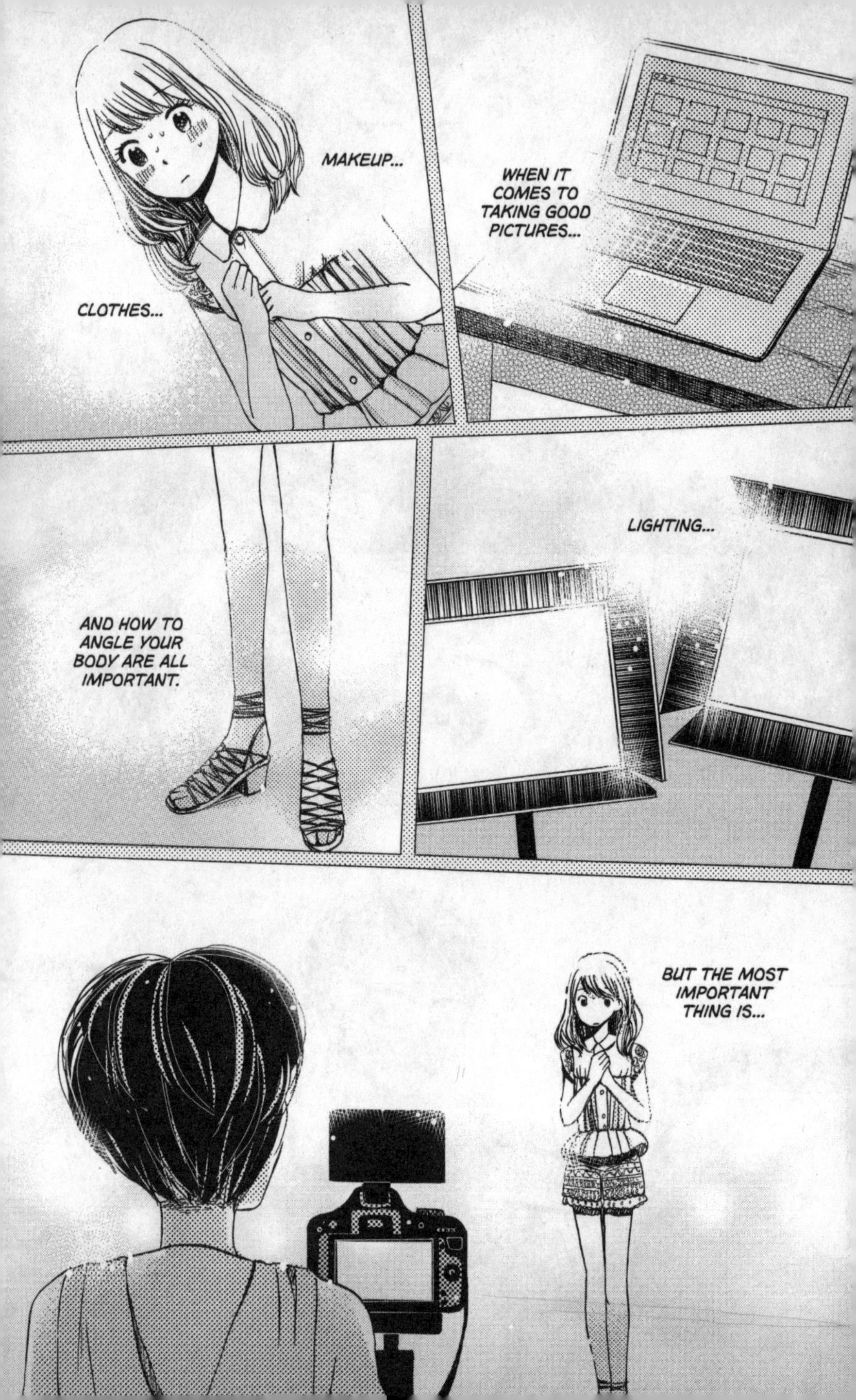
WHEN IT COMES TO TAKING GOOD PICTURES...
MAKEUP...
CLOTHES...
LIGHTING...
AND HOW TO ANGLE YOUR BODY ARE ALL IMPORTANT.
BUT THE MOST IMPORTANT THING IS...

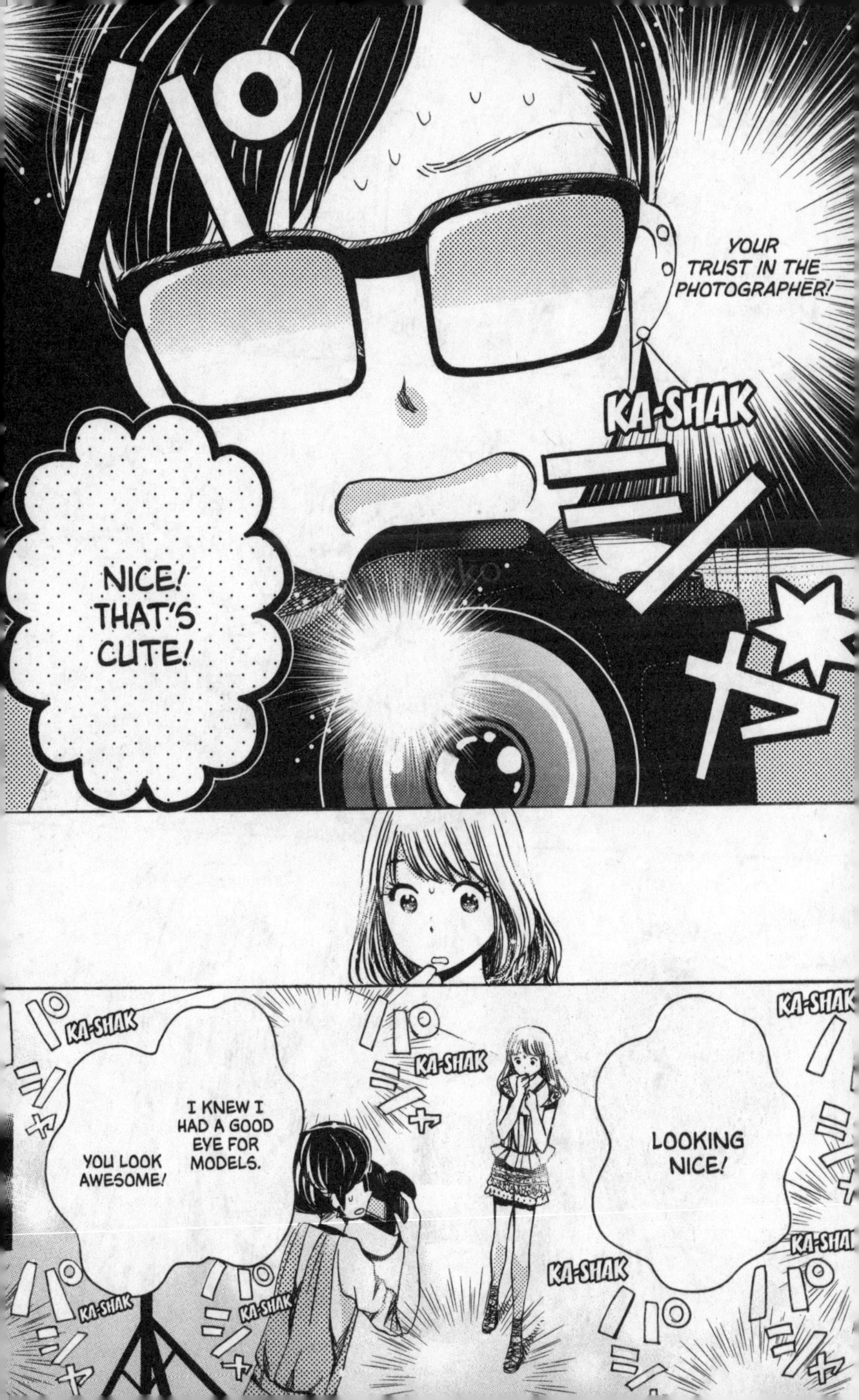
YOUR TRUST IN THE PHOTOGRAPHER!
KA-SHAK
NICE! THAT'S CUTE!
KA-SHAK
LOOKING NICE!
KA-SHAK
KA-SHAK
KA-SHAK
I KNEW I HAD A GOOD EYE FOR MODELS.
YOU LOOK AWESOME!
KA-SHAK
KA-SHAK
KA-SHAK

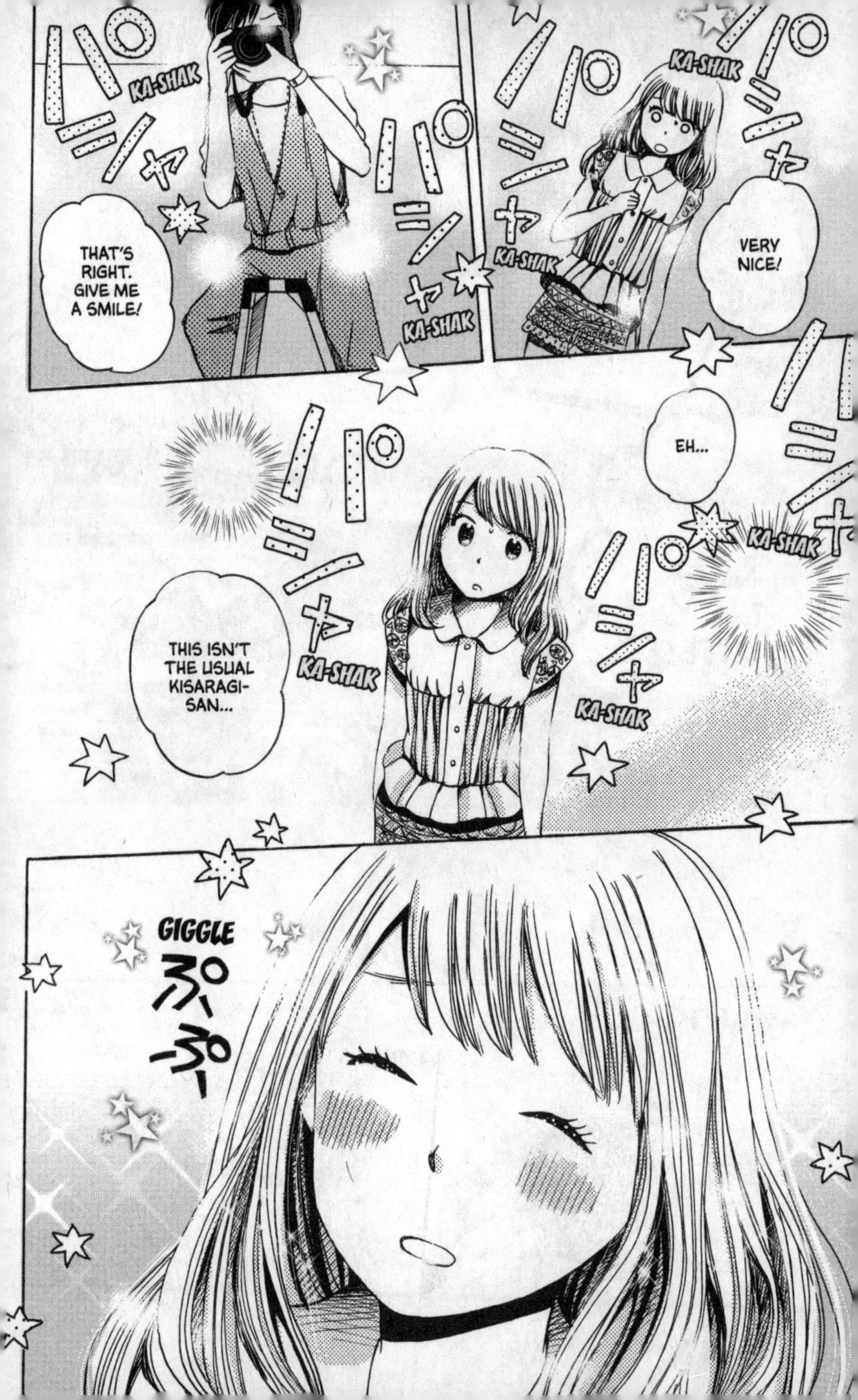

KA-SHAK
VERY NICE!
KA-SHAK
KA-SHAK
THAT'S RIGHT. GIVE ME A SMILE!
KA-SHAK
EH...
KA-SHAK
KA-SHAK
THIS ISN'T THE USUAL KISARAGI-SAN...
KA-SHAK
GIGGLE

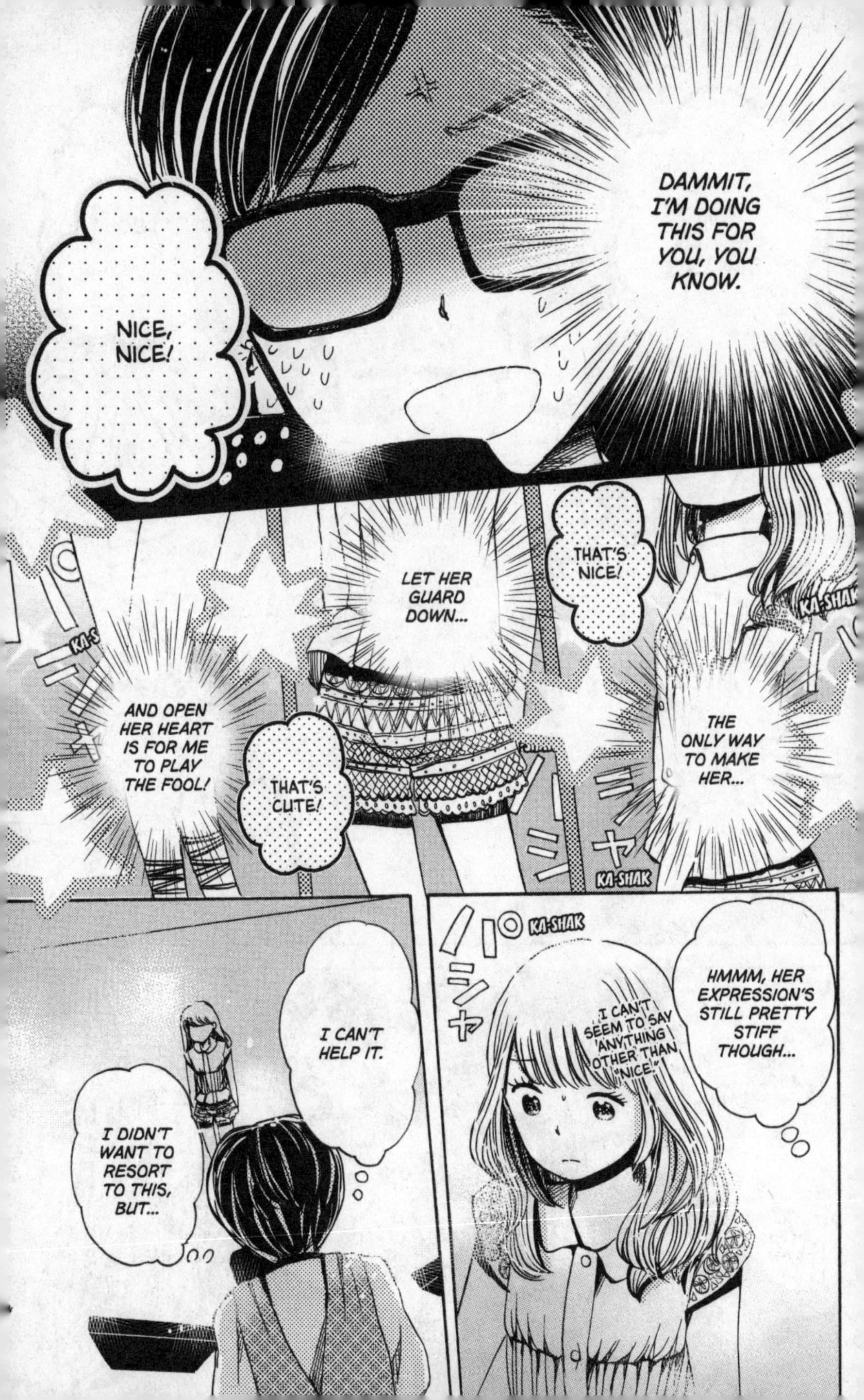
DAMMIT, I'M DOING THIS FOR YOU, YOU KNOW.
NICE, NICE!
THAT'S NICE!
KA-SHAK
THE ONLY WAY TO MAKE HER...
LET HER GUARD DOWN...
KA-SHAK
THAT'S CUTE!
AND OPEN HER HEART IS FOR ME TO PLAY THE FOOL!
KA-SHAK
HMMM, HER EXPRESSION'S STILL PRETTY STIFF THOUGH...
I CAN'T SEEM TO SAY ANYTHING OTHER THAN "NICE."
I CAN'T HELP IT.
I DIDN'T WANT TO RESORT TO THIS, BUT...

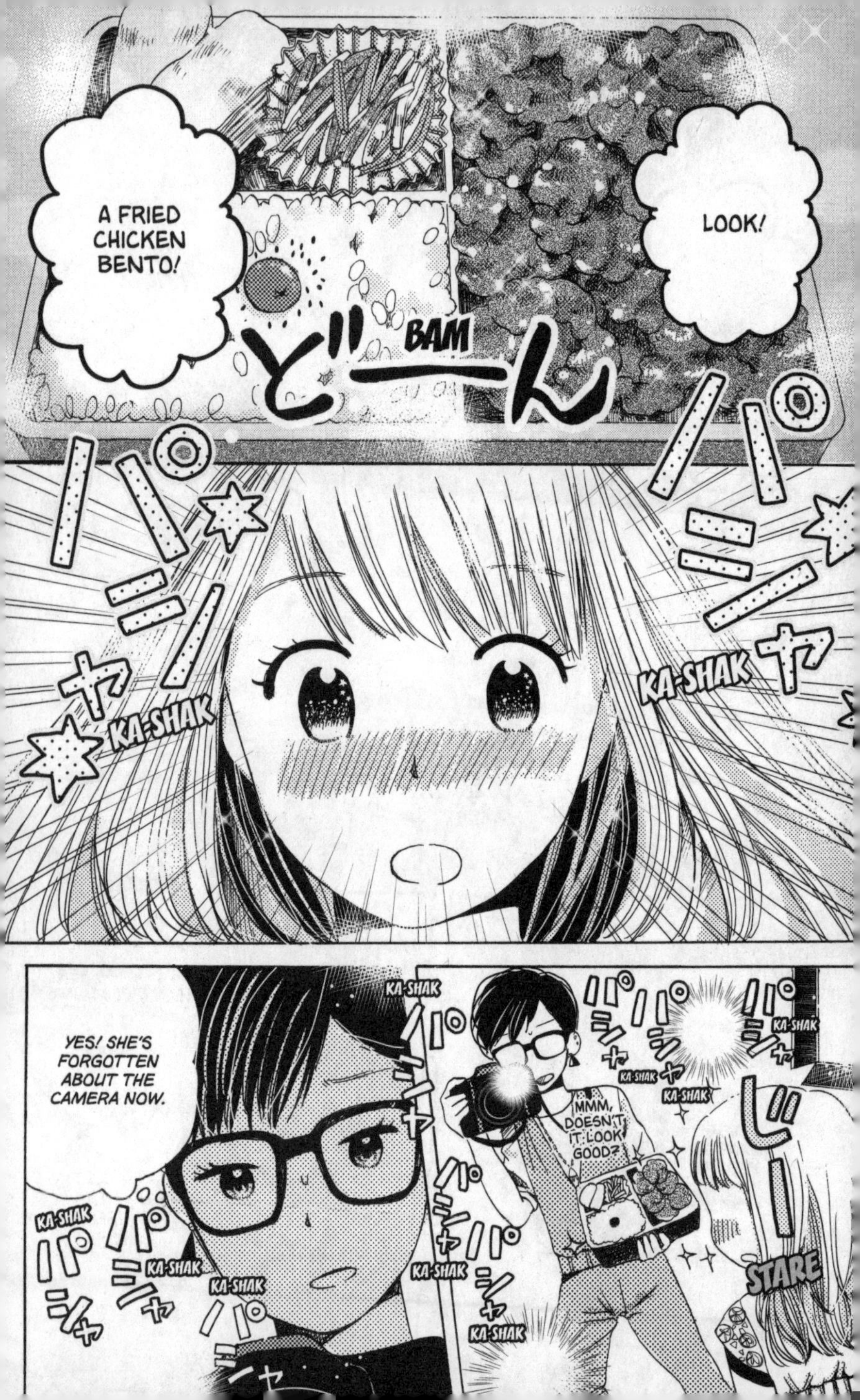
LOOK!
A FRIED CHICKEN BENTO!
どーん
BAM
パシャ
KA-SHAK
パシャ
KA-SHAK
じー
STARE
KA-SHAK
KA-SHAK
KA-SHAK
MMM, DOESN'T IT LOOK GOOD?
KA-SHAK
KA-SHAK
KA-SHAK
YES! SHE'S FORGOTTEN ABOUT THE CAMERA NOW.
KA-SHAK
KA-SHAK
KA-SHAK

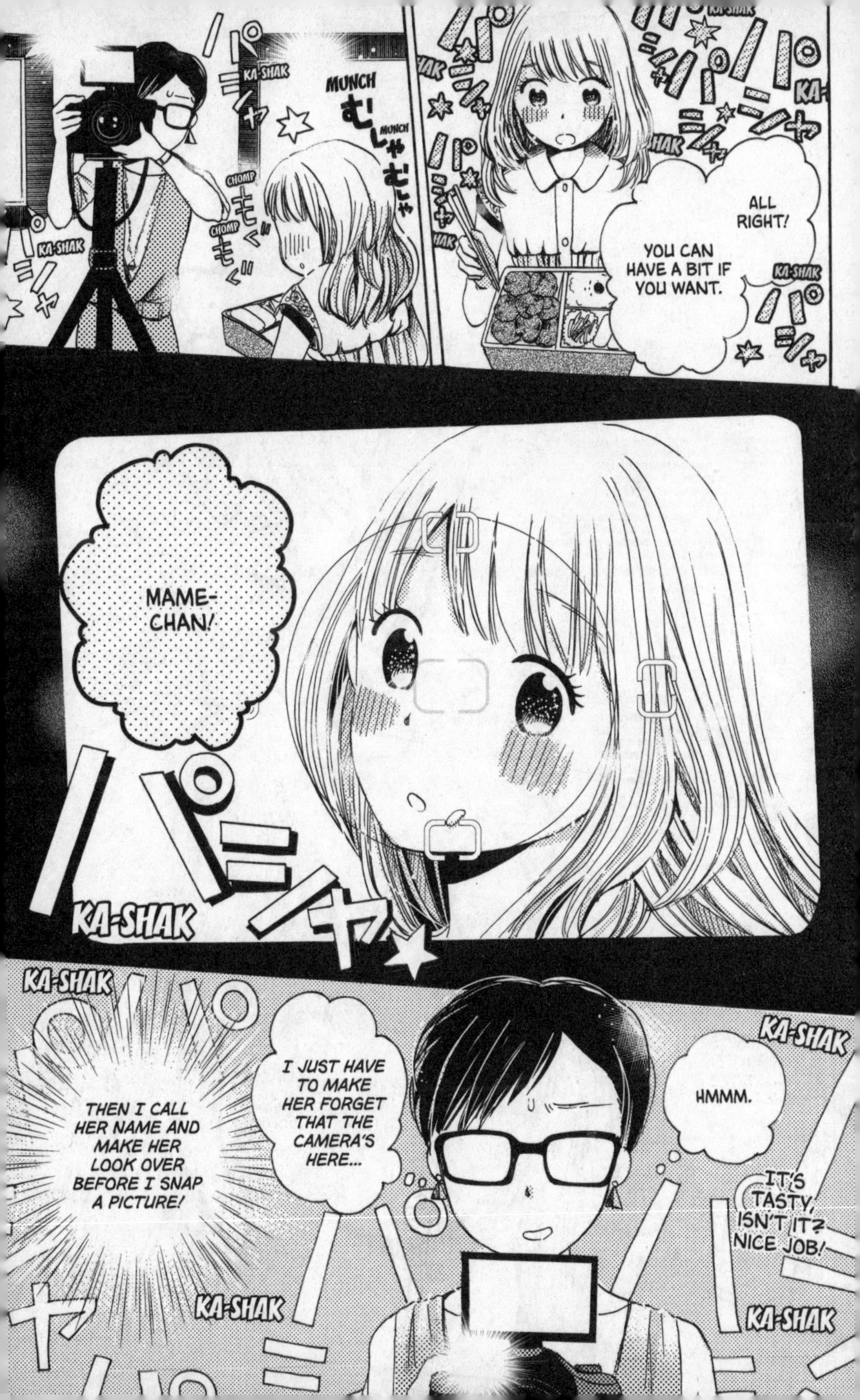
KA-SHAK
SHAK
ALL RIGHT!
YOU CAN HAVE A BIT IF YOU WANT.
KA-SHAK
KA-SHAK
MUNCH
MUNCH
CHOMP
CHOMP
KA-SHAK
MAME-CHAN!
KA-SHAK
KA-SHAK
HMMM.
IT'S TASTY, ISN'T IT? NICE JOB!
KA-SHAK
I JUST HAVE TO MAKE HER FORGET THAT THE CAMERA'S HERE...
THEN I CALL HER NAME AND MAKE HER LOOK OVER BEFORE I SNAP A PICTURE!
KA-SHAK
KA-SHAK

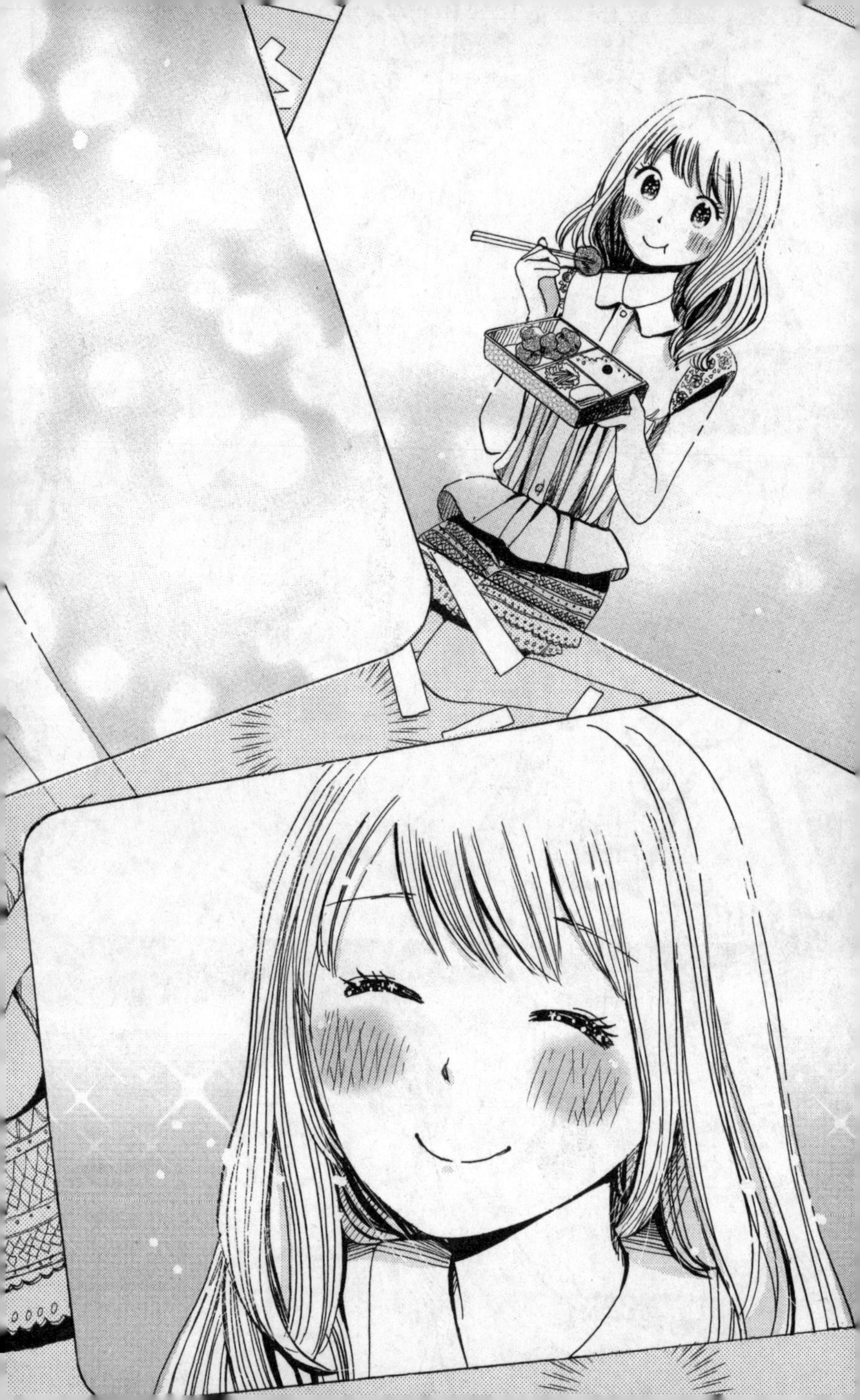

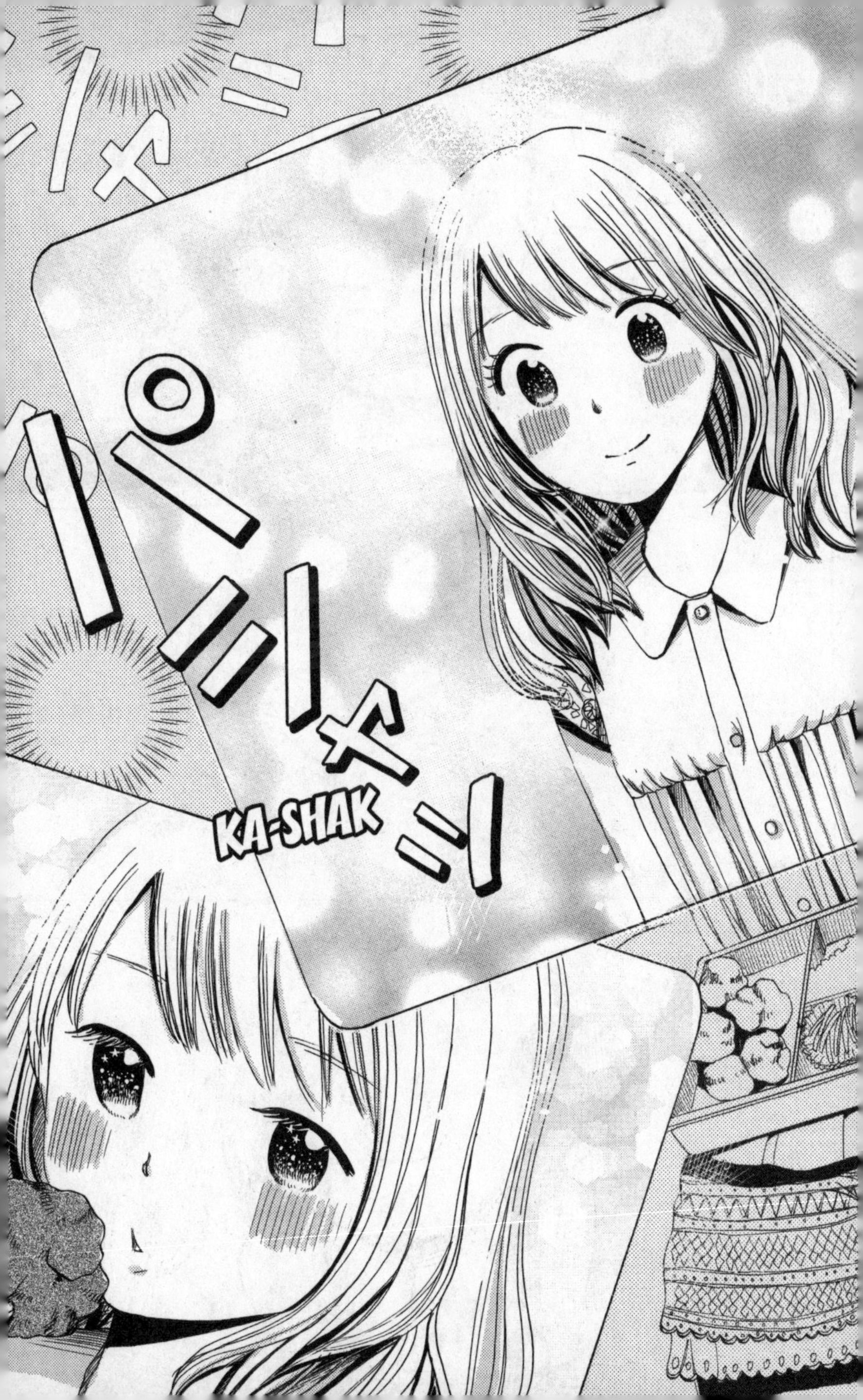
KA-SHAK

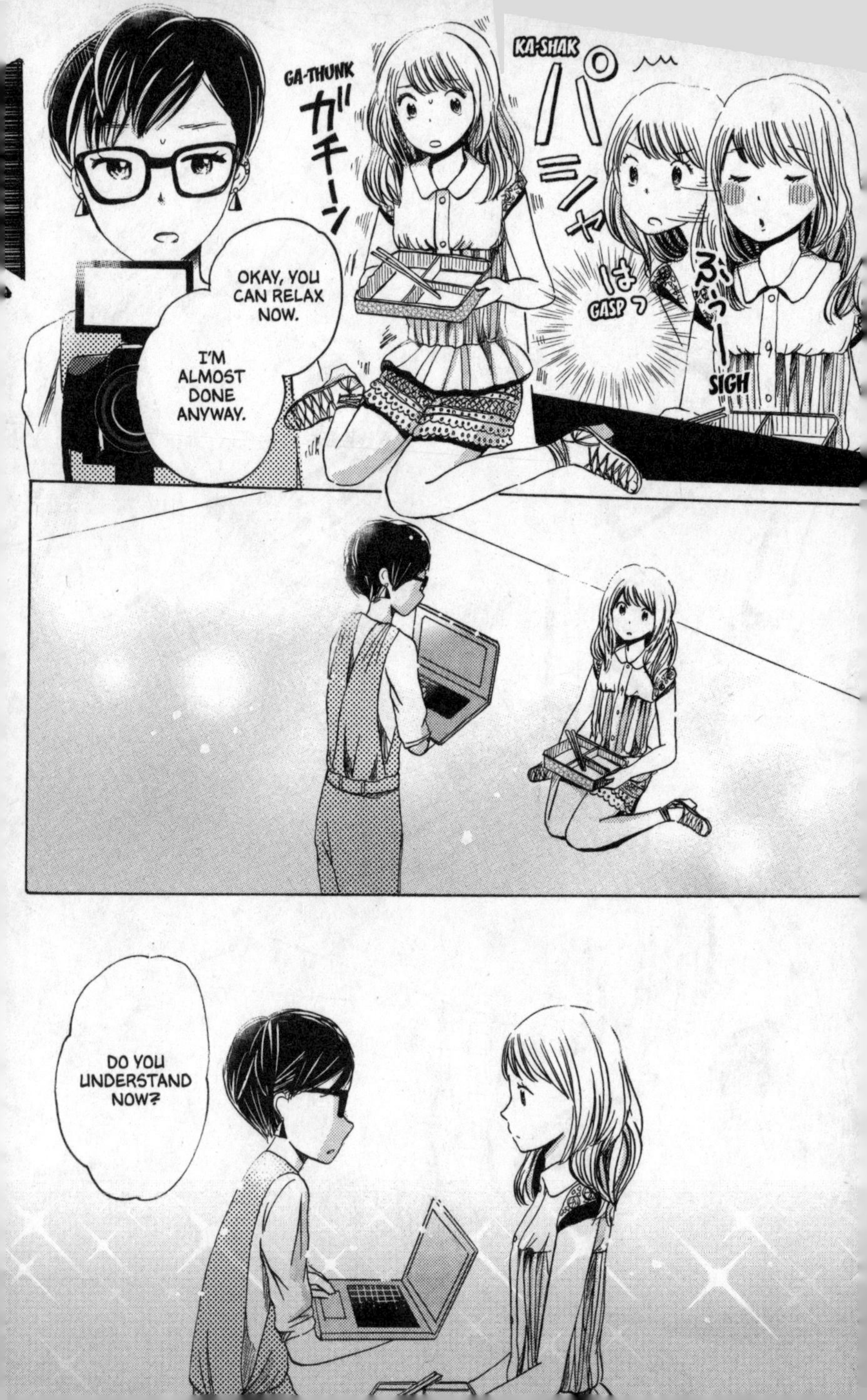
KA-SHAK
パシャ
はっ
GASP
ふぅー
SIGH
GA-THUNK
ガチーン
OKAY, YOU CAN RELAX NOW.
I'M ALMOST DONE ANYWAY.
DO YOU UNDERSTAND NOW?

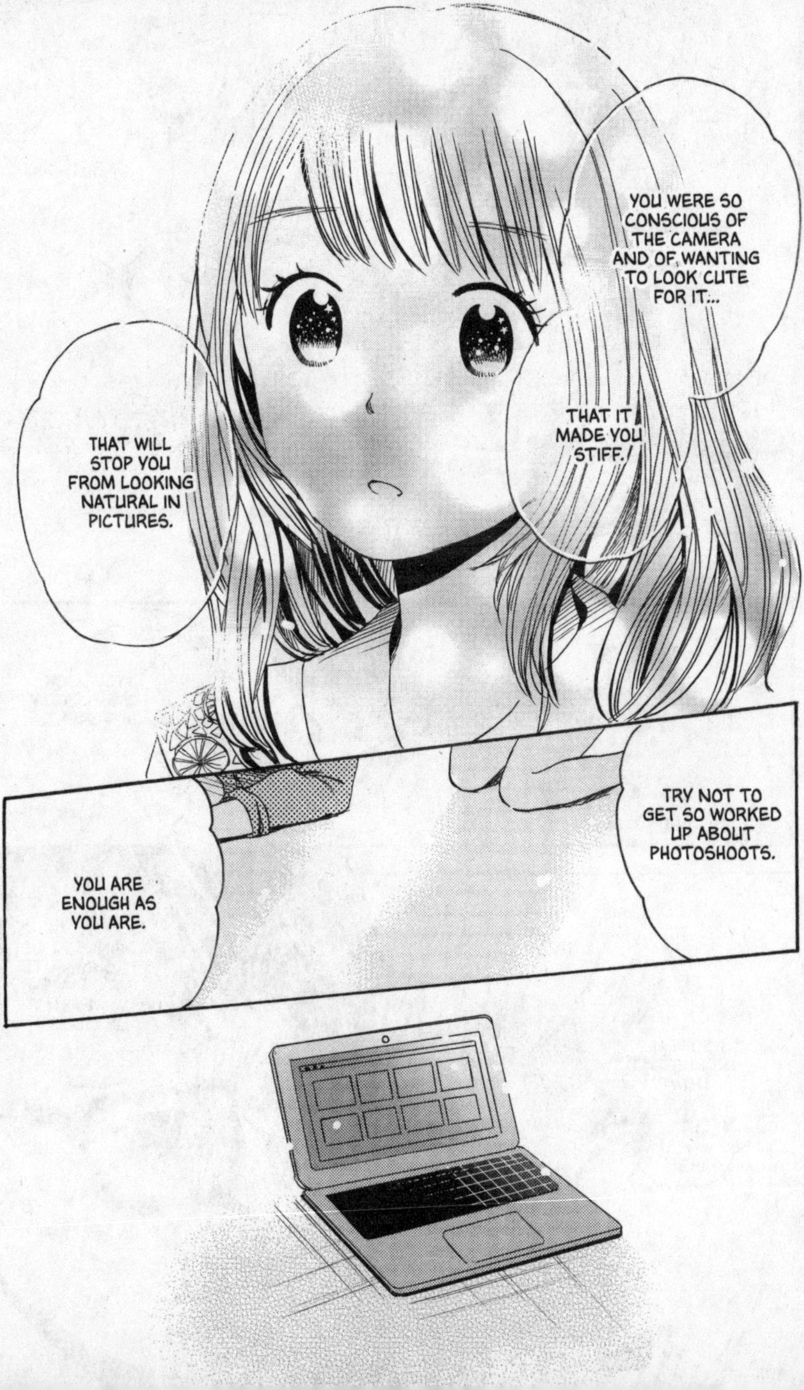
YOU WERE SO CONSCIOUS OF THE CAMERA AND OF WANTING TO LOOK CUTE FOR IT...
THAT IT MADE YOU STIFF.
THAT WILL STOP YOU FROM LOOKING NATURAL IN PICTURES.
TRY NOT TO GET SO WORKED UP ABOUT PHOTOSHOOTS.
YOU ARE ENOUGH AS YOU ARE.

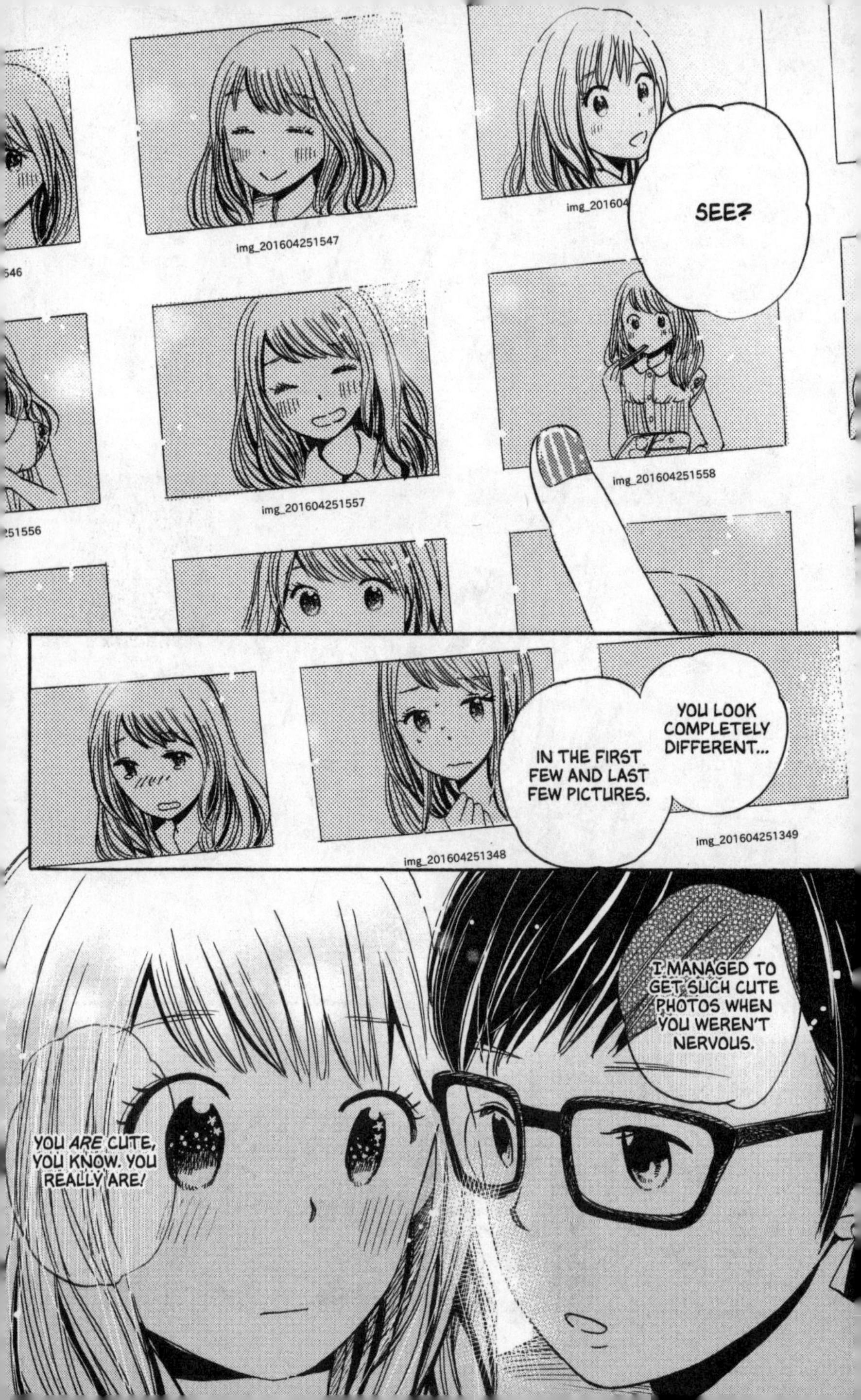
SEE?
img_201604251547
img_201604251558
img_201604251557
YOU LOOK COMPLETELY DIFFERENT...
IN THE FIRST FEW AND LAST FEW PICTURES.
img_201604251349
img_201604251348
I MANAGED TO GET SUCH CUTE PHOTOS WHEN YOU WEREN'T NERVOUS.
YOU *ARE* CUTE, YOU KNOW. YOU REALLY ARE!

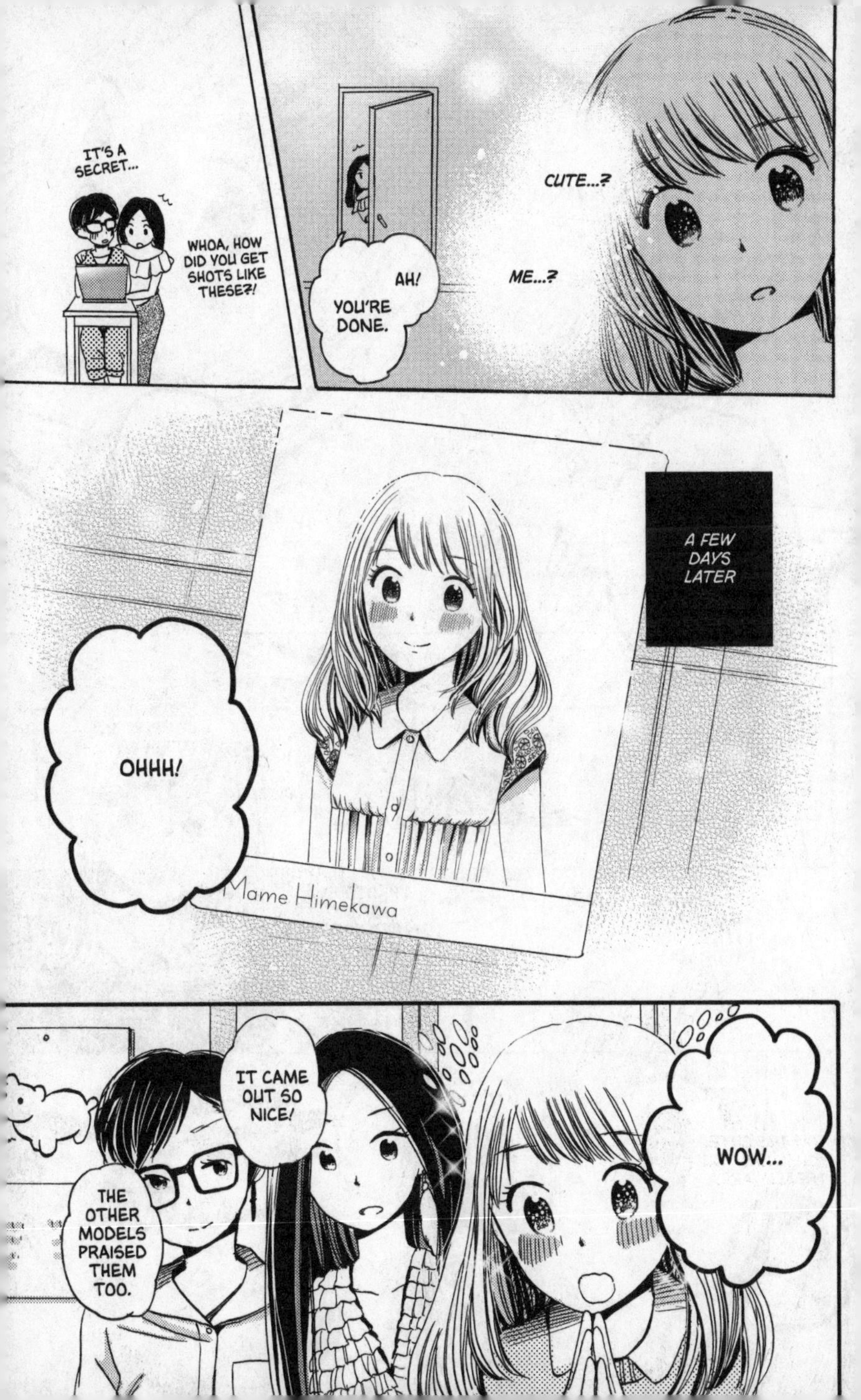
CUTE...?
ME...?
AH!
YOU'RE DONE.
WHOA, HOW DID YOU GET SHOTS LIKE THESE?!
IT'S A SECRET...
A FEW DAYS LATER
Mame Himekawa
OHHH!
WOW...
IT CAME OUT SO NICE!
THE OTHER MODELS PRAISED THEM TOO.

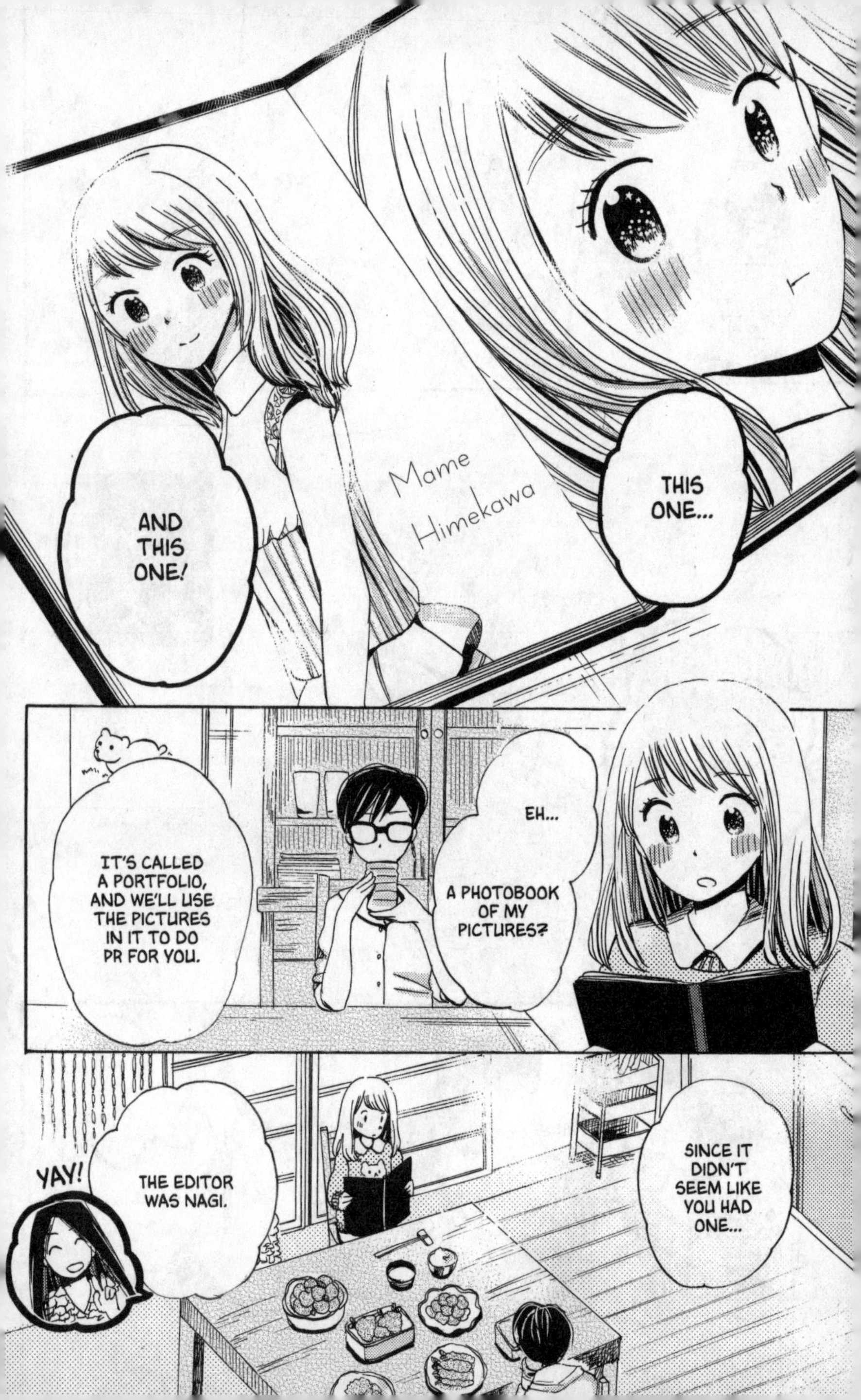
THIS ONE...
Mame Himekawa
AND THIS ONE!
EH...
A PHOTOBOOK OF MY PICTURES?
IT'S CALLED A PORTFOLIO, AND WE'LL USE THE PICTURES IN IT TO DO PR FOR YOU.
SINCE IT DIDN'T SEEM LIKE YOU HAD ONE...
THE EDITOR WAS NAGI.
YAY!

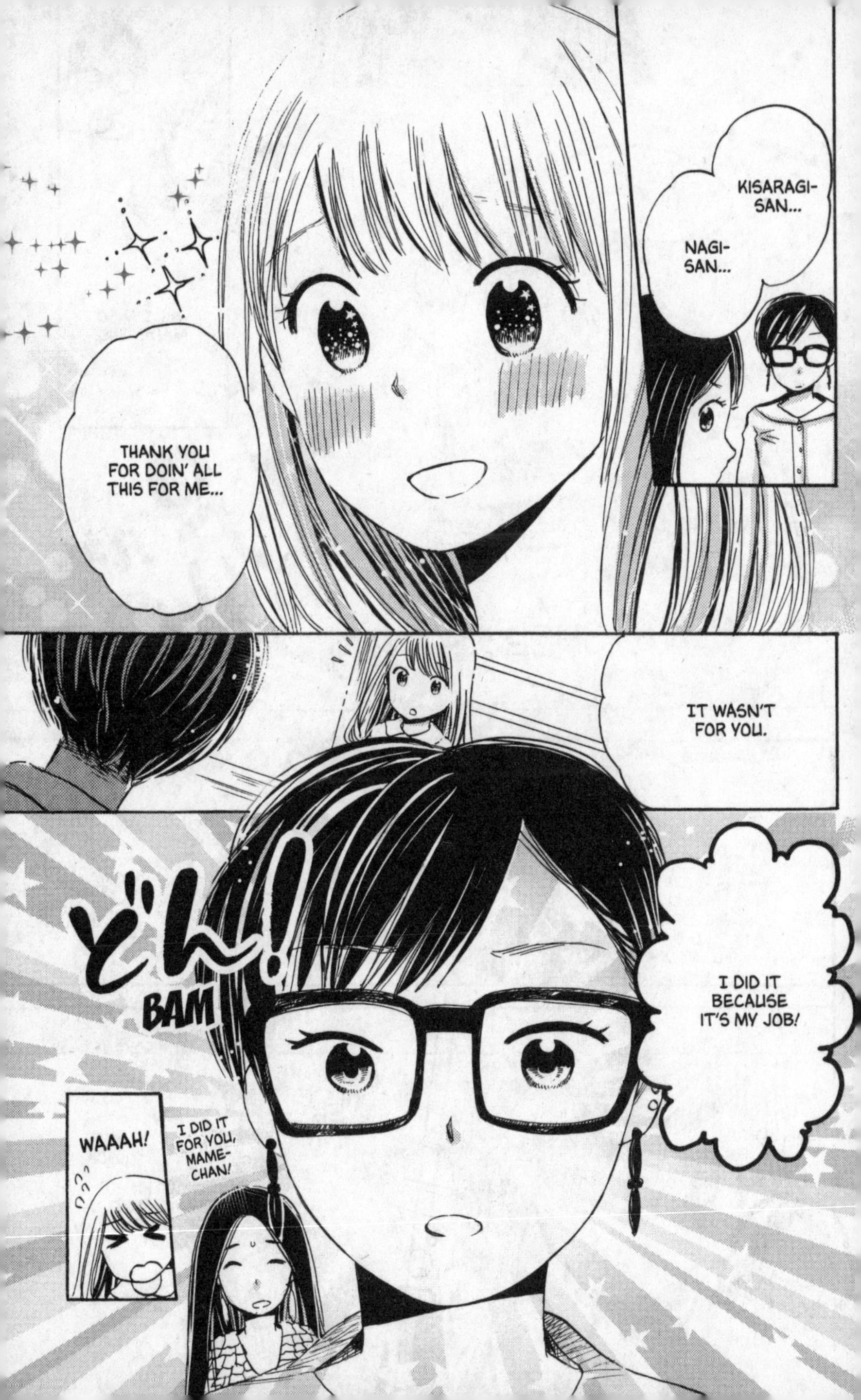
KISARAGI-SAN...
NAGI-SAN...
THANK YOU FOR DOIN' ALL THIS FOR ME...
IT WASN'T FOR YOU.
I DID IT BECAUSE IT'S MY JOB!
どん!
BAM
I DID IT FOR YOU, MAME-CHAN!
WAAAH!

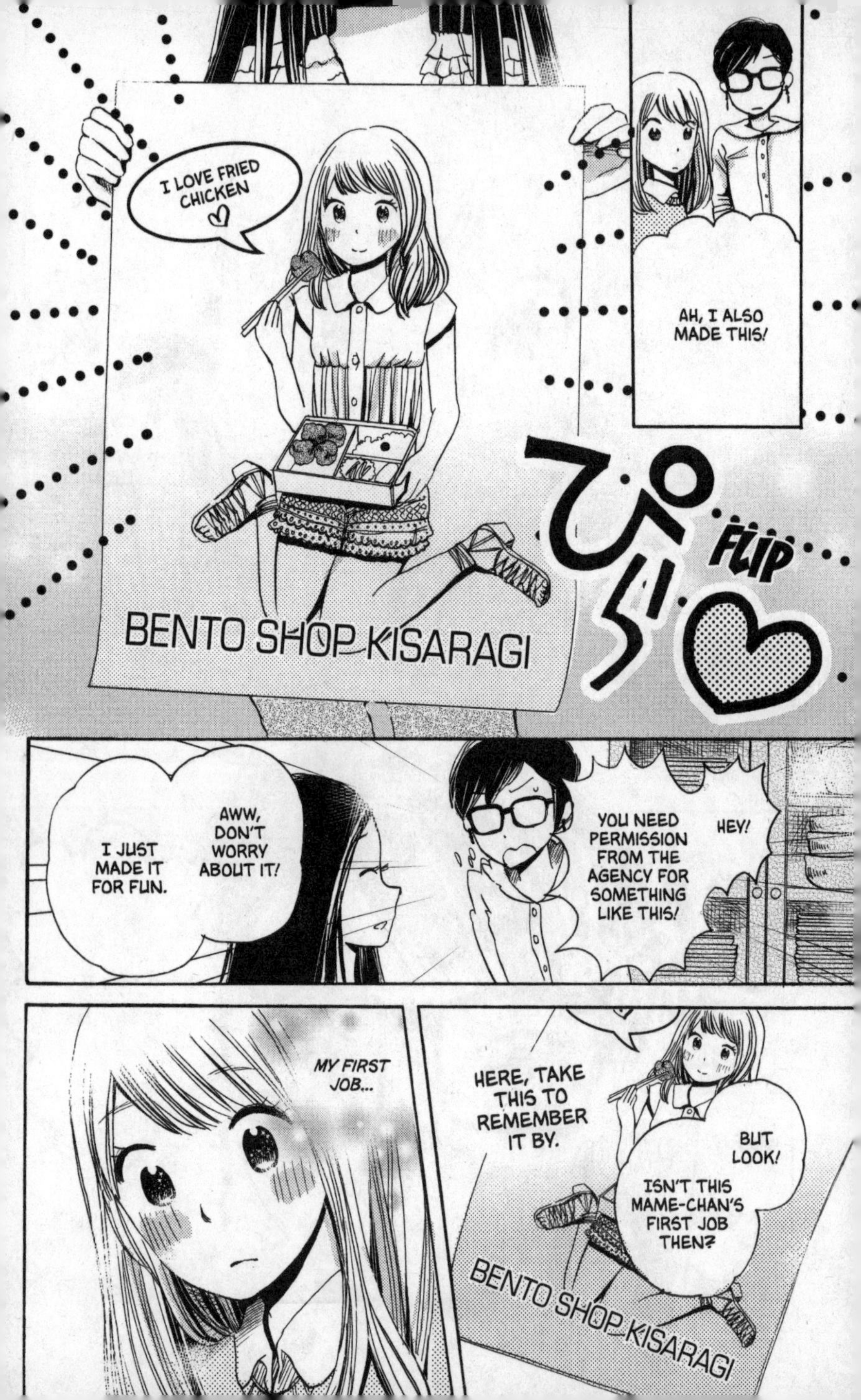
AH, I ALSO MADE THIS!
I LOVE FRIED CHICKEN ♡
BENTO SHOP KISARAGI
ぴら
FLIP
HEY!
YOU NEED PERMISSION FROM THE AGENCY FOR SOMETHING LIKE THIS!
AWW, DON'T WORRY ABOUT IT!
I JUST MADE IT FOR FUN.
BUT LOOK!
ISN'T THIS MAME-CHAN'S FIRST JOB THEN?
HERE, TAKE THIS TO REMEMBER IT BY.
BENTO SHOP KISARAGI
MY FIRST JOB...

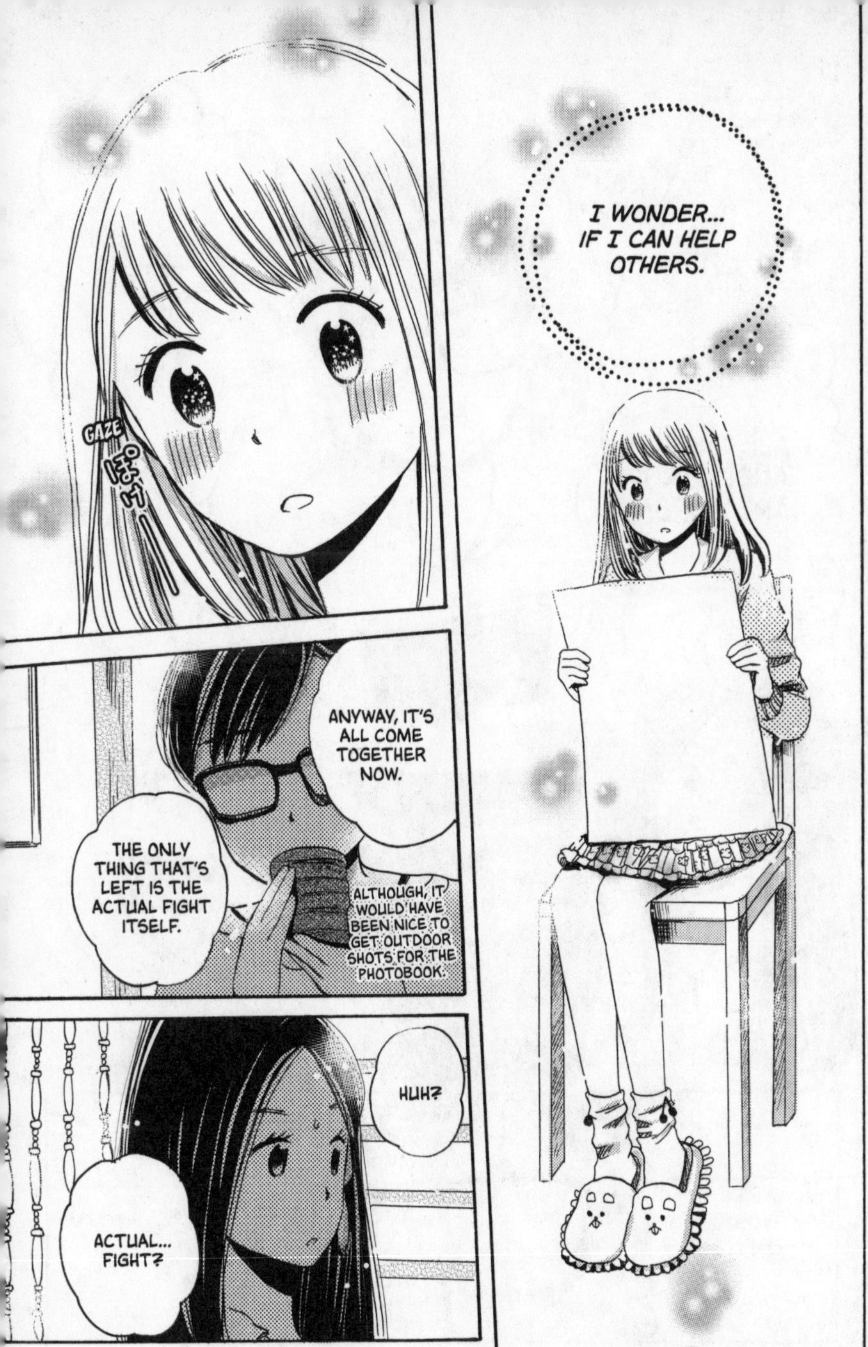
I WONDER... IF I CAN HELP OTHERS.
GAZE
ANYWAY, IT'S ALL COME TOGETHER NOW.
THE ONLY THING THAT'S LEFT IS THE ACTUAL FIGHT ITSELF.
ALTHOUGH, IT WOULD HAVE BEEN NICE TO GET OUTDOOR SHOTS FOR THE PHOTOBOOK.
HUH?
ACTUAL... FIGHT?

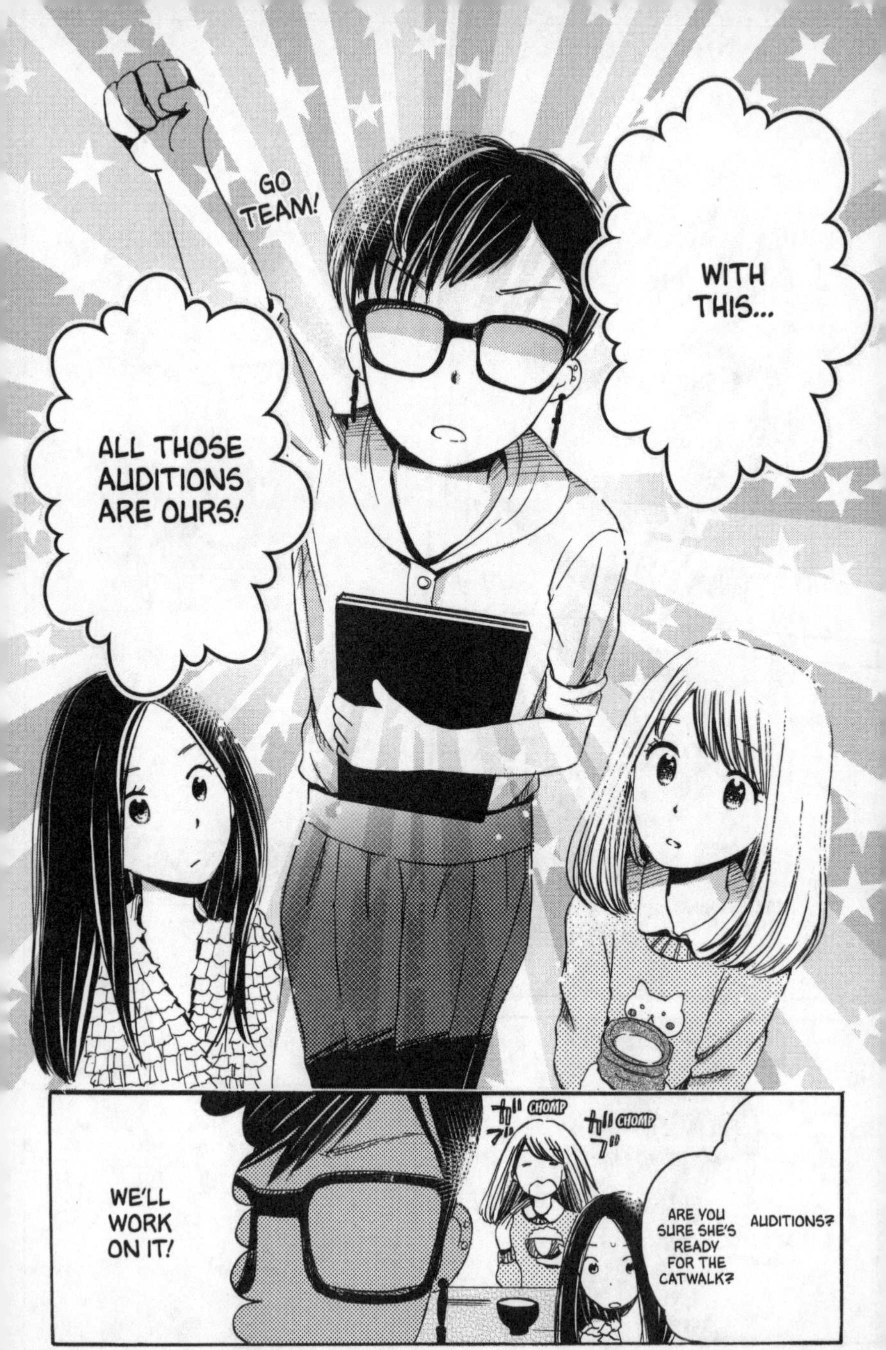
WITH THIS...
GO TEAM!
ALL THOSE AUDITIONS ARE OURS!
AUDITIONS?
ARE YOU SURE SHE'S READY FOR THE CATWALK?
CHOMP
CHOMP
WE'LL WORK ON IT!

M A M E
coordinate

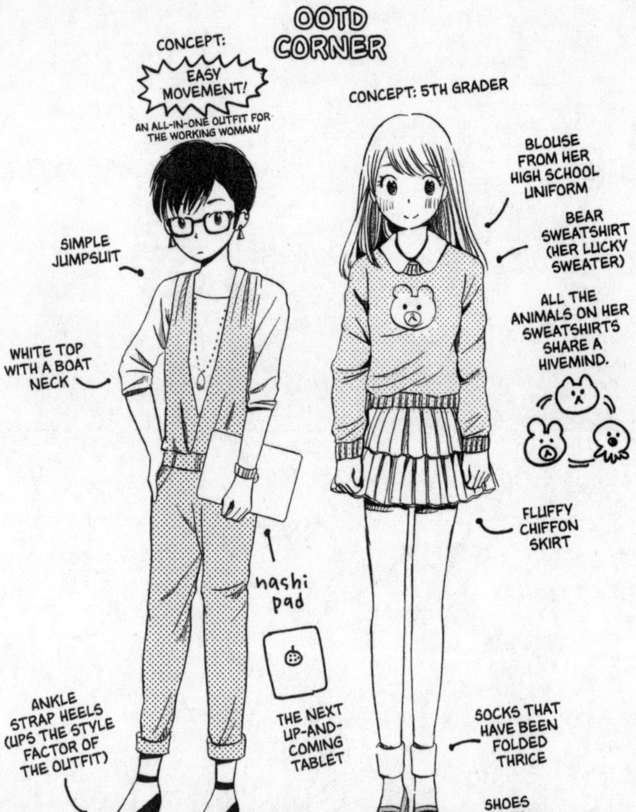

OOTD CORNER
CONCEPT: 5TH GRADER
BLOUSE FROM HER HIGH SCHOOL UNIFORM
BEAR SWEATSHIRT (HER LUCKY SWEATER)
ALL THE ANIMALS ON HER SWEATSHIRTS SHARE A HIVEMIND.
FLUFFY CHIFFON SKIRT
SOCKS THAT HAVE BEEN FOLDED THRICE
SHOES WITH STRAPS
CONCEPT:
EASY MOVEMENT!
AN ALL-IN-ONE OUTFIT FOR THE WORKING WOMAN!
SIMPLE JUMPSUIT
WHITE TOP WITH A BOAT NECK
nashi pad
THE NEXT UP-AND-COMING TABLET
ANKLE STRAP HEELS (UPS THE STYLE FACTOR OF THE OUTFIT)

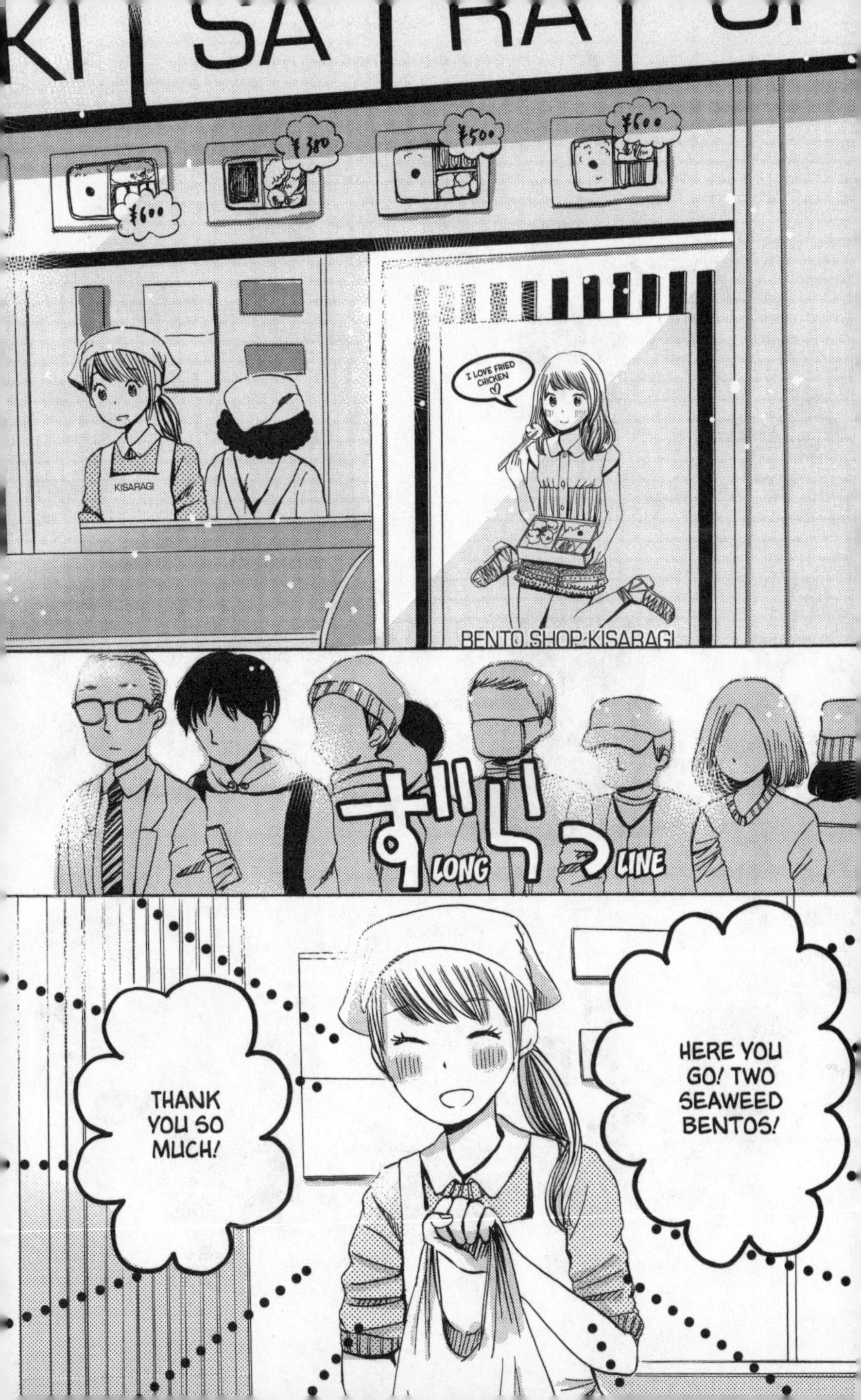
KI SA RA
KISARAGI
I LOVE FRIED CHICKEN
BENTO SHOP KISARAGI
ずらっ LONG LINE
HERE YOU GO! TWO SEAWEED BENTOS!
THANK YOU SO MUCH!

Chapter 4

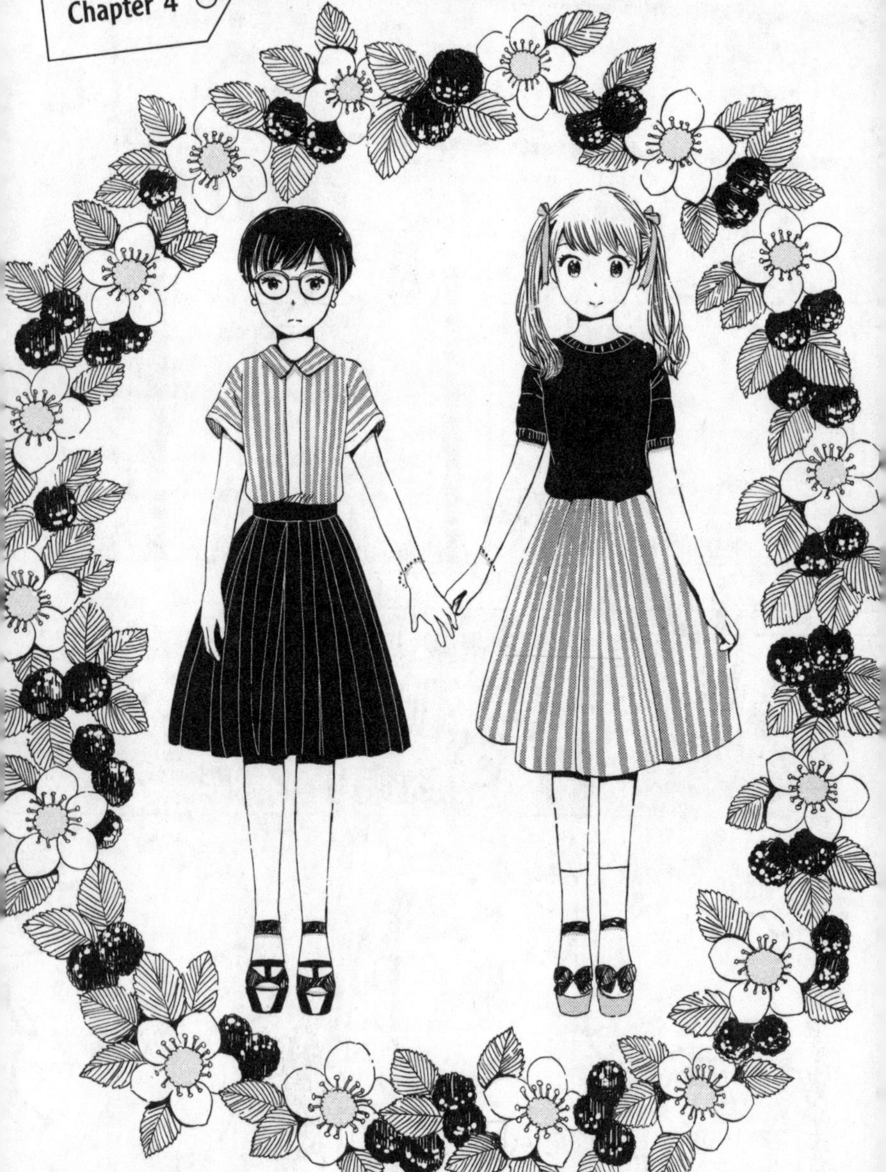

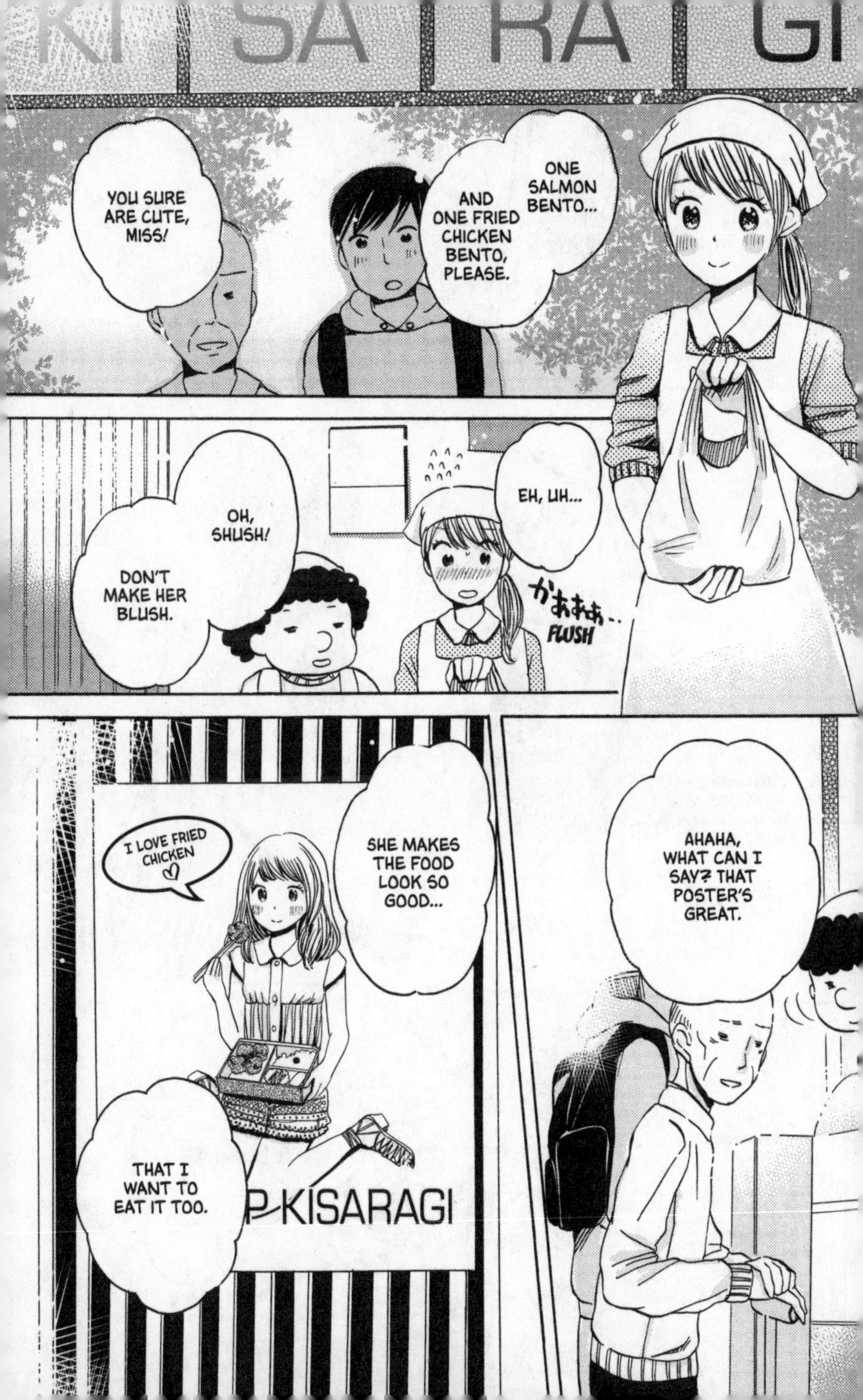
KI SA RA GI
ONE SALMON BENTO...
AND ONE FRIED CHICKEN BENTO, PLEASE.
YOU SURE ARE CUTE, MISS!
EH, UH...
かあああ..
FLUSH
OH, SHUSH!
DON'T MAKE HER BLUSH.
AHAHA, WHAT CAN I SAY? THAT POSTER'S GREAT.
SHE MAKES THE FOOD LOOK SO GOOD...
I LOVE FRIED CHICKEN ♡
P KISARAGI
THAT I WANT TO EAT IT TOO.

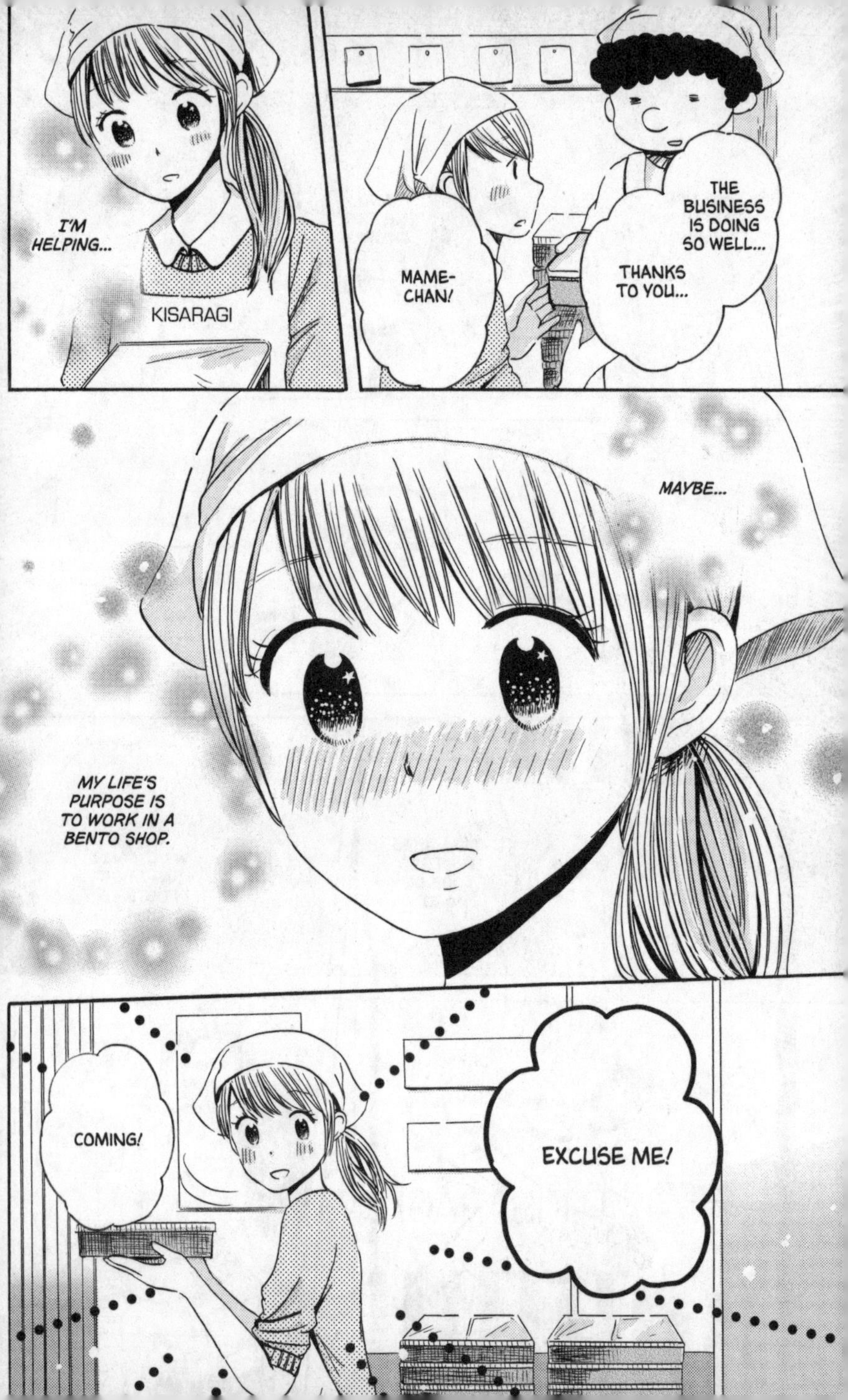
THE BUSINESS IS DOING SO WELL...
THANKS TO YOU...
MAME-CHAN!
I'M HELPING...
KISARAGI
MAYBE...
MY LIFE'S PURPOSE IS TO WORK IN A BENTO SHOP.
EXCUSE ME!
COMING!

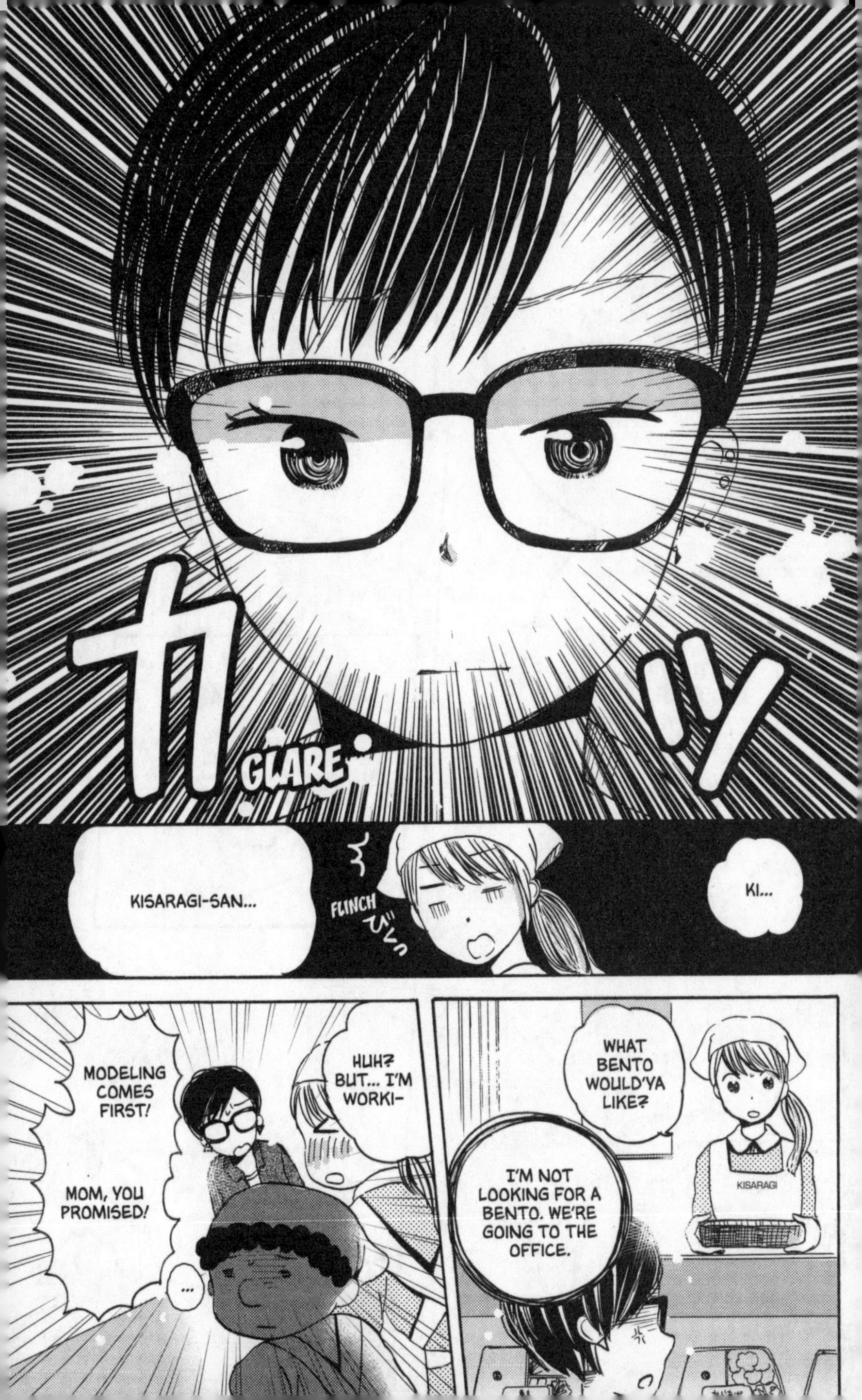
カッ
GLARE
KI...
FLINCH
びくっ
KISARAGI-SAN...
WHAT BENTO WOULD'YA LIKE?
KISARAGI
I'M NOT LOOKING FOR A BENTO. WE'RE GOING TO THE OFFICE.
HUH? BUT... I'M WORKI-
MODELING COMES FIRST!
MOM, YOU PROMISED!
...

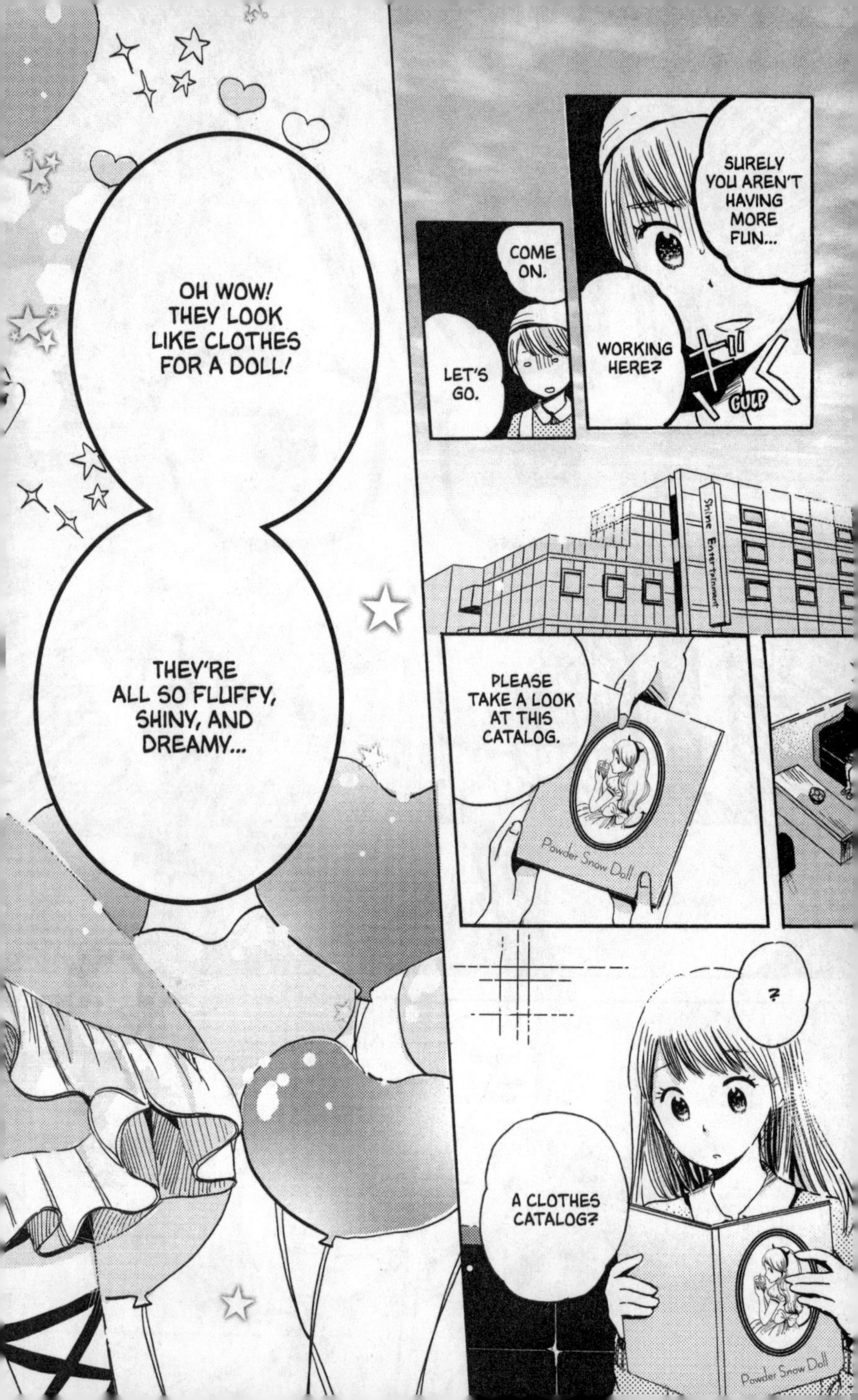
SURELY YOU AREN'T HAVING MORE FUN...
WORKING HERE?
GULP
COME ON.
LET'S GO.
Shine Entertainment
PLEASE TAKE A LOOK AT THIS CATALOG.
Powder Snow Doll
?
A CLOTHES CATALOG?
Powder Snow Doll
OH WOW! THEY LOOK LIKE CLOTHES FOR A DOLL!
THEY'RE ALL SO FLUFFY, SHINY, AND DREAMY...

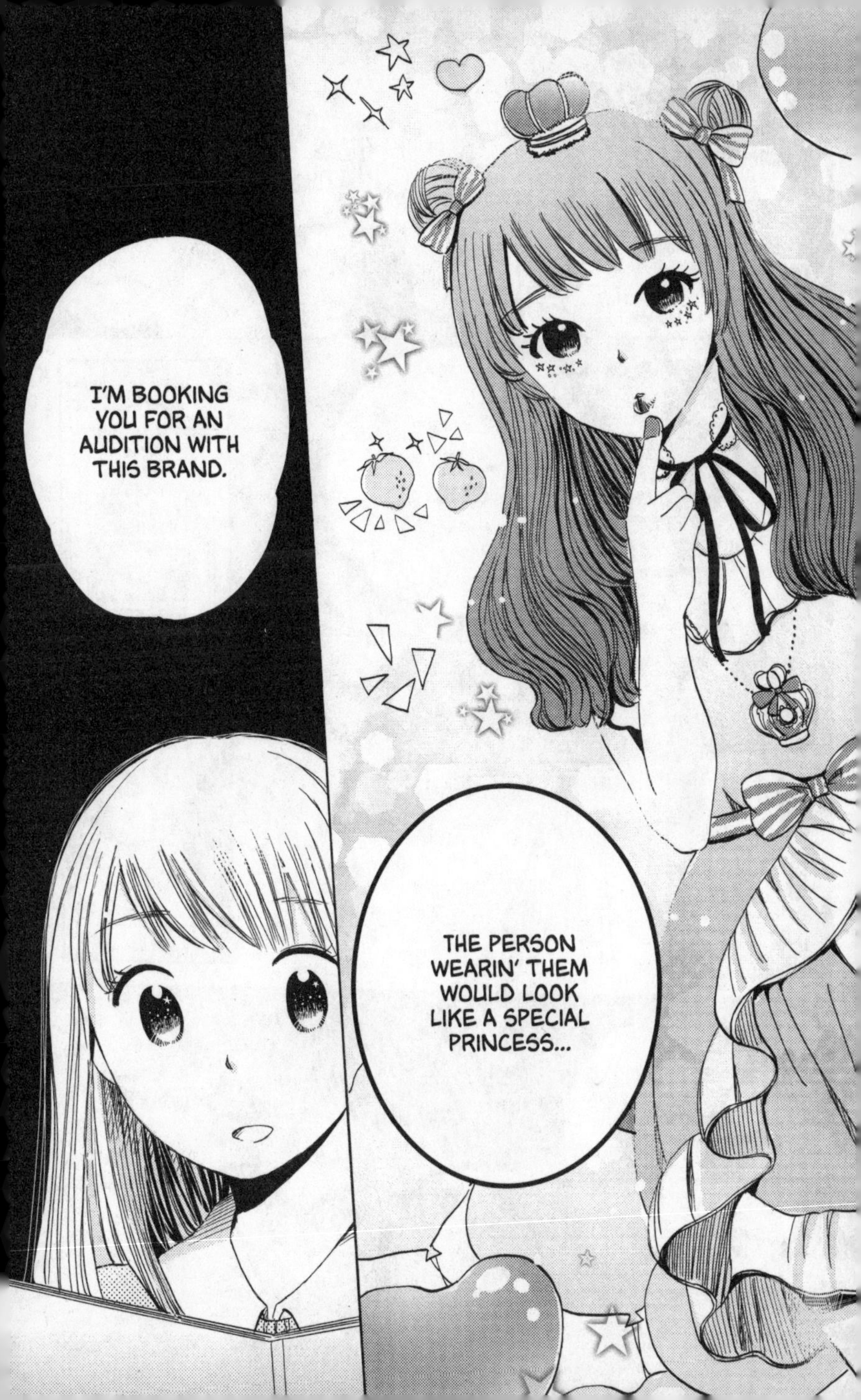
THE PERSON WEARIN' THEM WOULD LOOK LIKE A SPECIAL PRINCESS...
I'M BOOKING YOU FOR AN AUDITION WITH THIS BRAND.

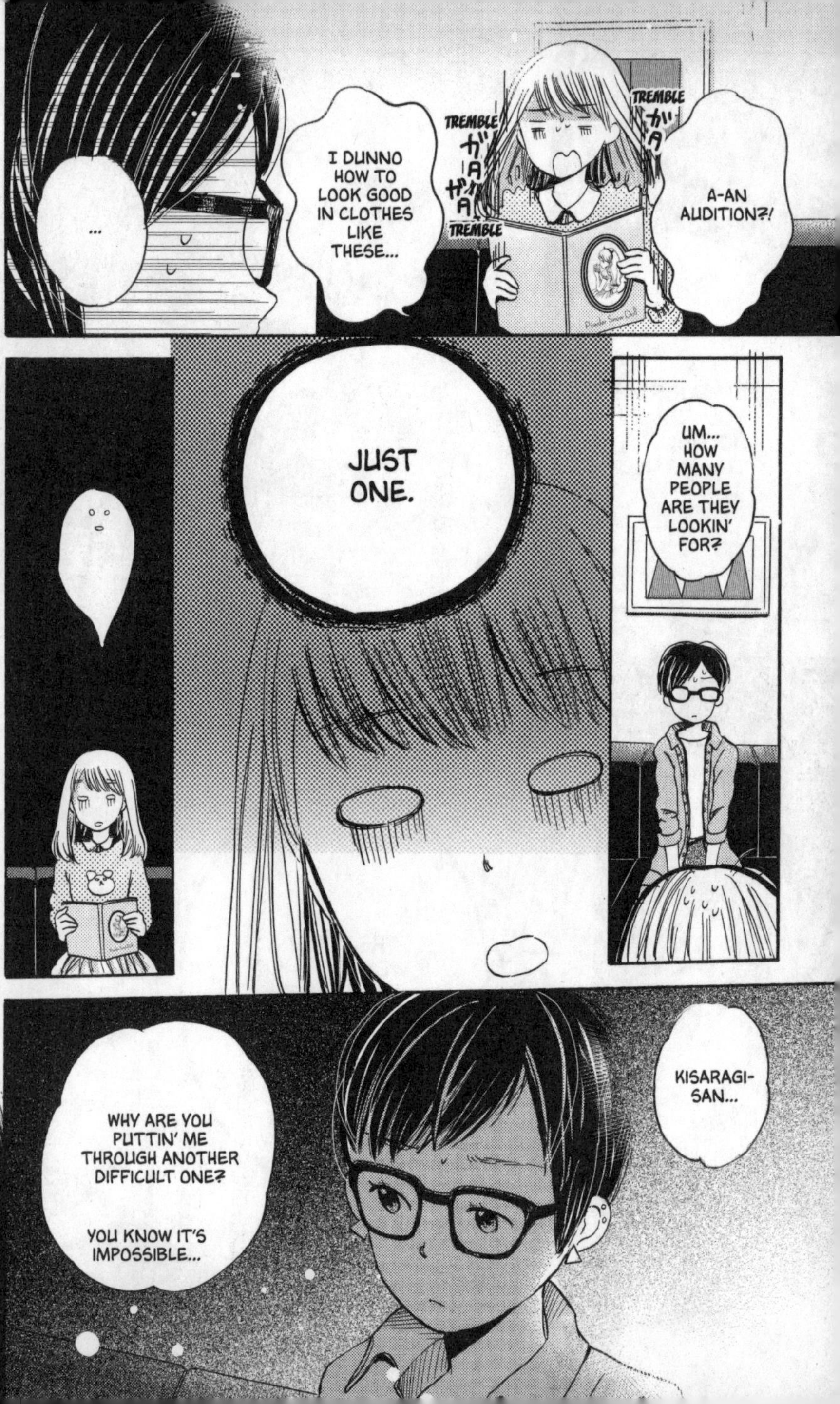
TREMBLE
TREMBLE
TREMBLE
A-AN AUDITION?!
I DUNNO HOW TO LOOK GOOD IN CLOTHES LIKE THESE...
...
UM... HOW MANY PEOPLE ARE THEY LOOKIN' FOR?
JUST ONE.
KISARAGI-SAN...
WHY ARE YOU PUTTIN' ME THROUGH ANOTHER DIFFICULT ONE?
YOU KNOW IT'S IMPOSSIBLE...

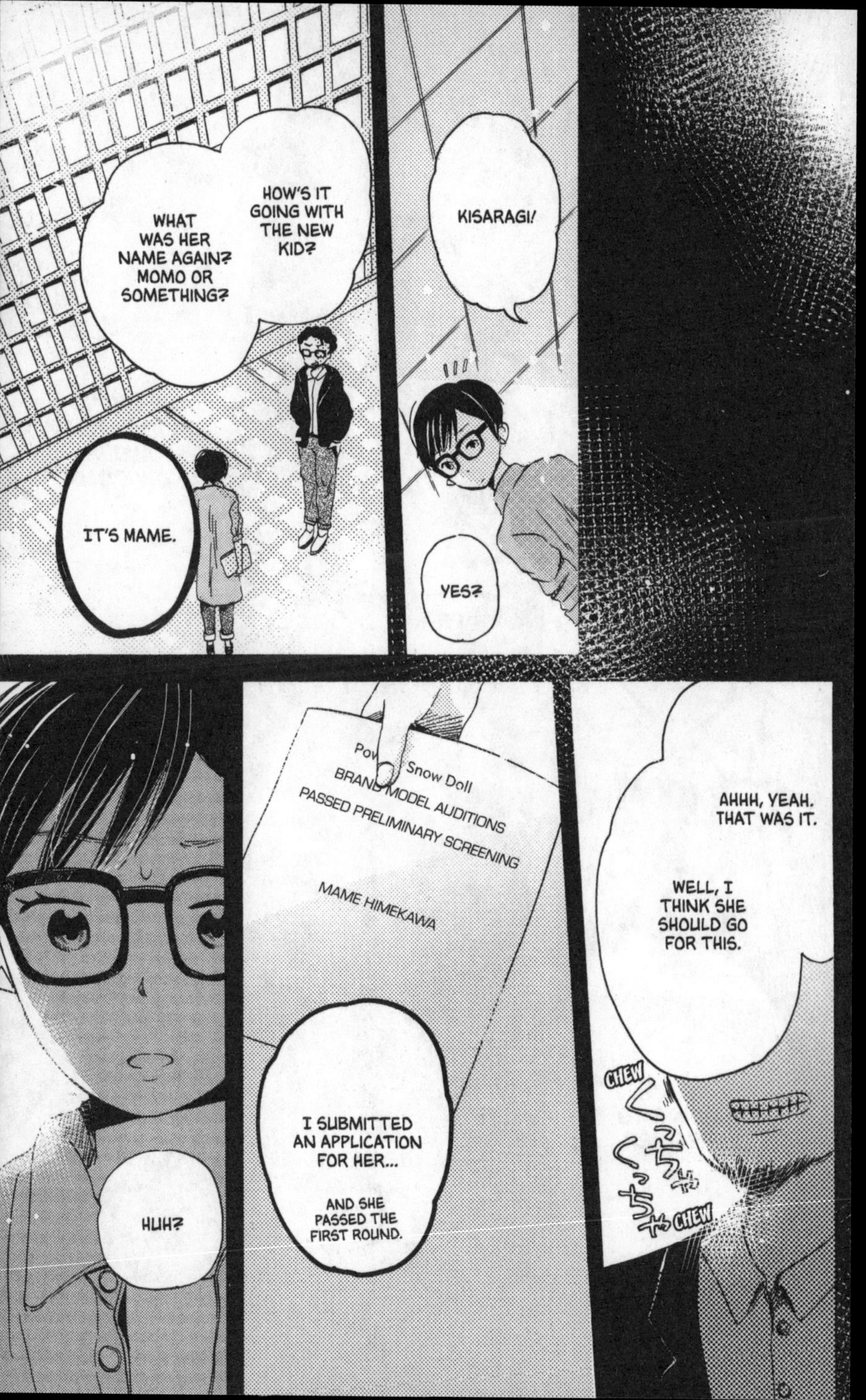
KISARAGI!
YES?
HOW'S IT GOING WITH THE NEW KID?
WHAT WAS HER NAME AGAIN? MOMO OR SOMETHING?
IT'S MAME.
AHHH, YEAH. THAT WAS IT.
WELL, I THINK SHE SHOULD GO FOR THIS.
CHEW
くっちゃ
くっちゃ
CHEW
Pow Snow Doll
BRAND MODEL AUDITIONS
PASSED PRELIMINARY SCREENING
MAME HIMEKAWA
I SUBMITTED AN APPLICATION FOR HER...
AND SHE PASSED THE FIRST ROUND.
HUH?

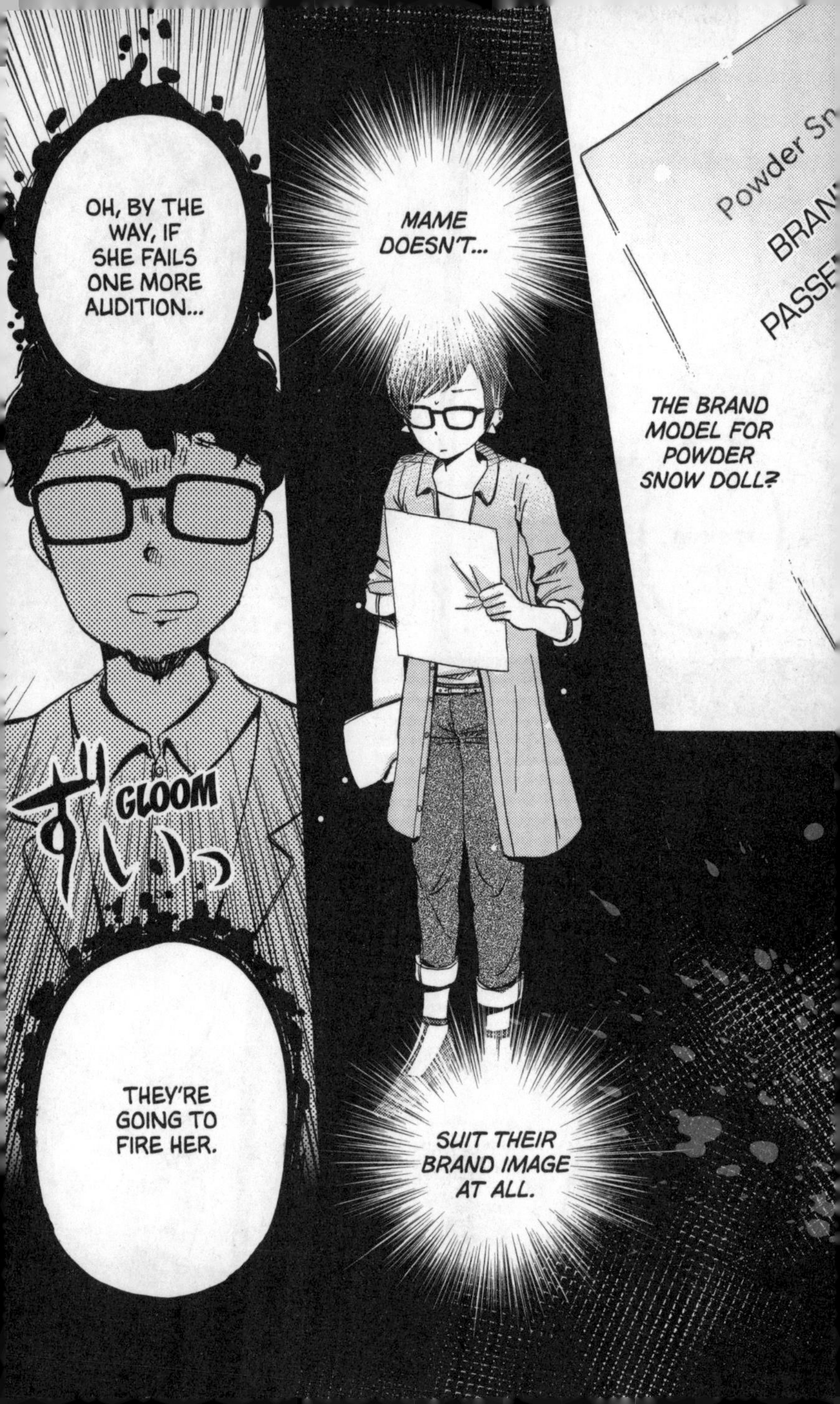
Powder Sn
BRAN
PASSE
THE BRAND MODEL FOR POWDER SNOW DOLL?
MAME DOESN'T...
SUIT THEIR BRAND IMAGE AT ALL.
OH, BY THE WAY, IF SHE FAILS ONE MORE AUDITION...
GLOOM
THEY'RE GOING TO FIRE HER.

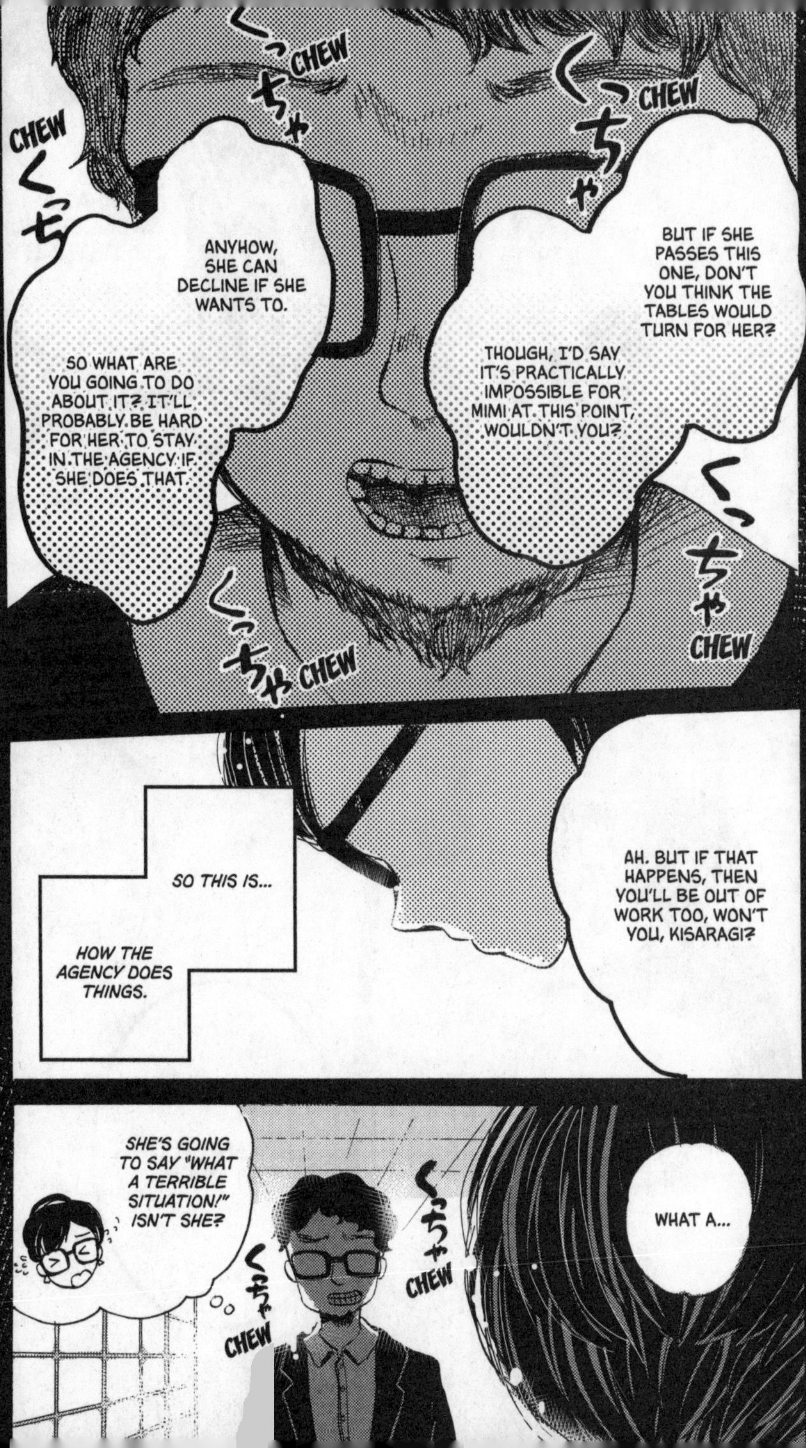
くっちゃ CHEW
くっちゃ CHEW
くっちゃ CHEW
BUT IF SHE PASSES THIS ONE, DON'T YOU THINK THE TABLES WOULD TURN FOR HER?
THOUGH, I'D SAY IT'S PRACTICALLY IMPOSSIBLE FOR MIMI AT THIS POINT, WOULDN'T YOU?
ANYHOW, SHE CAN DECLINE IF SHE WANTS TO.
SO WHAT ARE YOU GOING TO DO ABOUT IT? IT'LL PROBABLY BE HARD FOR HER TO STAY IN THE AGENCY IF SHE DOES THAT.
くっちゃ CHEW
くっちゃ CHEW
AH. BUT IF THAT HAPPENS, THEN YOU'LL BE OUT OF WORK TOO, WON'T YOU, KISARAGI?
SO THIS IS...
HOW THE AGENCY DOES THINGS.
WHAT A...
くっちゃ CHEW
くっちゃ CHEW
SHE'S GOING TO SAY "WHAT A TERRIBLE SITUATION!" ISN'T SHE?

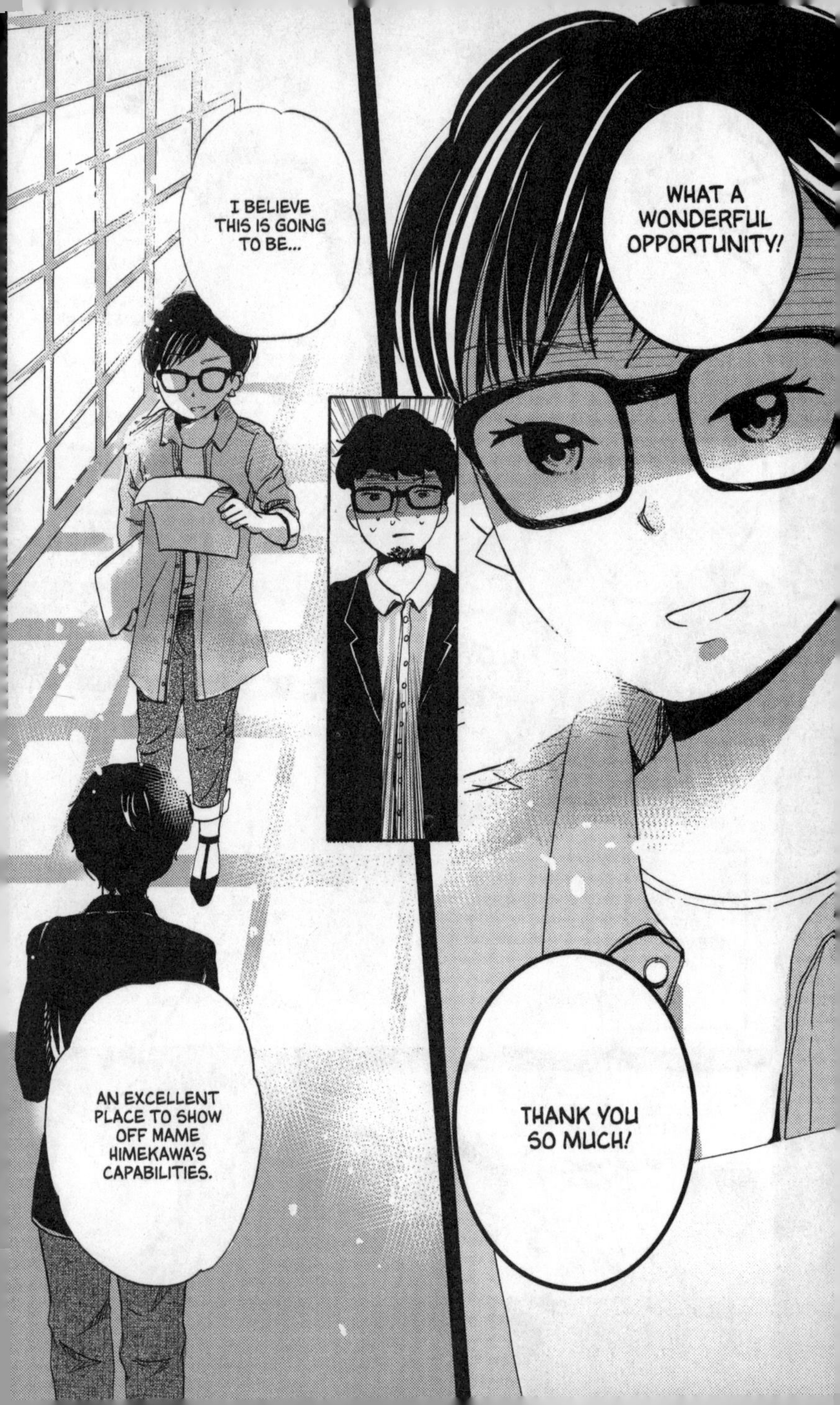
WHAT A WONDERFUL OPPORTUNITY!
THANK YOU SO MUCH!
I BELIEVE THIS IS GOING TO BE...
AN EXCELLENT PLACE TO SHOW OFF MAME HIMEKAWA'S CAPABILITIES.

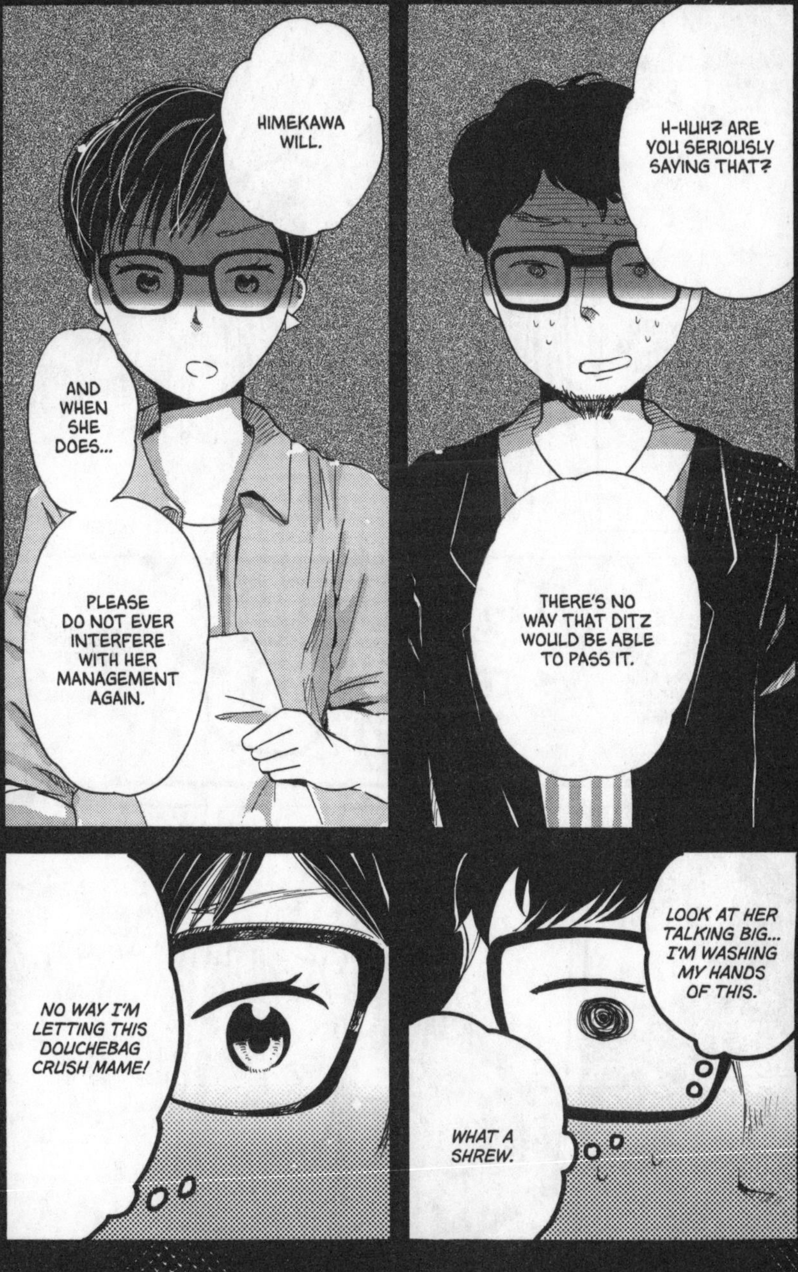
H-HUH? ARE YOU SERIOUSLY SAYING THAT?
THERE'S NO WAY THAT DITZ WOULD BE ABLE TO PASS IT.
HIMEKAWA WILL.
AND WHEN SHE DOES...
PLEASE DO NOT EVER INTERFERE WITH HER MANAGEMENT AGAIN.
LOOK AT HER TALKING BIG... I'M WASHING MY HANDS OF THIS.
WHAT A SHREW.
NO WAY I'M LETTING THIS DOUCHEBAG CRUSH MAME!

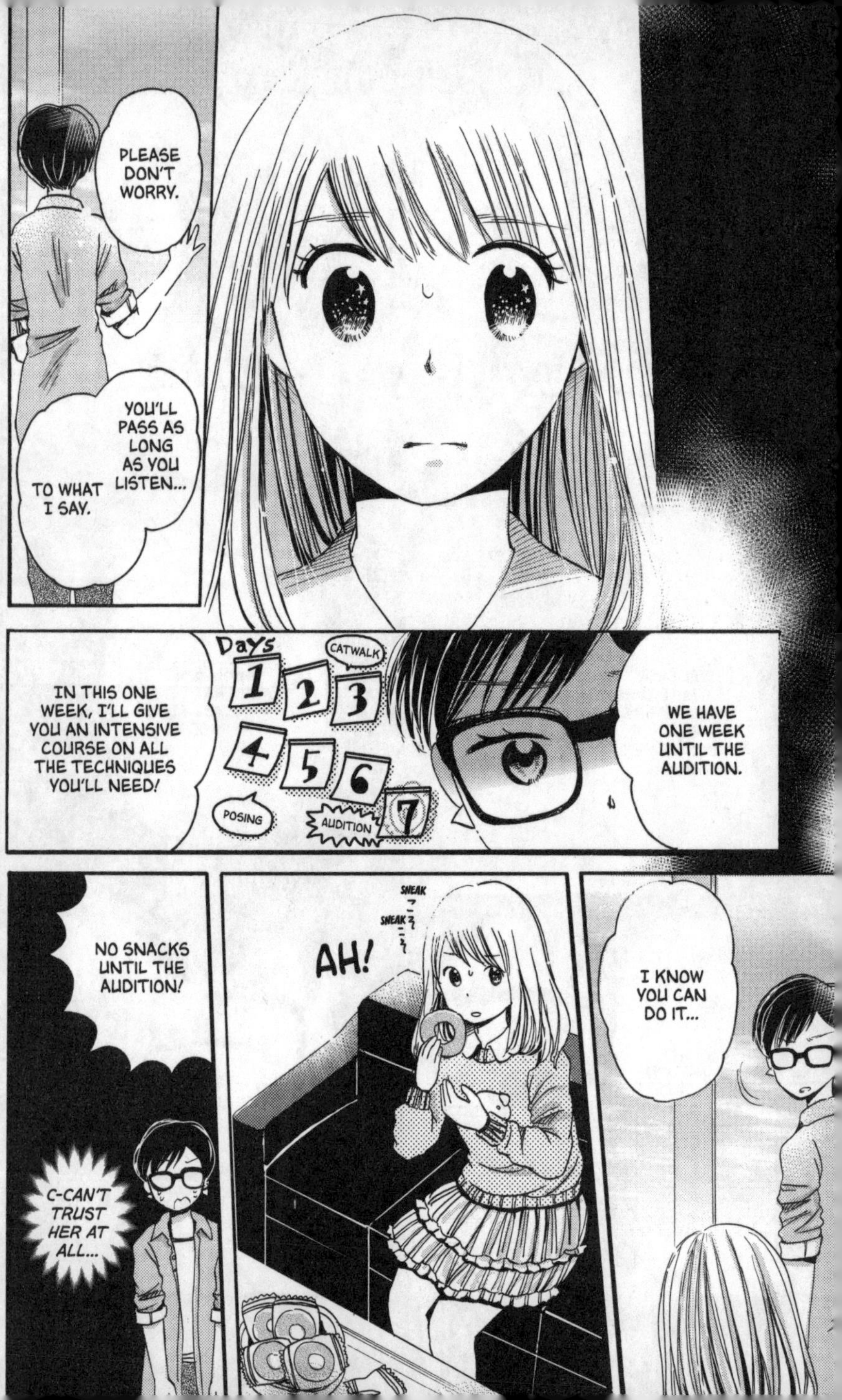
PLEASE DON'T WORRY.
YOU'LL PASS AS LONG AS YOU LISTEN...
TO WHAT I SAY.
WE HAVE ONE WEEK UNTIL THE AUDITION.
Days
1 2 3 4 5 6 7
CATWALK
POSING
AUDITION
IN THIS ONE WEEK, I'LL GIVE YOU AN INTENSIVE COURSE ON ALL THE TECHNIQUES YOU'LL NEED!
I KNOW YOU CAN DO IT...
SNEAK
SNEAK
AH!
NO SNACKS UNTIL THE AUDITION!
C-CAN'T TRUST HER AT ALL...

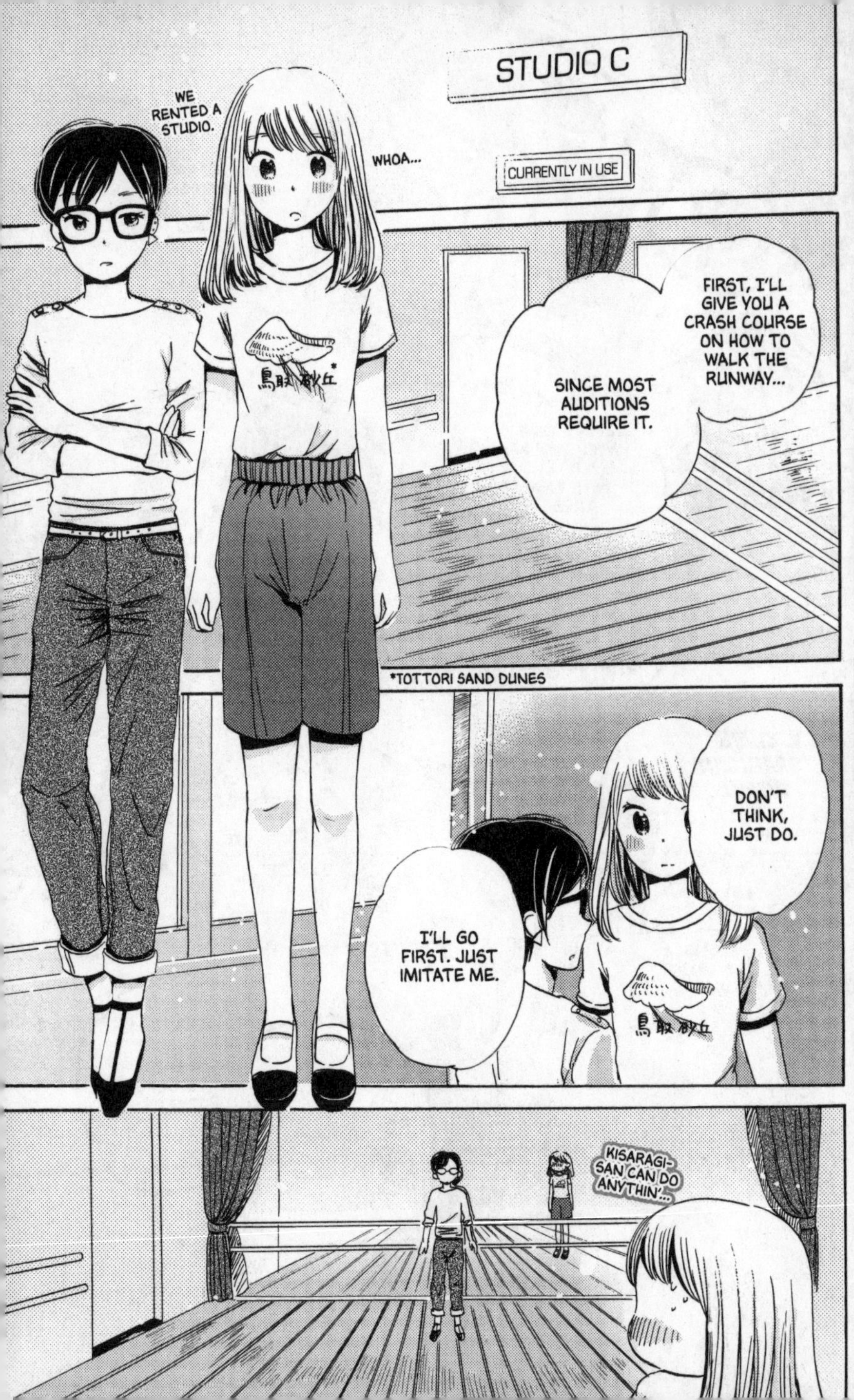
STUDIO C
CURRENTLY IN USE
FIRST, I'LL GIVE YOU A CRASH COURSE ON HOW TO WALK THE RUNWAY...
SINCE MOST AUDITIONS REQUIRE IT.
DON'T THINK, JUST DO.
I'LL GO FIRST. JUST IMITATE ME.
WHOA...
WE RENTED A STUDIO.
鳥取砂丘*
*TOTTORI SAND DUNES
KISARAGI-SAN CAN DO ANYTHIN'...

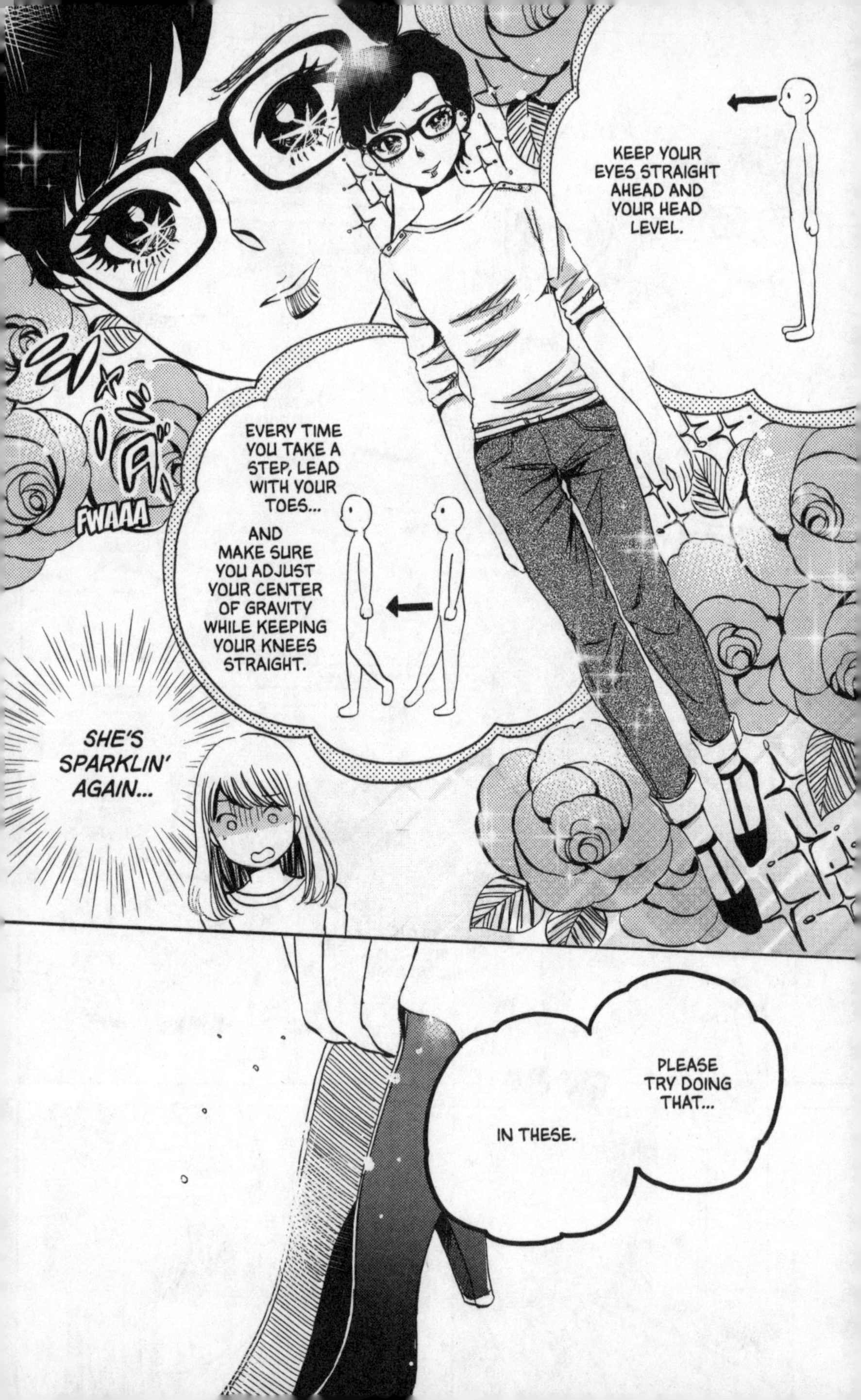
KEEP YOUR EYES STRAIGHT AHEAD AND YOUR HEAD LEVEL.
EVERY TIME YOU TAKE A STEP, LEAD WITH YOUR TOES...
AND MAKE SURE YOU ADJUST YOUR CENTER OF GRAVITY WHILE KEEPING YOUR KNEES STRAIGHT.
FWAAA
SHE'S SPARKLIN' AGAIN...
PLEASE TRY DOING THAT...
IN THESE.

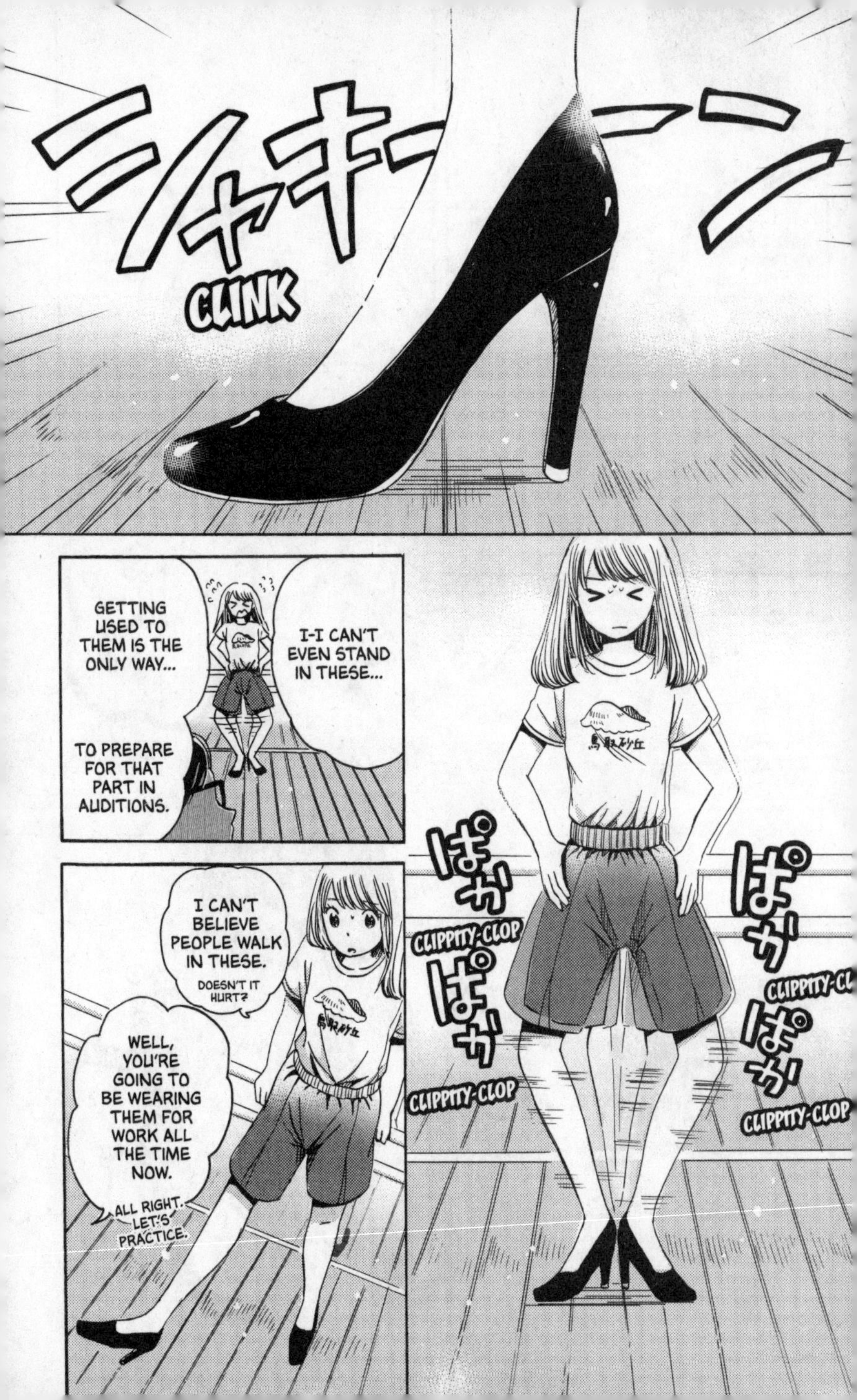
シャキーン
CLINK
ぱか
CLIPPITY-CL
ぱか
CLIPPITY-CLOP
ぱか
CLIPPITY-CLOP
ぱか
CLIPPITY-CLOP
I-I CAN'T EVEN STAND IN THESE...
GETTING USED TO THEM IS THE ONLY WAY...
TO PREPARE FOR THAT PART IN AUDITIONS.
I CAN'T BELIEVE PEOPLE WALK IN THESE.
DOESN'T IT HURT?
WELL, YOU'RE GOING TO BE WEARING THEM FOR WORK ALL THE TIME NOW.
ALL RIGHT. LET'S PRACTICE.

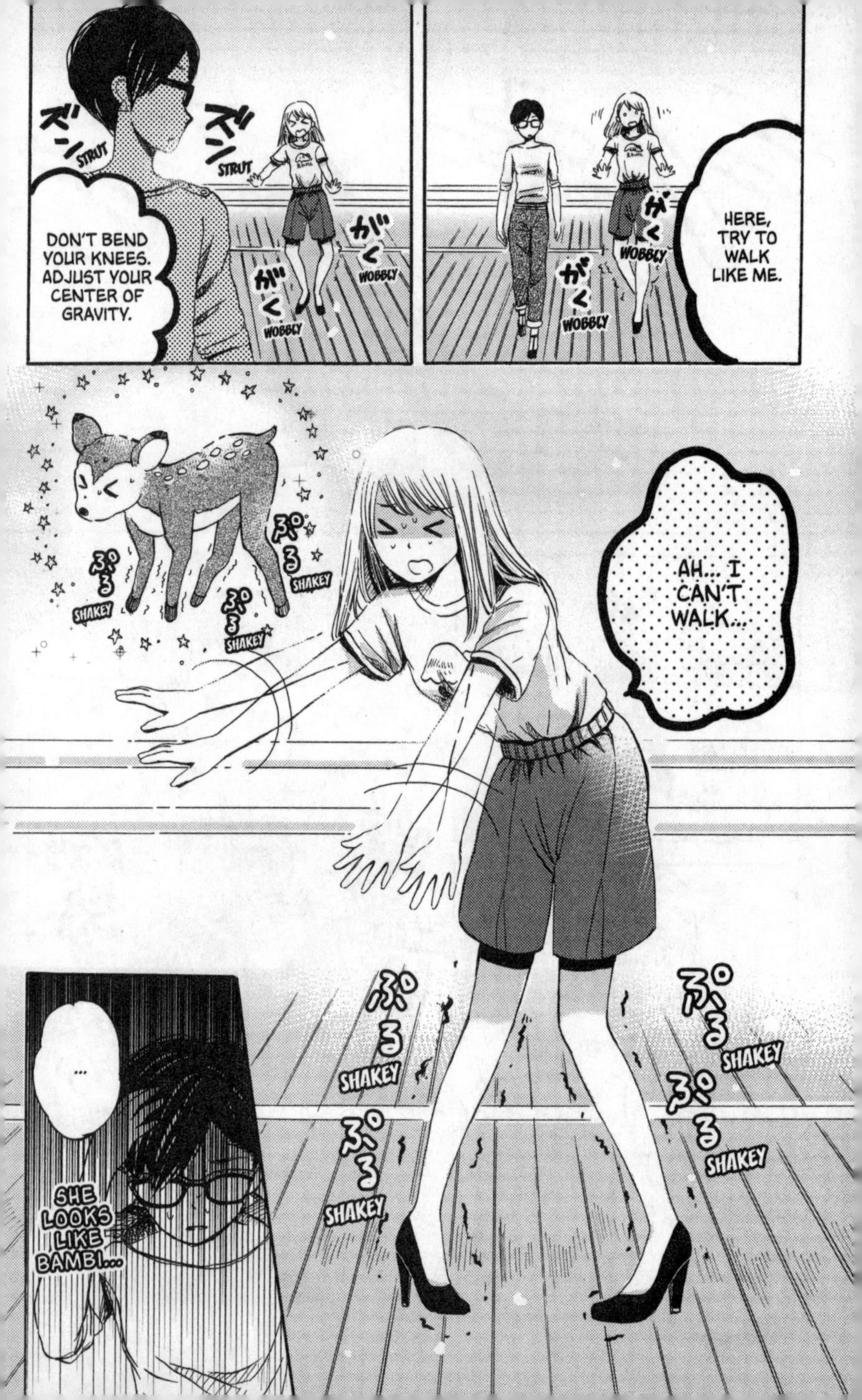
HERE, TRY TO WALK LIKE ME.
がく WOBBLY
がく WOBBLY
ズン STRUT
ズン STRUT
DON'T BEND YOUR KNEES. ADJUST YOUR CENTER OF GRAVITY.
がく WOBBLY
がく WOBBLY
AH... I CAN'T WALK...
ぷる SHAKEY
ぷる SHAKEY
ぷる SHAKEY
ぷる SHAKEY
ぷる SHAKEY
ぷる SHAKEY
ぷる SHAKEY
...
SHE LOOKS LIKE BAMBI...

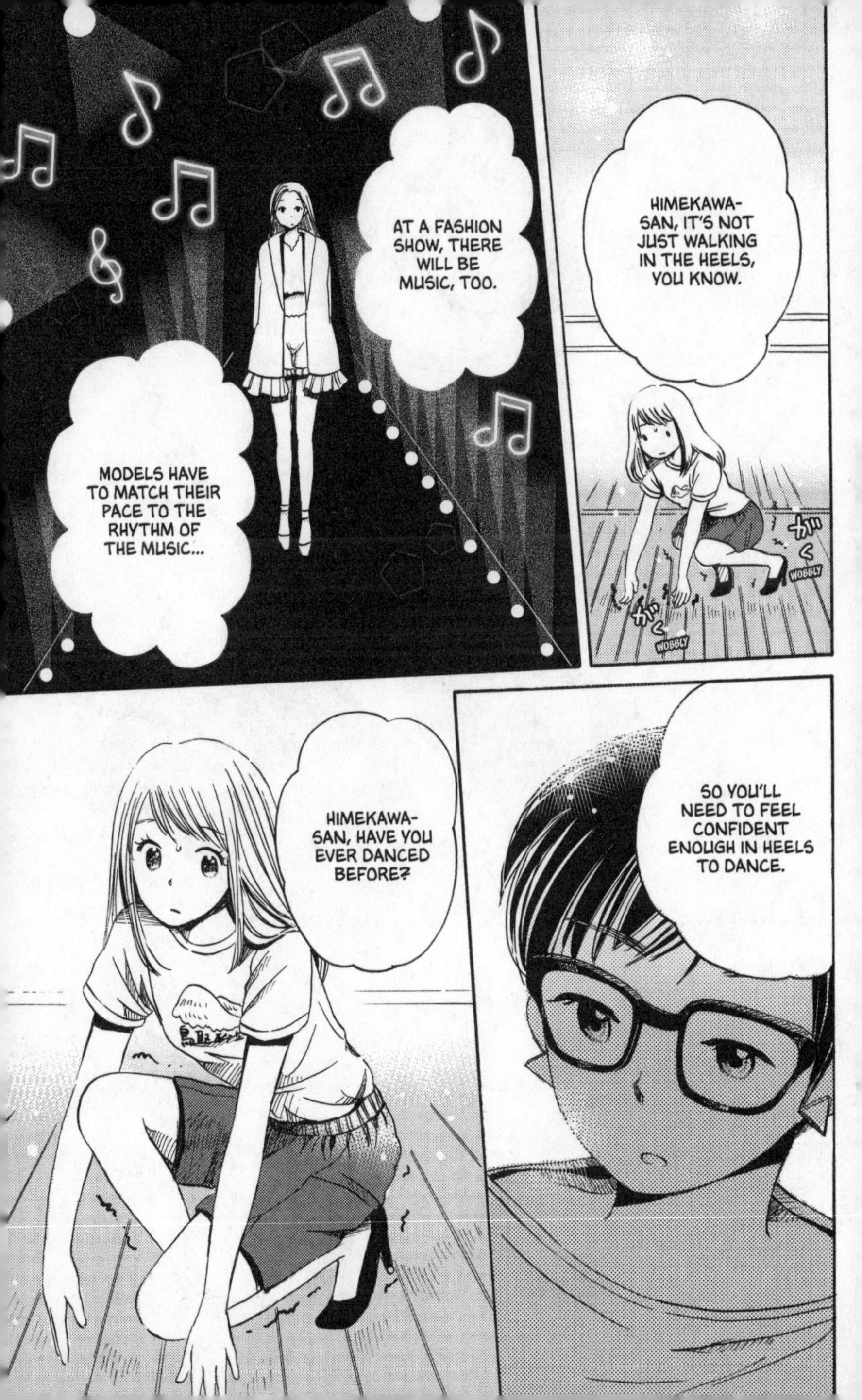
HIMEKAWA-SAN, IT'S NOT JUST WALKING IN THE HEELS, YOU KNOW.
WOBBLY
WOBBLY
AT A FASHION SHOW, THERE WILL BE MUSIC, TOO.
MODELS HAVE TO MATCH THEIR PACE TO THE RHYTHM OF THE MUSIC...
SO YOU'LL NEED TO FEEL CONFIDENT ENOUGH IN HEELS TO DANCE.
HIMEKAWA-SAN, HAVE YOU EVER DANCED BEFORE?

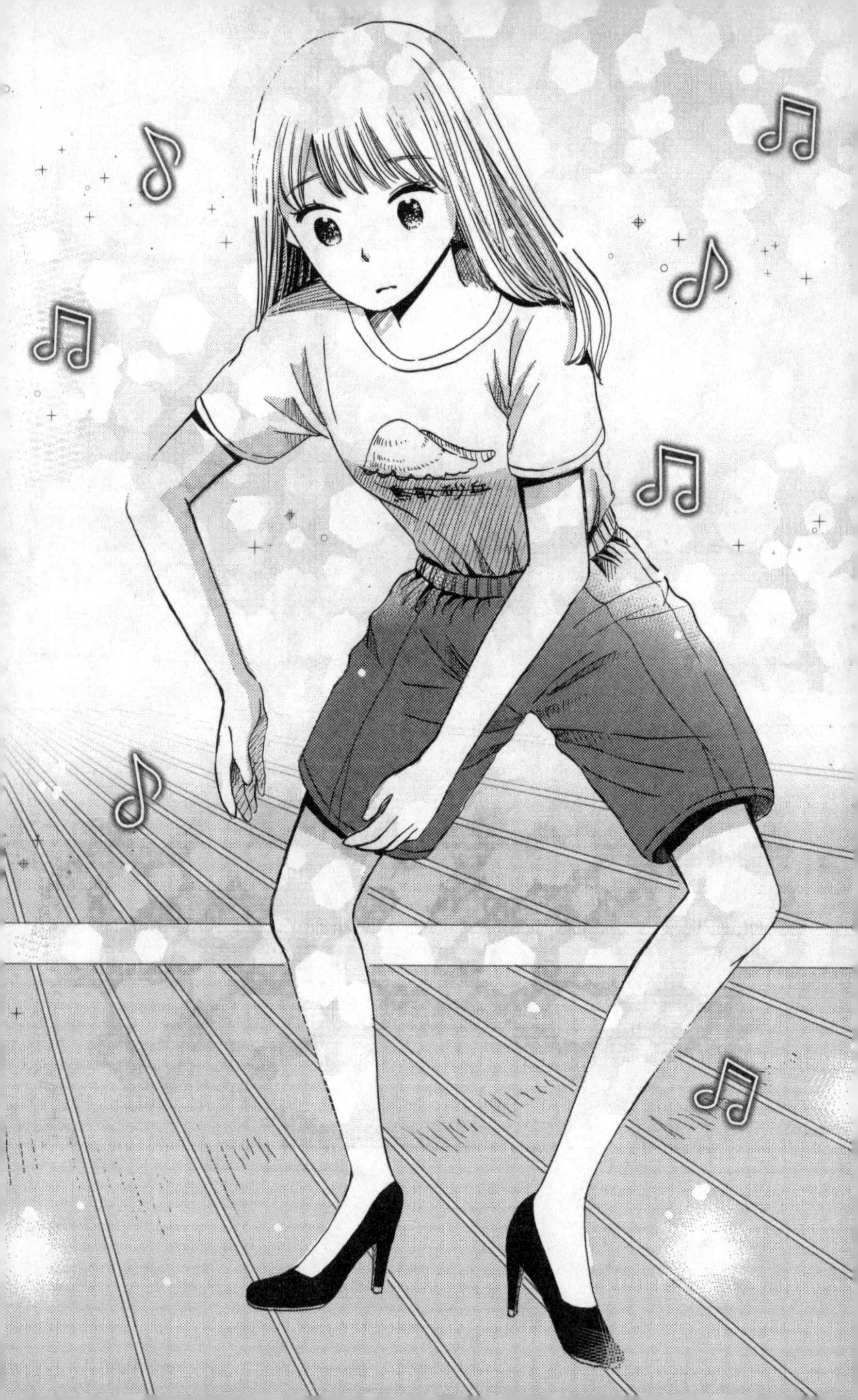

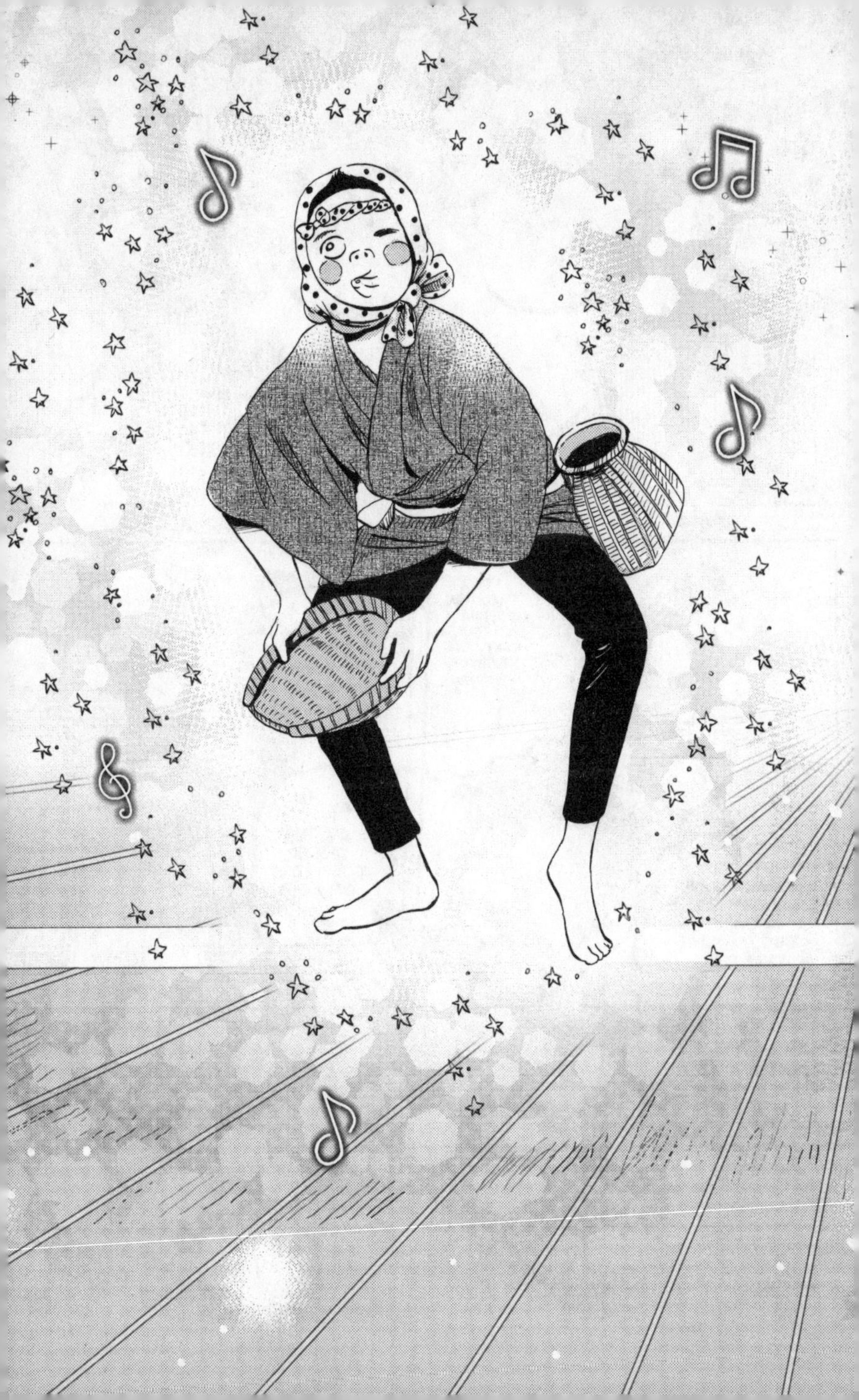

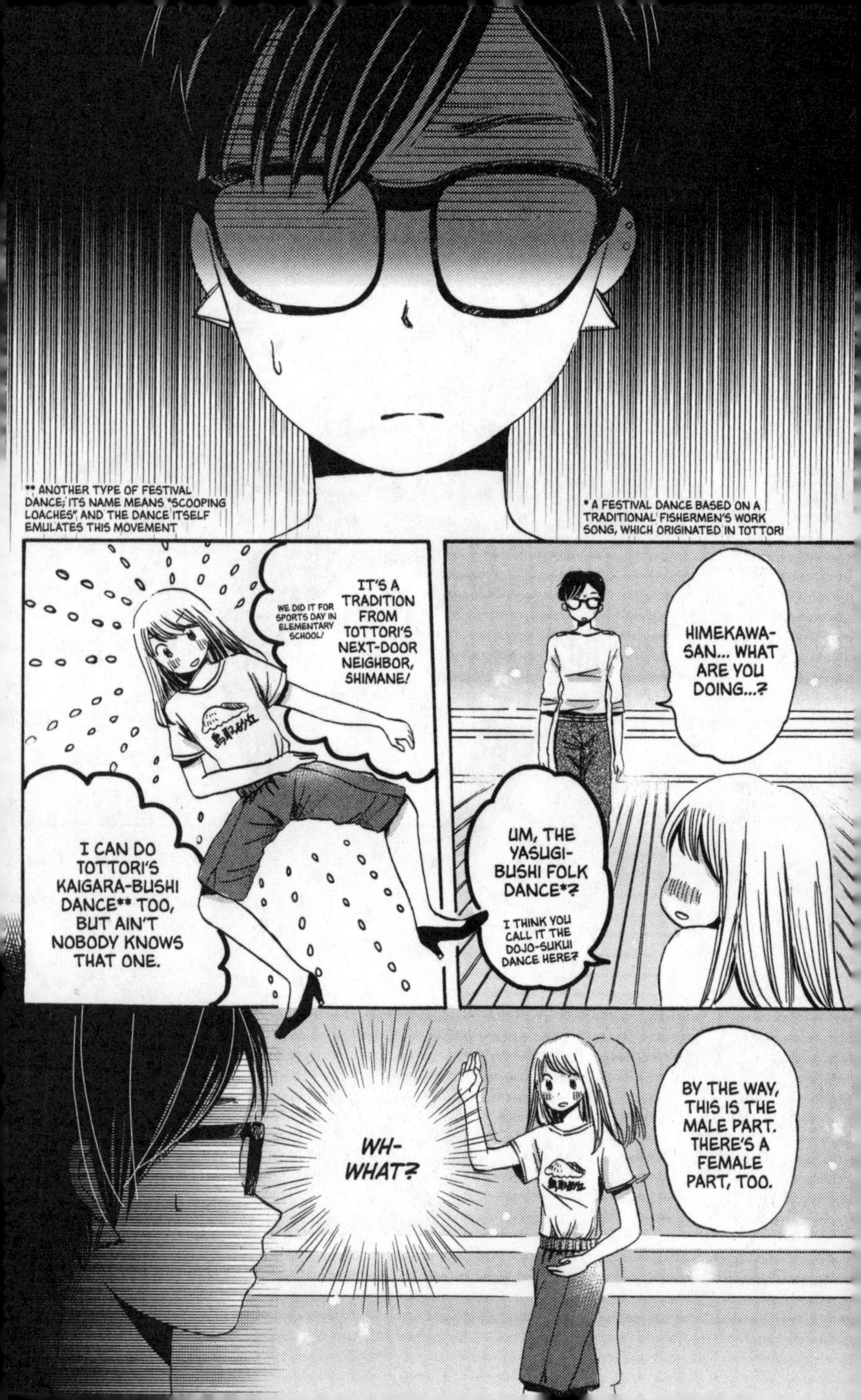
* A FESTIVAL DANCE BASED ON A TRADITIONAL FISHERMEN'S WORK SONG, WHICH ORIGINATED IN TOTTORI
** ANOTHER TYPE OF FESTIVAL DANCE; ITS NAME MEANS "SCOOPING LOACHES", AND THE DANCE ITSELF EMULATES THIS MOVEMENT
HIMEKAWA-SAN... WHAT ARE YOU DOING...?
UM, THE YASUGI-BUSHI FOLK DANCE*?
I THINK YOU CALL IT THE DOJO-SUKUI DANCE HERE?
IT'S A TRADITION FROM TOTTORI'S NEXT-DOOR NEIGHBOR, SHIMANE!
WE DID IT FOR SPORTS DAY IN ELEMENTARY SCHOOL!
I CAN DO TOTTORI'S KAIGARA-BUSHI DANCE** TOO, BUT AIN'T NOBODY KNOWS THAT ONE.
BY THE WAY, THIS IS THE MALE PART. THERE'S A FEMALE PART, TOO.
WH-WHAT?

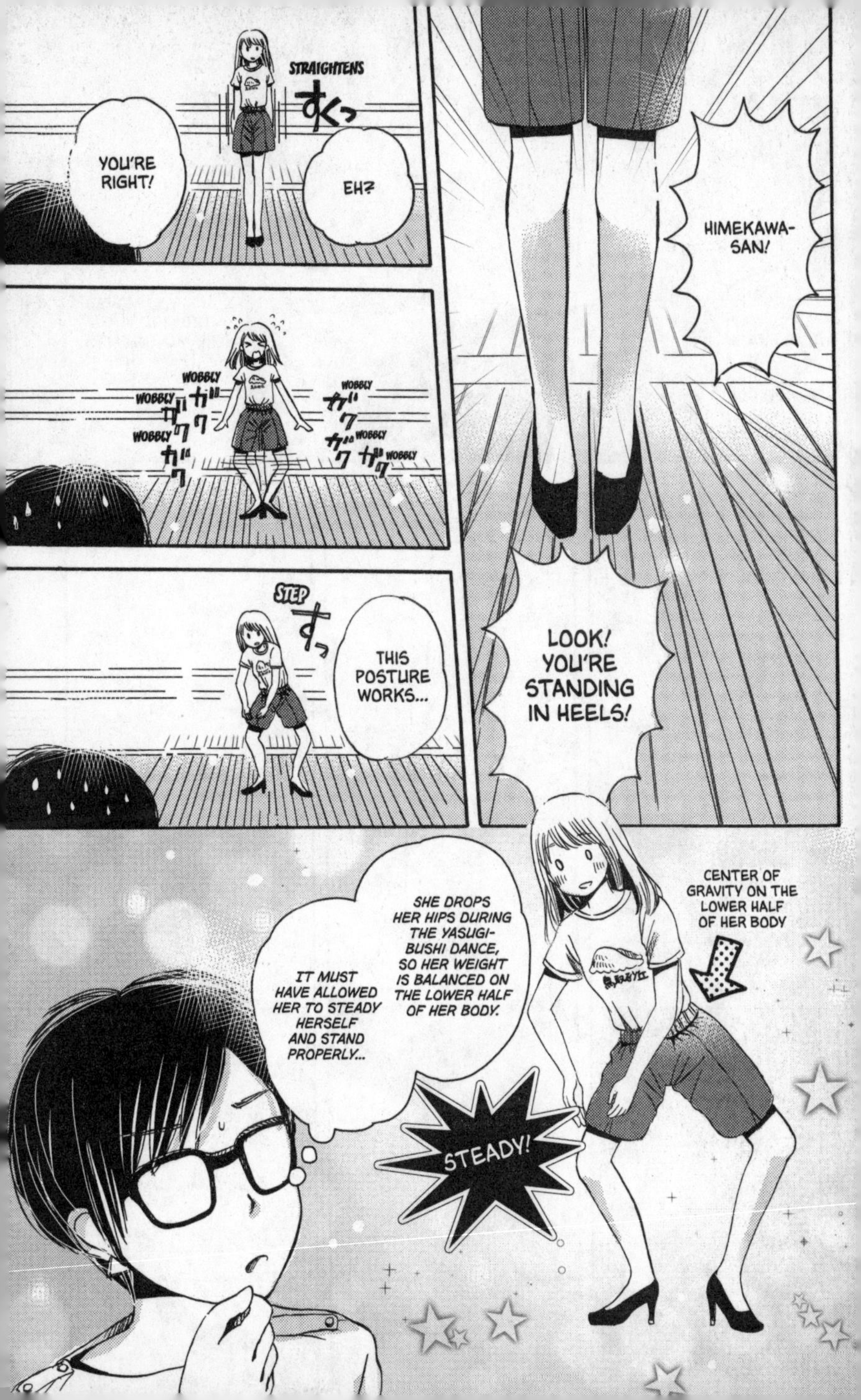
HIMEKAWA-SAN!
LOOK! YOU'RE STANDING IN HEELS!
STRAIGHTENS
すくっ
EH?
YOU'RE RIGHT!
WOBBLY
ガク
WOBBLY
ガク
WOBBLY
ガク
WOBBLY
ガク
WOBBLY
ガク
WOBBLY
ガク
STEP
すっ
THIS POSTURE WORKS...
CENTER OF GRAVITY ON THE LOWER HALF OF HER BODY
SHE DROPS HER HIPS DURING THE YASUGI-BUSHI DANCE, SO HER WEIGHT IS BALANCED ON THE LOWER HALF OF HER BODY.
IT MUST HAVE ALLOWED HER TO STEADY HERSELF AND STAND PROPERLY...
STEADY!

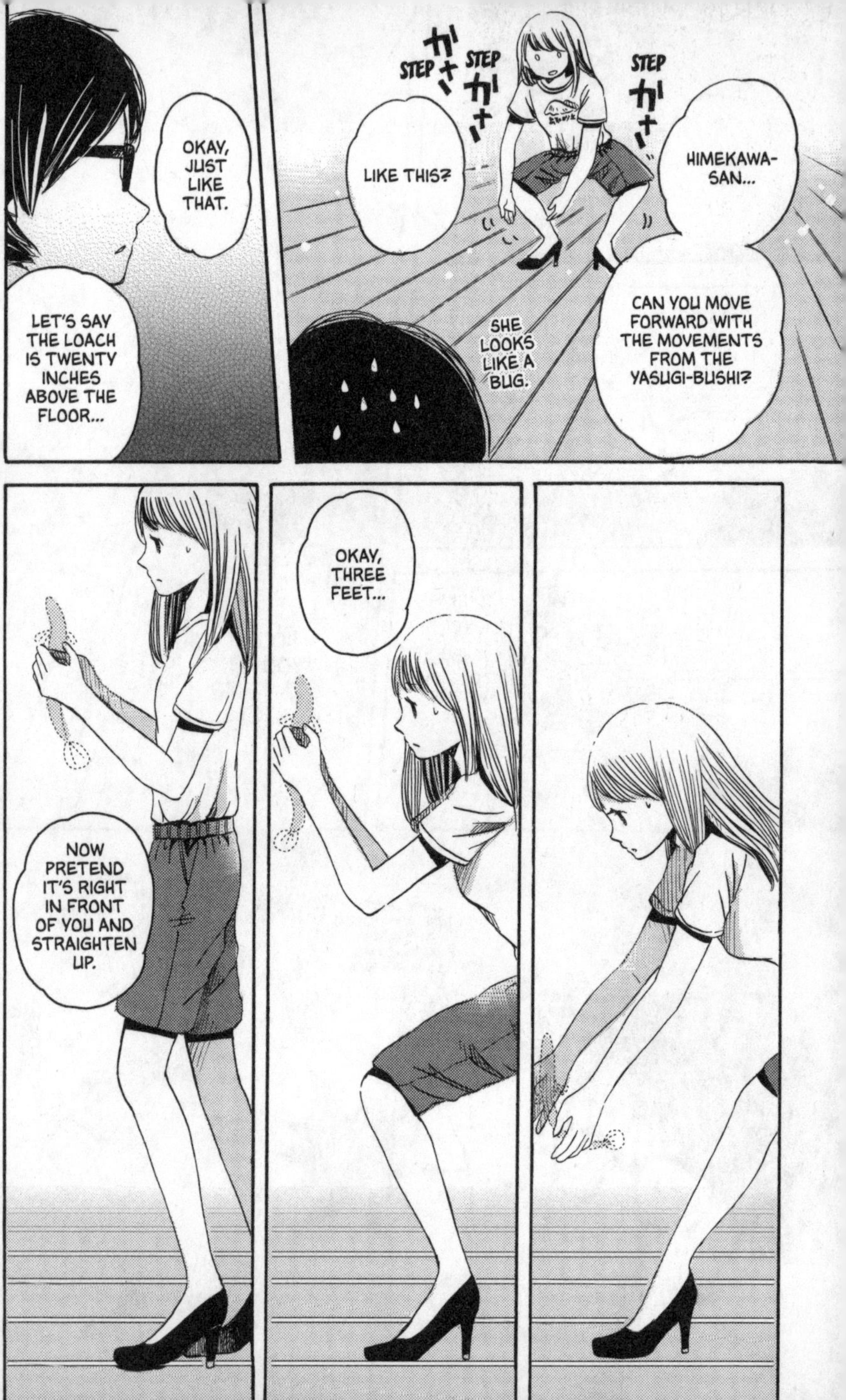

STEP がさ
HIMEKAWA-SAN...
CAN YOU MOVE FORWARD WITH THE MOVEMENTS FROM THE YASUGI-BUSHI?
STEP がさ
STEP がさ
LIKE THIS?
SHE LOOKS LIKE A BUG.
OKAY, JUST LIKE THAT.
LET'S SAY THE LOACH IS TWENTY INCHES ABOVE THE FLOOR...
OKAY, THREE FEET...
NOW PRETEND IT'S RIGHT IN FRONT OF YOU AND STRAIGHTEN UP.

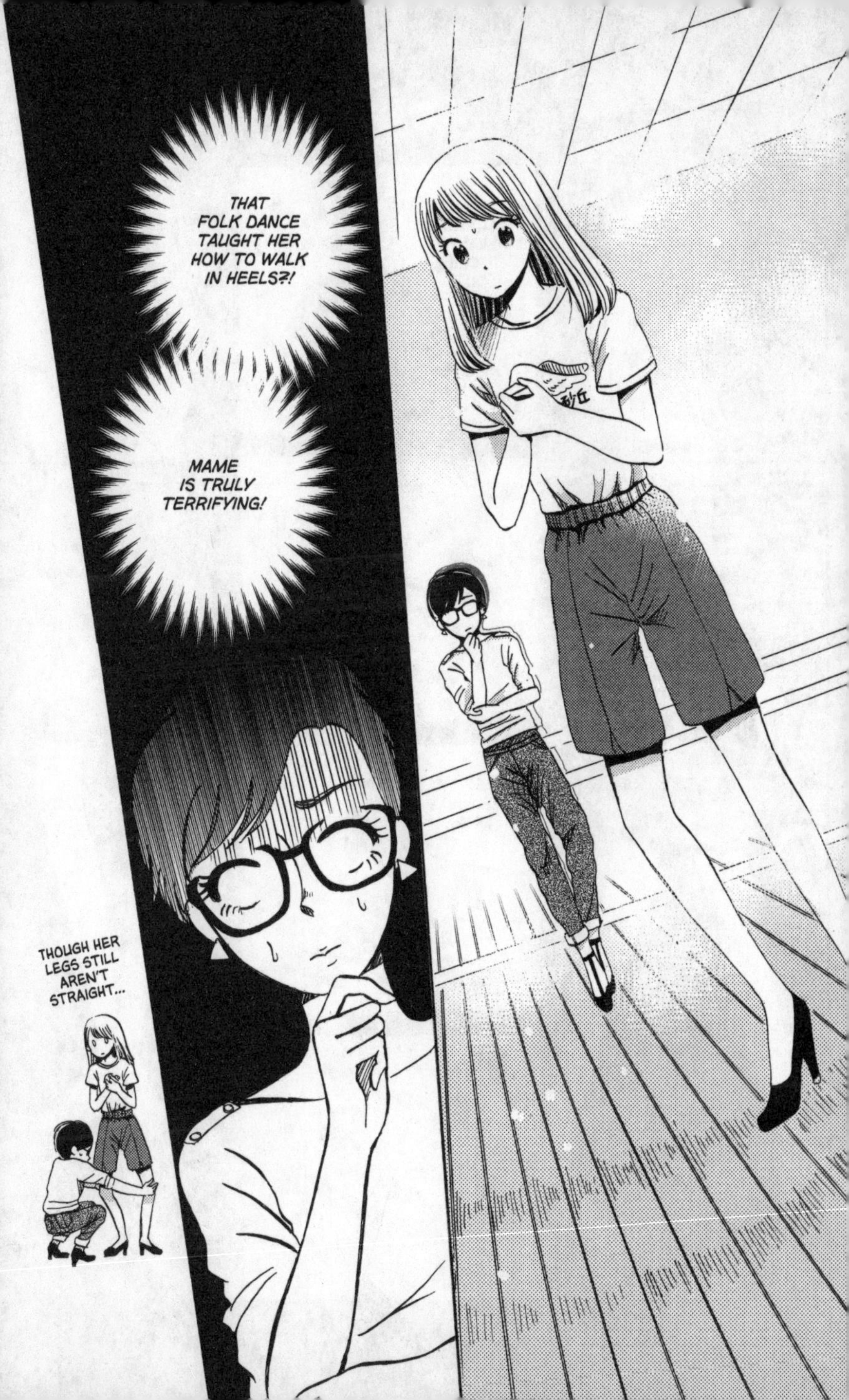
THAT FOLK DANCE TAUGHT HER HOW TO WALK IN HEELS?!
MAME IS TRULY TERRIFYING!
THOUGH HER LEGS STILL AREN'T STRAIGHT...

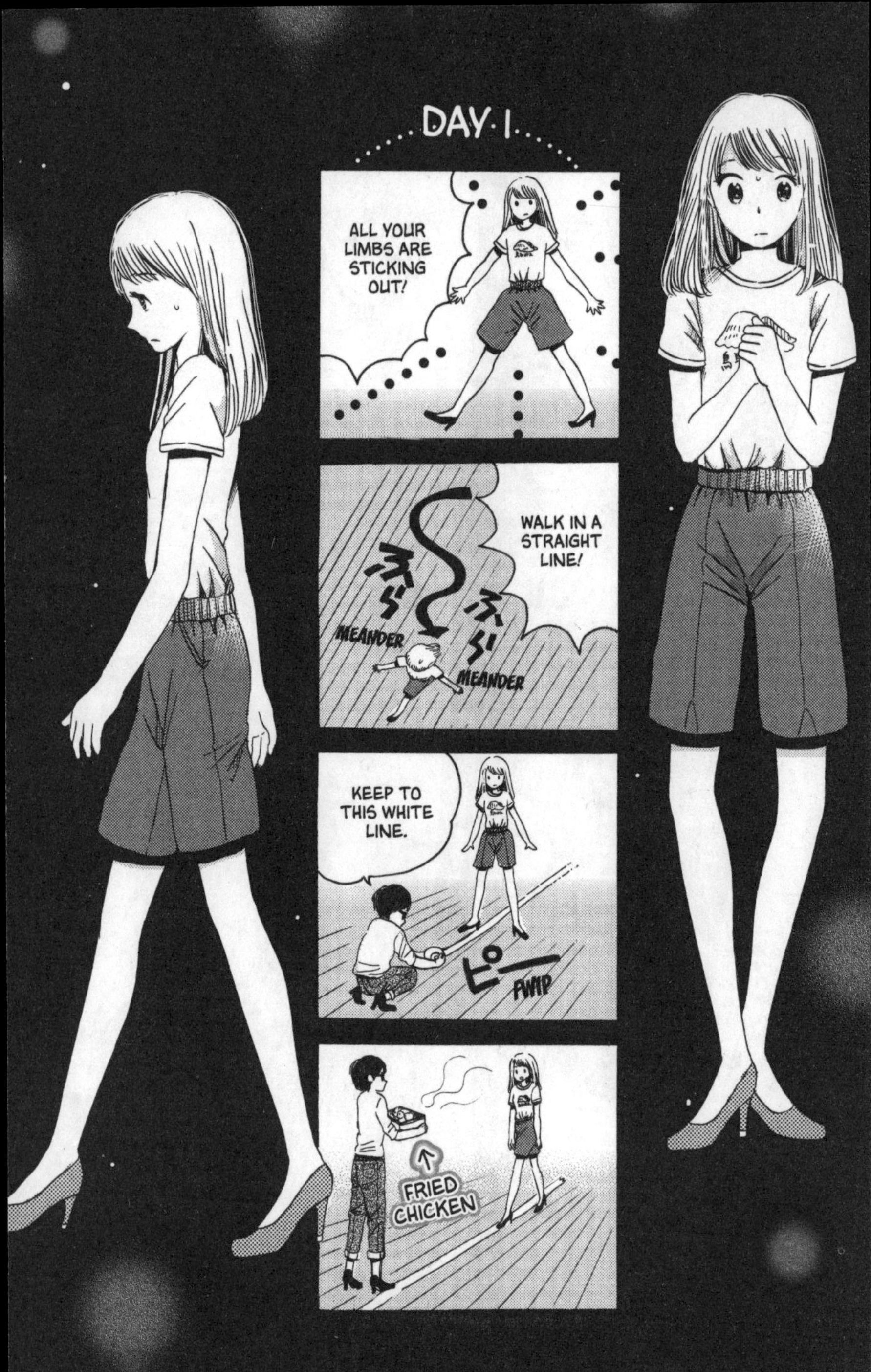
DAY 1
ALL YOUR LIMBS ARE STICKING OUT!
WALK IN A STRAIGHT LINE!
ふら MEANDER
ふら MEANDER
KEEP TO THIS WHITE LINE.
ピー PWIP
FRIED CHICKEN

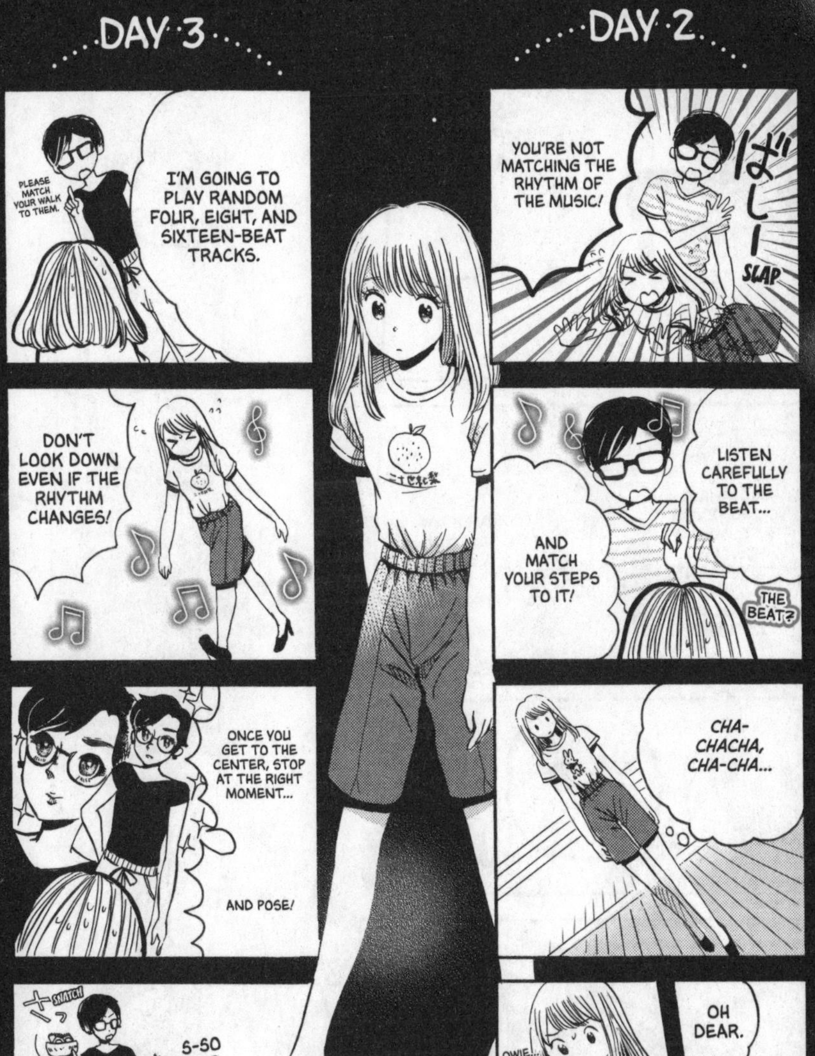
DAY 2
YOU'RE NOT MATCHING THE RHYTHM OF THE MUSIC!
ばしー
SLAP
LISTEN CAREFULLY TO THE BEAT...
AND MATCH YOUR STEPS TO IT!
THE BEAT?
CHA-CHACHA, CHA-CHA...
OH DEAR.
SO MANY BLISTERS...
OWIE...
ふー
BLOW
DAY 3
I'M GOING TO PLAY RANDOM FOUR, EIGHT, AND SIXTEEN-BEAT TRACKS.
PLEASE MATCH YOUR WALK TO THEM.
DON'T LOOK DOWN EVEN IF THE RHYTHM CHANGES!
ONCE YOU GET TO THE CENTER, STOP AT THE RIGHT MOMENT...
AND POSE!
S-SO TIRED...
SNATCH
NO SNACKS!

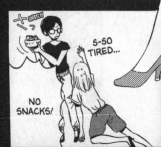

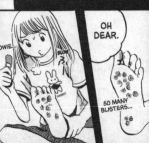

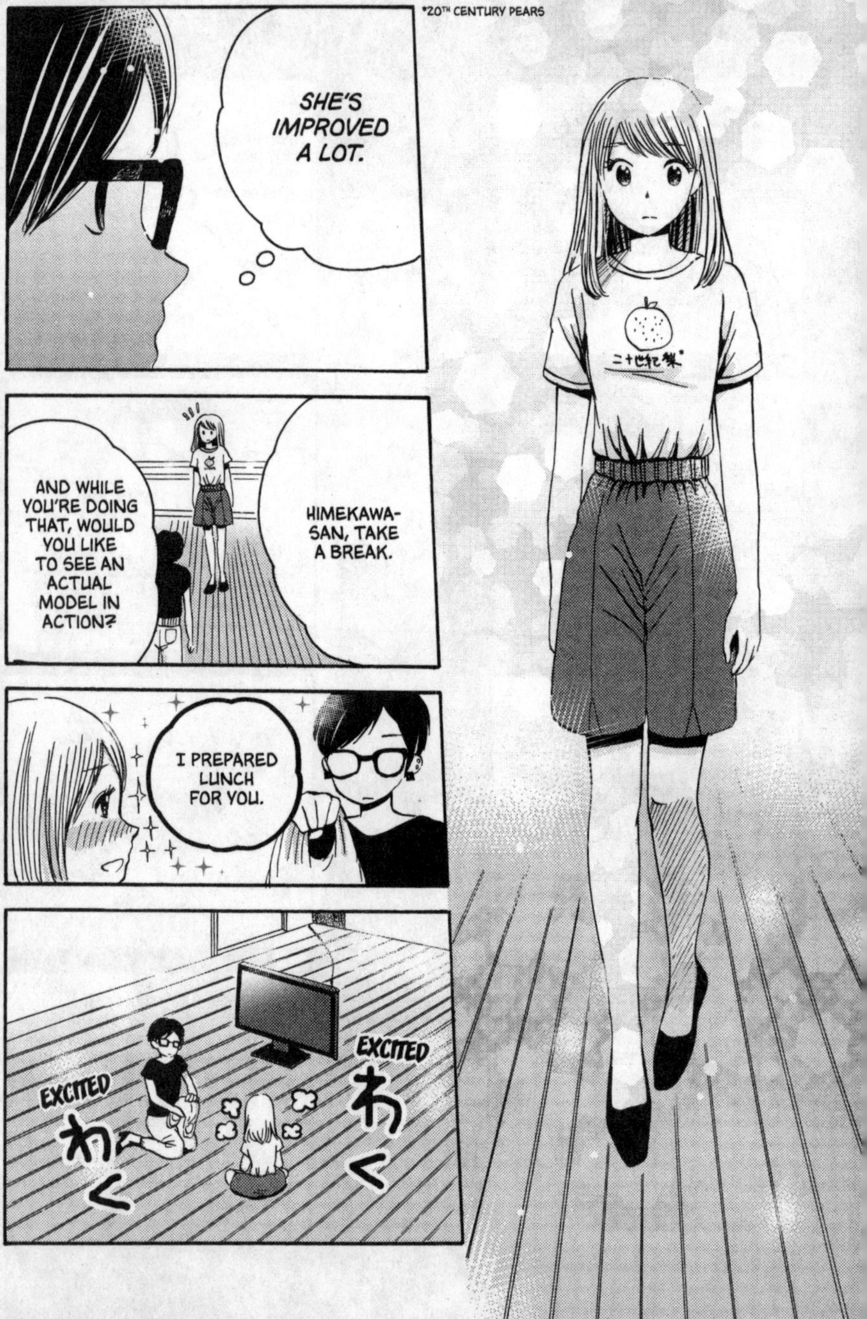
二十世紀梨*
*20TH CENTURY PEARS
SHE'S IMPROVED A LOT.
HIMEKAWA-SAN, TAKE A BREAK.
AND WHILE YOU'RE DOING THAT, WOULD YOU LIKE TO SEE AN ACTUAL MODEL IN ACTION?
I PREPARED LUNCH FOR YOU.
EXCITED
わく
EXCITED
わく

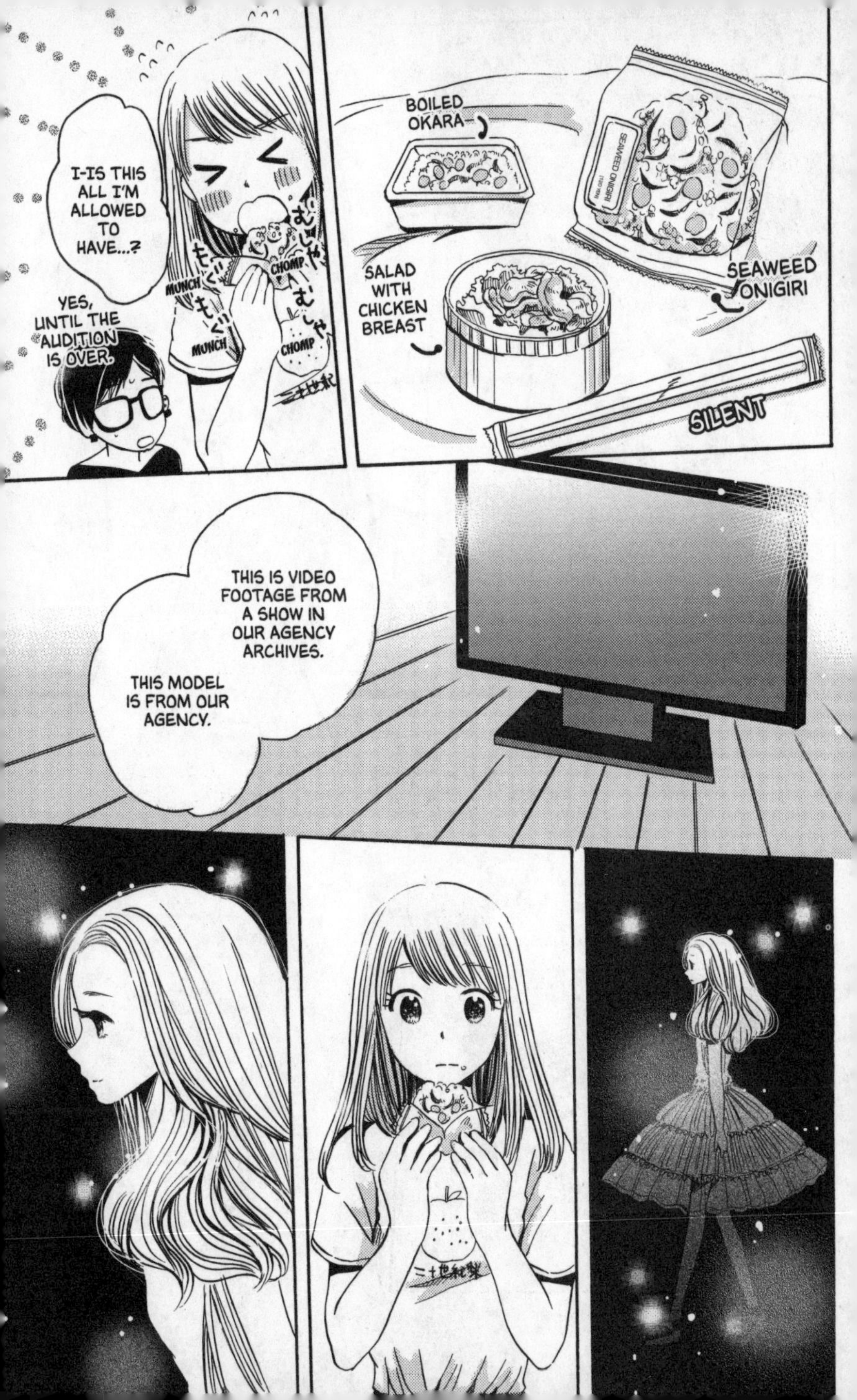
BOILED OKARA
SEAWEED ONIGIRI
SEAWEED ONIGIRI
SALAD WITH CHICKEN BREAST
SILENT
I-IS THIS ALL I'M ALLOWED TO HAVE...?
MUNCH
MUNCH
CHOMP
CHOMP
YES, UNTIL THE AUDITION IS OVER.
THIS IS VIDEO FOOTAGE FROM A SHOW IN OUR AGENCY ARCHIVES.
THIS MODEL IS FROM OUR AGENCY.

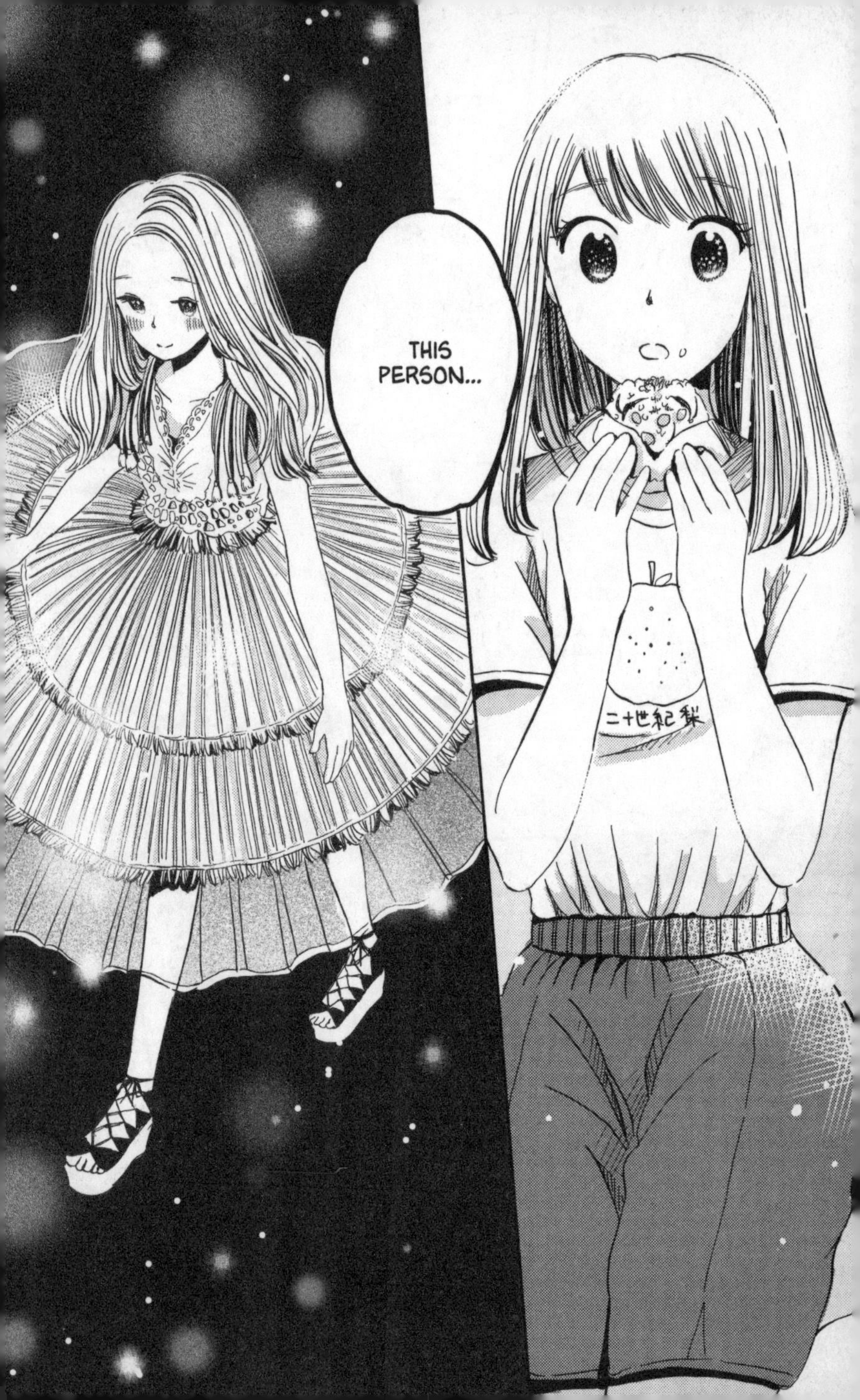
THIS PERSON...
二十世紀梨

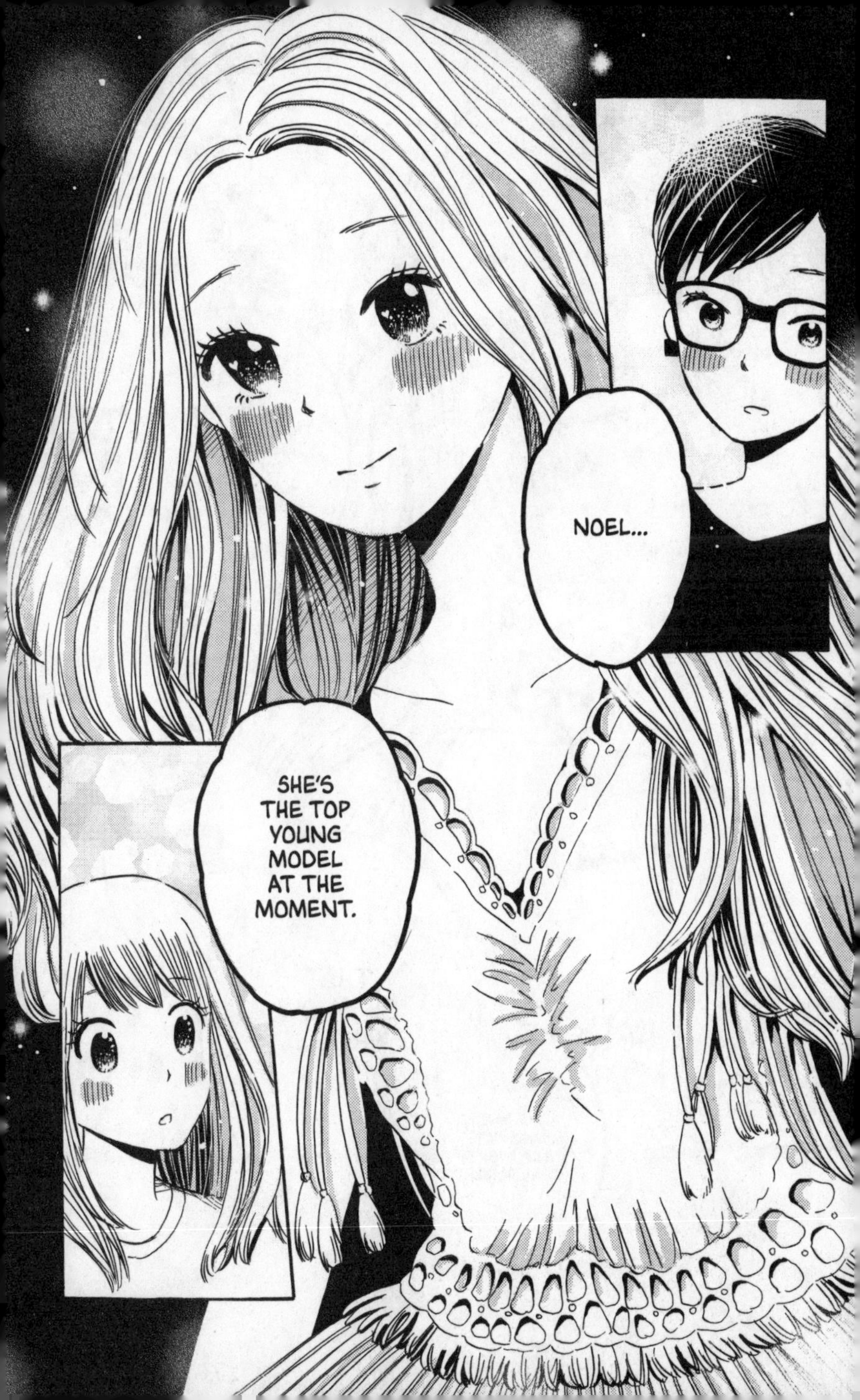
NOEL...
SHE'S THE TOP YOUNG MODEL AT THE MOMENT.

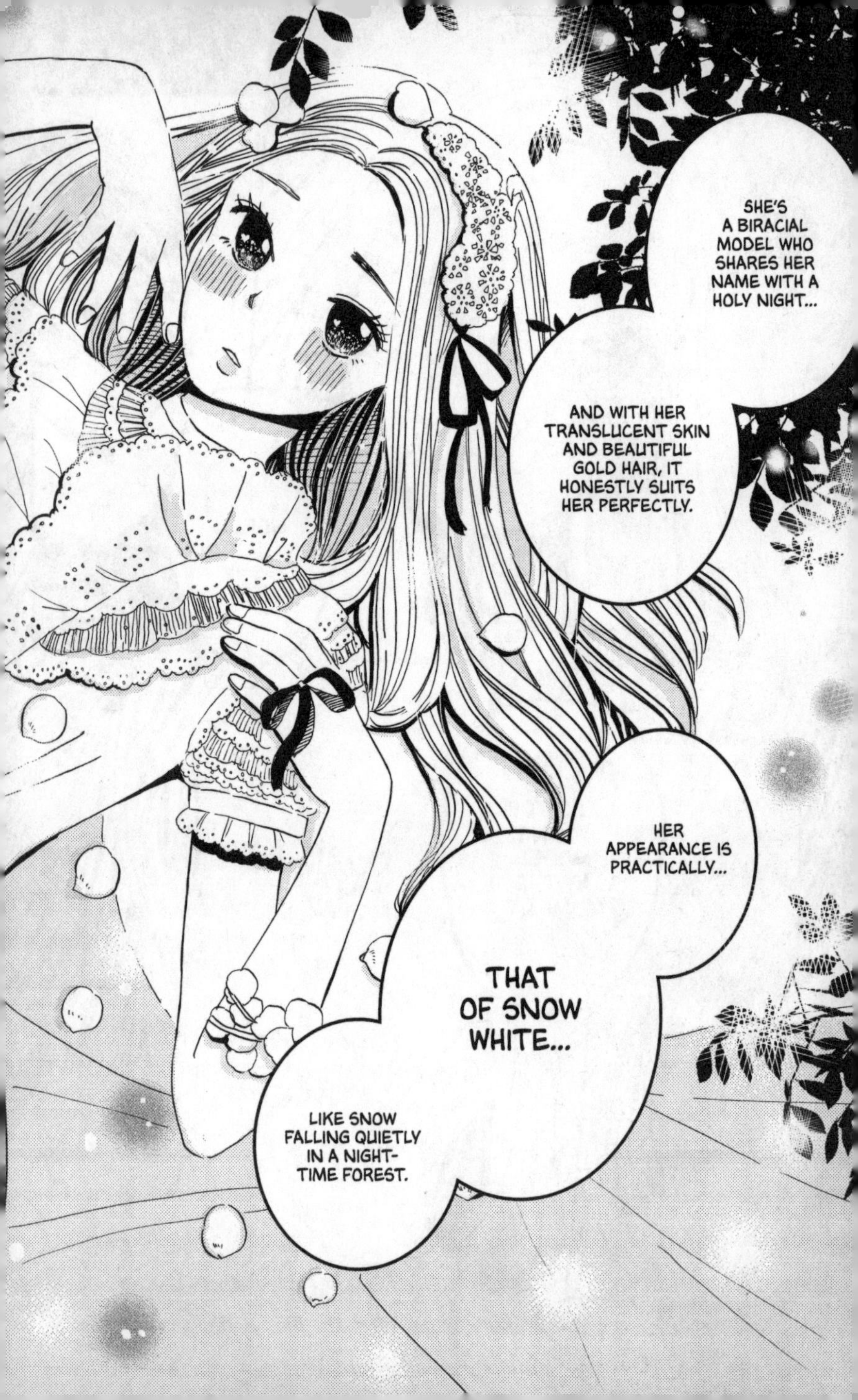
SHE'S A BIRACIAL MODEL WHO SHARES HER NAME WITH A HOLY NIGHT...
AND WITH HER TRANSLUCENT SKIN AND BEAUTIFUL GOLD HAIR, IT HONESTLY SUITS HER PERFECTLY.
HER APPEARANCE IS PRACTICALLY...
THAT OF SNOW WHITE...
LIKE SNOW FALLING QUIETLY IN A NIGHT-TIME FOREST.

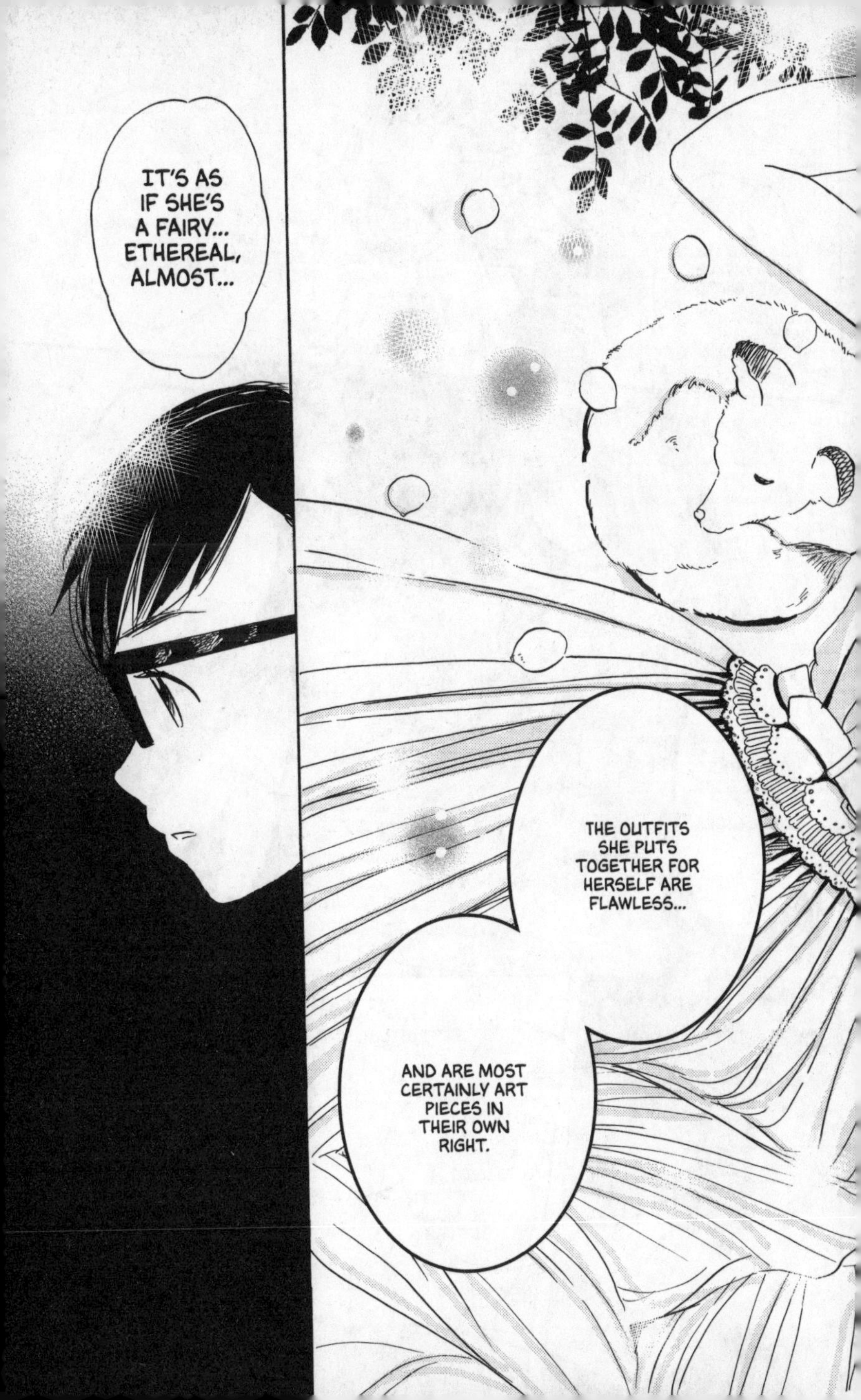
THE OUTFITS SHE PUTS TOGETHER FOR HERSELF ARE FLAWLESS...
AND ARE MOST CERTAINLY ART PIECES IN THEIR OWN RIGHT.
IT'S AS IF SHE'S A FAIRY... ETHEREAL, ALMOST...

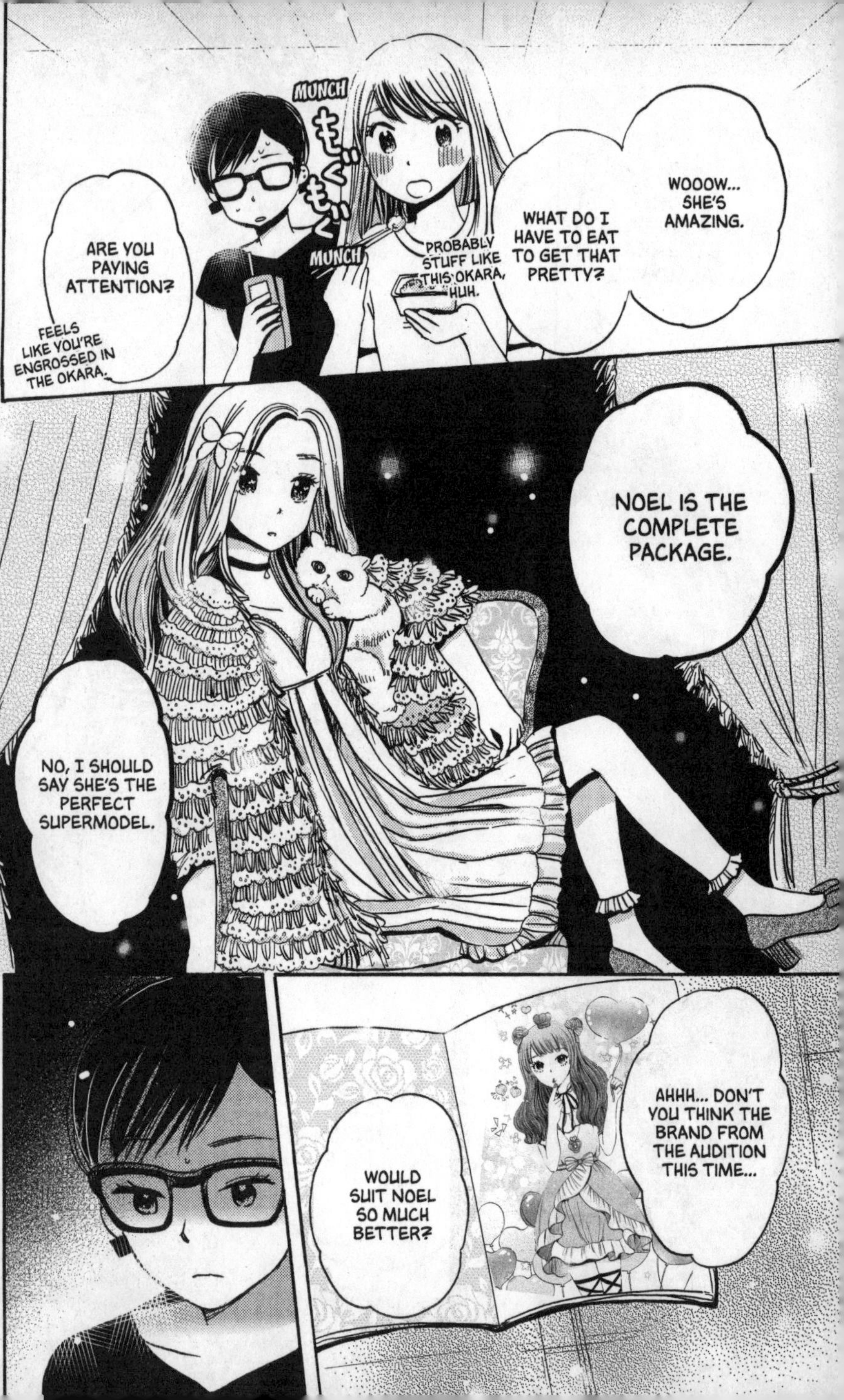
WOOOW... SHE'S AMAZING.
WHAT DO I HAVE TO EAT TO GET THAT PRETTY?
PROBABLY STUFF LIKE THIS OKARA, HUH.
MUNCH
もぐもぐ
MUNCH
ARE YOU PAYING ATTENTION?
FEELS LIKE YOU'RE ENGROSSED IN THE OKARA.
NOEL IS THE COMPLETE PACKAGE.
NO, I SHOULD SAY SHE'S THE PERFECT SUPERMODEL.
AHHH... DON'T YOU THINK THE BRAND FROM THE AUDITION THIS TIME...
WOULD SUIT NOEL SO MUCH BETTER?

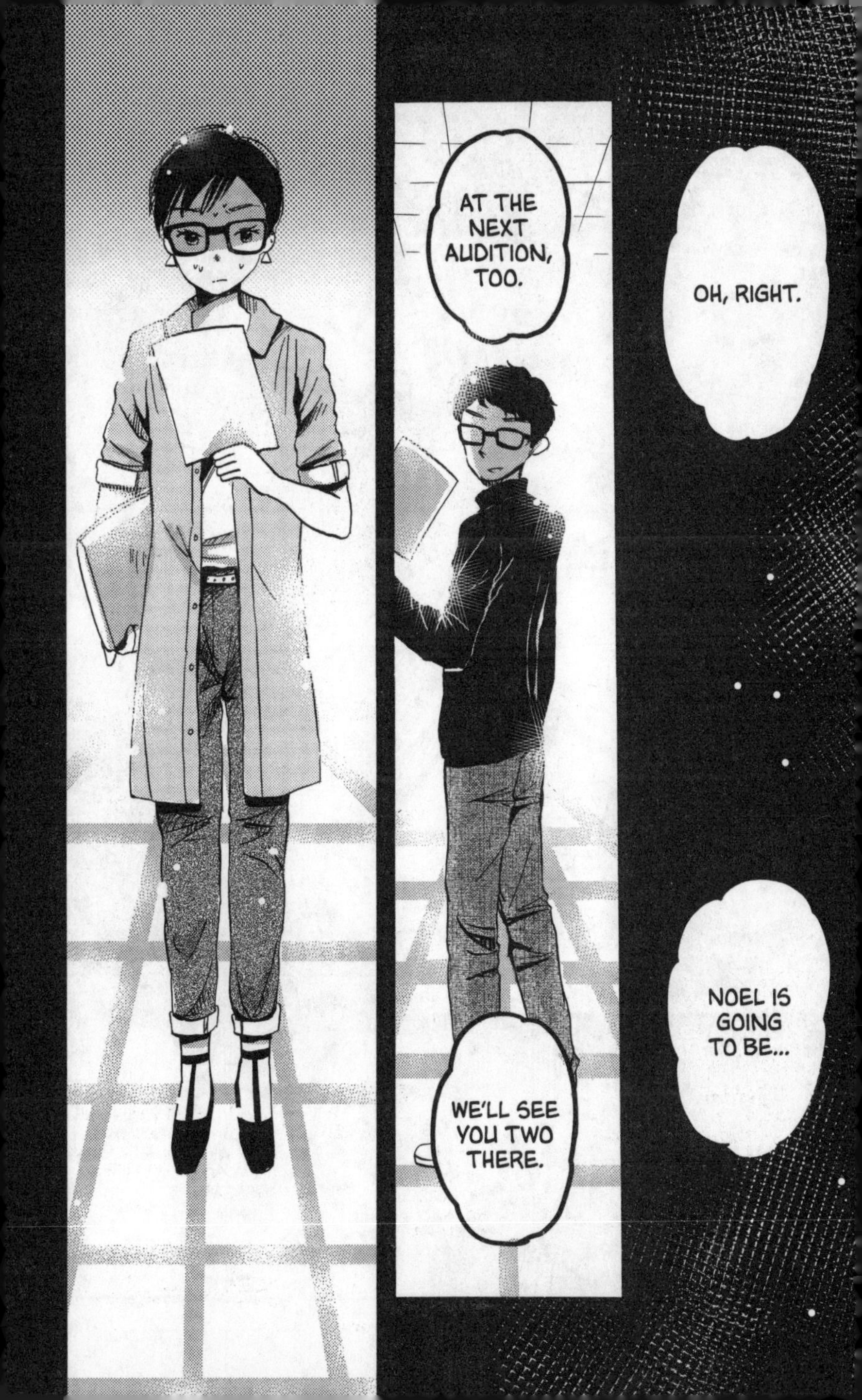
OH, RIGHT.
NOEL IS GOING TO BE...
AT THE NEXT AUDITION, TOO.
WE'LL SEE YOU TWO THERE.

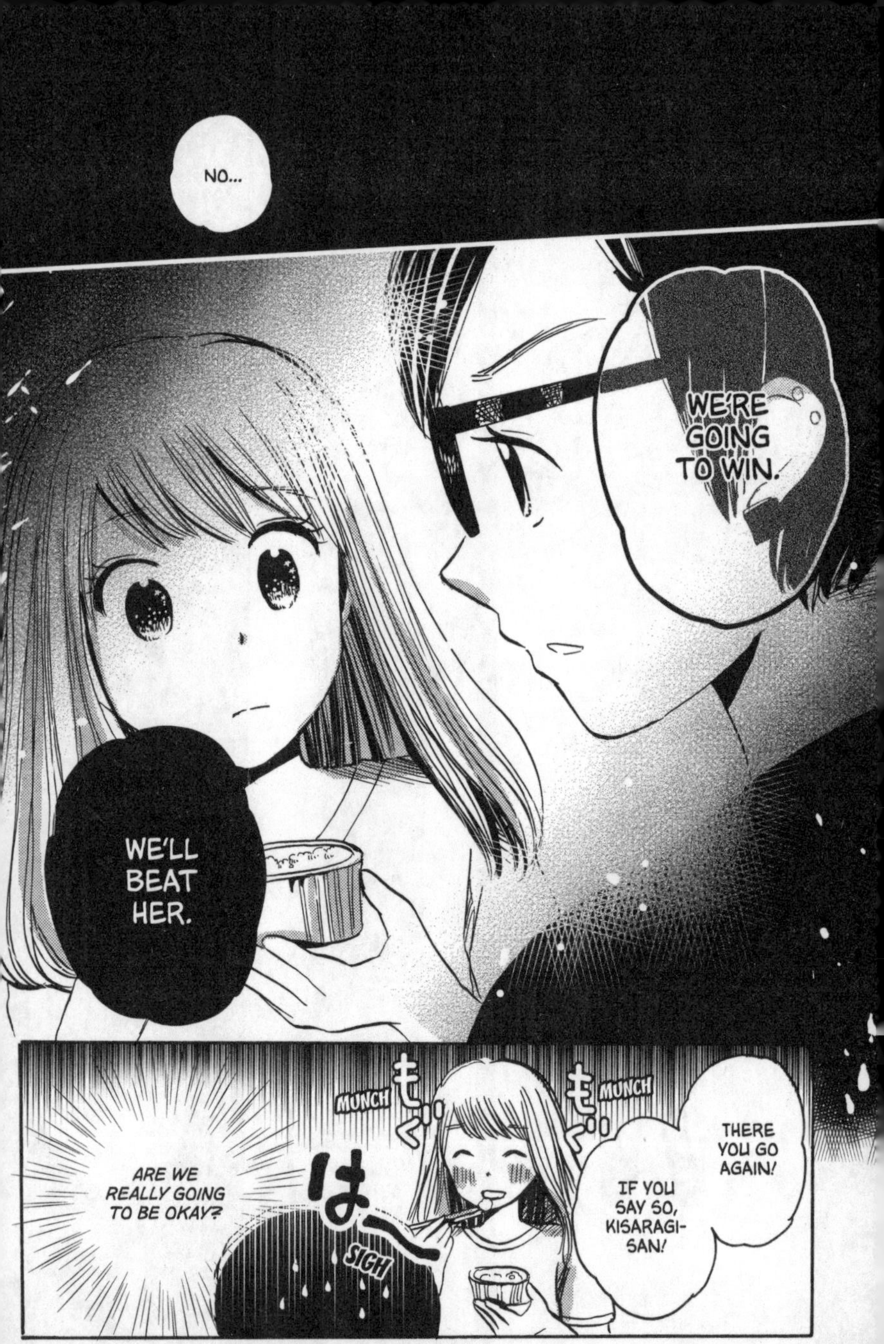
NO...
WE'RE GOING TO WIN.
WE'LL BEAT HER.
THERE YOU GO AGAIN!
IF YOU SAY SO, KISARAGI-SAN!
もぐ MUNCH
もぐ MUNCH
はー SIGH
ARE WE REALLY GOING TO BE OKAY?

MAME
coordinate

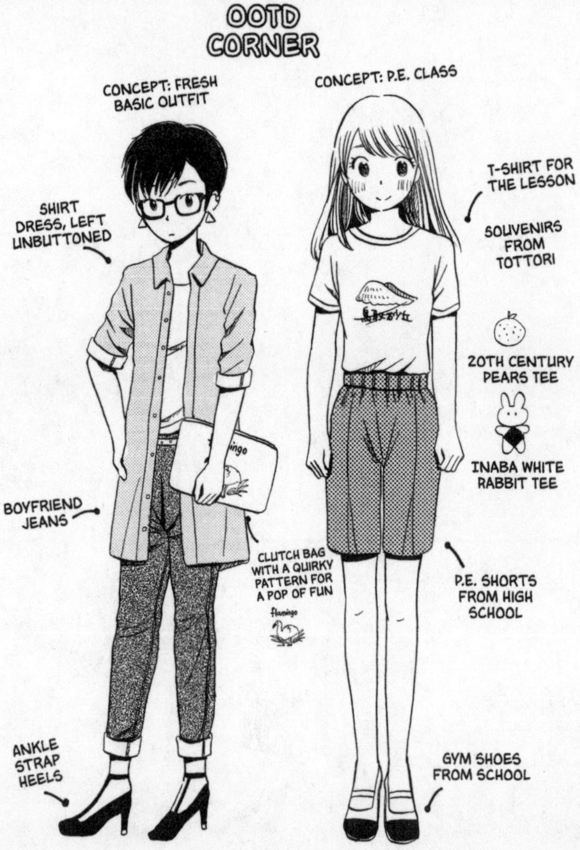
OOTD
CORNER
CONCEPT: P.E. CLASS
T-SHIRT FOR THE LESSON
SOUVENIRS FROM TOTTORI
20TH CENTURY PEARS TEE
INABA WHITE RABBIT TEE
P.E. SHORTS FROM HIGH SCHOOL
GYM SHOES FROM SCHOOL
CONCEPT: FRESH BASIC OUTFIT
SHIRT DRESS, LEFT UNBUTTONED
BOYFRIEND JEANS
CLUTCH BAG WITH A QUIRKY PATTERN FOR A POP OF FUN
flamingo
ANKLE STRAP HEELS

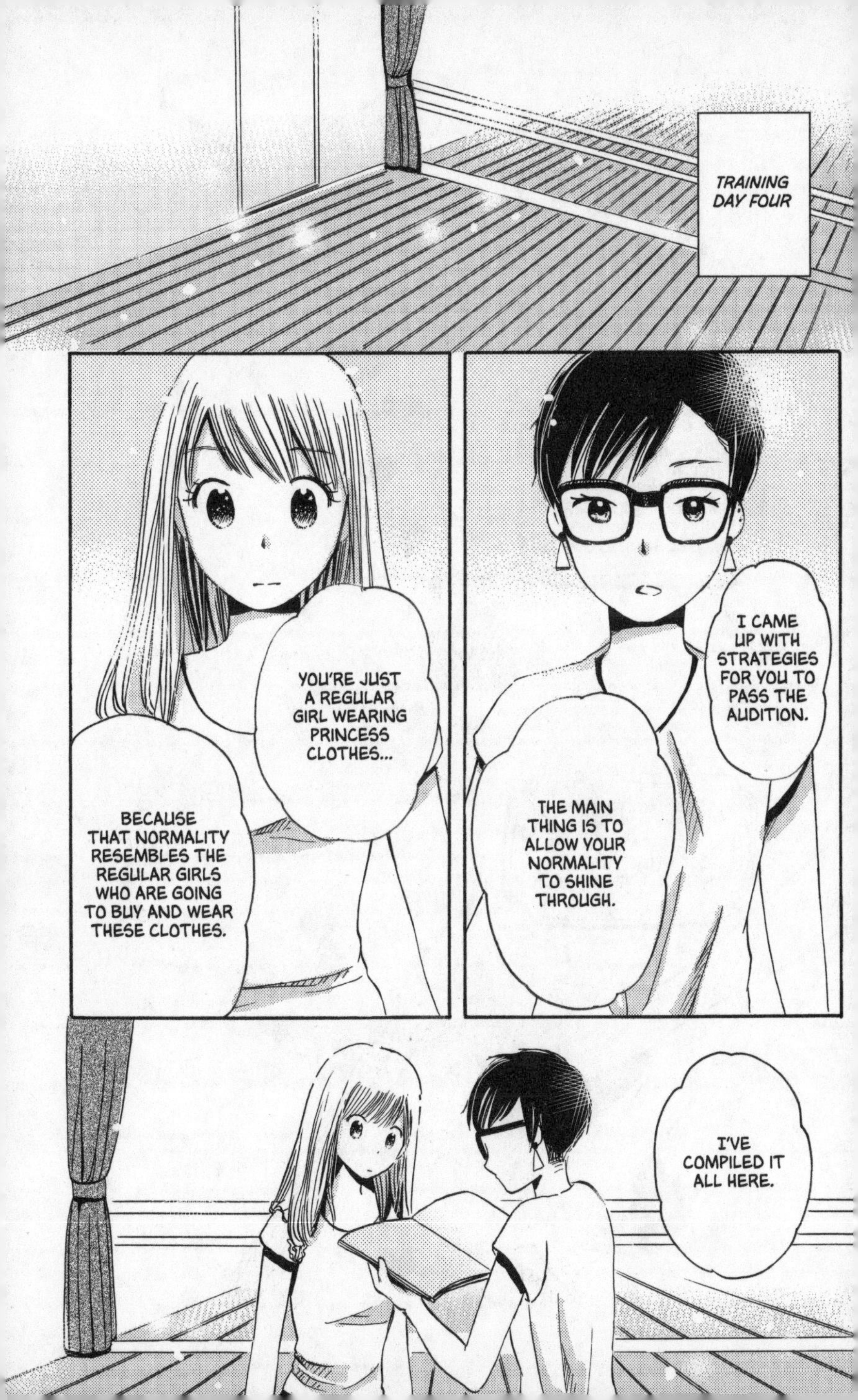
TRAINING DAY FOUR
I CAME UP WITH STRATEGIES FOR YOU TO PASS THE AUDITION.
THE MAIN THING IS TO ALLOW YOUR NORMALITY TO SHINE THROUGH.
YOU'RE JUST A REGULAR GIRL WEARING PRINCESS CLOTHES...
BECAUSE THAT NORMALITY RESEMBLES THE REGULAR GIRLS WHO ARE GOING TO BUY AND WEAR THESE CLOTHES.
I'VE COMPILED IT ALL HERE.

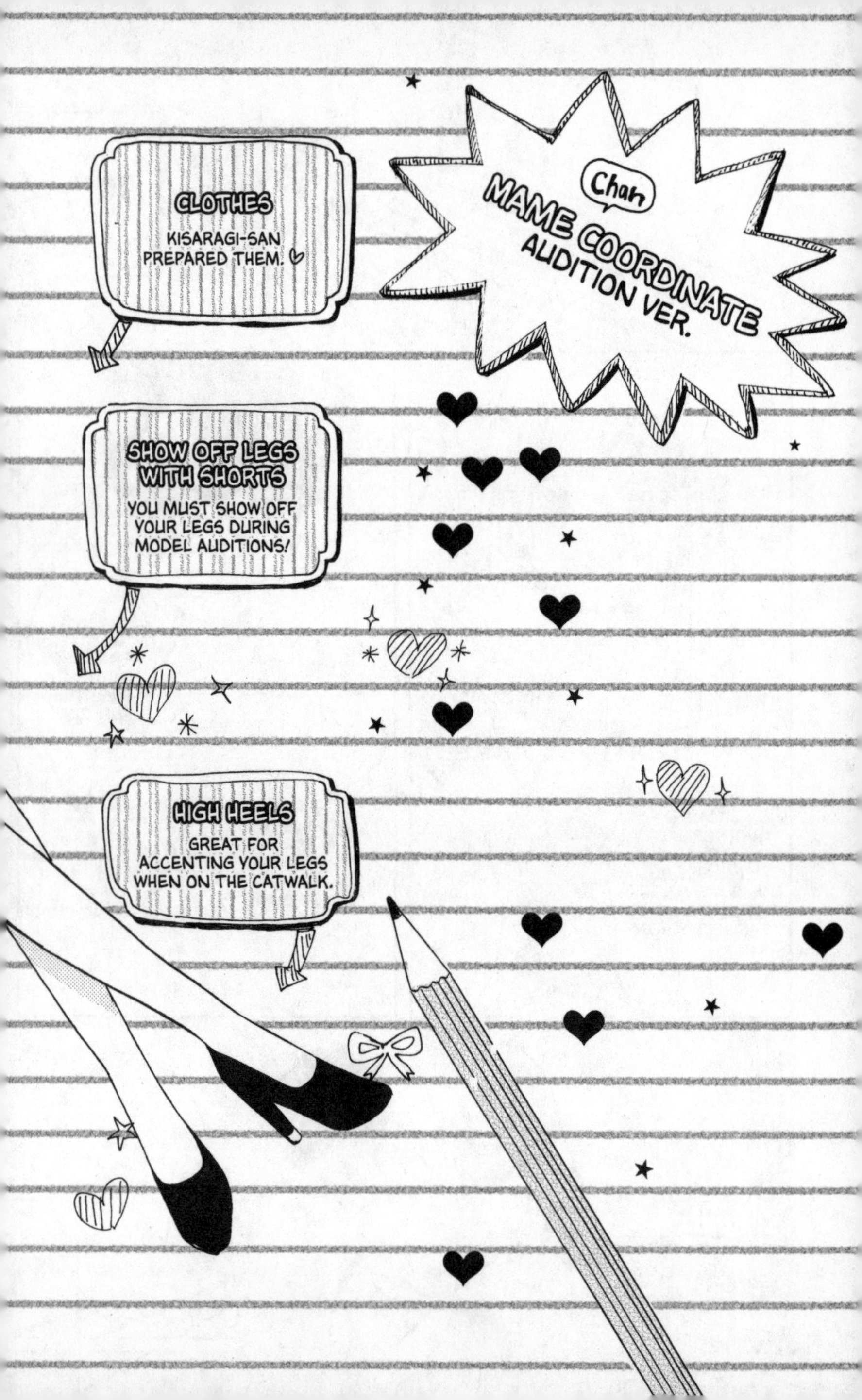
Chan
MAME COORDINATE
AUDITION VER.
CLOTHES
KISARAGI-SAN PREPARED THEM.
SHOW OFF LEGS WITH SHORTS
YOU MUST SHOW OFF YOUR LEGS DURING MODEL AUDITIONS!
HIGH HEELS
GREAT FOR ACCENTING YOUR LEGS WHEN ON THE CATWALK.

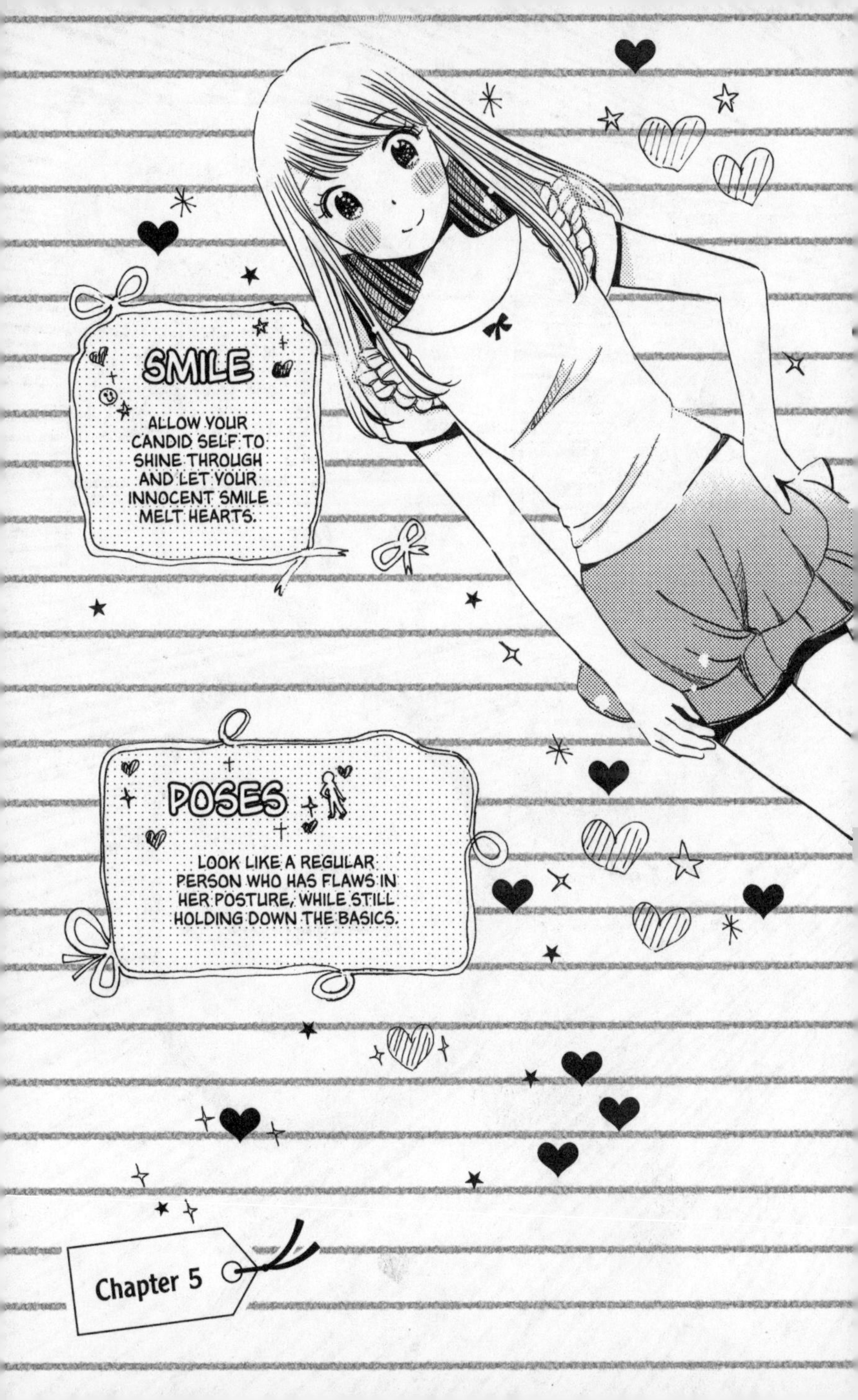
SMILE
ALLOW YOUR CANDID SELF TO SHINE THROUGH AND LET YOUR INNOCENT SMILE MELT HEARTS.
POSES
LOOK LIKE A REGULAR PERSON WHO HAS FLAWS IN HER POSTURE, WHILE STILL HOLDING DOWN THE BASICS.
Chapter 5

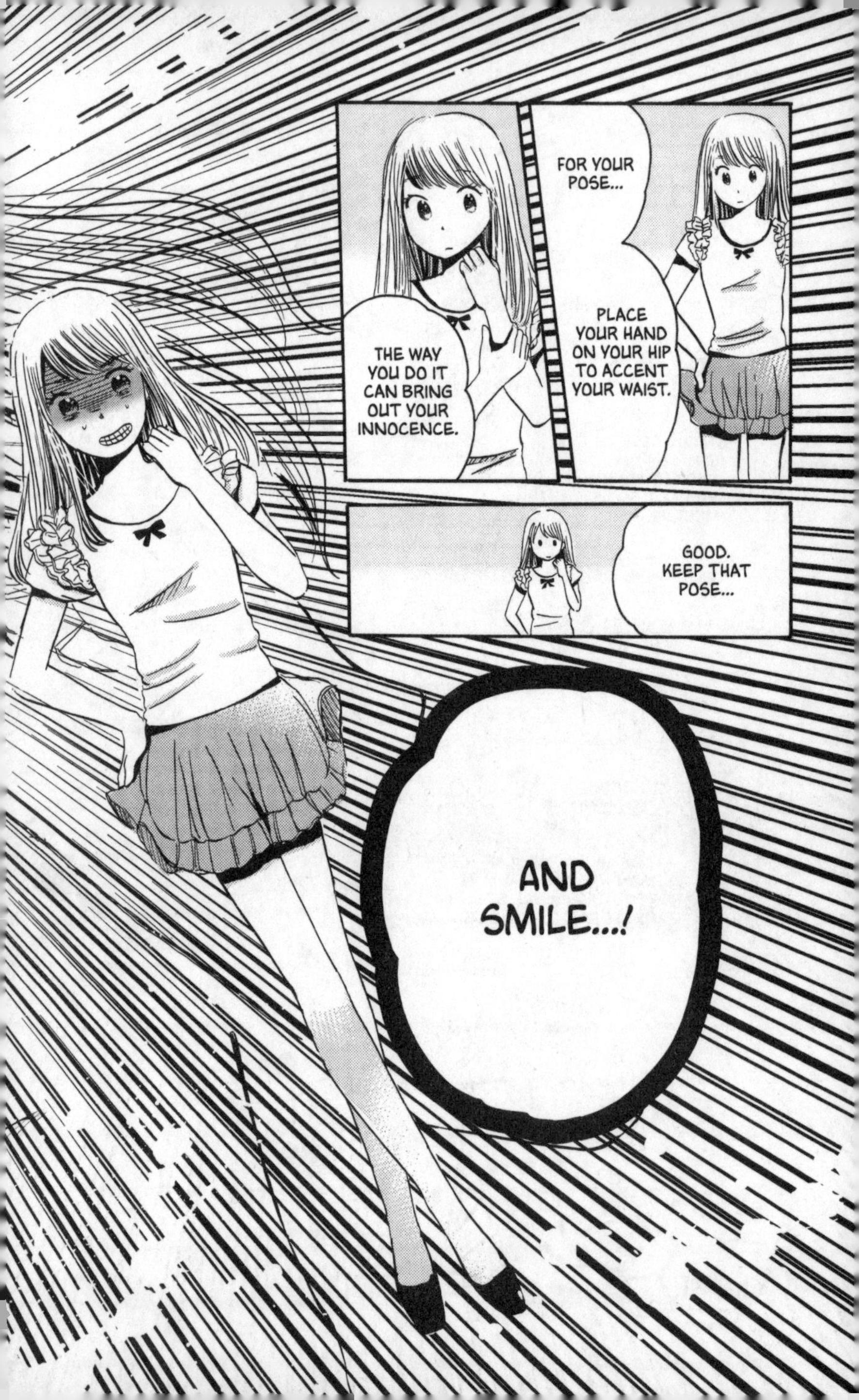
FOR YOUR POSE...
PLACE YOUR HAND ON YOUR HIP TO ACCENT YOUR WAIST.
THE WAY YOU DO IT CAN BRING OUT YOUR INNOCENCE.
GOOD. KEEP THAT POSE...
AND SMILE...!

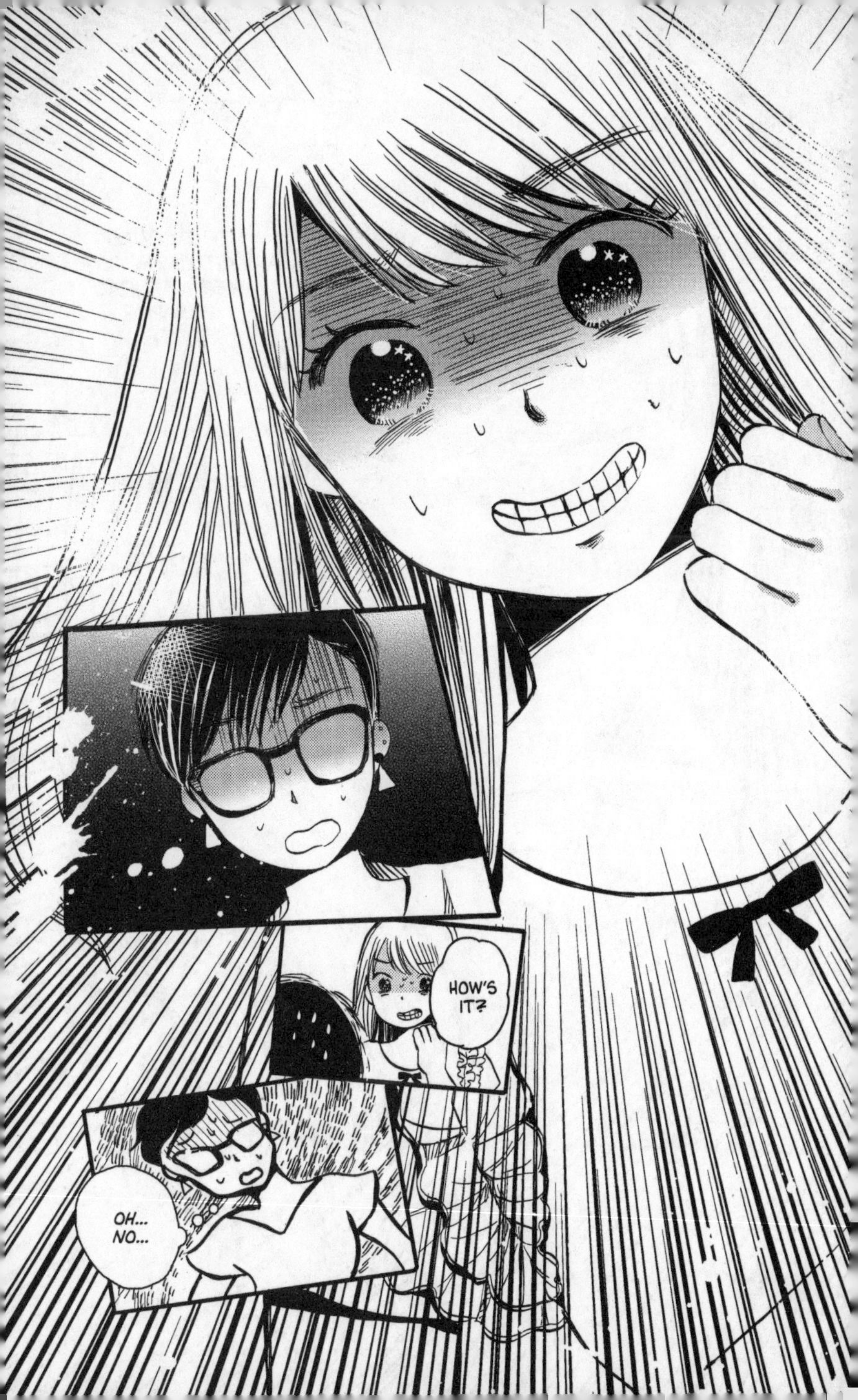
HOW'S IT?
OH... NO...

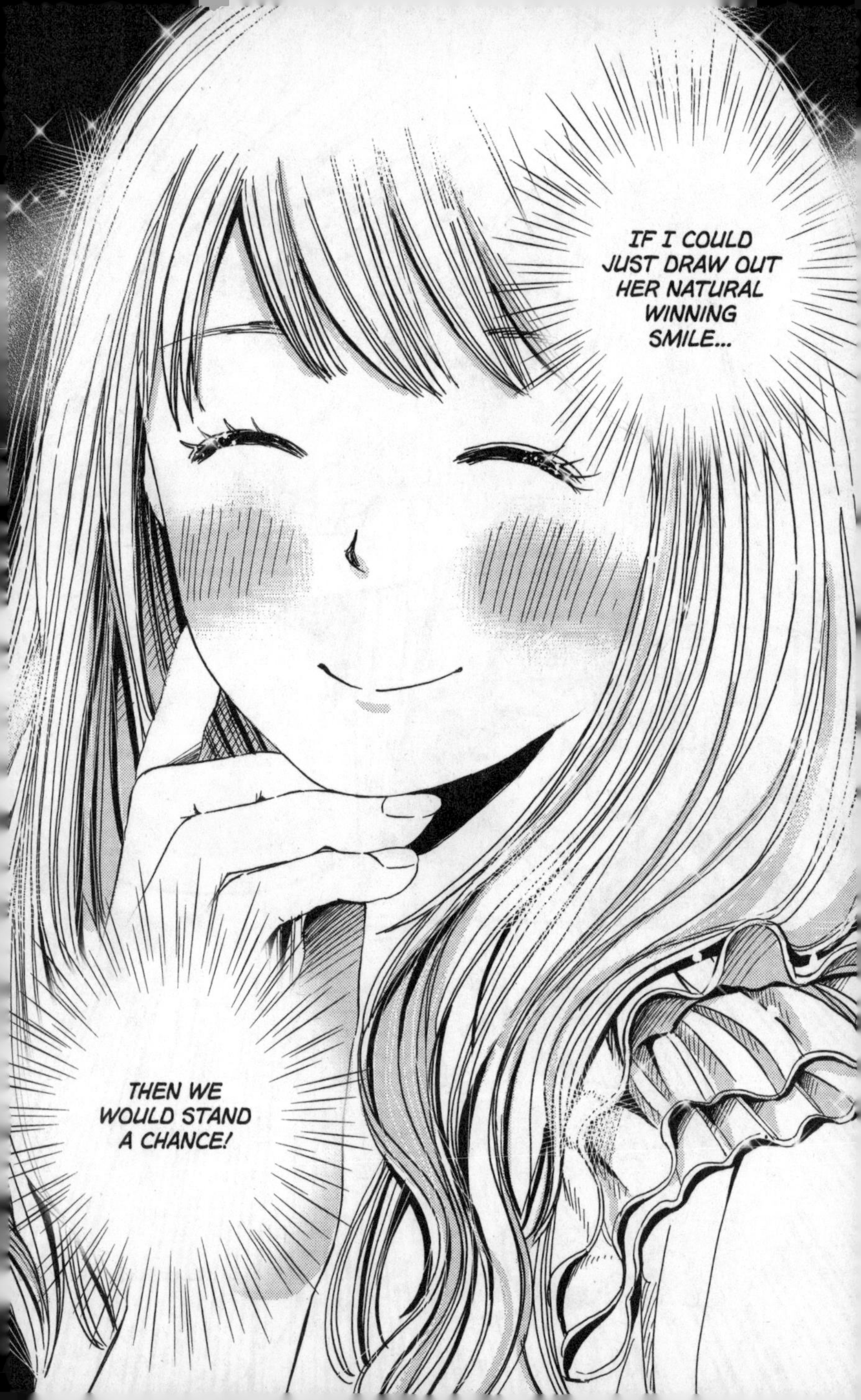
IF I COULD JUST DRAW OUT HER NATURAL WINNING SMILE...
THEN WE WOULD STAND A CHANCE!

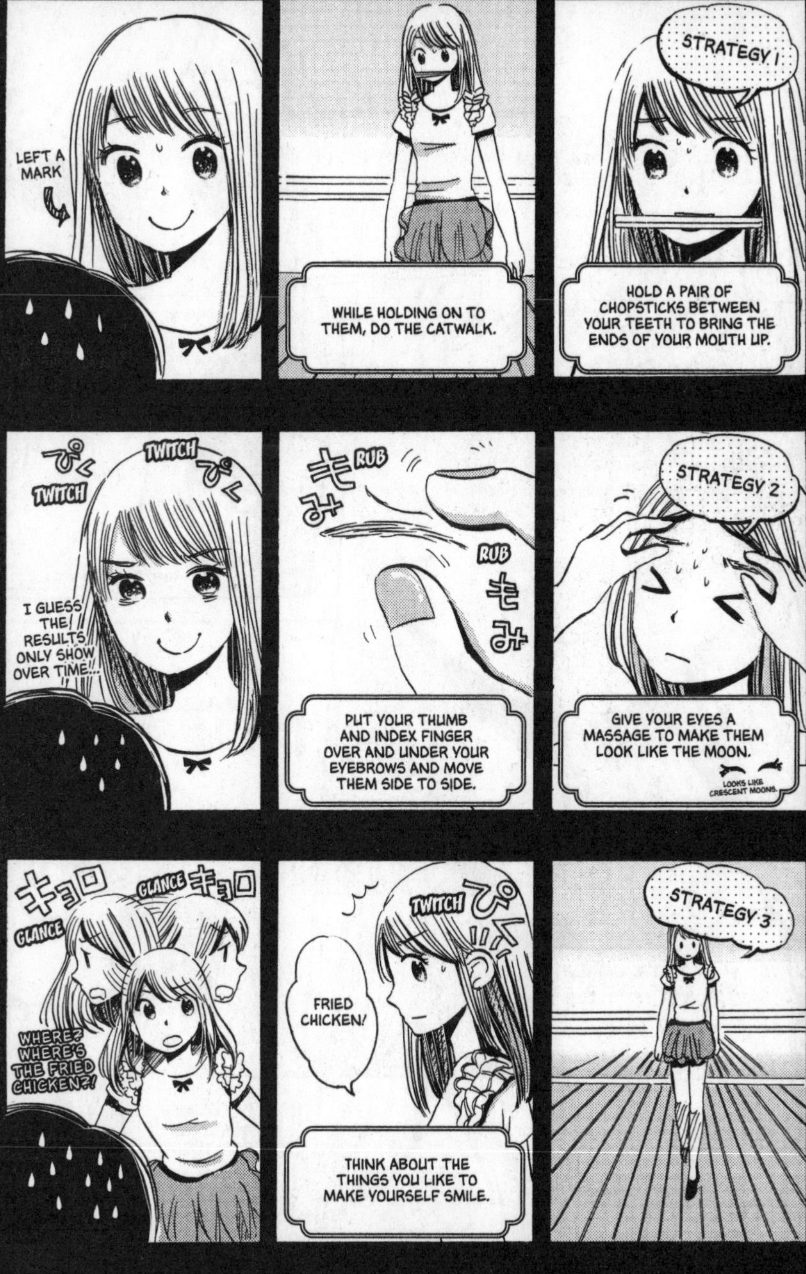

STRATEGY 1
HOLD A PAIR OF CHOPSTICKS BETWEEN YOUR TEETH TO BRING THE ENDS OF YOUR MOUTH UP.
WHILE HOLDING ON TO THEM, DO THE CATWALK.
LEFT A MARK
STRATEGY 2
GIVE YOUR EYES A MASSAGE TO MAKE THEM LOOK LIKE THE MOON.
LOOKS LIKE CRESCENT MOONS.
もみ RUB
もみ RUB
PUT YOUR THUMB AND INDEX FINGER OVER AND UNDER YOUR EYEBROWS AND MOVE THEM SIDE TO SIDE.
ぴく TWITCH
ぴく TWITCH
I GUESS THE RESULTS ONLY SHOW OVER TIME!...
STRATEGY 3
ぴく TWITCH
FRIED CHICKEN!
THINK ABOUT THE THINGS YOU LIKE TO MAKE YOURSELF SMILE.
キョロ GLANCE
キョロ GLANCE
WHERE? WHERE'S THE FRIED CHICKEN?!

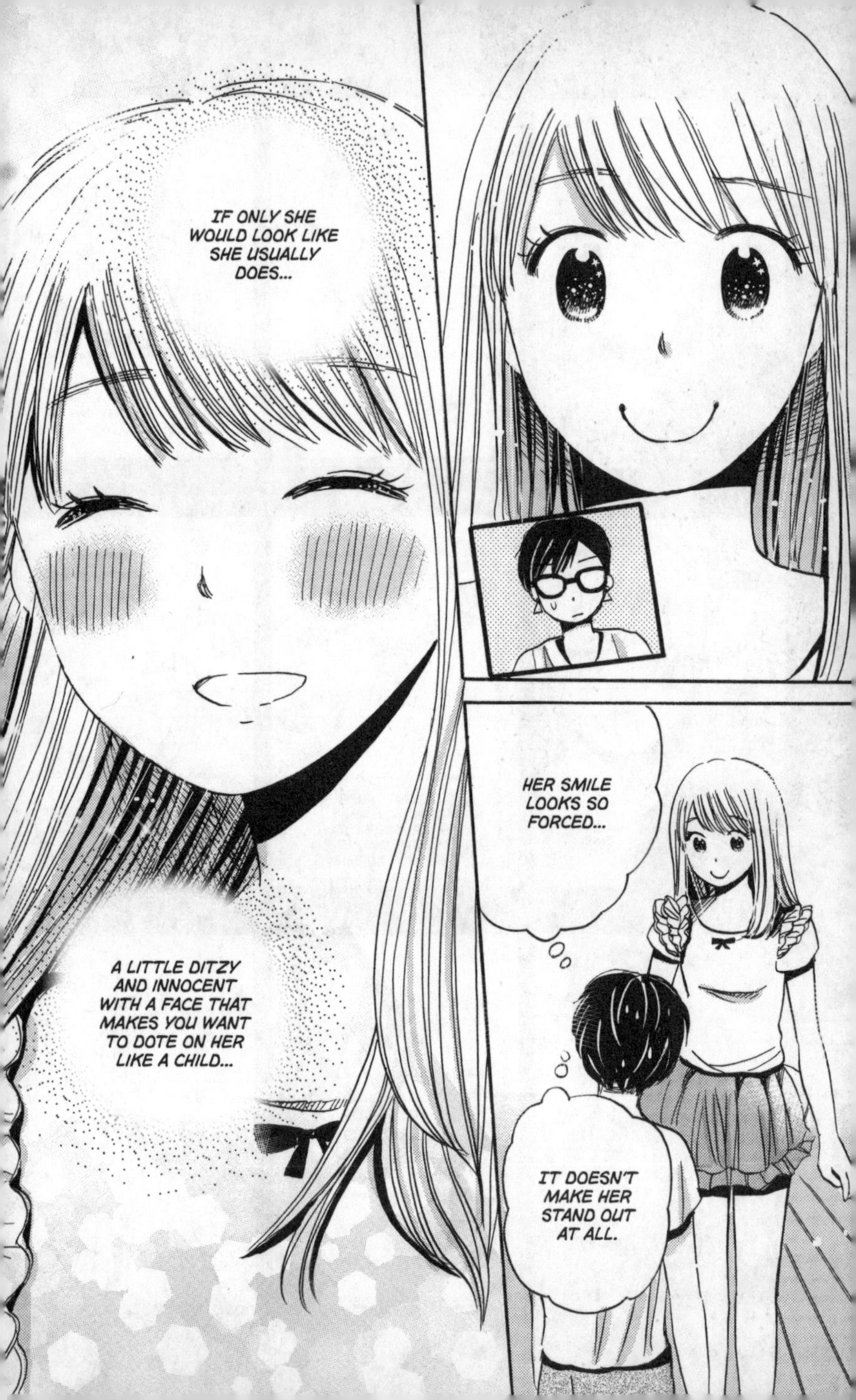
HER SMILE LOOKS SO FORCED...
IT DOESN'T MAKE HER STAND OUT AT ALL.
IF ONLY SHE WOULD LOOK LIKE SHE USUALLY DOES...
A LITTLE DITZY AND INNOCENT WITH A FACE THAT MAKES YOU WANT TO DOTE ON HER LIKE A CHILD...

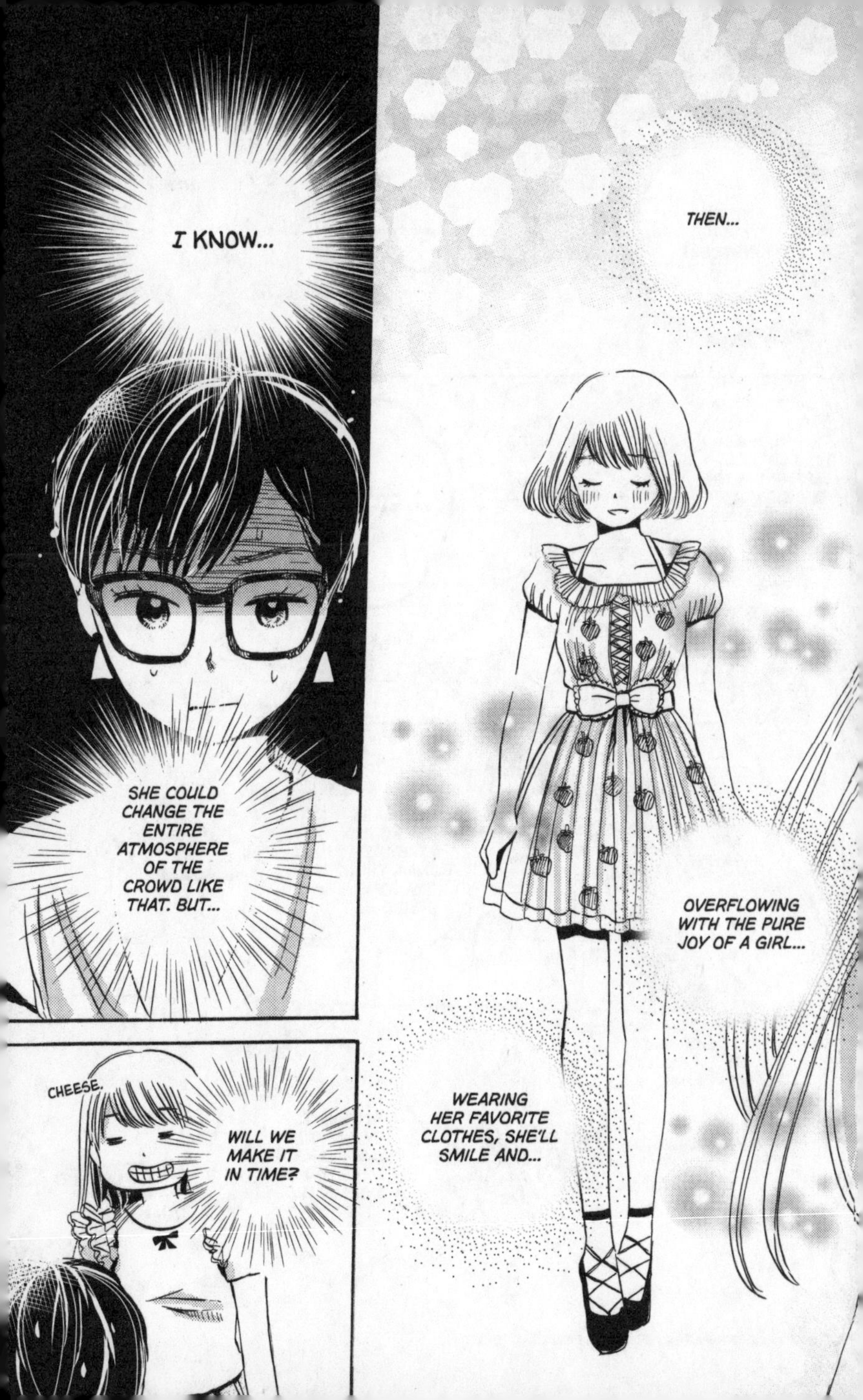
THEN...
OVERFLOWING WITH THE PURE JOY OF A GIRL...
WEARING HER FAVORITE CLOTHES, SHE'LL SMILE AND...
I KNOW...
SHE COULD CHANGE THE ENTIRE ATMOSPHERE OF THE CROWD LIKE THAT. BUT...
WILL WE MAKE IT IN TIME?
CHEESE.

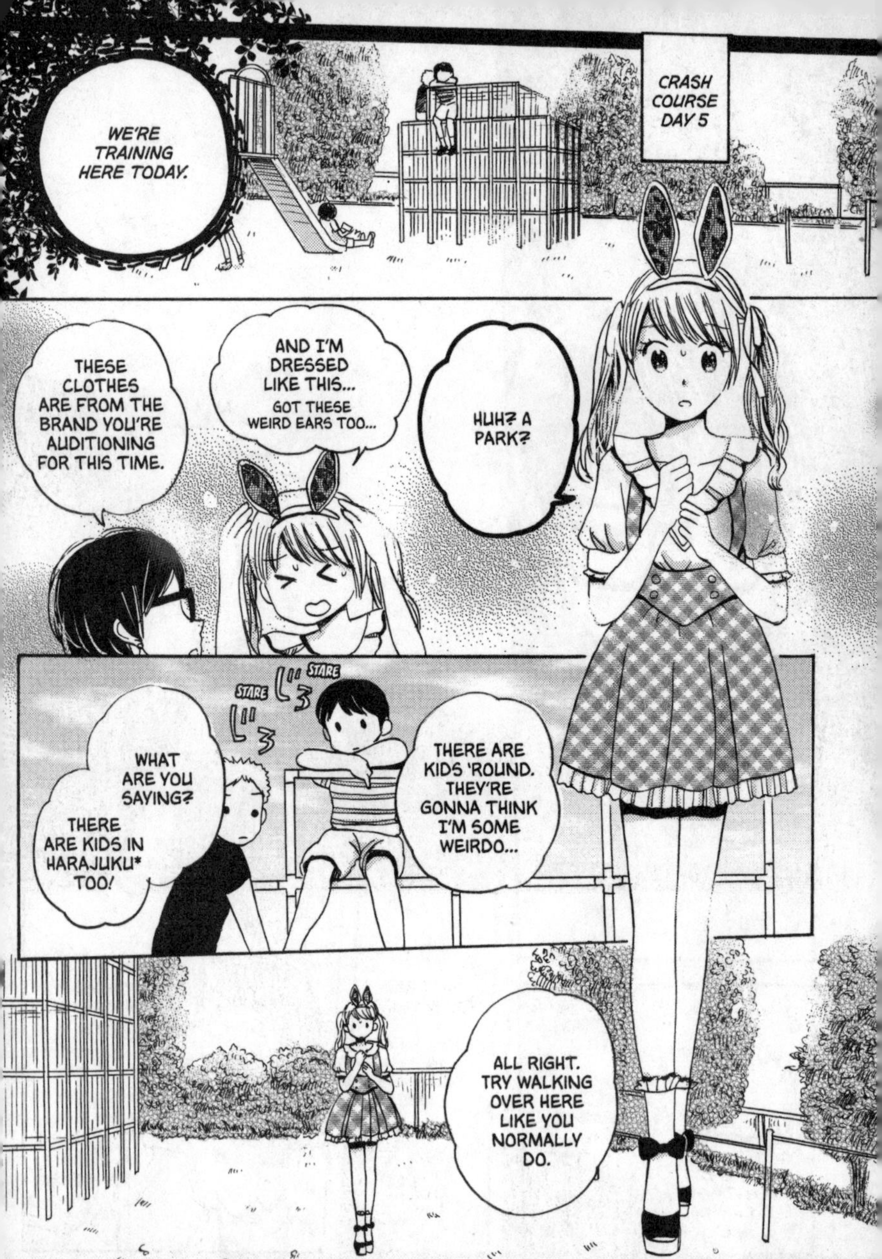
CRASH COURSE DAY 5
WE'RE TRAINING HERE TODAY.
HUH? A PARK?
AND I'M DRESSED LIKE THIS... GOT THESE WEIRD EARS TOO...
THESE CLOTHES ARE FROM THE BRAND YOU'RE AUDITIONING FOR THIS TIME.
THERE ARE KIDS 'ROUND. THEY'RE GONNA THINK I'M SOME WEIRDO...
STARE
STARE
WHAT ARE YOU SAYING? THERE ARE KIDS IN HARAJUKU* TOO!
ALL RIGHT. TRY WALKING OVER HERE LIKE YOU NORMALLY DO.

* A TRENDY SHOPPING AREA FOR YOUNG PEOPLE IN TOKYO

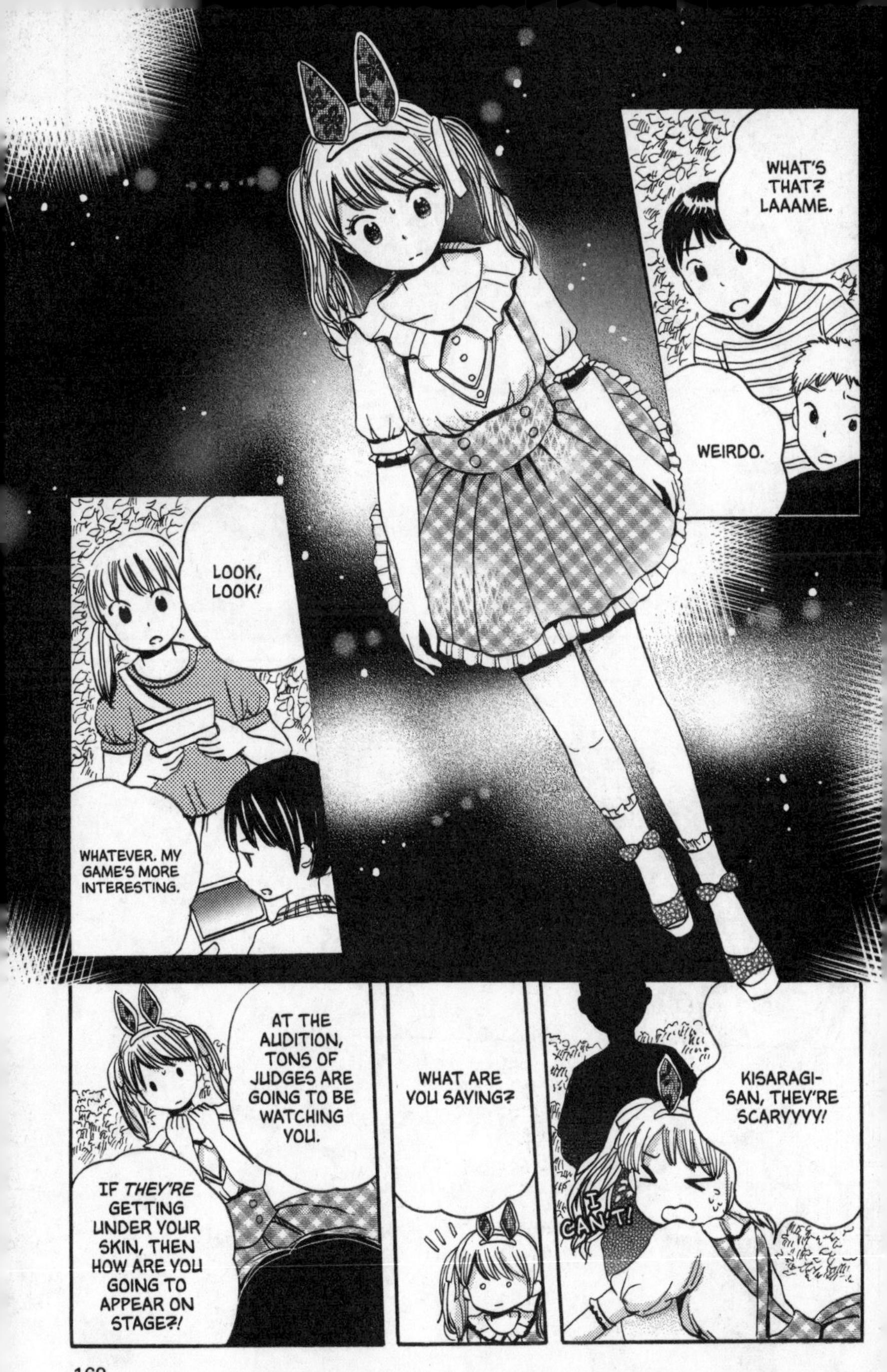
WHAT'S THAT? LAAAME.
WEIRDO.
LOOK, LOOK!
WHATEVER. MY GAME'S MORE INTERESTING.
KISARAGI-SAN, THEY'RE SCARYYYY!
I CAN'T!
WHAT ARE YOU SAYING?
AT THE AUDITION, TONS OF JUDGES ARE GOING TO BE WATCHING YOU.
IF *THEY'RE* GETTING UNDER YOUR SKIN, THEN HOW ARE YOU GOING TO APPEAR ON STAGE?!

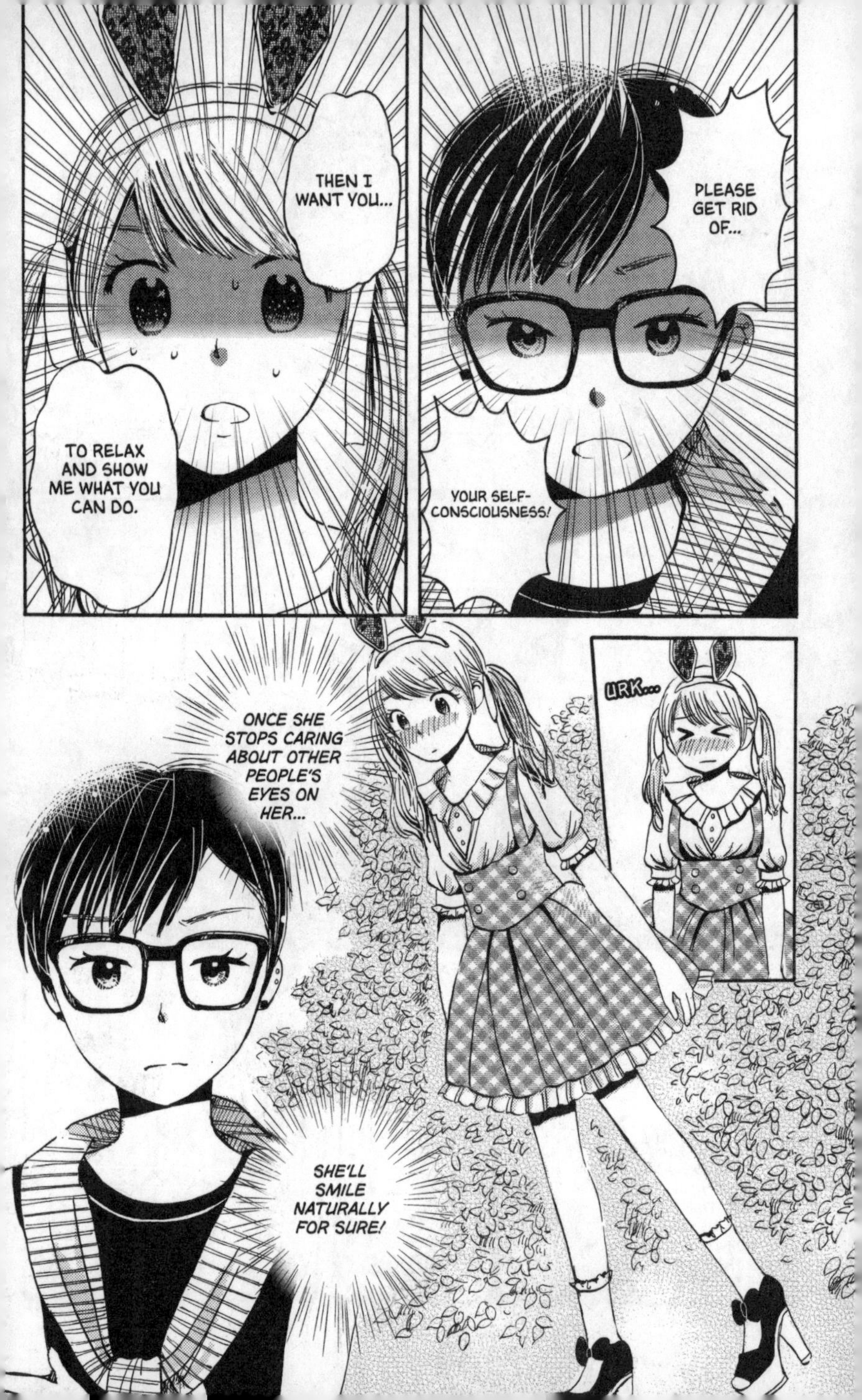
PLEASE GET RID OF...
YOUR SELF-CONSCIOUSNESS!
THEN I WANT YOU...
TO RELAX AND SHOW ME WHAT YOU CAN DO.
URK...
ONCE SHE STOPS CARING ABOUT OTHER PEOPLE'S EYES ON HER...
SHE'LL SMILE NATURALLY FOR SURE!

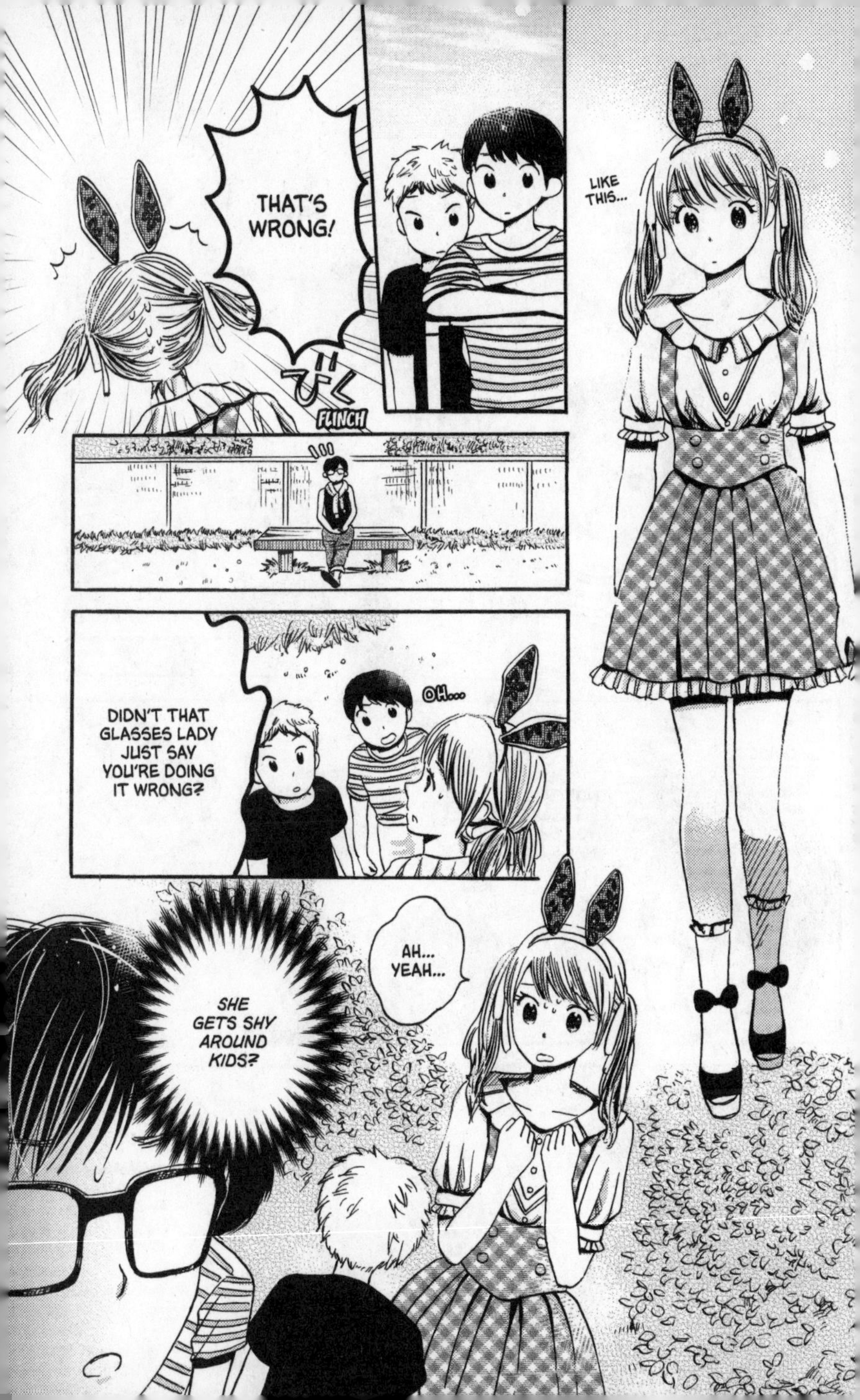

LIKE THIS...
THAT'S WRONG!
びく
FLINCH
OH...
DIDN'T THAT GLASSES LADY JUST SAY YOU'RE DOING IT WRONG?
AH... YEAH...
SHE GETS SHY AROUND KIDS?

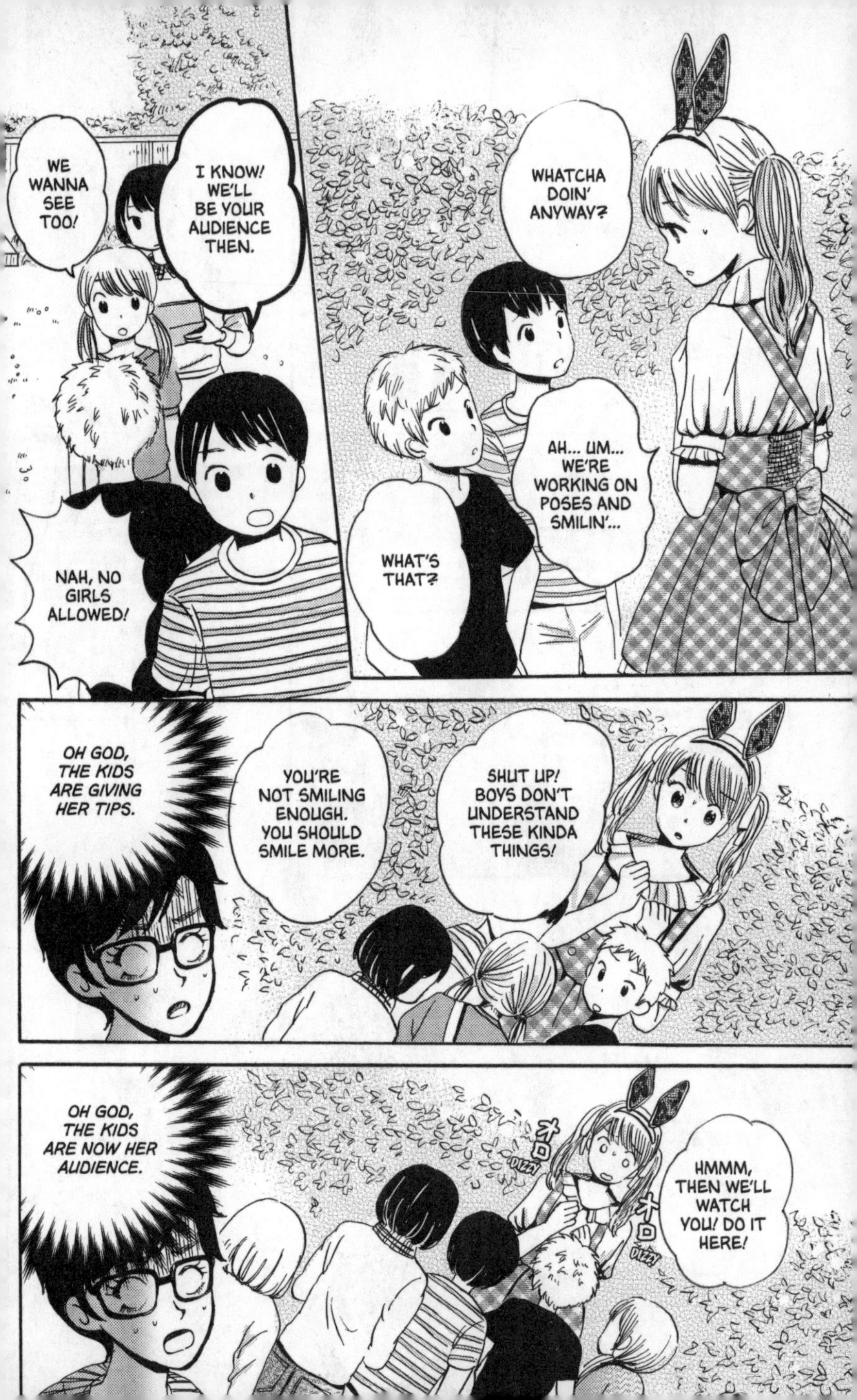
WHATCHA DOIN' ANYWAY?
AH... UM... WE'RE WORKING ON POSES AND SMILIN'...
WHAT'S THAT?
I KNOW! WE'LL BE YOUR AUDIENCE THEN.
WE WANNA SEE TOO!
NAH, NO GIRLS ALLOWED!
SHUT UP! BOYS DON'T UNDERSTAND THESE KINDA THINGS!
YOU'RE NOT SMILING ENOUGH. YOU SHOULD SMILE MORE.
OH GOD, THE KIDS ARE GIVING HER TIPS.
HMMM, THEN WE'LL WATCH YOU! DO IT HERE!
オロ DIZZY
オロ DIZZY
OH GOD, THE KIDS ARE NOW HER AUDIENCE.

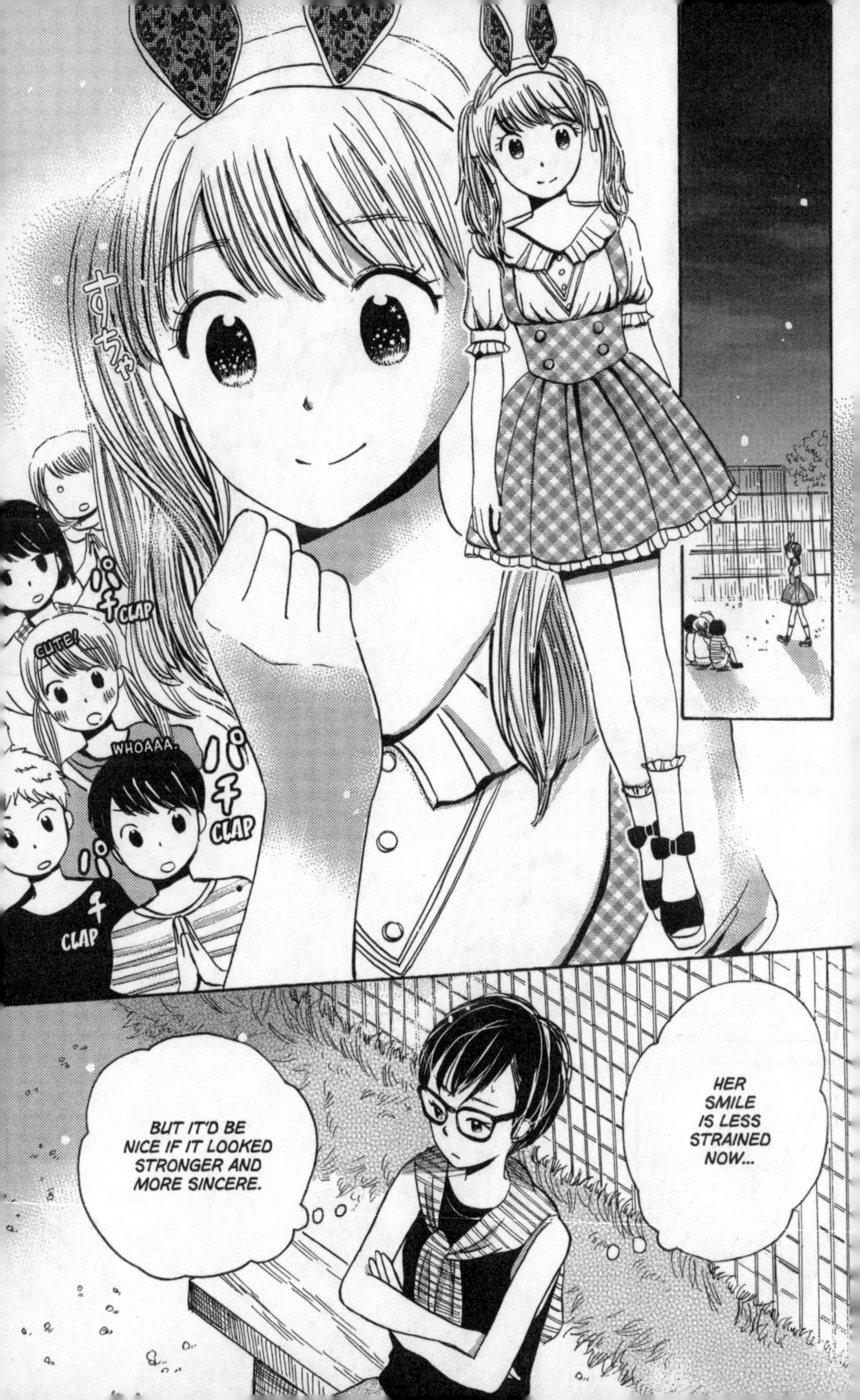
すちゃ
パチ CLAP
パチ CLAP
CUTE!
WHOAAA.
パチ CLAP
HER SMILE IS LESS STRAINED NOW...
BUT IT'D BE NICE IF IT LOOKED STRONGER AND MORE SINCERE.

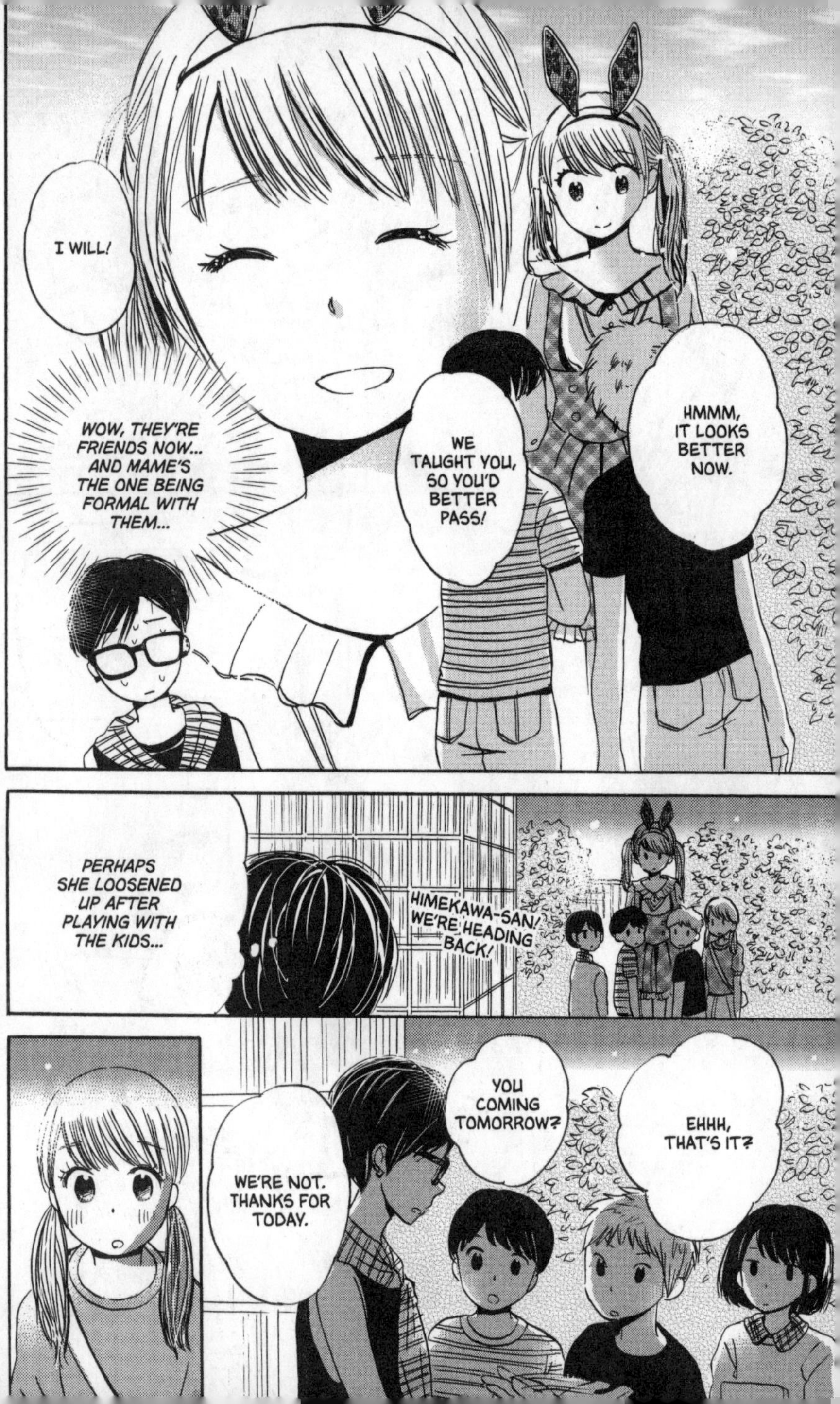
HMMM, IT LOOKS BETTER NOW.
WE TAUGHT YOU, SO YOU'D BETTER PASS!
I WILL!
WOW, THEY'RE FRIENDS NOW... AND MAME'S THE ONE BEING FORMAL WITH THEM...
HIMEKAWA-SAN! WE'RE HEADING BACK!
PERHAPS SHE LOOSENED UP AFTER PLAYING WITH THE KIDS...
EHHH, THAT'S IT?
YOU COMING TOMORROW?
WE'RE NOT. THANKS FOR TODAY.

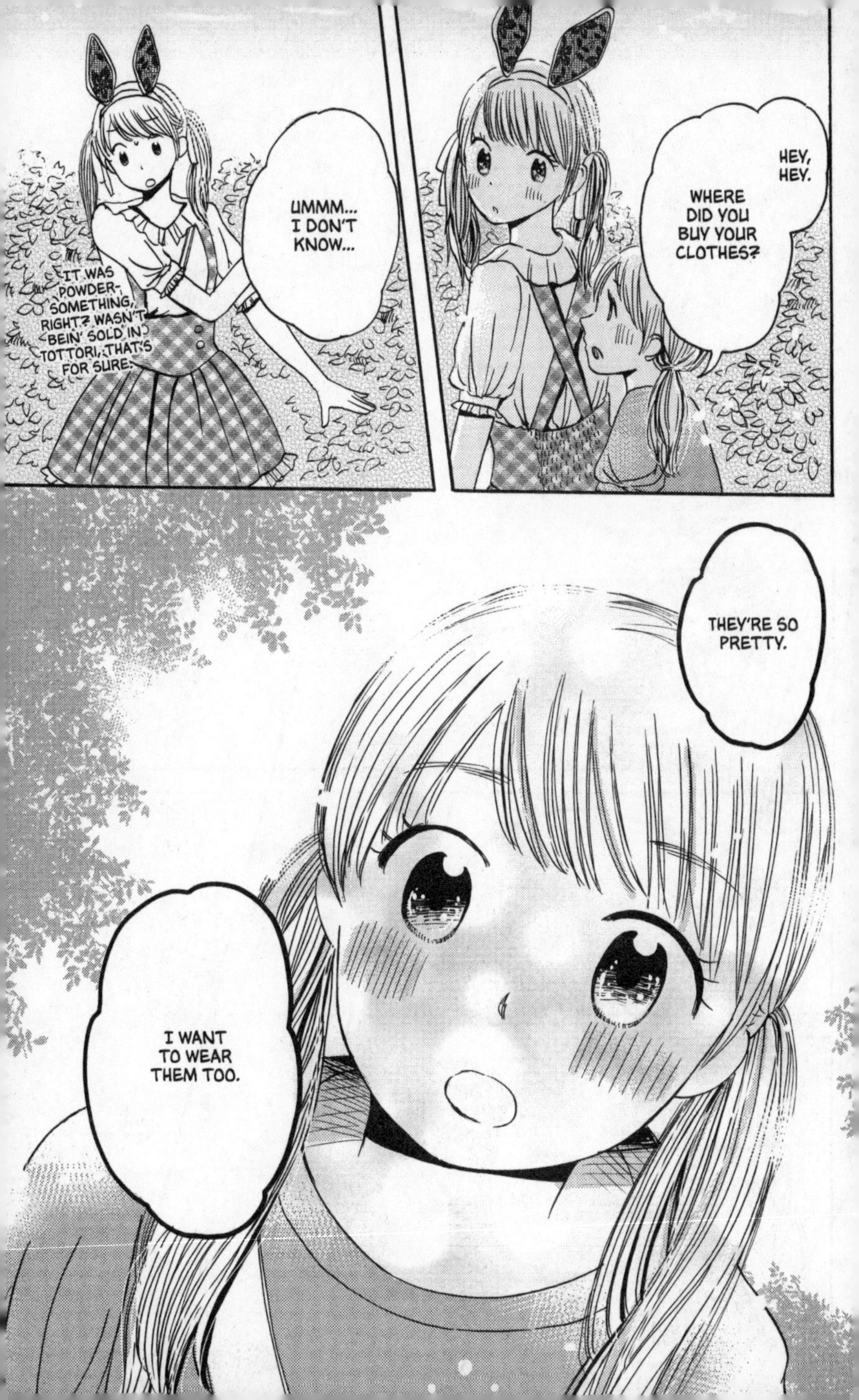

HEY, HEY. WHERE DID YOU BUY YOUR CLOTHES?
UMMM... I DON'T KNOW...
IT WAS POWDER-SOMETHING, RIGHT? WASN'T BEIN' SOLD IN TOTTORI, THAT'S FOR SURE.
THEY'RE SO PRETTY.
I WANT TO WEAR THEM TOO.

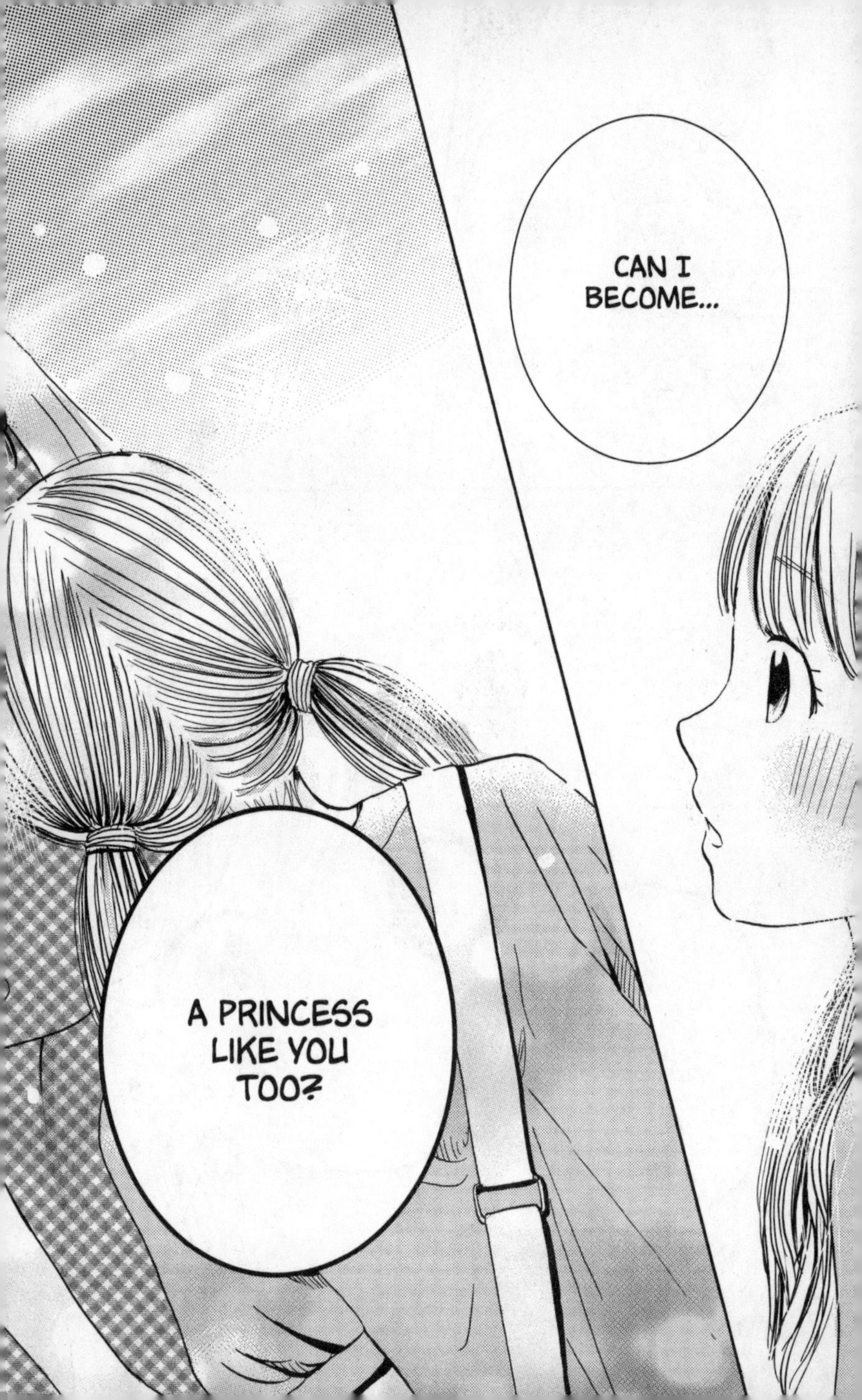
CAN I BECOME...
A PRINCESS LIKE YOU TOO?

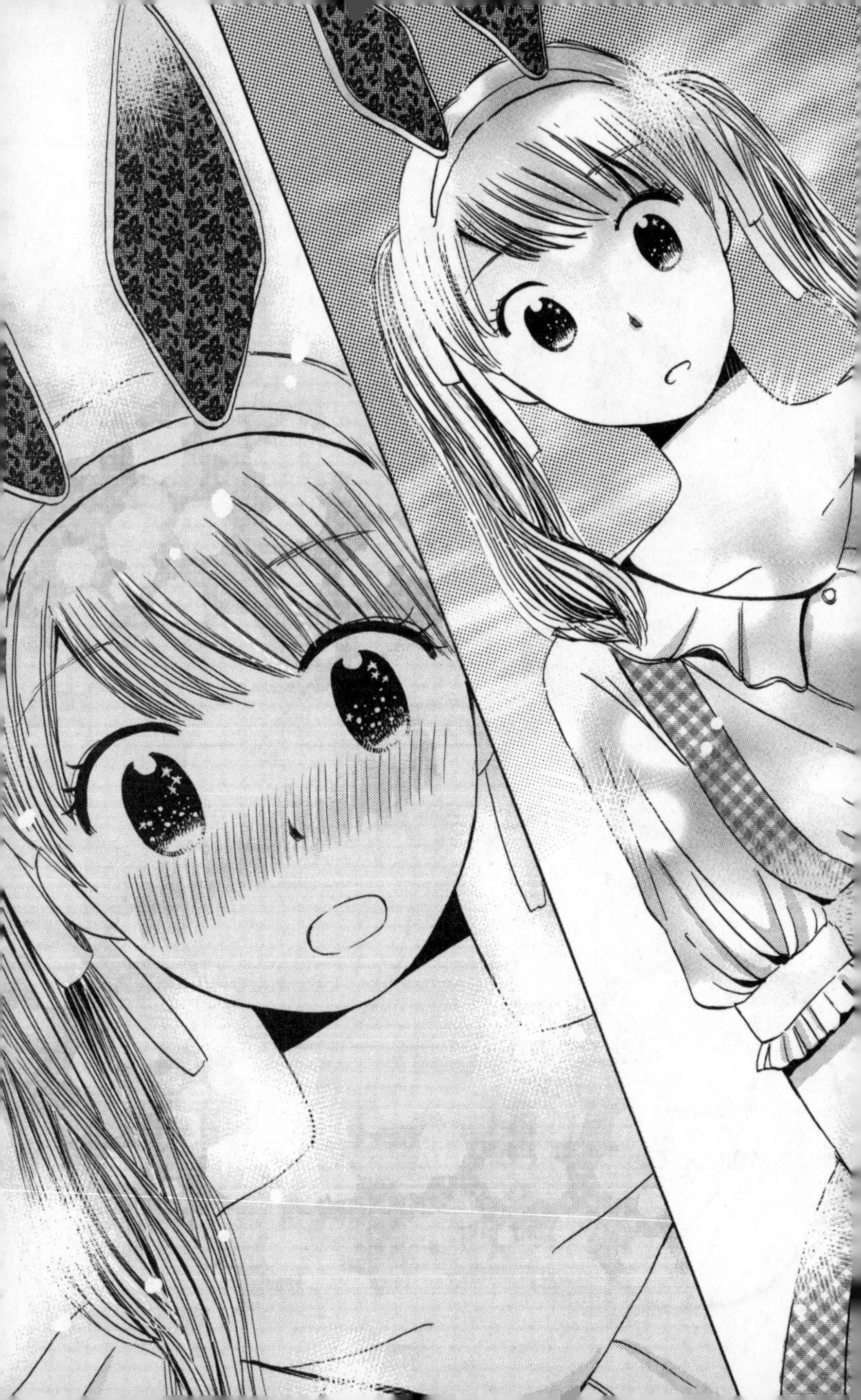

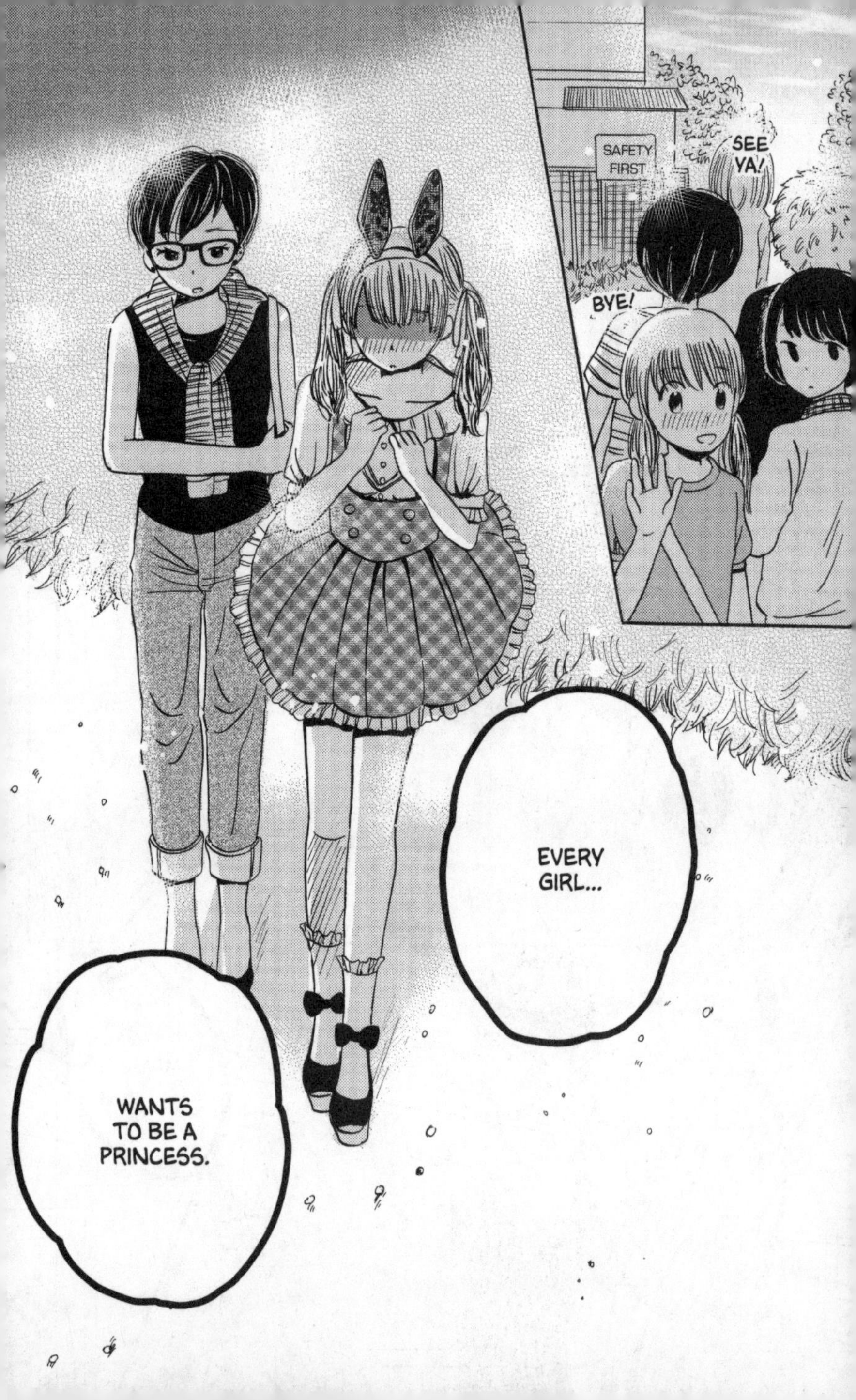
SEE YA!
SAFETY FIRST
BYE!
EVERY GIRL...
WANTS TO BE A PRINCESS.

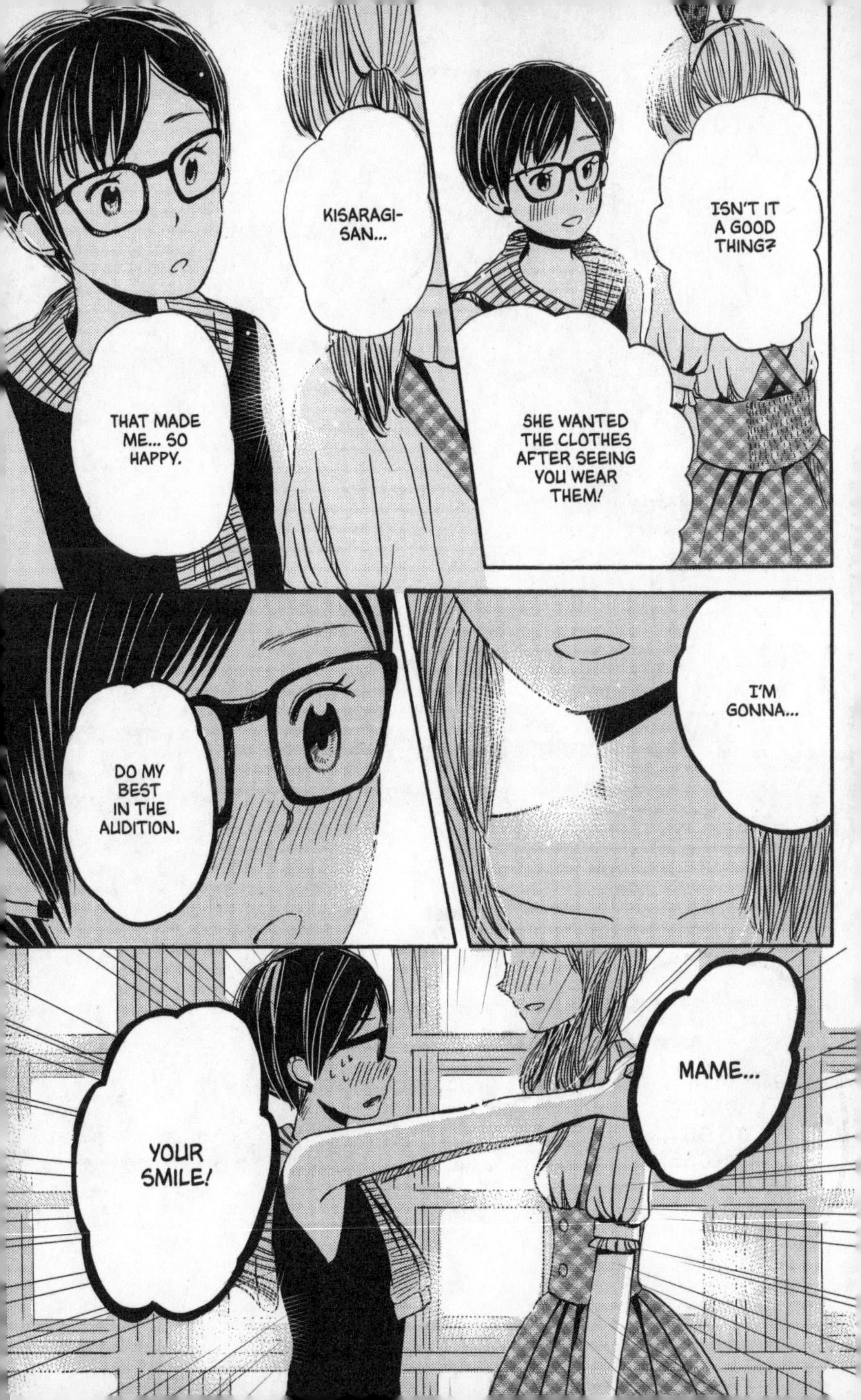
ISN'T IT A GOOD THING?
SHE WANTED THE CLOTHES AFTER SEEING YOU WEAR THEM!
KISARAGI-SAN...
THAT MADE ME... SO HAPPY.
I'M GONNA...
DO MY BEST IN THE AUDITION.
MAME...
YOUR SMILE!

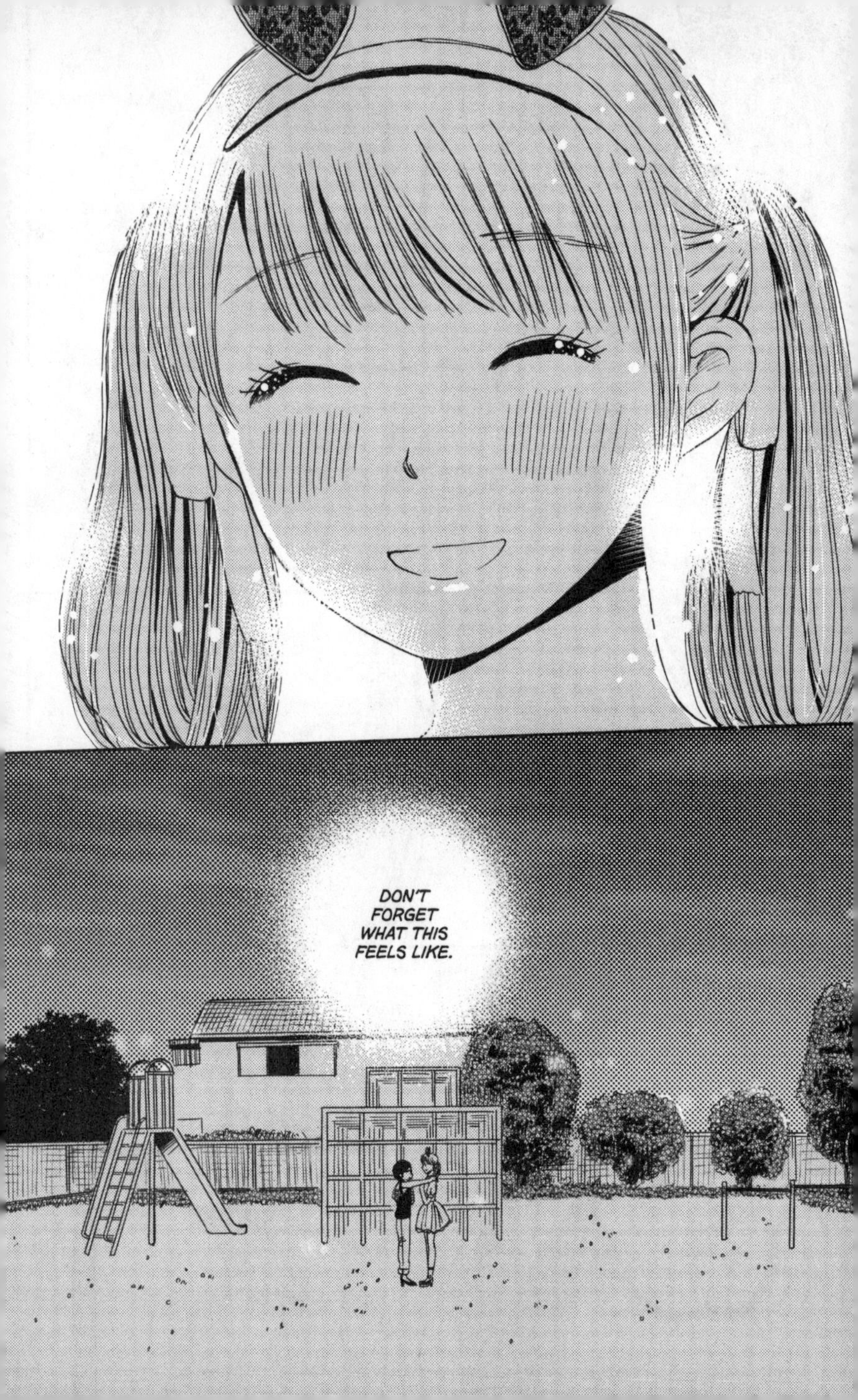
DON'T FORGET WHAT THIS FEELS LIKE.

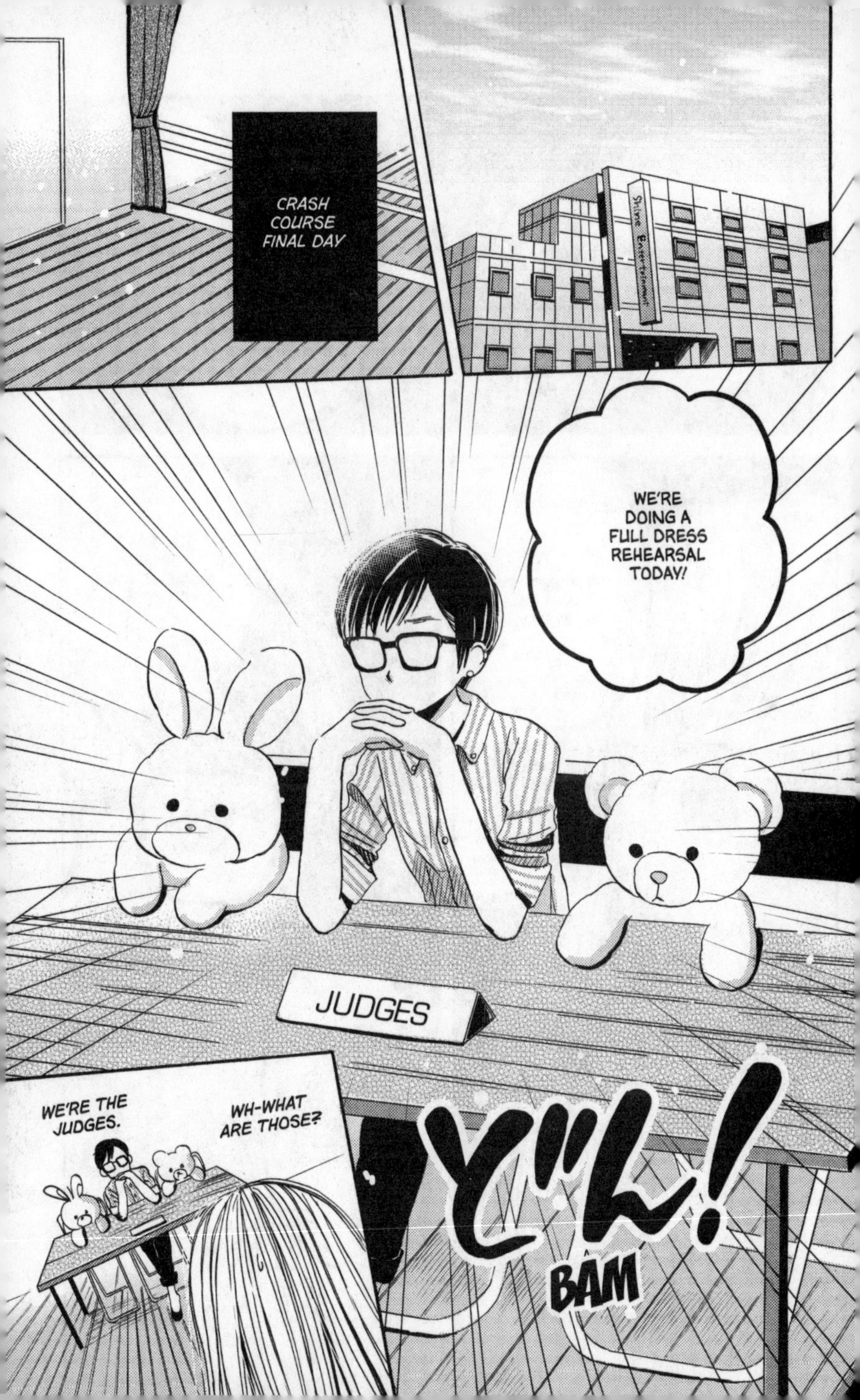
CRASH COURSE FINAL DAY
WE'RE DOING A FULL DRESS REHEARSAL TODAY!
JUDGES
BAM
WH-WHAT ARE THOSE?
WE'RE THE JUDGES.

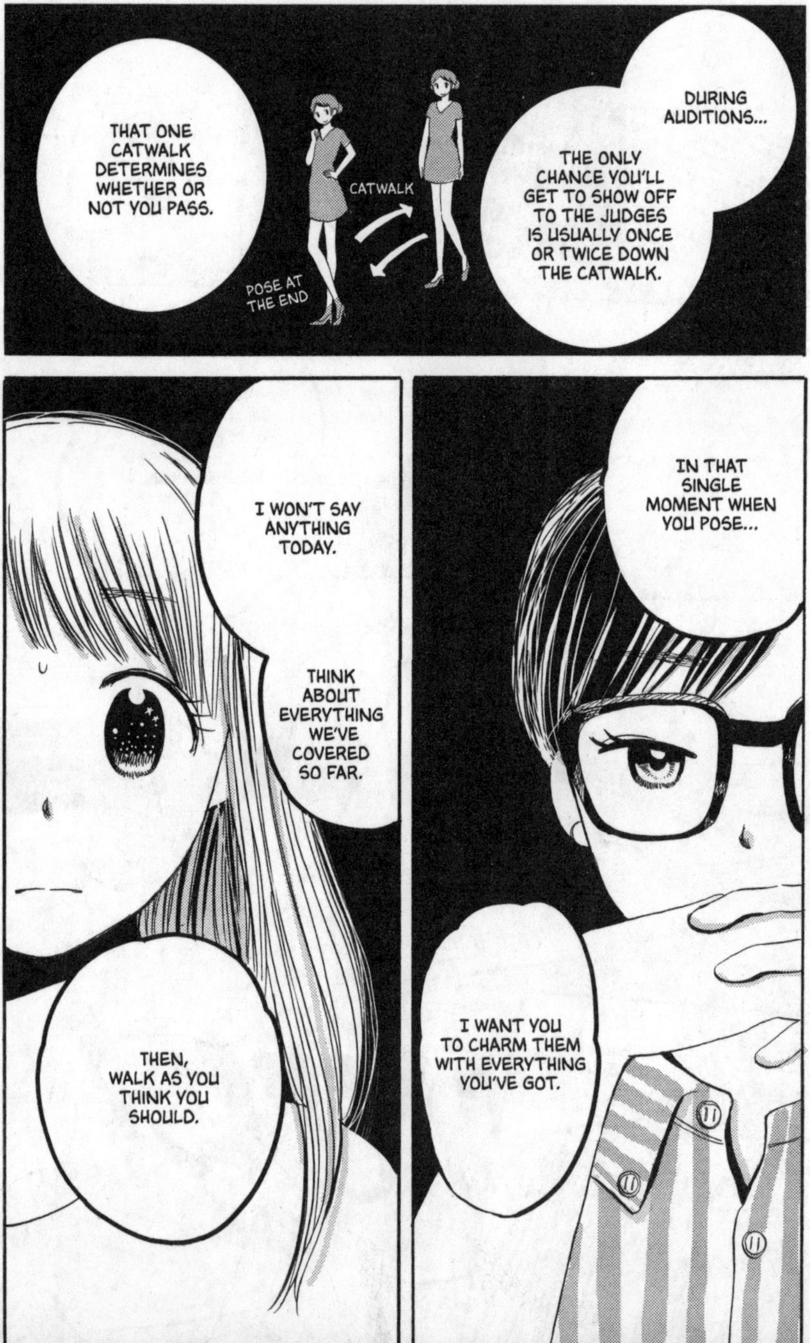
DURING AUDITIONS...
THE ONLY CHANCE YOU'LL GET TO SHOW OFF TO THE JUDGES IS USUALLY ONCE OR TWICE DOWN THE CATWALK.
CATWALK
POSE AT THE END
THAT ONE CATWALK DETERMINES WHETHER OR NOT YOU PASS.
IN THAT SINGLE MOMENT WHEN YOU POSE...
I WANT YOU TO CHARM THEM WITH EVERYTHING YOU'VE GOT.
I WON'T SAY ANYTHING TODAY.
THINK ABOUT EVERYTHING WE'VE COVERED SO FAR.
THEN, WALK AS YOU THINK YOU SHOULD.

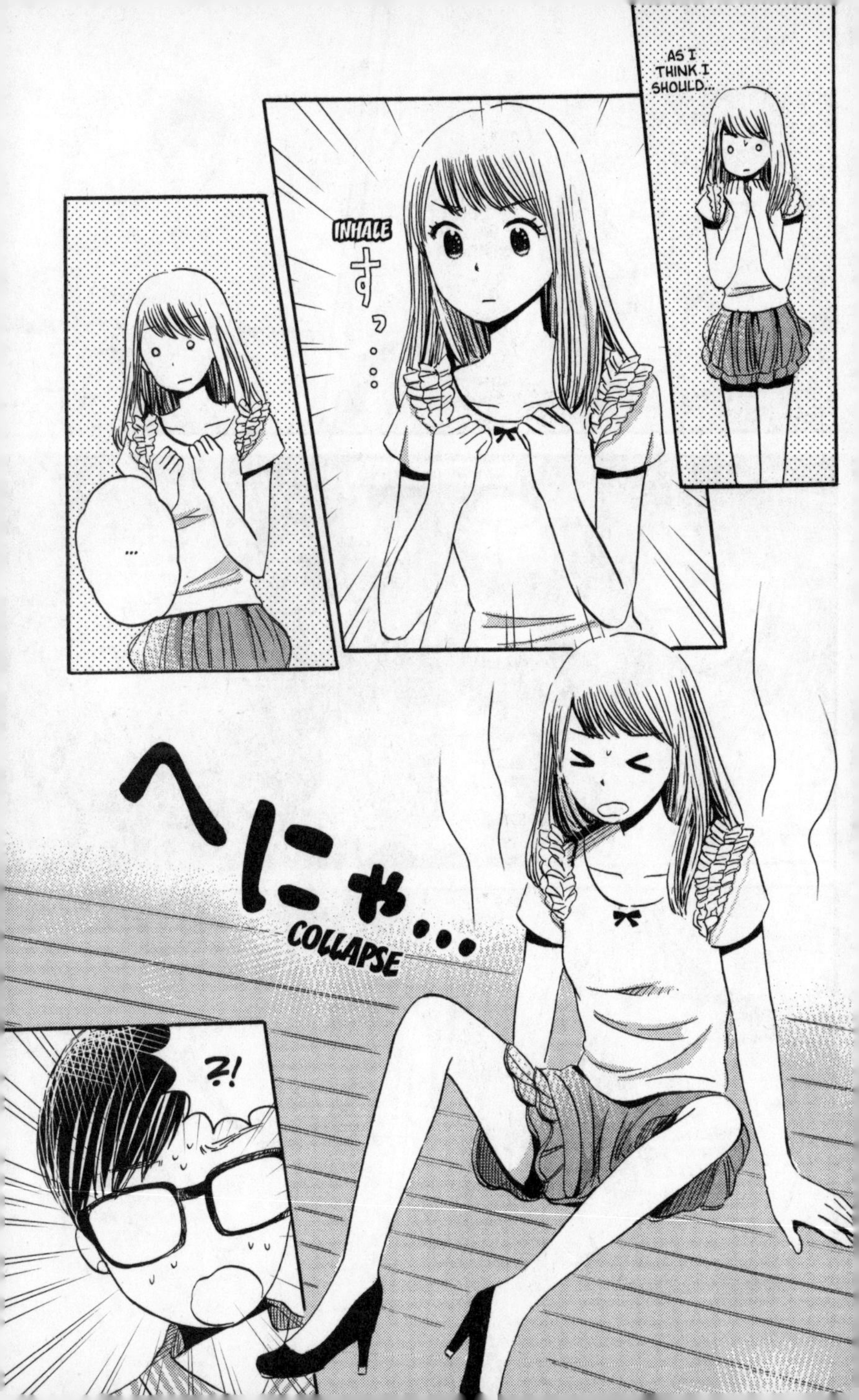
AS I THINK I SHOULD...
INHALE
すっ...
...
へにゃ...
COLLAPSE
?!

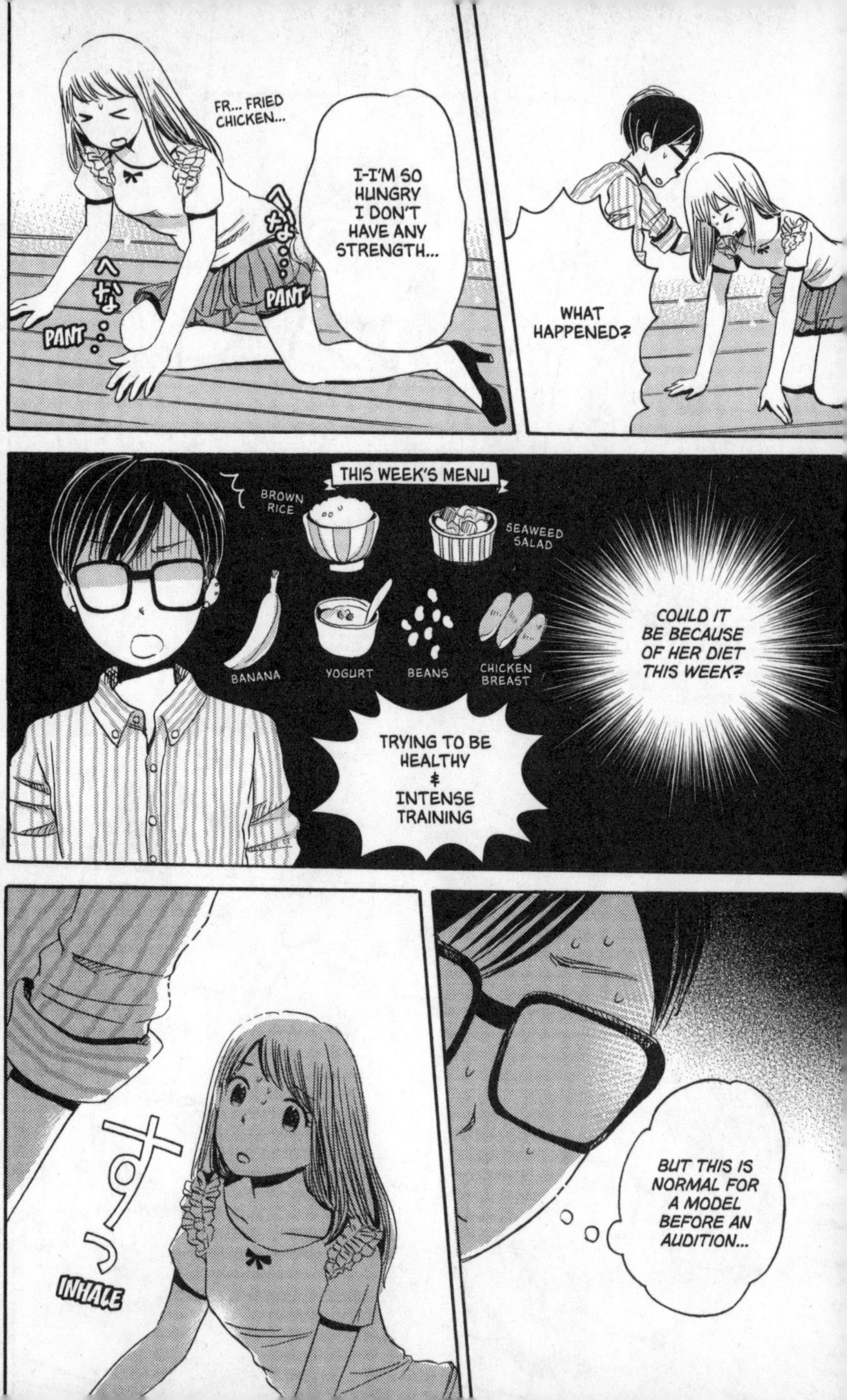
WHAT HAPPENED?
I-I'M SO HUNGRY I DON'T HAVE ANY STRENGTH...
FR... FRIED CHICKEN...
へな
PANT
へな
PANT
COULD IT BE BECAUSE OF HER DIET THIS WEEK?
THIS WEEK'S MENU
SEAWEED SALAD
BROWN RICE
CHICKEN BREAST
BEANS
YOGURT
BANANA
TRYING TO BE HEALTHY & INTENSE TRAINING
BUT THIS IS NORMAL FOR A MODEL BEFORE AN AUDITION...
すっ
INHALE

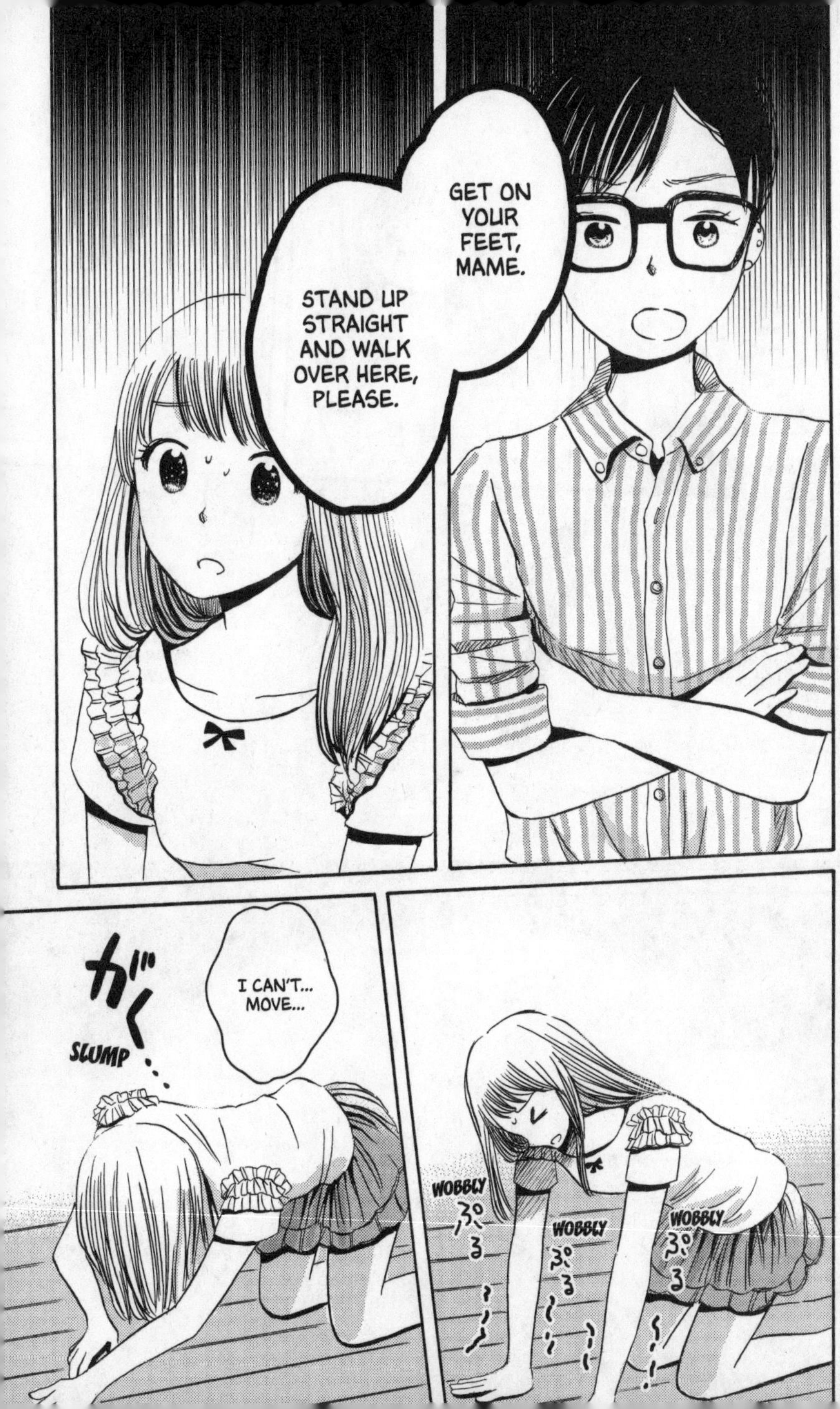
GET ON YOUR FEET, MAME.
STAND UP STRAIGHT AND WALK OVER HERE, PLEASE.
WOBBLY ぶる〜
WOBBLY ぶる〜
WOBBLY ぶる〜
がく
SLUMP
I CAN'T... MOVE...

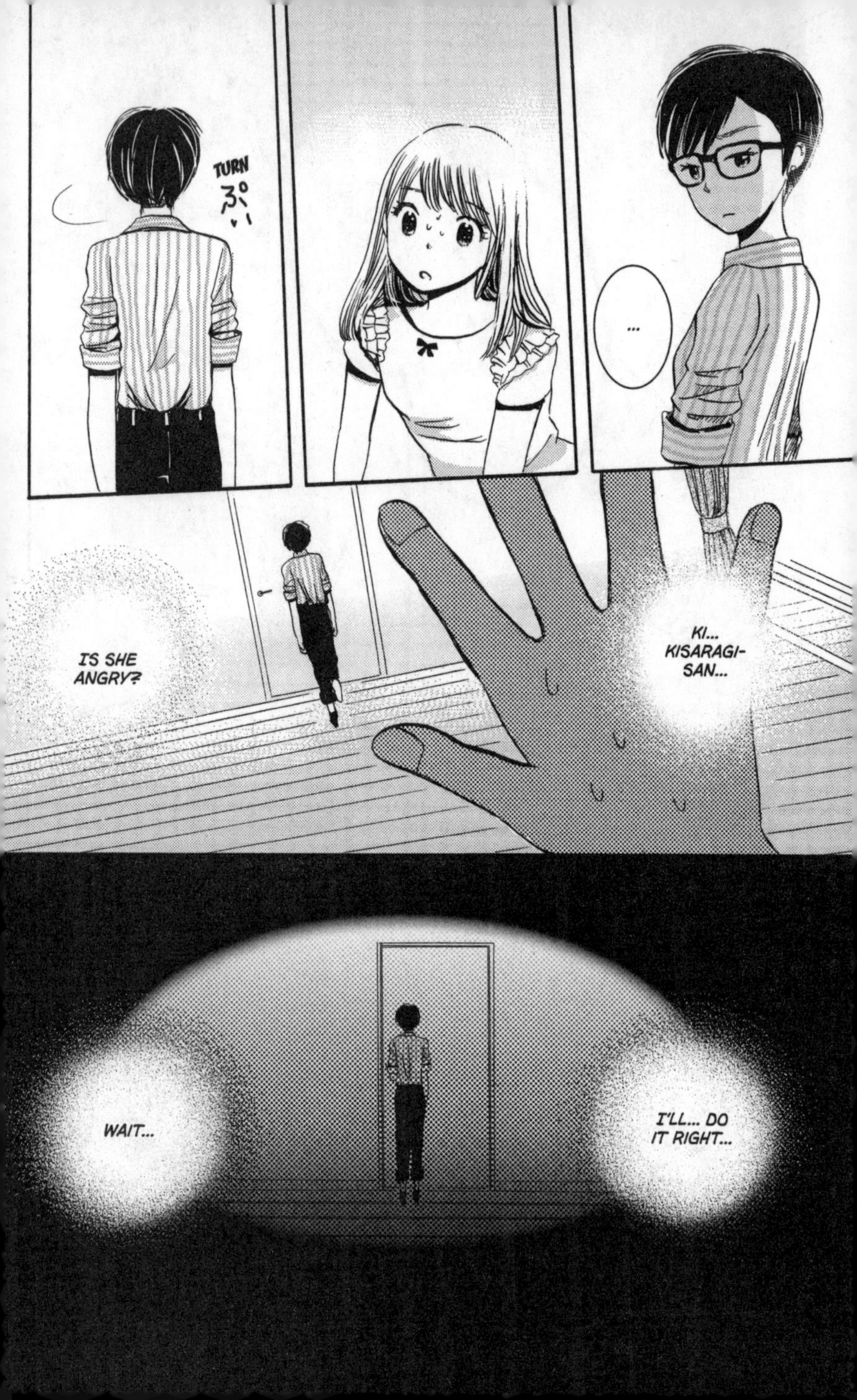
...
TURN
ぷい
KI... KISARAGI-SAN...
IS SHE ANGRY?
I'LL... DO IT RIGHT...
WAIT...

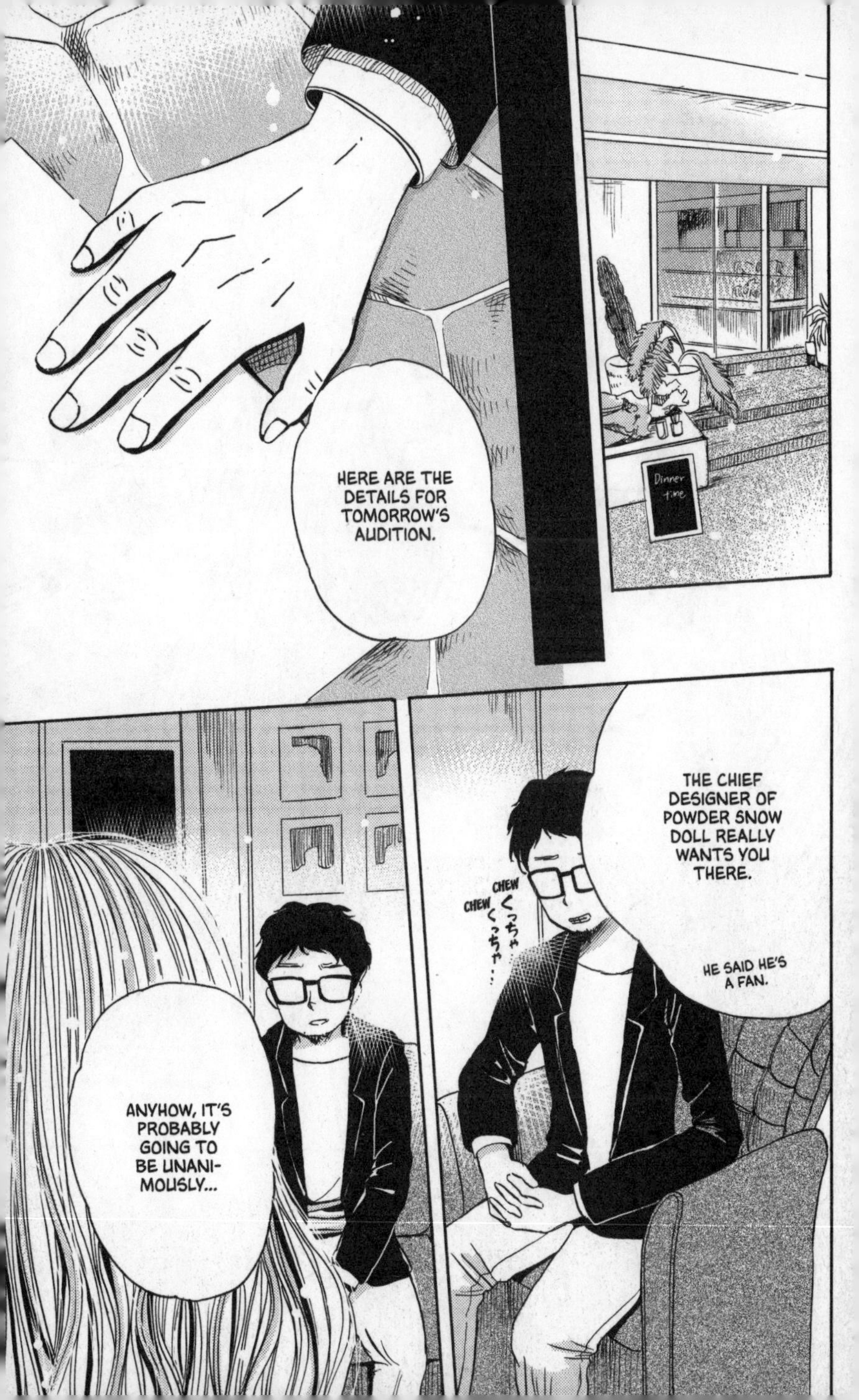
Dinner time
HERE ARE THE DETAILS FOR TOMORROW'S AUDITION.
THE CHIEF DESIGNER OF POWDER SNOW DOLL REALLY WANTS YOU THERE.
HE SAID HE'S A FAN.
CHEW CHEW
くっちゃ くっちゃ…
ANYHOW, IT'S PROBABLY GOING TO BE UNANI-MOUSLY...

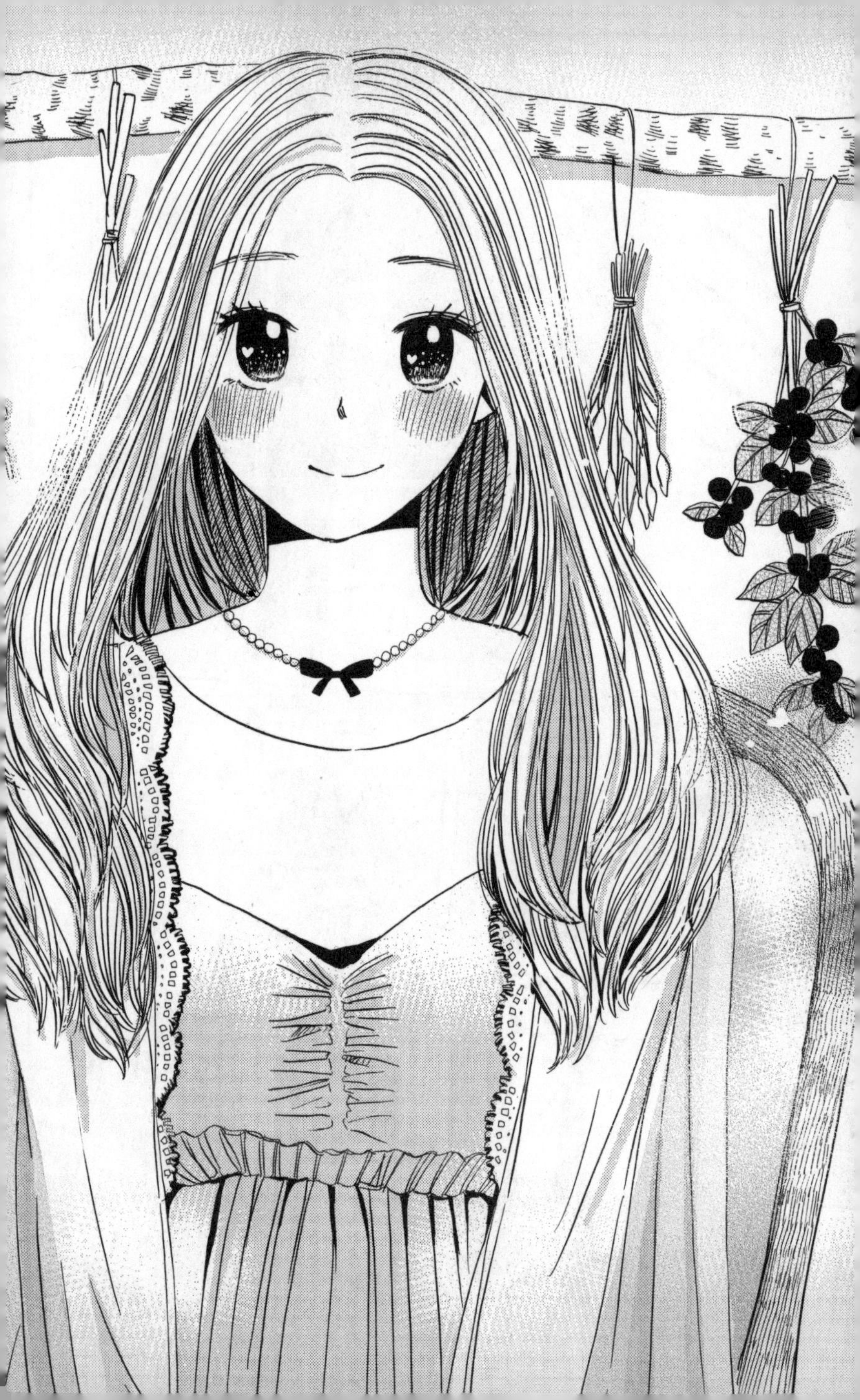

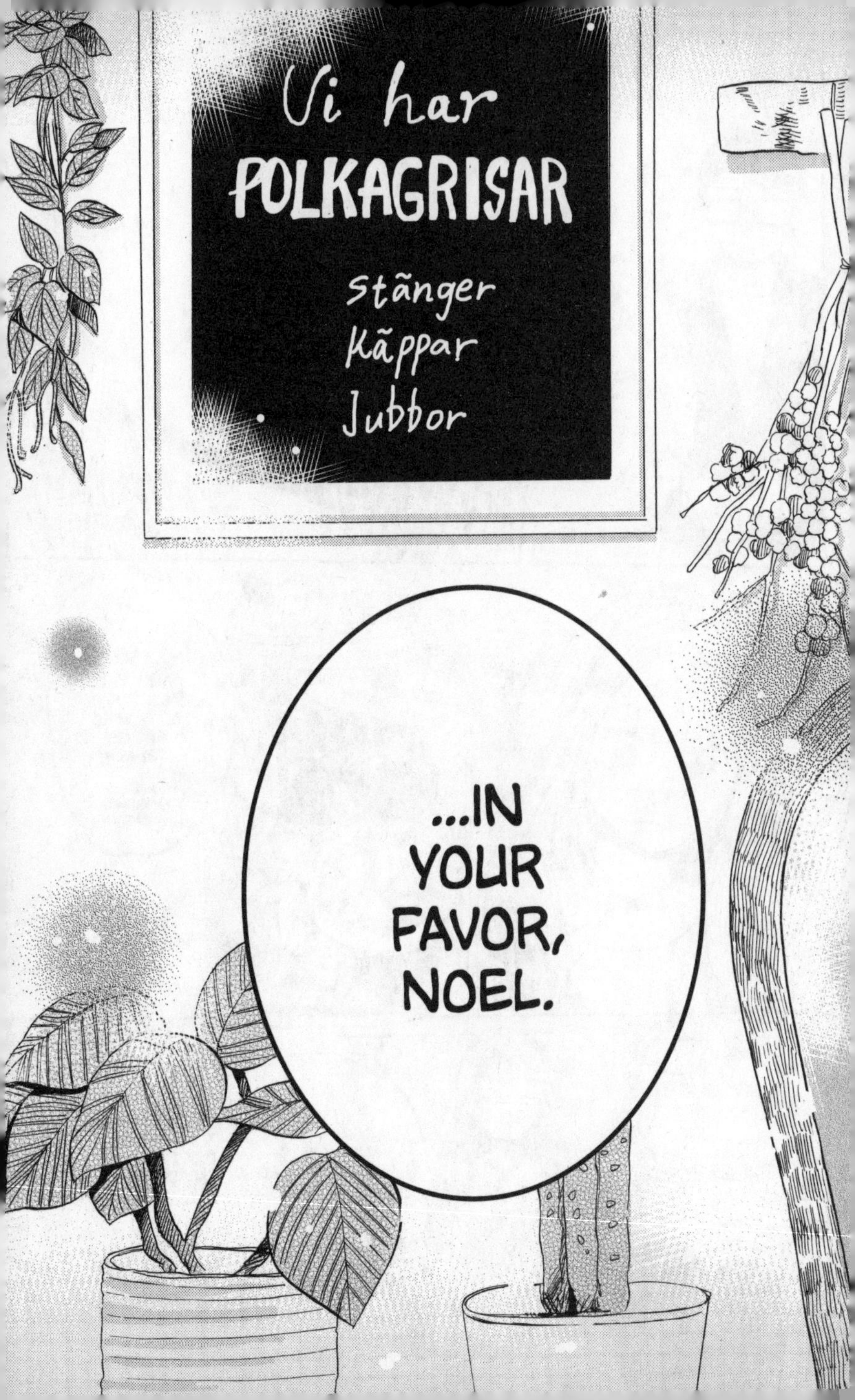
Vi har
POLKAGRISAR
Stãnger
Kãppar
Jubbor
...IN YOUR FAVOR, NOEL.

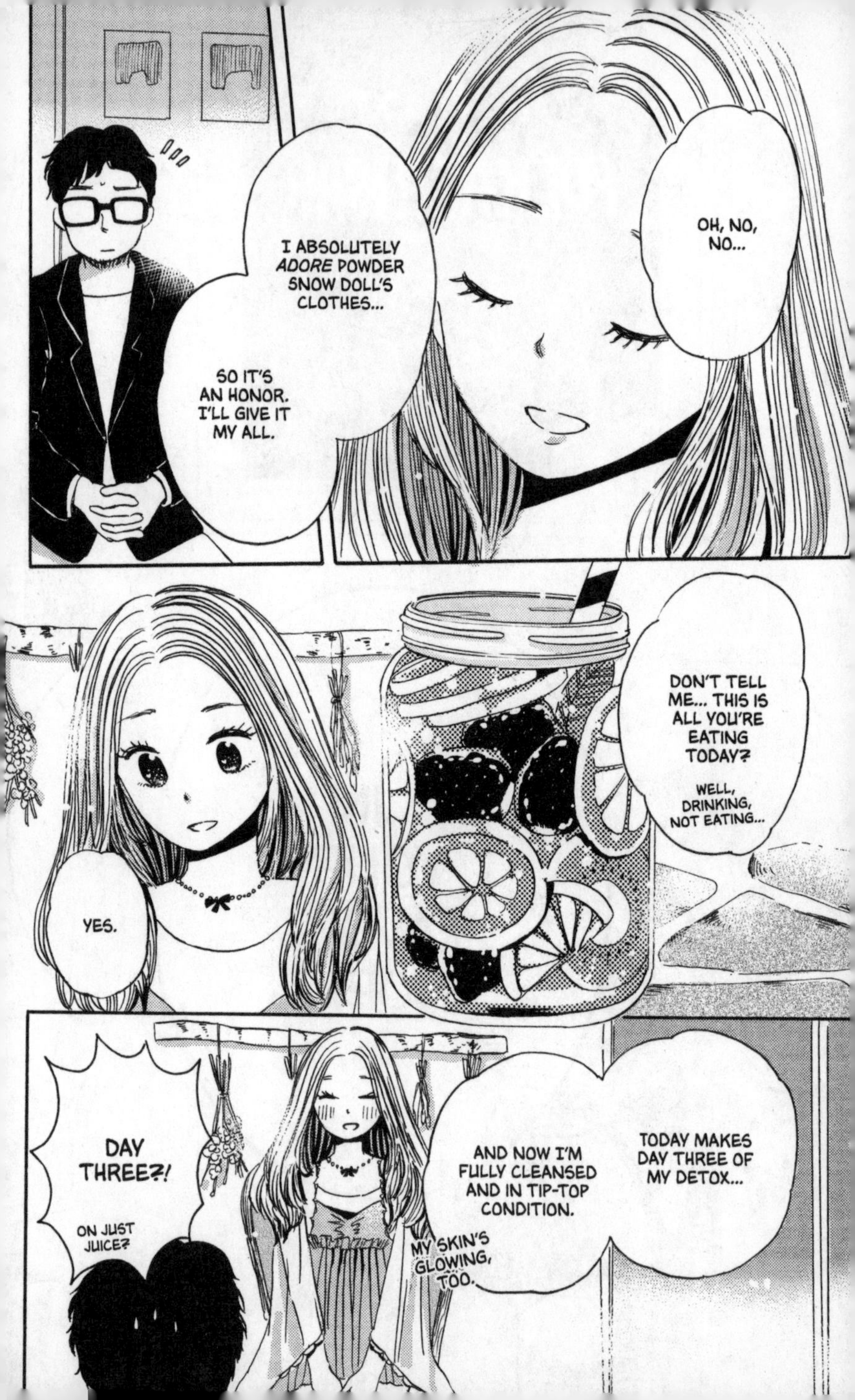
OH, NO, NO...
I ABSOLUTELY *ADORE* POWDER SNOW DOLL'S CLOTHES...
SO IT'S AN HONOR. I'LL GIVE IT MY ALL.
DON'T TELL ME... THIS IS ALL YOU'RE EATING TODAY?
WELL, DRINKING, NOT EATING...
YES.
TODAY MAKES DAY THREE OF MY DETOX...
AND NOW I'M FULLY CLEANSED AND IN TIP-TOP CONDITION.
MY SKIN'S GLOWING, TOO.
DAY THREE?!
ON JUST JUICE?

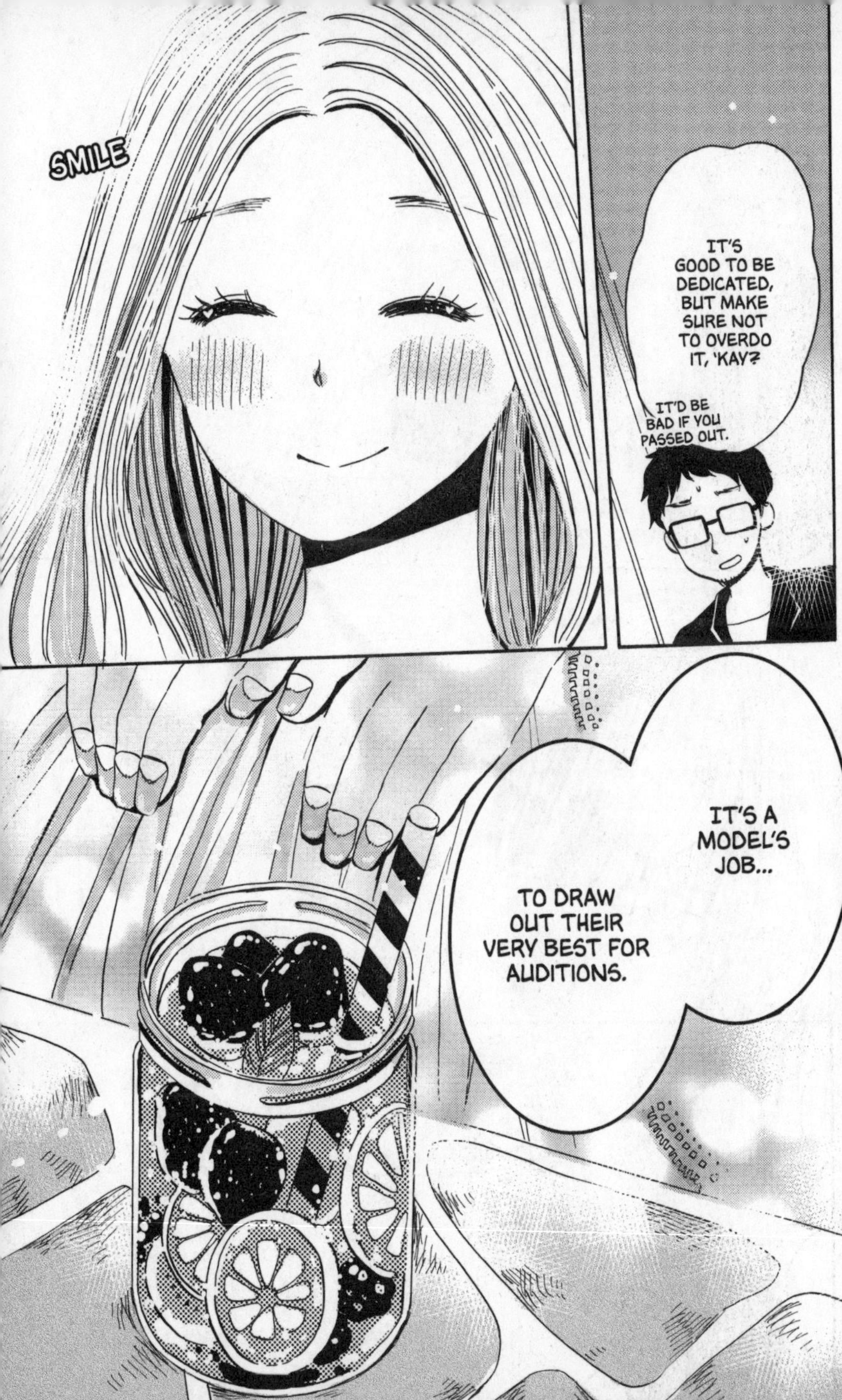
IT'S GOOD TO BE DEDICATED, BUT MAKE SURE NOT TO OVERDO IT, 'KAY?
IT'D BE BAD IF YOU PASSED OUT.
SMILE
IT'S A MODEL'S JOB...
TO DRAW OUT THEIR VERY BEST FOR AUDITIONS.

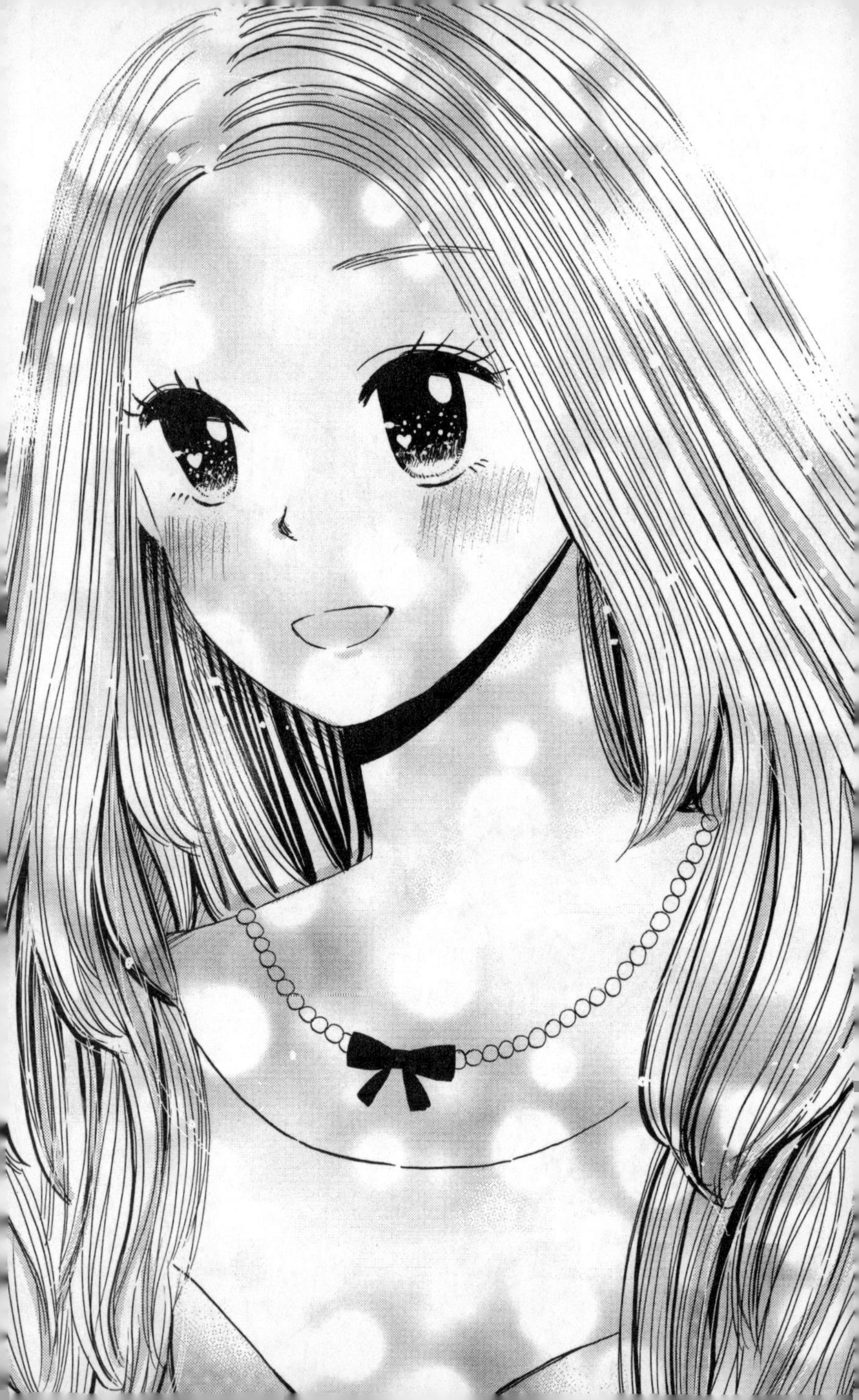

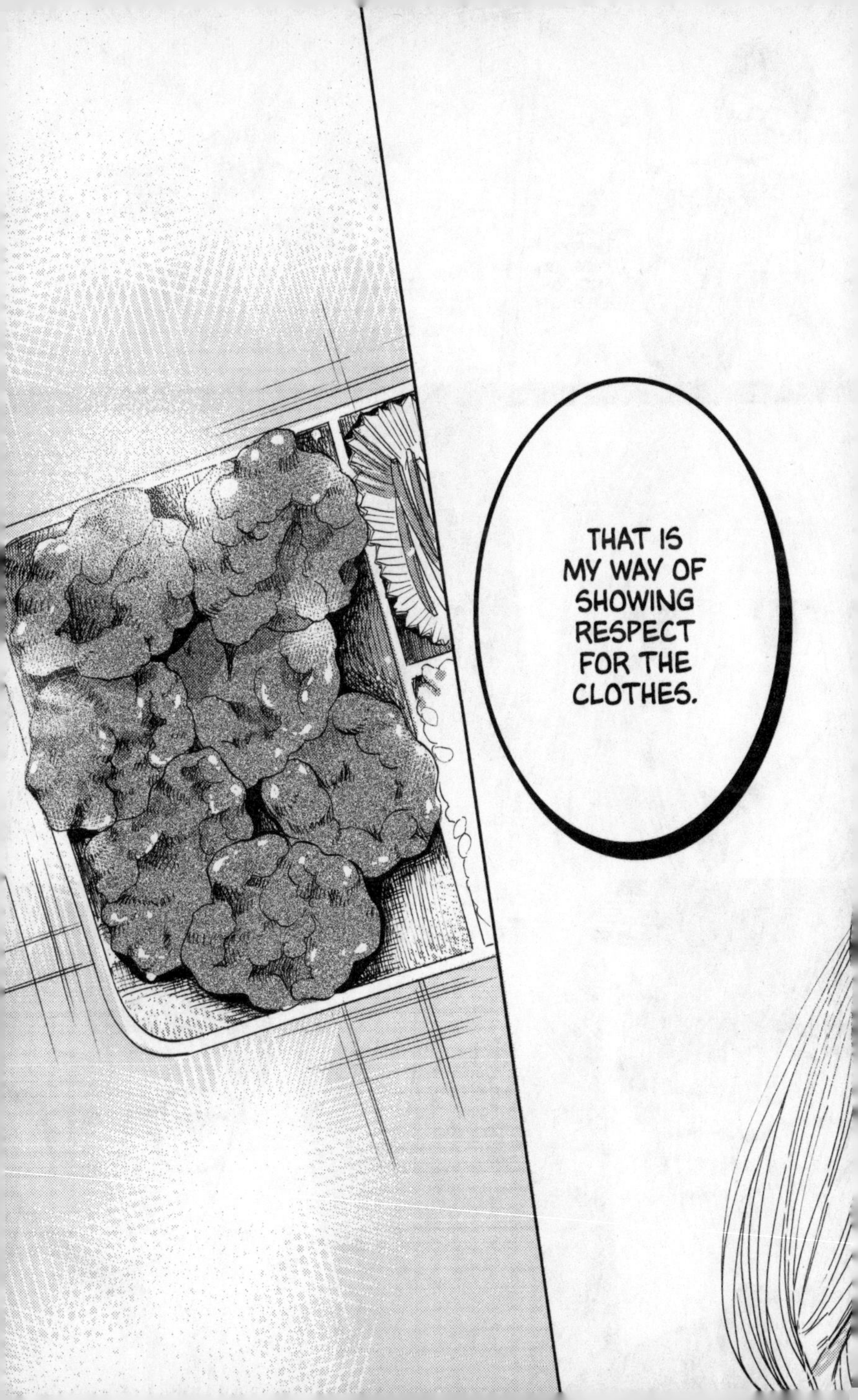
THAT IS MY WAY OF SHOWING RESPECT FOR THE CLOTHES.

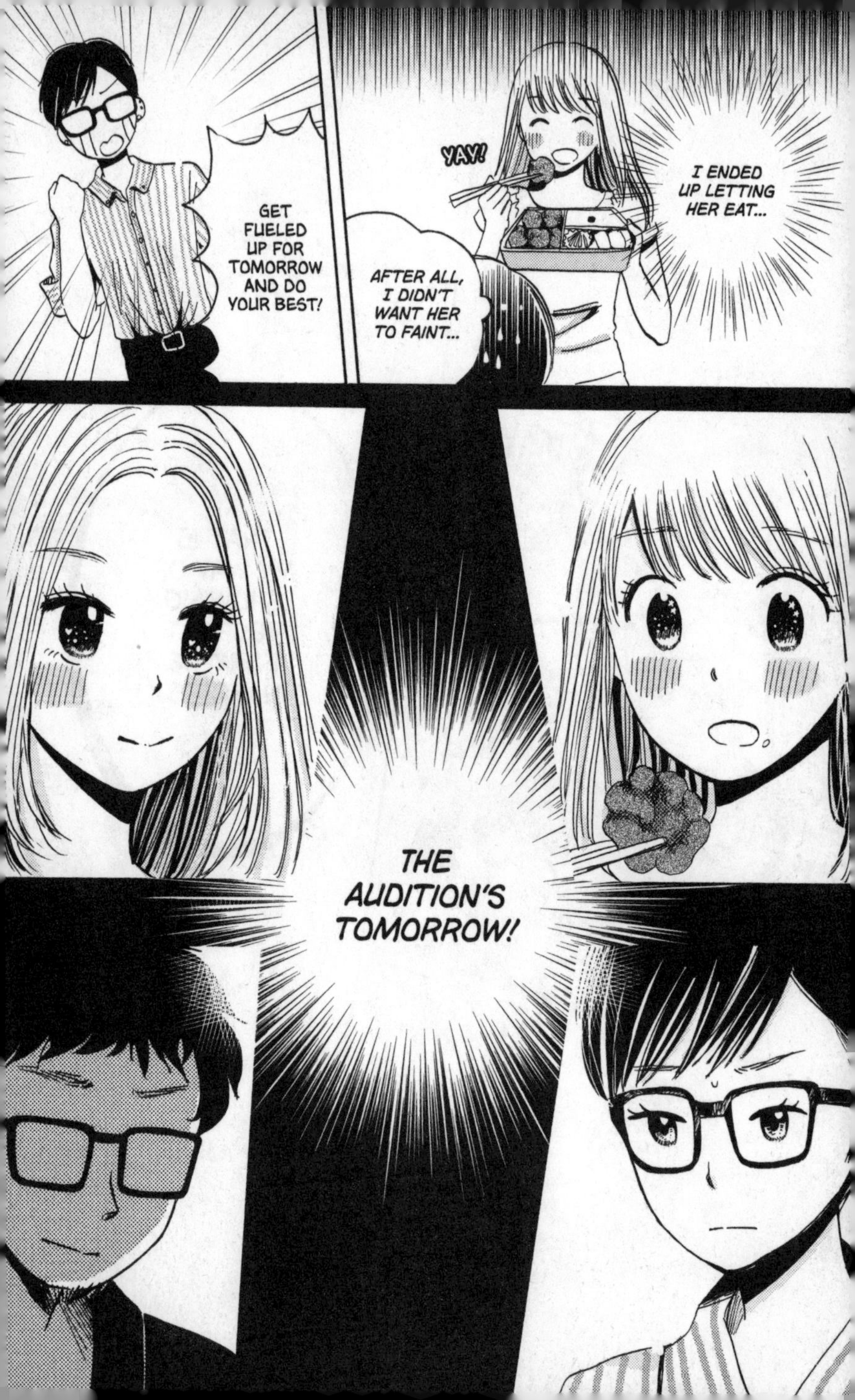
I ENDED UP LETTING HER EAT...
YAY!
AFTER ALL, I DIDN'T WANT HER TO FAINT...
GET FUELED UP FOR TOMORROW AND DO YOUR BEST!
THE AUDITION'S TOMORROW!

Thank you for buying *Mame Coordinate* Volume 1! I hope to see you in the next one too!

– Sachi Miyabe

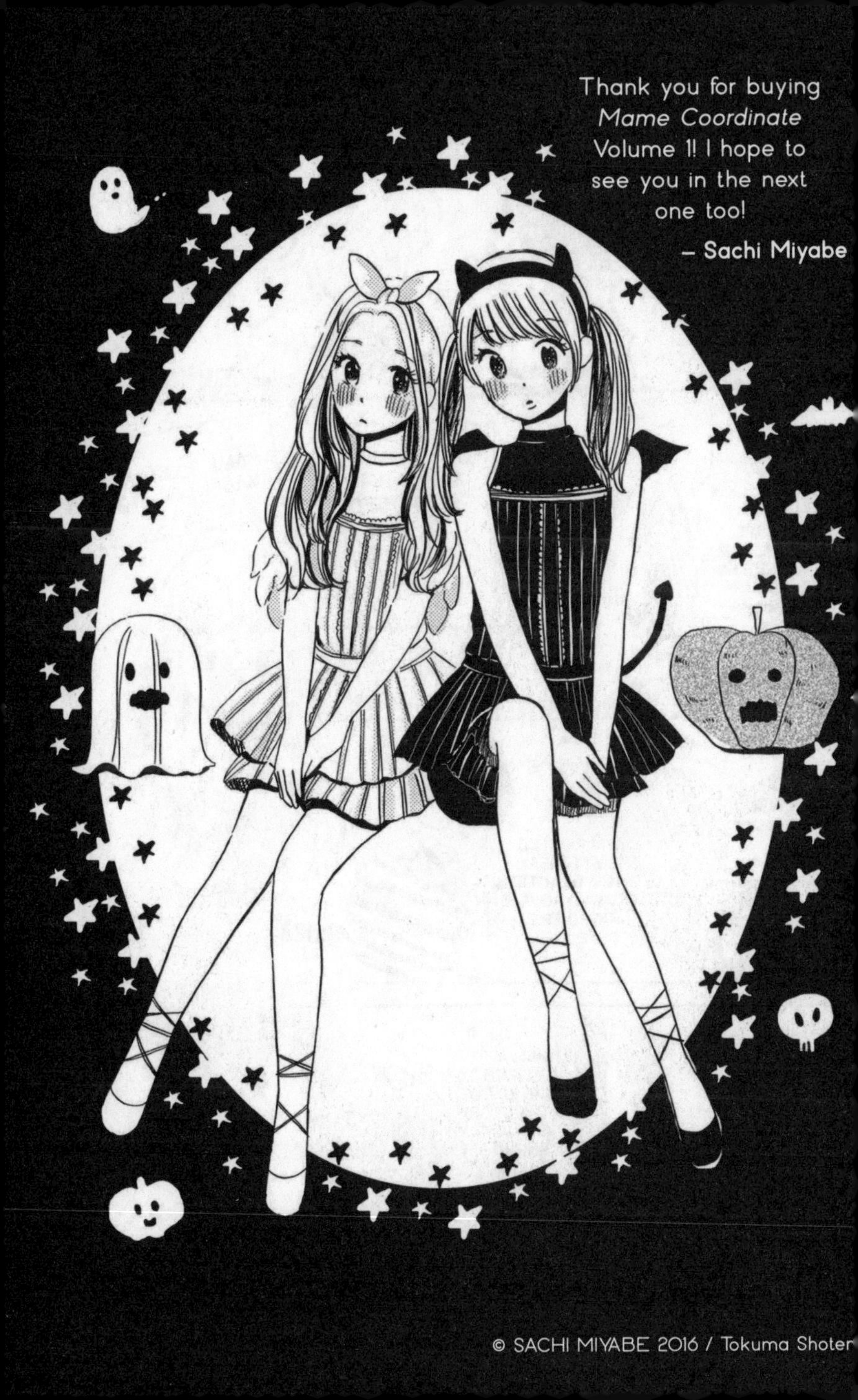

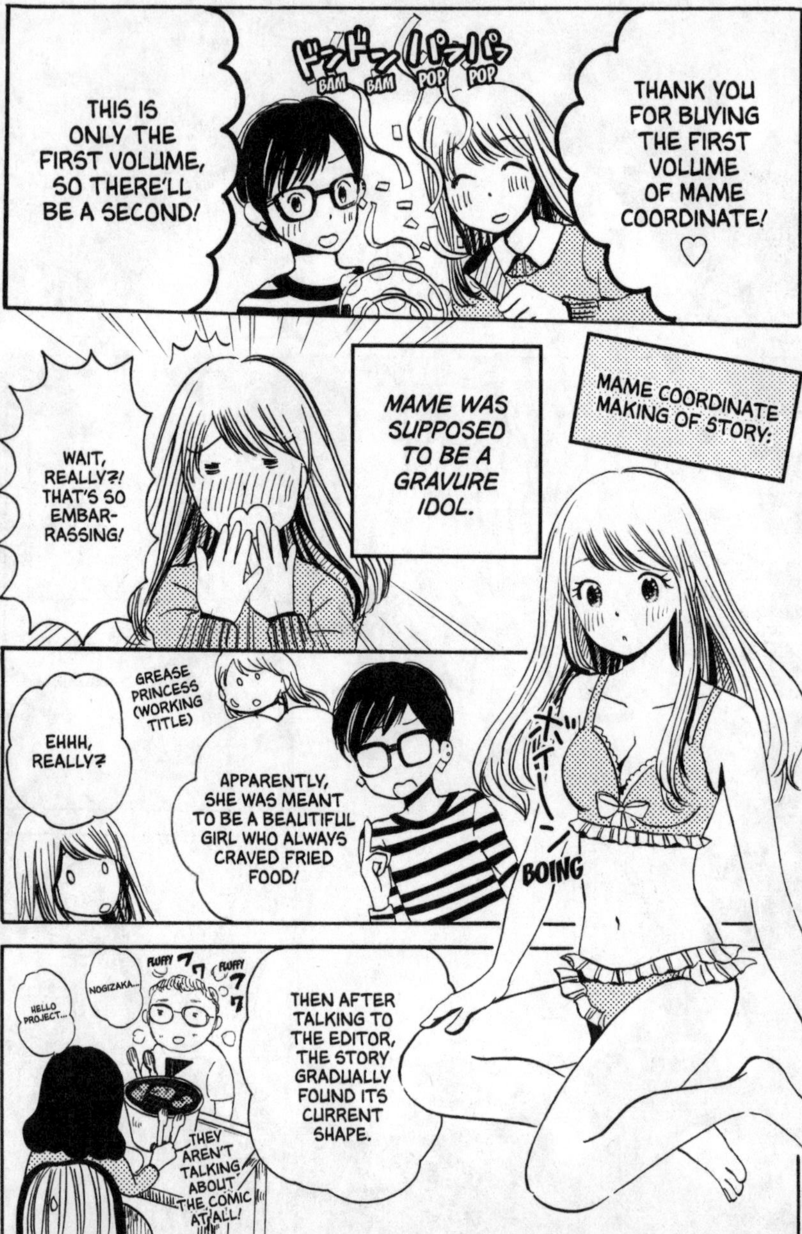
THANK YOU FOR BUYING THE FIRST VOLUME OF MAME COORDINATE! ♡
ドンドン パフパフ
BAM BAM POP POP
THIS IS ONLY THE FIRST VOLUME, SO THERE'LL BE A SECOND!
MAME COORDINATE MAKING OF STORY:
MAME WAS SUPPOSED TO BE A GRAVURE IDOL.
WAIT, REALLY?! THAT'S SO EMBAR-RASSING!
BOING
APPARENTLY, SHE WAS MEANT TO BE A BEAUTIFUL GIRL WHO ALWAYS CRAVED FRIED FOOD!
GREASE PRINCESS (WORKING TITLE)
EHHH, REALLY?
THEN AFTER TALKING TO THE EDITOR, THE STORY GRADUALLY FOUND ITS CURRENT SHAPE.
FLUFFY FLUFFY
NOGIZAKA...
HELLO PROJECT...
THEY AREN'T TALKING ABOUT THE COMIC AT ALL!

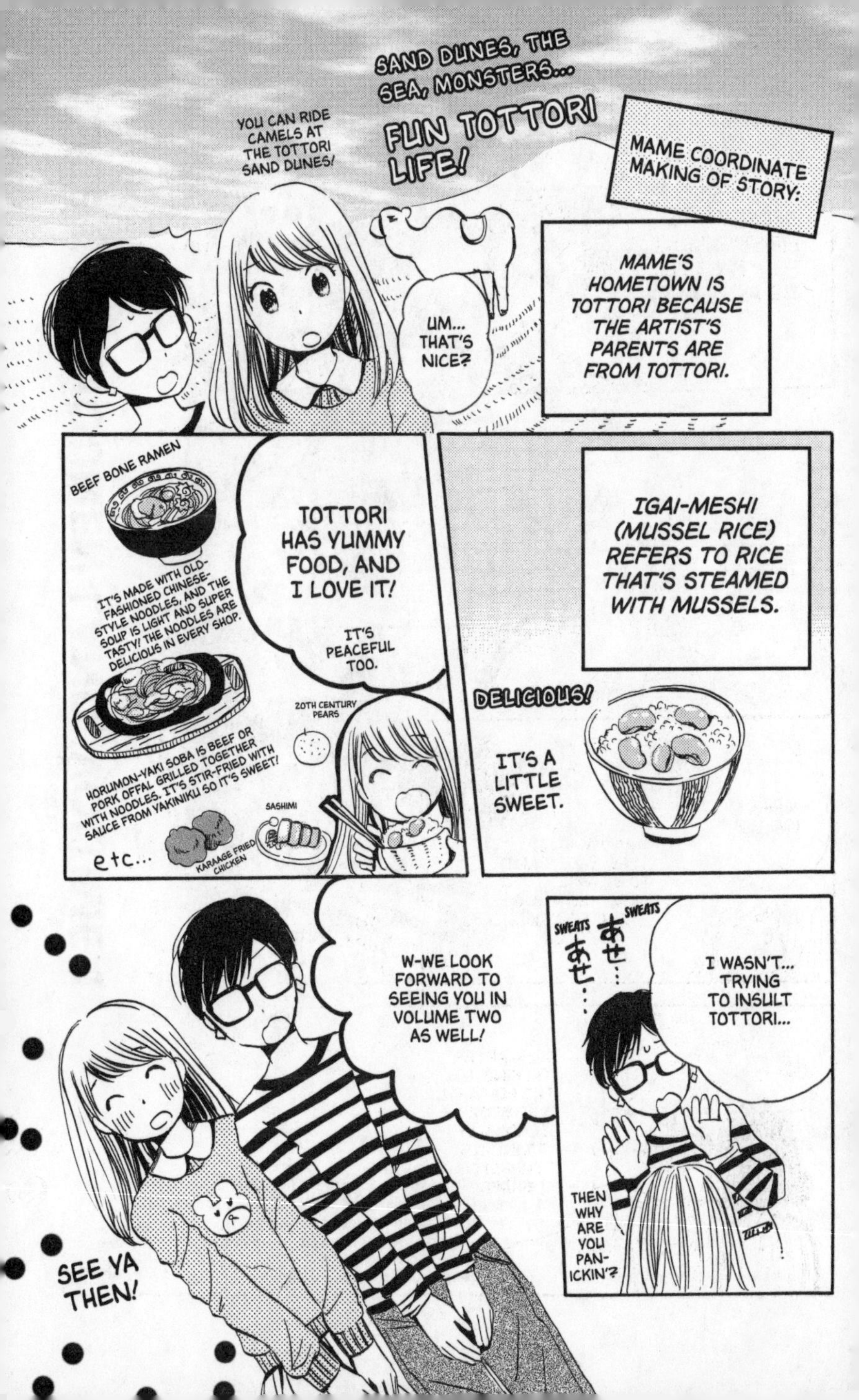
MAME COORDINATE MAKING OF STORY:
SAND DUNES, THE SEA, MONSTERS...
FUN TOTTORI LIFE!
MAME'S HOMETOWN IS TOTTORI BECAUSE THE ARTIST'S PARENTS ARE FROM TOTTORI.
YOU CAN RIDE CAMELS AT THE TOTTORI SAND DUNES!
UM... THAT'S NICE?
IGAI-MESHI (MUSSEL RICE) REFERS TO RICE THAT'S STEAMED WITH MUSSELS.
DELICIOUS!
IT'S A LITTLE SWEET.
TOTTORI HAS YUMMY FOOD, AND I LOVE IT!
IT'S PEACEFUL TOO.
BEEF BONE RAMEN
IT'S MADE WITH OLD-FASHIONED CHINESE-STYLE NOODLES, AND THE SOUP IS LIGHT AND SUPER TASTY! THE NOODLES ARE DELICIOUS IN EVERY SHOP.
HORUMON-YAKI SOBA IS BEEF OR PORK OFFAL GRILLED TOGETHER WITH NOODLES. IT'S STIR-FRIED WITH SAUCE FROM YAKINIKU SO IT'S SWEET!
20TH CENTURY PEARS
SASHIMI
KARAAGE FRIED CHICKEN
etc...
SWEATS あせ...
SWEATS あせ...
I WASN'T... TRYING TO INSULT TOTTORI...
THEN WHY ARE YOU PAN-ICKIN'?
W-WE LOOK FORWARD TO SEEING YOU IN VOLUME TWO AS WELL!
SEE YA THEN!

Yushi
Kawata &
Yukito

COMEDY

Alice Kagami is an ordinary high school girl who doesn't really get her friend Tamami's obsession with idol games. There's more to life than handsome digital boys, dating sims, and mini-games, right? But then, Tamami is "chosen" as one of the top idol fangirls in the country and gets drawn into the game — and hapless Alice gets pulled in too!

Between dealing with the mismatched members of her idol group to intense pressure to spend real money on gachas, how is a total idol game newbie supposed to take them to the top?

ALICE IN KYOTO FOREST, VOLUME 1

Mai Mochizuki, Haruki Niwa

Alice in Kyoto Forest

1

Haruki Niwa
Mai Mochizuki

TOKYOPOP

FANTASY

After being orphaned when she was very young, Alice has lived with her aunt for most of her childhood, but her uncle clearly doesn't want her around. At fifteen years old, Alice decides to return home to Kyoto and train as a maiko, an apprentice with the hopes of eventually becoming a full-fledged geisha.

But when she arrives back to the city where she was born, she finds that Kyoto has changed quite a bit in the years since she left it. Almost as if it's a completely different world...

Check out *LOVExLOVE.info* for all kinds of romance!

TOKYOPOP believes all types of romances deserve to be celebrated. *LOVE x LOVE* was born from that idea and our commitment to representing a variety of stories and voices as diverse as our fans.

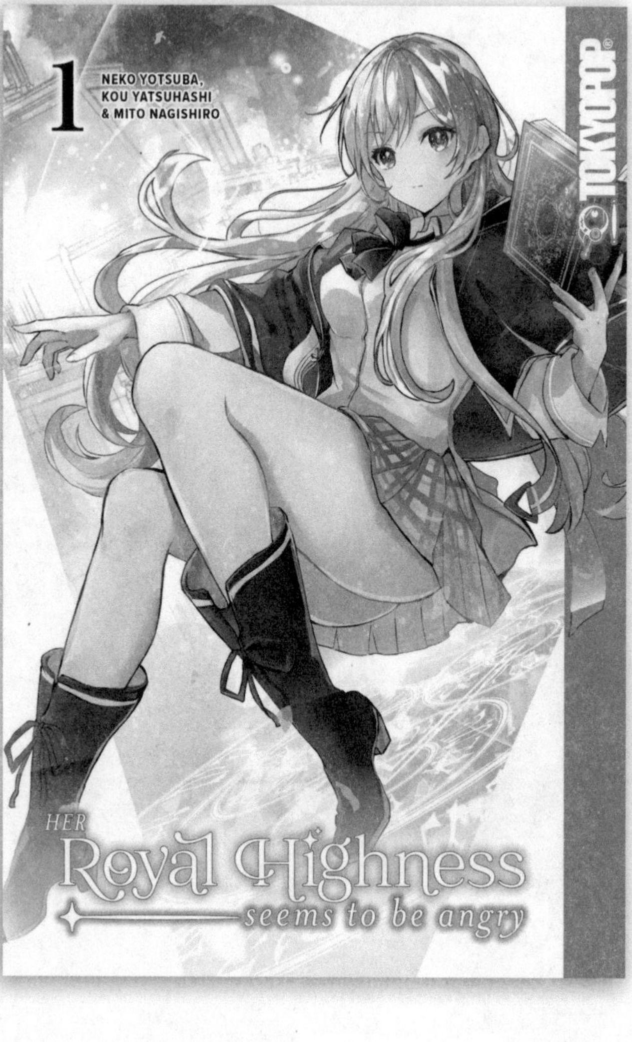
1
NEKO YOTSUBA,
KOU YATSUHASHI
& MITO NAGISHIRO
TOKYOPOP
HER
Royal Highness
seems to be angry

HER ROYAL HIGHNESS SEEMS TO BE ANGRY, VOLUME 1

Neko Yotsuba, Kou Yatsuhashi, Mito Nagishiro

LOVE-x-LOVE

In a remote kingdom, there lived a princess, adored by her subjects and wielding powerful magic. But as her land was ravaged by an endless war, she lost everything: her people, her family, her loved ones, and eventually, her own life. Until she opened her eyes and awoke in a place she'd never seen before! A thousand years have passed, and she finds herself reincarnated into someone else's body. Realizing the person she's now living as is despised by her own family and even her fiancé, the former princess struggles to understand this new world and the events that have transpired since her death. There's a lot to be upset about, but first on the list: how in the world did future magic turn out so lame?

TOKYOPOP

I WAS REINCARNATED AS THE VILLAINESS IN AN OTOME GAME BUT THE BOYS LOVE ME ANYWAY!, VOLUME 1

Ataka, Sou Inaida, Hachipisu Wan

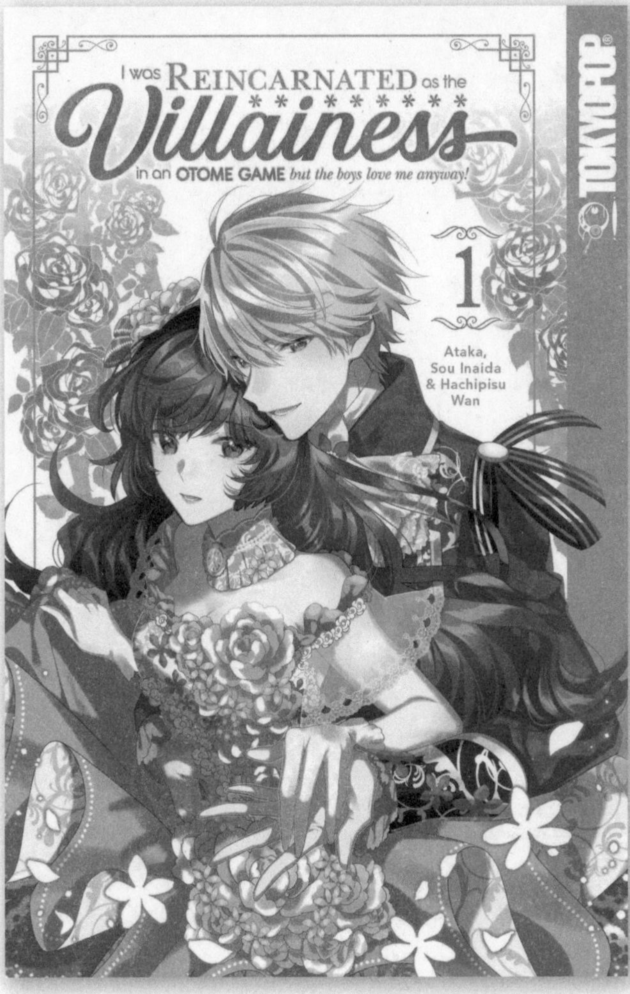
I was REINCARNATED as the
Villainess
in an OTOME GAME but the boys love me anyway!
1
Ataka,
Sou Inaida
& Hachipisu
Wan
TOKYOPOP

LOVE-x-LOVE

TOKYOPOP

Fated to die as the villainess of an otome game, Mystia sets out to change her own unhappy ending! Mystia Aren is the daughter of a noble family, and she just started high school. She's surrounded by a group of adoring classmates and her charming fiancé. Everything seems perfect. Except that this world is actually a dating sim called Kyun-Love, and Mystia knows she's been reincarnated into the role of the main character's evil rival! Mystia is determined to do everything she can to avoid her fate, but it's not as easy as it sounds. Especially when all the boys keep falling in love with her!

SPRINGTIME BY THE WINDOW, VOLUME 1

Suzuyuki

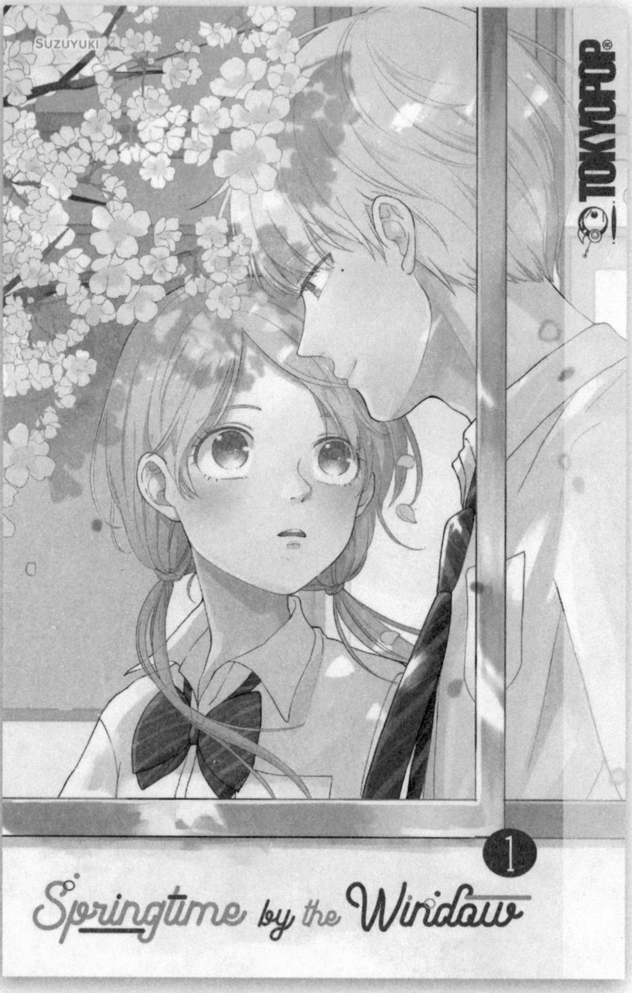
SUZUYUKI
TOKYOPOP
1
Springtime by the Window

LOVE-x-LOVE

Cool and collected second-year Yamada is in love with his childhood friend, Seno. His classmates Akama and Toda are also starting to think about romance, though neither of them realizes yet that they might actually feel the same way about each other...High school love in the spring of adolescence blooms with earnest, messy emotions.

TOKYOPOP

FUTARIBEYA: A ROOM FOR TWO, VOL 1

Yukiko

Futaribeya
A ROOM FOR TWO
TOKYOPOP
1
YUKIKO

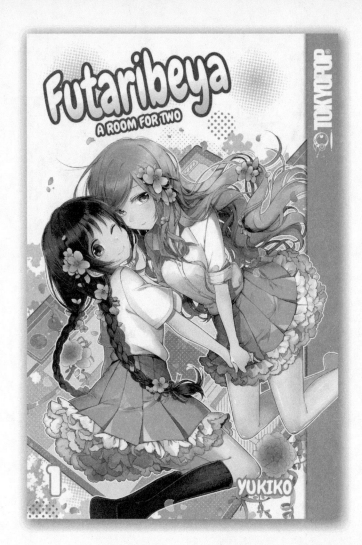

♀LOVE-x-LOVE♀

As her exciting first year of high school begins, Sakurako Kawawa settles into her new lodgings. There, she meets her roommate — the stunningly beautiful Kasumi Yamabuki, who lives life at her own pace. From day one, responsible, level-headed Sakurako and lazy, easygoing Kasumi find themselves at odds with one another... But with their matching mugs and one bed to share, Sakurako and Kasumi's friendship is just beginning!

You Kajika

THE TREASURE OF THE KING AND THE CAT

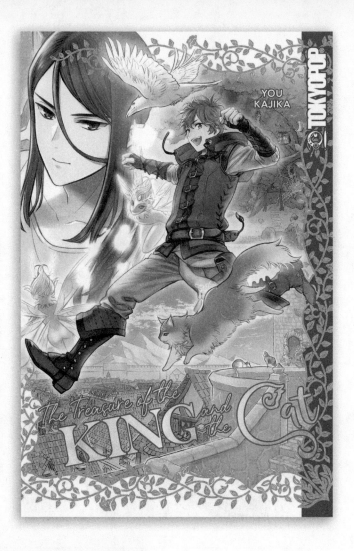

YOU
KAJIKA

◊LOVE-x-LOVE◊

One day, a large number of people suddenly disappeared in the royal capital. When young King Castio goes out to investigate this occurrence, he comes across the culprit... but the criminal puts a spell on him! To help him out, the king calls the wizard O'Feuille to his castle, along with Prince Volks and his loyal retainer Nios. Together, they're determined to solve this strange, fluffy mystery full of cats, swords and magic!

KATAKOI LAMP

Kyohei Azumi

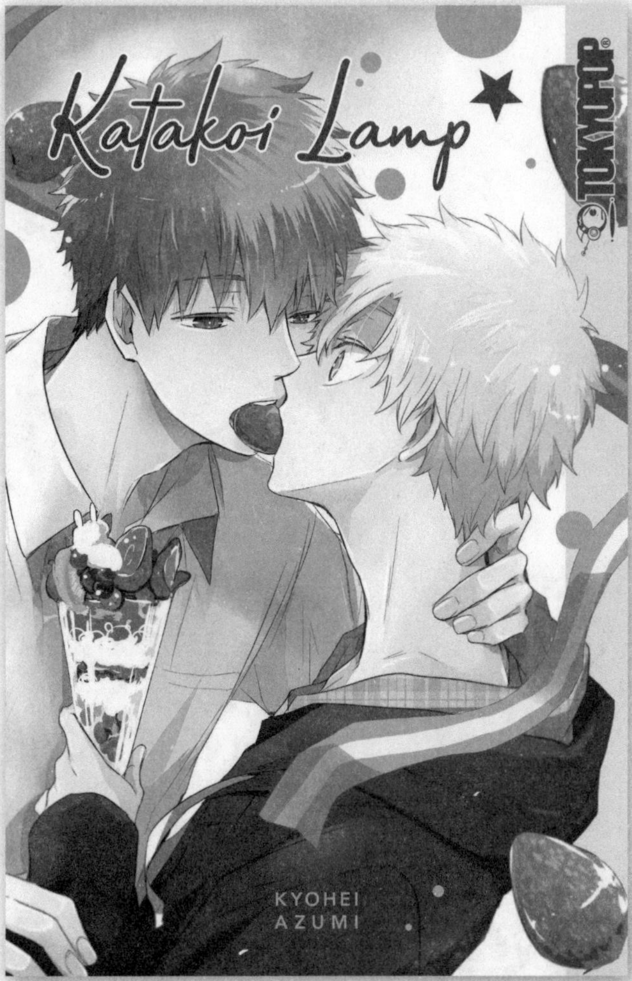
Katakoi Lamp
TOKYOPOP
KYOHEI
AZUMI

LOVE-x-LOVE

Kazuto Muronoi runs a cute little coffee shop, where many people enjoy doing some work or writing papers for school. Among his coffee shop's regulars is a college student named Jun, who often studies there. It was love at first sight for Kazuto! Will Kazuto be able to find the courage to confess his crush before Jun graduates college and stops frequenting the shop? And to make matters even more complicated... it seems Jun has his sights set on another worker at the café!

TOKYOPOP

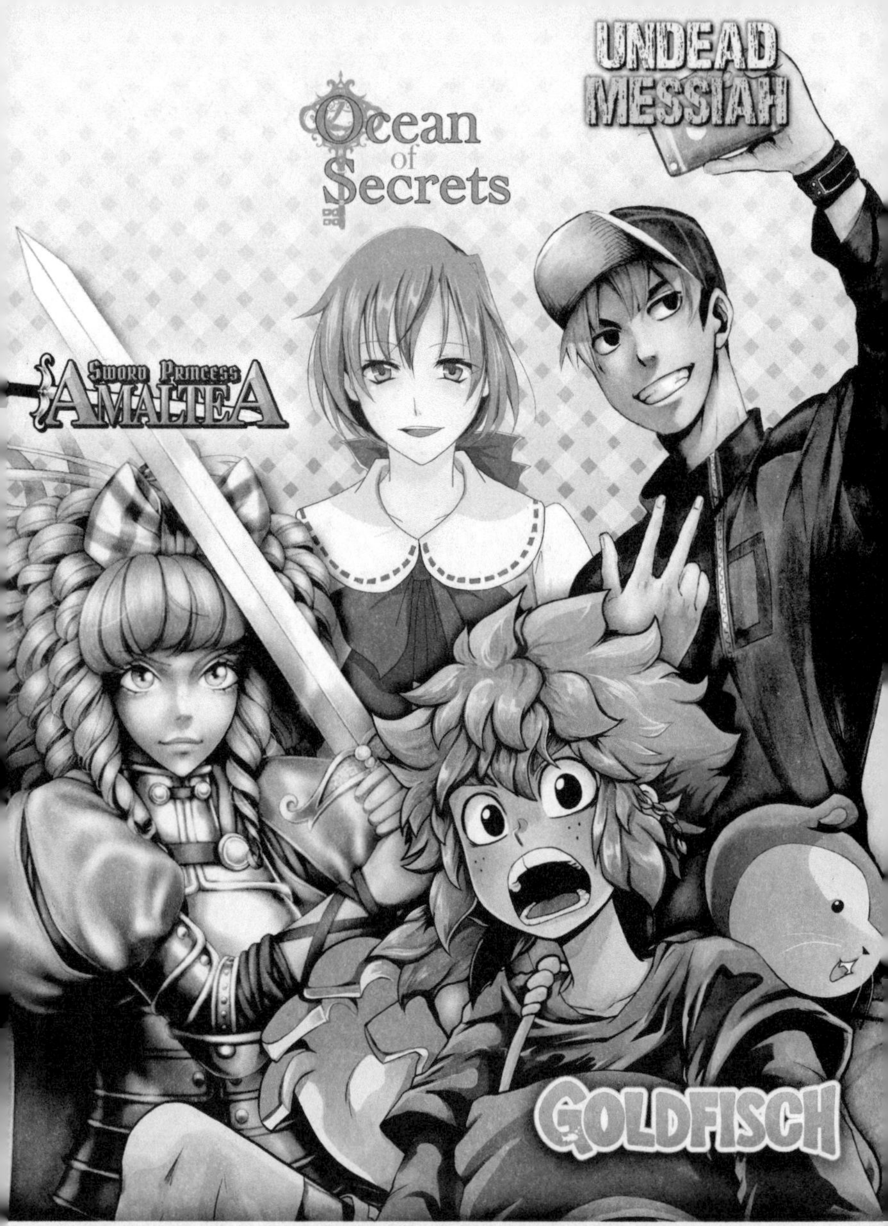
UNDEAD MESSIAH
Ocean of Secrets
SWORD PRINCESS AMALTEA
GOLDFISCH

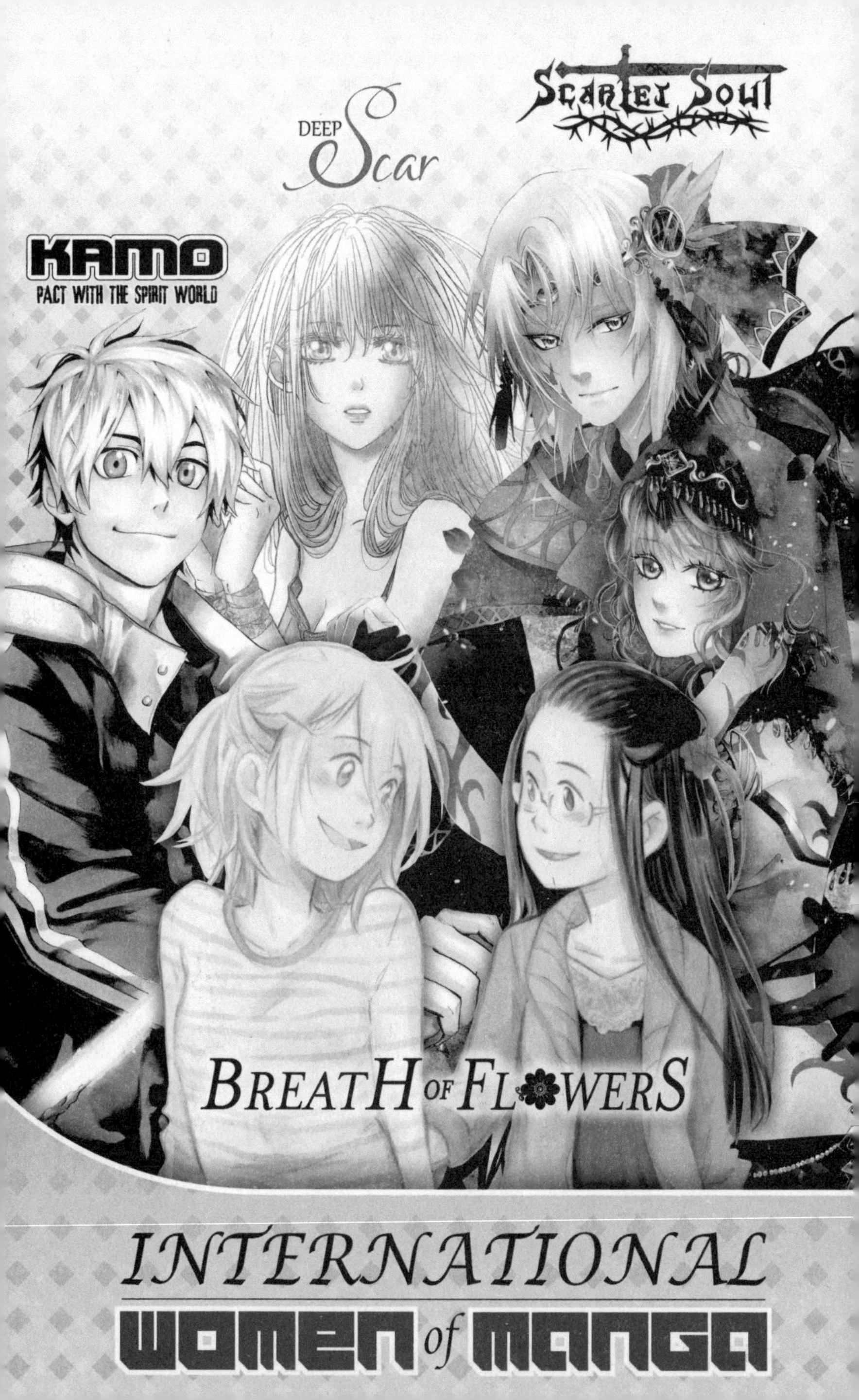
Scarlet Soul
DEEP Scar
KAMO
PACT WITH THE SPIRIT WORLD
BREATH OF FLOWERS
INTERNATIONAL
Women of Manga

Mame Coordinate, Volume 1
Manga by Sachi Miyabe

Editor	-	Lena Atanassova
Translator	-	Caroline Wong
Quality Check	-	Nina Sawada
Proofreader	-	Katie Kimura
Copy Editor	-	M. Cara Carper
Cover & Logo Designer	-	Sol DeLeo
Editorial Associate	-	Janae Young
Marketing Associate	-	Kae Winters
Digital Marketing Assistant	-	Kitt Burgess
Retouching and Lettering	-	Vibrraant Publishing Studio
Licensing Specialist	-	Arika Yanaka
Editor-in-Chief & Publisher	-	Stu Levy

A  Manga

TOKYOPOP and 🐾 are trademarks or registered trademarks of TOKYOPOP Inc.

TOKYOPOP Inc.
4136 Del Rey Ave., Suite 502
Marina del Rey, CA 90292-5604

E-mail: info@TOKYOPOP.com
Come visit us online at www.TOKYOPOP.com

f www.facebook.com/TOKYOPOP
🐦 www.twitter.com/TOKYOPOP
📷 www.instagram.com/TOKYOPOP

ISBN: 978-1-4278-6792-6
First TOKYOPOP Printing: April 2022
Printed in CANADA

STOP

THIS IS THE BACK OF THE BOOK!

How do you read manga-style? It's simple! Let's practice -- just start in the top right panel and follow the numbers below!

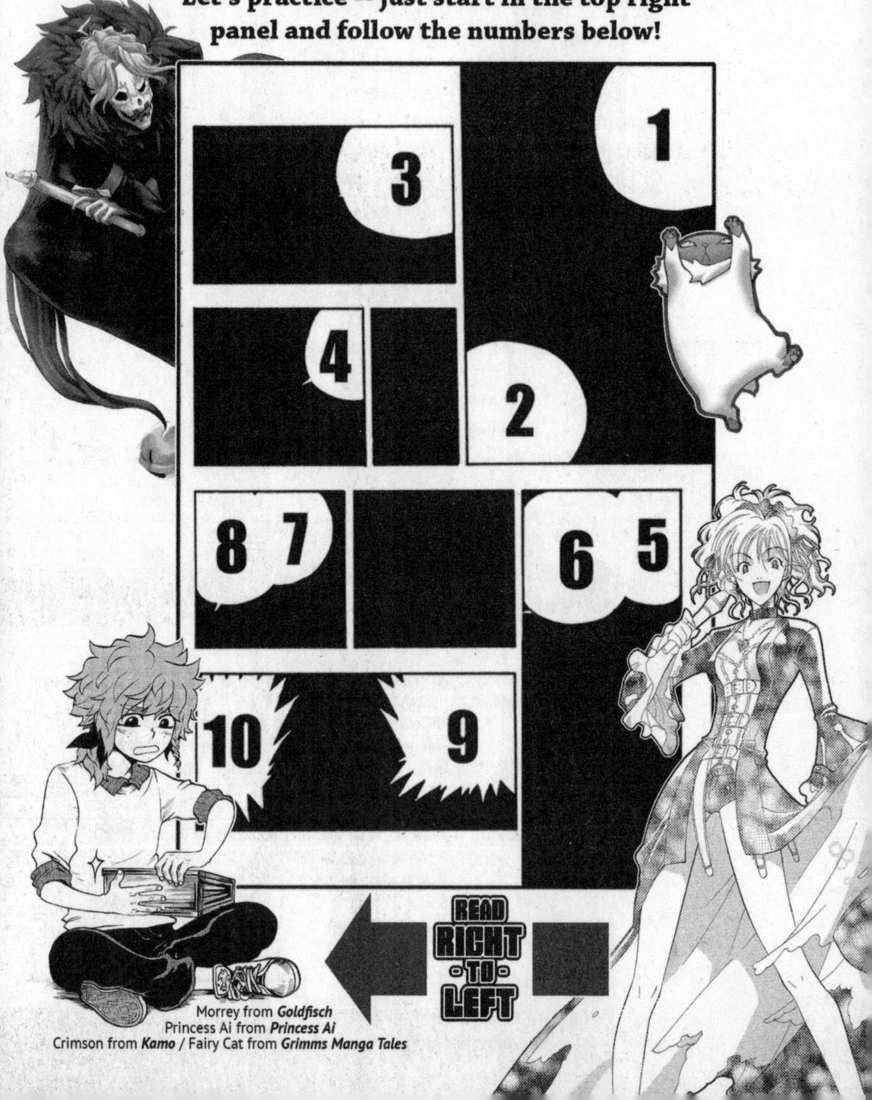
1
2
3
4
5
6
7
8
9
10
READ
RIGHT
-TO-
LEFT

Morrey from *Goldfisch*
Princess Ai from *Princess Ai*
Crimson from *Kamo* / Fairy Cat from *Grimms Manga Tales*